# Tapping the Government Grapevine

# Tapping the Government Grapevine

## The User-Friendly Guide to U.S. Government Information Sources

### Second Edition

by Judith Schiek Robinson

ORYX PRESS
1993

The rare Arabian Oryx is believed to have inspired the myth of the unicorn. This desert antelope became virtually extinct in the early 1960s. At that time several groups of international conservationists arranged to have 9 animals sent to the Phoenix Zoo to be the nucleus of a captive breeding herd. Today the oryx population is over 800, and nearly 400 have been returned to reserves in the Middle East.

Copyright © 1988, 1993 by The Oryx Press
First edition published 1988. Second edition 1993.
4041 North Central at Indian School Road
Phoenix, Arizona 85012-3397

Published simultaneously in Canada

Printed and bound in the United States of America

(∞) The paper used in this publication meets the minimum requirements of American National Standard for Information Science—Permanence of Paper for Printed Library Materials, ANZI Z39.48, 1984.

Library of Congress Cataloging-in-Publication Data
Robinson, Judith Schiek, 1947–
    Tapping the government grapevine : the user friendly guide to U.S.
Government publications / by Judith Schiek Robinson. —2nd ed.
        p.    cm.
    Includes bibliographical references and index.
    ISBN 0-89774-712-7
    I. Title.
Z1223.Z7R633   1993
[J83]                                        92-40201
025.17'34—dc20                               CIP

079466

# Contents

To Kristen Wilhelm, who helped research and write this book, and Bev Porter Federspiel, both treasured colleagues; and to Bru.

# Preface

The purpose of this book is to dispel the government information mystique. It has been written for users and potential users of government information: librarians, library school students, researchers, teachers, citizens—anyone with the need to track down information generated by government. Although much of the discussion is directed toward librarians, anyone can learn to harvest government information by reading these pages.

The second edition of *Tapping the Government Grapevine* has been enhanced with expanded and updated information, search tips, glossaries, new summary tables and information boxes, access tips, practice exercises following many chapters, and a suggested inexpensive documents reference collection (Appendix 4, "Documents Toolkit"). The practice exercises not only provide answers, they also trace the thought processes that retrieve the answers, differentiating among similar sources and noting their unique qualities. Some practice questions have been repeated in more than one chapter because they can be answered with several types of sources.

This book does not tell the reader everything about documents and their history but selects the most practical information needed to use and make sense of government information. Just as one doesn't learn to drive by reading the description of a car, reading annotated bibliographies of document titles is not the formula for mastery of government information retrieval. Without differentiation between similar sources, identification of idiosyncrasies and potential pitfalls, and guidance in effective searching techniques, using these sources becomes a trial-and-error struggle. This book aims to provide that guidance in a readable, interesting, and straightforward format. *Tapping the Government Grapevine*, Second Edition, describes not only information resources but also the personalities, events, and ironies behind them. It may be browsed to identify government infor-

mation for a specific need or read cover to cover to learn about government information in general. Most chapters begin with a summary of scope in a *what, why, when, where, who* format. Key information is highlighted in summary tables that offer a source of quick referral or review. Sample entries from documents aren't simply reproduced, they are explained. Superintendent of Documents classification (SuDocs) numbers are provided throughout the text and in an appendix for quick referral. Further research is aided by chapter references and an appendix of *Library Literature* subject headings relevant to each chapter's content. Use the index to find additional material on topics, since some are scattered throughout book in various chapters.

The book is not limited to print resources and their microfiche offspring but also includes information on databases, electronic bulletin boards, CD-ROMs, audiovisual materials, archival collections and other primary resources, including government experts, clearinghouses, and research laboratories. U.S. federal resources are emphasized, but information about foreign, state, and local publications is also provided in chapters 14 and 15. A practicing librarian, Karen Smith, has contributed the chapter on foreign documents. Karen is coordinator of the Business and Government Documents Reference Center in Lockwood Library at the State University of New York at Buffalo, a depository for European Community documents. She has also worked with international documents in the SUNYAB Law Library.

*Note*: If you have additional ideas for solutions to exercises or favorite inexpensive references that belong in the documents toolkit, please forward them to the author for inclusion in the third edition: Dr. Judith Robinson, Associate Professor, School of Information and Library Studies, 381 Baldy Hall, Buffalo, New York 14260-1020, (716) 645-3327 LISROBIN@UBVM.BITNET.

# Tapping the Government Grapevine

# CHAPTER 1
# Introduction to Government Information Resources

*Government after all is a very simple thing.*
—Warren G. Harding

Governments have been part of civilization since prehistoric times, originally recording their activities on stone, animal skins, parchment, and clay tablets, and later on paper, microforms, and, more recently, CD-ROMs and other electronic media. National, state, and local governments all publish records of their activities, with the U.S. government holding the distinction as the world's most prolific publisher (see Figure 1.1). In 1990 alone, the U.S. Government Printing Office cranked out 1.9 billion items. Laid end to end, these publications could circle the globe eleven times.

*The documents of a nation preserve its memory, the record of its errors and triumphs, and offer the citizens of a republic the means to understanding and judgment.*
—National Study Commission on Records and Documents of Federal Officials

Some people enjoy characterizing government publishing as frivolous and whimsical, an example of the randomness of the universe. But government publishing actually reflects government-agency missions. The statutory authority that establishes a government agency dictates its purpose and role. Publications are generated as part of the daily business of government, to fulfill agency missions and serve the public. While some government publications are targeted especially toward the general public, most are issued to record actions or deliberations, to meet legal requirements, or to fulfill administrative needs.

As deadly as this may sound, government publications can be the richest of information sources. Covering thousands of topics, they range from light, informative pamphlets to ponderous treatises, and come in familiar formats: books, journals, pamphlets, indexes and abstracts, reference tomes, electronic databases, and audiovisuals. Government publications are distinguished from other informational materials in that (1) they emanate

from government agencies rather than commercial publishers, and (2) traditional library skills may not always retrieve them.

Bibliographic control of government publications—keeping records of their existence—dwells in a parallel universe that only occasionally overlaps with that of traditional bibliographic control. Both library users and librarians should be alerted that some library catalogs may be poor sources for identifying documents, since they may list only those titles shelved with the regular collection. This is changing rapidly, however. Today, with computerized documents cataloging available through OCLC and other vendors, more and more depositories are "mainstreaming" documents by listing holdings in the library's online catalog. Many libraries, however, continue to own more documents than are represented in their public catalogs. In these cases, it is helpful to remember that the documents department often maintains a shelf list in SuDocs number order, showing locations of all depository documents.

The adept seeker of government information distrusts the library catalog, bypasses the traditional classification systems, and disregards traditional indexes and abstracts. These trusted standbys can be inadequate when it comes to government searches, which rely instead upon a unique corps of catalogs and indexes to pilot the gentle reader. These sources are specialized, but not difficult. The biggest danger is overlooking them altogether.

*Information is the currency of democracy.*
—Thomas Jefferson

Why would it matter if the keys to searching government publications were overlooked? Because government information offers a treasure trove of research material. From diaries of the Lewis and Clark expeditions to the latest cancer research results, they spin a historical and up-to-the-minute record of our nation that cannot be surpassed. The Rogers Commission report on the space shuttle *Challenger* accident is a good example. For months Americans read and watched accounts of the commission's discoveries as it traced the causes of the January 28, 1986, disaster. After a five-month wait, the first volume of the official report was released. With its twenty-six full-page color photographs, verbatim testimony, and numerous drawings and diagrams, the 256-page report read like a gripping detective novel in which a knotty puzzle is unraveled clue by clue. Why then were most Americans satisfied with a two-column synopsis in the newspaper or a five-minute summary on the evening news? How many people knew that the report itself can be checked out from many government depository libraries as easily as a library book?

Although the United States enjoys an openness of information unparalleled anywhere in the world, few citizens exercise it. The nation monitors its government through newspaper front pages and television screens, rather than through the elaborate system of libraries and laws set up to guarantee our right to the truth, if only we will dig for it. The public lets the "professionals" do that for them: the scholars, reporters, consumer advocates, and special-interest groups for whom tracking down facts is all in a day's work. But, as happens with gossip, when information is filtered through second and third parties, it risks oversimplification and distortion. By depending on others to interpret our nation's daily activities, we risk information helplessness and dependency.

We as a society have a freedom that threatens to atrophy if not exercised. Tracking down government information requires a sophisticated literacy that transcends the basic skills of reading and writing. Government information literacy, the ability to find and use government information for research and daily life, begs to be counted among the other "literacies" being promoted today. It is no less essential to our quality of life than computer, math, visual, or other popular literacies that have captured recent media attention.

If you are unfamiliar with government information resources, you are handicapping yourself in the race for information. Whether you are a student, teacher, historian, librarian, doctor, lawyer, grocer, or consumer there is government information you can use. Questions handled by the Consumer Information Center (CIC), a source of free and inexpensive government pamphlets, provide a glimpse at the range of information available from government. The CIC fields requests for information about housing, health, federal programs, food, travel, hobbies, money management, cars, weight control, and exercise.[1] Depository libraries have shelves full of free information on these topics and more, not just for researchers, but covering aspects of everyday life: child care, nutrition, travel, gardening, business management, and hundreds of other subjects. Alongside these practical pamphlets await the historical and current records of our government: city maps from the turn of the century, addresses of government agencies, voting records of legislators, regulations on food additives, transcripts of the Iran-Contra hearings. Depository collections in every state are augmented by primary resources in the National Archives, Library of Congress, the presidential libraries; government-agency experts; clearinghouses, and research labs; plus government-produced audiovisual materials, electronic bulletin boards and databases.

## GOVERNMENT INFORMATION DEFINED

*DOCUMENT: A piece of paper that has been sanctified by a bureaucrat.* —Hugh Rawson

*[A government publication is] informational matter which is published as an individual document at government expense, or as required by law.*
—Federal Depository Library Act of 1962

Although the terms "government publication" and "government document" are usually used interchangeably in this country, some nations and intergovernmental organizations distinguish between them. When the distinction is made, "documents" are defined as internal-use-only records (such as minutes of meetings), while "publications" are those available to outsiders (such as informational pamphlets). Government documents and publications are components of the broader notion of *government information*, including not only print and other formats such as CD-ROMs and databases, but also published and unpublished information and both restricted and publicly available information. In other words, not all government information is available to the public or published. This book focuses on publicly available government information, both published and unpublished (archival collections, for example), in numerous formats.

Government information is produced by or for a government agency. Although the terms "document" and "publication" indicate printed paper format, government-produced information comes in many other media, including microfiche, CD-ROMs, databases, electronic bulletin boards, and audiovisual materials. In the late 1980s, the proportion of federal information in paper slowly decreased, while electronic products tripled. But, despite the General Services Administration's vision of a paperless electronic government by the year 2000, the federal government is expected to remain paper-documented for a long while. And, although it's unlikely that electronic formats will soon supplant paper, formats like online databases, magnetic tape, floppy disks, and CD-ROMs are making swift gains, especially for bibliographic, reference, statistical, scientific, and technical data. Electronic media have already eclipsed microfiche, which faces a diminished future predominately as a records storage and archives medium.

Because official definitions have not kept pace with new technologies, the 1962 definition of a government publication has become something of an anachronism. Congress has been grappling with the need for legislation to broaden legal definitions to encompass government-generated information reproduced in any way. This updated definition, which would incorporate newer electronic materials such as CD-ROMs and databases, would involve revising Title 44 of the *U.S. Code*.

Why are definitions so important? Partly because they determine what will be available in depository libraries, the public's primary source of government information. In practice, the Government Printing Office, which administers the Depository Library Program, defines a depository "publication" as not only print and microfiche, but also any informational matter produced for public dissemination, in any format. Unfortunately, GPO's liberal interpretation of ambiguous pre-electronic era legal language is not always shared by government issuing agencies. Many neglect their responsibility to supply GPO with depository copies of their information products, allowing thousands of government-produced materials to slip through loopholes in the depository library net.

## THE IMPACT OF NEW TECHNOLOGIES

Equity of access to government information was the polemic of the 1980s. New technologies, unforeseen when our information laws were drafted, prompted concern about erosion of public access to government information. Organizations like the American Library Association, the Association of Research Libraries, the Information Industry Association, and the National Commission on Libraries and Information Science issued policy statements defending public access to government information in all formats. The National Commission on Libraries and Information Science, for example, described public information as a "national resource" owned by the people, and worried that "basic principles regarding its creation, use and dissemination are in danger of being neglected and even forgotten."[2]

In 1988, the long-awaited Congressional Office of Technology Assessment (OTA) analysis of the nation's information collection, processing, and dissemination was released as *Informing the Nation: Federal Information Dissemination in an Electronic Age* (Y 3.T 22/2:2 In 3/9). Assessing the implications of electronic technology for GPO, the Superintendent of Documents, NTIS, and depository libraries, OTA pinpointed two thorny issues: equity of access, and defining government and private-sector roles in information dissemination. The report

**FIGURE 1.1: The Government of the United States.**

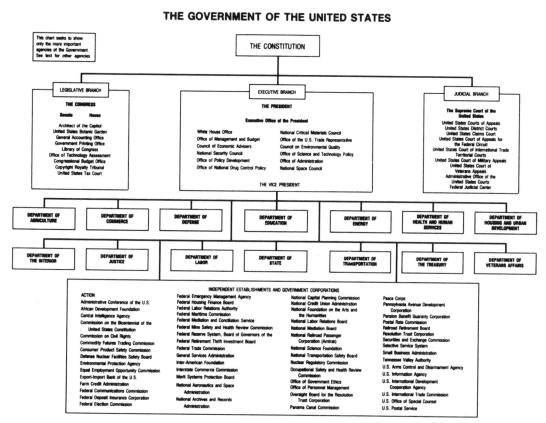

Source: *U.S. Government Manual*, 1991–92.

portrayed a nation at a crossroads heaped with opportunities and challenges, and called for legislation to resolve urgent federal information dissemination issues and set the nation's course.

Although the Office of Management and Budget (OMB) oversees government information policies, the United States lacks a unified national information policy. As the only major industrialized nation without such a policy, the U.S. trails behind nations like Japan, France, Brazil, and Canada. Instead, the U.S. operates under what has been called a "de facto national information policy," a potpourri of "mini-policies" emanating from laws, regulatory decisions, budget priorities, bureaucratic decisions, and congressional oversight.[3] Several key laws dominate the national information policy mosaic: the Printing Act of 1895, the Depository Library Act of 1962, the Freedom of Information Act, Copyright Act, and Paperwork Reduction Act. Numerous philosophical questions complicate the development of a unified national information policy. Citizen access must be balanced against national needs, private-sector interests, and the options and restrictions born of new technologies.

## BIBLIOGRAPHIC CONTROL

> *Unfortunately, no one—not the GPO, the JCP, nor the OMB—can make more than an educated guess as to how many information products are issued annually by the federal government.* —David Brown, GPO

The quest for government information requires two steps: first, verifying its existence, sometimes called "intellectual access," and then obtaining it, or "physical access."[4] This quest is symbolized by two questions: What information has the government generated, and where can I find it? Bibliographic control involves creating records of publications (citations) so they may be identified and obtained, fostering both intellectual and physical access. Bibliographic access tools for government publications include government and commercially published catalogs and indexes and databases such as OCLC, the Online Computer Library Center. OCLC maintains an online union catalog that is the world's largest database of library bibliographic information.

Government information that eludes bibliographic documentation hovers in an informational black hole, untraceable because it lacks a bibliographic record. Legions of other government titles enjoy intellectual access, but their physical access is thwarted. This is the situation when a title is listed in the *Monthly Catalog*, for example, but not distributed to depository libraries.

Federal government information activity is decentralized. That can mean that sometimes the right hand doesn't know what the left hand is doing. In this case, instead of two hands, the government has around 5,800—that's about the number of government departments and

agencies in the federal government. A 1983 survey identified 449 federal information dissemination facilities besides those of the Superintendent of Documents: clearinghouses, special libraries, depositories, information analysis and referral centers, databases, and agency sales and distribution outlets.[5] This proliferation of information dissemination options adds to the challenge of interagency coordination. While no single agency regulates all government information activity, a "Big Two" oversee federal information production and dissemination: (1) congress's Joint Committee on Printing, which guides the Government Printing Office, and (2) the Office of Management and Budget (OMB), authorized by the Paperwork Reduction Act of 1980 to oversee the entire life cycle of government information, from collection to dissemination. In addition, there are two major printing and distribution organs, the Government Printing Office (GPO) and the National Technical Information Service (NTIS), plus numerous clearinghouses, depository programs, archival collections, and information centers.

## GPO: The Mother Lode

While the Government Printing Office is not the sole source of federal publications, it is the federal government's primary information reproducer and distributor. GPO's responsibilities include not only printing for the federal government, but also disseminating government information to the public through the Superintendent of Documents and depository library program. Since federal law mandates that agencies send GPO copies of any federally funded information products for depository distribution, GPO is positioned to monitor government publishing and oversee its bibliographic control. It is, therefore, one of the primary indexers and distributors of federal publications.

## NTIS: The Other Lode

The National Technical Information Service (NTIS) is the nation's clearinghouse for unclassified technical reports of government-sponsored research. NTIS collects, indexes, abstracts, and sells U.S. and foreign research reports, not just on scientific and technical subjects, but also in the behavioral and social sciences. Technically, NTIS qualifies as the nation's most prolific publisher, making available some 80,000 titles yearly. GPO, by comparison, releases only about 30,000 titles each year. As a matter of fact, NTIS's output of individual titles exceeds that of GPO and all United States commercial publishers put together. All of these titles are stored at NTIS forever and can be reproduced indefinitely, never going out of print. Unfortunately though, many NTIS titles are unavailable for depository distribution and are not listed in the *Monthly Catalog*. Instead, they must be traced using specialized indexes and databases.

## Falling through the Cracks: The "Non's"

*We can lick gravity, but sometimes the paperwork is overwhelming.* —Wernher von Braun

Nondepository publications are those not earmarked to be sent to federal depository libraries. Non-GPO publications are those not produced under the auspices of the GPO. Because both nondepository and non-GPO materials exist, neither GPO nor depository libraries provide access to all federal government information.

Since non-GPO publications do not grind through the GPO machinery, they are often missed by GPO's bibliographic net of catalogs and indexes. Although agencies are required to supply copies of non-GPO publications for depository distribution and *Monthly Catalog* documentation, noncompliance is common. Educated estimates calculate that as many as half of all federal publications elude "national announcement."[6] Such lost publications are sometimes called "fugitive" documents. One Department of Health and Human Services official has estimated that 80 percent of HHS publications, including many grant-related technical reports, never go through the GPO system. This is typical of technical report literature, much of which is not funneled through GPO and therefore evades depository distribution. Not only will these publications fail to appear on the shelves of depository libraries, they often will not be listed in any of GPO's bibliographic control tools. To find out they exist and to get copies to read, one must go through different channels, for instance, NTIS.

Not funneled through GPO or NTIS, not announced, not listed in mainstream government publication catalogs, indexes, or databases, fugitive publications are available only to those who know to ask for them. They include products considered of limited interest, such as those of the National Cancer Institute, those printed in-house by agencies or produced by contractors or grantees, in-house-distribution-only titles, and many promotional brochures, leaflets, and press releases. Thousands of fugitive publications slip through the bibliographic net each year, many because they were not printed through GPO, others because they were never "printed" at all, evading GPO's machinery through electronic and other nontraditional routes.

## THE QUEST

*If you think education is expensive, try ignorance.*
—Derek Bok,
Harvard University President

Consider the tomato. Shunned as poisonous, the plump red fruit held our ancestors at bay until the early nineteenth century. The spell was broken in 1820, when Colonel Robert Johnson ate a basket of tomatoes in full view of his Salem, New Jersey, neighbors. The crowd that watched Johnson's suicidal act cheered when he survived, and the tomato's reputation was transformed.

Government publications are a lot like tomatoes. To this day their potential remains shrouded not by one misconception, but by many. Among uninitiated librarians they enjoy a mystique that is fueled by unfamiliarity. To the general public they remain largely unexplored, an informational fourth dimension perceived as inaccessible to the masses. As a result, government publications have been the province of a self-selected elite for over two centuries.

Meanwhile, like tomatoes which spawned new varieties through horticultural experimentation, government publications have evolved in the wake of technology. The concept of "publication" or "document" has been eclipsed by the broader notion of *government information*. Printed publications now make up only one channel of government information, which comprises CD-ROMS, microfiche, audiovisuals, electronic databases and bulletin boards, clearinghouses and research laboratories, agency subject experts, and primary resources in the collections of the National Archives, the Library of Congress, and the presidential libraries. All are accessible to the public and await exploration.

Don't feel guilty if you've never experienced the joy of government information. Government documents can make even seasoned library users and senior librarians cringe, like vampires recoiling from sunlight. Why? Much user reluctance can be chalked up to a sketchy awareness that documents are "different," coupled with lack of practice using them. The apparatus of government information is specialized, but not difficult. You should be proficient by the time you finish this text.

## FREEBIES

The following subject bibliography is free from U.S. Government Printing Office, Superintendent of Documents, Washington, DC 20402:

141. Federal Government

## REFERENCES

1. Judith Waldrop, "Educating the Customer," *American Demographics* 13 (September 1991):46.

2. "Principles of Public Information" adopted by the U.S. National Commission on Libraries and Information Science, June 29, 1990.

3. *Federal Information Dissemination Policies and Practices. Hearings before the Government Information, Justice, and Agriculture Committee of the Committee on Government Operations House of Representatives, 101st Congress, 1st Session, April 18, May 23, and July 11, 1989.* GPO, 1990. (Y4.G74/7:In3/22), p. 302. (Testimony of Harold Shill, librarian.)

4. William S. Buddington, "Access to Information," in *Advances in Librarianship*, vol. 2, ed. by Melvin J. Voigt. (New York: Seminar Press, 1971), pp. 1-43.

5. *Federal Information Dissemination Policies and Practices*, p. 262.

6. Depository Library Council to the Public Printer, *First Report to the Public Printer, 1972-1976* (GPO, 1978), p. 65 (GP 1.35:972-76); also Cynthia Bower, "Federal Fugitives, DNDs and Other Aberrants: A Cosmology," *Documents to the People* 17 (September 1989):121.

## FURTHER READING

Congress. Office of Technology Assessment. *Informing the Nation: Federal Information Dissemination in an Electronic Age.* (OTA-CIT-396) GPO, 1988. (Y 3.T 22/2:2 In 3/9)

A summary of the report is free from OTA; the report is the focus of "Symposium on the U.S. Office of Technology Assessment Report: Informing the Nation: Federal Information Dissemination in an Electronic Age," in *Government Information Quarterly* 6/3 (1989), pp. 131-71.

Gore, Albert, Jr., "Infrastructure for the Global Village: Computers, Networks and Public Policy." *Scientific American* 265 (September 1991):150-53.

"Exformation," surpluses of untapped data, result in unused information "rotting" while questions are left unanswered and problems are left unsolved.

Hernon, Peter. "Discussion Forum: Government Information Safety Nets." *Government Information Quarterly* 7 (August 1990):249-57.

An exploration of the concept of safety nets for ensuring access to federal government information.

Hernon, Peter and Charles R. McClure. *Public Access to Government Information: Issues, Trends, and Strategies.* 2nd ed. Norwood, NJ: Ablex Publishing Corp., 1988.

Issues, trends, and strategies for public access to government information.

McClure, Charles R., Peter Hernon, and Harold C. Relyea. *United States Government Information Policies: Views and Perspectives.* Norwood, NJ: Ablex Publishing Corp., 1989.

The role of government information in American society is thoroughly explored.

Redmond, Mary. "From Backwater to Mainstream: Government Documents in the Online Catalog." *The Bookmark* 47 (Spring 1989): 161-65.

How and why government publications are being incorporated into library online catalogs.

# CHAPTER 2
# Access to Government Information

## A FREE AND OPEN SOCIETY

*To secure these rights, Governments are instituted among Men, deriving their just powers from the consent of the governed.*
—The Declaration of Independence

Access to government information is truly essential to the American way of life, which relies upon its citizens to make informed public decisions. The free flow of information between government and the public has been called "the mortar of our society."[1] Libraries, especially depositories, which archive government information in every state of the union, provide a vital link between citizens and their government.

*A popular Government without popular information, or the means of acquiring it, is but as Prologue to a Farce or a Tragedy; or perhaps both. Knowledge will forever govern ignorance: And a people who mean to be their own Governors, must arm themselves with the power which knowledge gives.* —James Madison

The doctrine of government accountability to citizens emerged during our nation's infancy, but not without controversy. The colonies' closed legislative proceedings and the secrecy surrounding the constitutional convention both incited public criticism. Opening congressional proceedings to the public was debated during the Continental Congress, but the Senate continued to meet in secret sessions until 1795, when the public galleries were opened to reporters. Until the early 1800s, newspaper articles were the public's only means of monitoring congressional activities.

Arguing for the public's right to an impartial record of government activities, proponents of the people's right to know eventually triumphed. Citizen access to government information was seen as a way to ensure government accountability and informed citizen decision making. The Government Printing Office and the depository library system were created, charged with printing and archiving government records.

Government publishing was nurtured by a law exempting government publications from copyright restrictions. The first federal publications documented official activities with a sober stream of laws, treaties, court rulings, and congressional proceedings. Later, as agencies plunged into their missions, popular and informational publications began to roll off the presses: reports of geological surveys, first-person accounts of the opening of the West, "how-to" guides for farmers, and navigational aids.

## THE FREE FLOW OF INFORMATION

*Information, the lifeblood of the federal government.*
—*Informing the Nation*

We tend to take our open government for granted until we compare it with more repressive societies. In Rumania, for example, typewriters must be licensed. In Russia, controls over typewriters were only recently lifted, along with the threat of imprisonment for unauthorized photocopying. The 1980s saw President Gorbachev's policy of *glasnost*, or "openness," sanction the release of information Soviet citizens had heretofore been denied. Information kept under wraps for decades began emerging: the first statistics on suicide released since 1928, plus secret files on the Russian Orthodox Church, the Bolshevik Revolution, and the czarist secret police. The Soviets coined the word "informatization" to describe their process of adapting to the new climate of information exchange.

Fox Butterfield, the *New York Times* China correspondent, describes that country as "one of the most secretive societies in the world."[2] China controls citizen use of copy machines, and forbids foreigners to read certain newspapers or to enter "classified" sections of bookstores. One American visitor discovered that even Chinese government-published city maps are purposely distorted to foil foreign intelligence efforts. China's list of classified state secrets includes anything about the country's military, foreign affairs, culture, public health, ethnic minorities, warehouses, and even weather forecasts. Try planning a picnic in Beijing.

In Great Britain, known as the world's most secretive democracy, most government information is routinely classified for at least thirty years. The British Official Secrets Act encourages classification of government information as "state secrets," outlawing unauthorized disclosure of any government information, no matter how innocuous.[3] Britons lack freedom of information laws protecting the public's right to know, or any "bill of rights" guaranteeing basic liberties. British concern about government secrecy led to hiring Ralph Nader as a consultant in the battle for access to government records.

> *Those who expect to reap the blessing of freedom, must, like men, undergo the fatigue of supporting it.*
> —Thomas Paine

In contrast, it is acknowledged that the spy trying to dig up facts about the United States haunts libraries, legally reading publicly available, unclassified publications. At a 1985 conference on The International Flow of Scientific and Technical Information, attendees were shown slides of two military planes, one U.S., one Soviet. The Soviet airplane was an exact copy of its U.S. counterpart, although the U.S. plane had been designed first and was never mass-produced. How did the Soviets copy it? They didn't need to see the actual plane; they simply located drawings of it published in U.S. literature.

---

**Government Publications in Action**

Testifying before a congressional committee, consumer advocate Ralph Nader recalled having his own subscription to the *Congressional Record* as a high school student in the 1950s. Although the subscription price was then a walloping $12, young Nader received daily issues of the *Congressional Record* free. He had simply written his Senator (Prescott Bush, father of former President George Bush) and requested one of the Senator's allocation of free constituent subscriptions.

---

A favorite KGB hangout has traditionally been the Library of Congress, offering free use of unclassified reports and technical publications, comfortable seating, and modern rest rooms. KGB agents openly attended congressional hearings, educational seminars, and trade shows, devouring openly accessible public information. In the 1980s, the "Decade of the Spy," the FBI estimated that 90 percent of Soviet intelligence about the U.S. was gathered from open, public sources.[4]

There are two typical reactions to exploitation of our open society. Proponents of limiting access to government information argue that our government should not be "the world's largest free library-reference service."[5] Others contend that although abuses are distasteful, it would be equally distasteful for our democratic principles to be compromised. As columnist Kenneth C.

Bass explained, "When it comes to spies, Americans hate the disease. But we hate the cure as well."[6]

---

**Government Publications in Action**

On December 17, 1969, the Secretary of the Air Force announced the termination of Project Blue Book, the official investigations of unidentified flying objects. Of the 12,618 UFO sightings investigated between 1947 and 1969, seven hundred remained "unexplained," but not considered extraterrestrial. Project Blue Book is open to researchers on site in the National Archives Microfilm Reading Room, or through copies of the microfilm rolls of sighting reports and photographs that can be purchased for about $23 each.

---

## THE COST OF FREE INFORMATION

> *[Government] publications are among the most cost-effective of all government activities, for they empower citizens to use the laws themselves.*
> —Ralph Nader

The proper balance between cost-effectiveness and ready citizen access to government information has been debated for decades. A writer in 1895 complained that junk shops were stacked with tons of public documents waiting to be ground into scrap while the Capitol's vaults were heaped with unused books and documents. At the turn of the century the Superintendent of Documents contended that a surplus of documents made them seem cheap and contemptible to the public. He characterized the problem as "chronic document indigestion."

Almost a century later, the battle continues between government cost cutters and right-to-know advocates. Reevaluation of public access to information was spurred by *Information Resources Management* (Y 3.P 19:2In 3), a 1977 Commission on Federal Paperwork report, which argued that information is not free and limitless "like air and sunshine, simply ours for the asking." Instead, the report maintained, the information supply is limited, its handling expensive, and as a result the government should reconsider providing so much of it free to the public. The Commission on Federal Paperwork's recommendations were incarnated in the Paperwork Reduction Act of 1980 (PRA), which sought to reduce the public's burden of reporting to government, but also tapped the Office of Management and Budget to oversee government information policies.

In 1981, OMB spearheaded a campaign to eliminate wasteful spending on publications and audiovisuals, and by 1984, one-quarter of all federal publications had been eliminated. OMB's Circular A-130, "Management of Federal Information Resources," outlined a framework for carrying out PRA requirements through cost-benefit analysis, privatization, and user charges. Widely criticized, Circular A-130 is slated for revision, and PRA reauthorization is on the agenda of the 102nd Congress (1991-92). A proposed revision of A-130 appeared in the *Federal Register* in April 1992, with a call for public comments (57 FR 18296). Congress is expected to use the next PRA reauthorization to review policy governing government-produced electronic information and OMB's regulatory authority.

The 1980s witnessed termination and consolidation of publications, price hikes, user fees, curtailment of freebies, intensified classification, and elimination of information collection and dissemination programs. Other moves included substituting electronic formats for paper, weakening the Freedom of Information Act, and transferring government publications to private publishers ("privatization"). Critics cautioned that while these actions appeared to save taxpayers money, they also restricted free information access, creating other, incalculable, costs.

## NEW TECHNOLOGIES

*The "document" of the future will vary radically from what it is now.*
—The Effects of Electronic Recordkeeping on the Historical Record of the U.S. Government

Information access is also affected by changes in depository document formats. The shift from paper to microfiche saved money, but meant inconvenience, scattered collections, and confusion for many users. The newest challenge to public access is electronic-format-only information, with no paper counterpart. The 1980s witnessed a surge of electronic government information, with a concomitant decline in printed publications. Federal agencies are opting to save money and time by disseminating information electronically through databases, floppy disks, CD-ROMs, and electronic bulletin boards. Many of these become "fugitive documents," government information products missed by the Depository Library Program. When agencies contract with commercial vendors to disseminate electronic information, the taxpayer pays twice: once for agency information collection, and again to access it. Those who can't afford to pay are blocked from perusing government information. Unfortunately, our national information dissemination policies were developed when today's new communications media were undreamed of. The print mind-set of our printing and distribution laws has lent urgency to appeals for an expanded legal definition of government "printing" to guarantee free depository library access to machine-readable formats. As Wayne P. Kelley, Superintendent of Documents explained, "The core principle is that the public has paid for the collection, compilation, and publication of Federal information—and should have access to it without further cost."

## FEDERAL AMNESIA

*With the use of paper, the development of policies was simple to trace. Successive drafts indicated the evolution of decisions. With computers, though, drafts no longer exist. Instead, policy papers evolve and each new version is written over the previous one.*
—Patricia Aronsson, National Archives and Records Administration

Although electronic technologies allow faster, cheaper, and more efficient information handling, they pose a threat to historical documentation. Because many electronic records are ephemeral, the danger of losing the nation's "memory" is a mounting concern among historians, archivists, and researchers. Electronic record-keeping could extinguish documentation of federal programs and decisions whenever historically significant first drafts, marginal notes, and attachments are lost. Some observers rank the danger of information loss as more grave than that of deteriorating acid-paper in books. Fearing "federal amnesia," they have urged solutions be found "if our history is not to stop short in the 1980's."[7]

A recent National Archives' assessment determined that so far parallel paper records systems have preserved electronic policy and decision-making records but "it is only a matter of time" before serious losses occur.[8] Electronic records are vulnerable because of their fragility, rapid obsolescence, and ease of erasure or alteration, coupled with a lack of "historical awareness" on the part of government employees, and the low priority given records management. Meanwhile, government officials have expressed fears that a silent FOIA (Freedom of Information Act) backlash has made "electronic shredding" of sensitive material a routine method of avoiding FOIA disclosure.[9]

*Will we all need a passport to enter a public library?*
—Robert A. Simons, DIALOG lawyer

Unlike printed publications, copies of which are scattered coast to coast, the plug can easily be pulled on access to electronic information. In late 1986, the National Security Council and the Pentagon launched a campaign to restrict or monitor use of "sensitive but unclassified" federal information accessible through nongovernment sources such as DIALOG, NEXIS, and LEXIS. President Reagan issued National Security Directive 145 to protect national security by thwarting foreign access to unclassified scientific, technical, and economic information used to piece together intelligence information. Opposition from the library community, information industry, Congress, and the public culminated in The Computer Security Act of 1987, which limited the Defense Department's authority over computer security policy for unclassified data systems.[10]

## PUBLIC ACCESS LEGISLATION

*Secrecy is the bane of democracy because it is the enemy of accountability.*
—Arthur Schlesinger, Jr., historian

The Freedom of Information and Privacy Acts are key means of public access to federal government records. The Freedom of Information Act opens agency administrative files to the public, while the Privacy Act protects personal information amassed by government. Both laws are founded on the principle of the people's right to know what their government is doing. Both are also beginning to show their age. Conceived when most federal records were stashed in filing cabinets, the two laws have stumbled into the electronic era bereft of clauses specifying access to computerized files. *Informing the Nation* explored potential problems in administering antiquated access laws. Until the Freedom of Information and Privacy Acts are modernized, requesters remain dependent on agency and judicial expansiveness in interpreting the spirit of the laws.

## The Freedom of Information Act (FOIA)

Originally enacted on Independence Day, 1966, after eleven years of congressional debate, FOIA (pronounced "foy-ah") provided a formal request procedure for public access to federal executive agency records. The law was toughened in 1974, after congressional oversight hearings cited "five years of foot-dragging by the Federal bureaucracy," plus loopholes that allowed long response delays and high fees.

The amended FOIA, for which Congress overrode a presidential veto, made it easier, quicker, and cheaper to get information from federal agency files. It placed a time limit of ten working days for agencies to acknowledge requests, set reasonable photocopying charges, allowed for appeals when information was denied, and required publication of indexes in the *Federal Register* to aid in tracking down information.

### Who Uses FOIA?

Although the law was designed with journalists, consumer groups, and private citizens in mind, its heaviest use has been from business. Corporations use FOIA as a marketing aid, for defending themselves in court, and for corporate "espionage" to gather information about competitors. A FOIA request for a competitor's affirmative action data is an example of how FOIA can indirectly reveal company secrets. The numbers of employees in each department might be deduced from the data, allowing guesses about how well certain products are selling. Such uses of the law have resulted in reverse Freedom of Information lawsuits to prevent release of trade secrets.

Journalists, consumers, and citizens do use FOIA, although not as often as Congress anticipated. Ralph Nader's successful campaign against the carcinogenic Red Dye No. 2 was bolstered by documents acquired under FOIA. The sons of executed spies Julius and Ethel Rosenberg made dozens of FOIA requests in their quest to clear their parents' names. FOIA requests led to disclosure of the My Lai massacre and uncovered files on unsafe nuclear reactors, contaminated drinking water, CIA mind experiments, $600 military coffeepots, ineffective drugs, and hazardous television sets.

The Freedom of Information Act has been called "the bread and butter of investigative journalism," yet a 1989 survey by the Society of Professional Journalists uncovered widespread frustration over denials and delays that stalled some requests for years.[11] More chilling was the admission by government officials that a silent protest against FOIA has probably left some agency actions undocumented and encouraged "electronic shredding" of sensitive material.

---

**Government Publications in Action**

When reference librarian David Kusche began researching mysterious disappearances in the Bermuda Triangle, many popular explanations already existed, including time warps, reverse gravity fields, death rays from Atlantis, black holes, and UFOs. Kusche traced each incident back to primary sources and concluded that the Bermuda Triangle is a "manufactured mystery," nurtured by careless research, misconceptions, and sensationalism. His primary research for his book, *The Bermuda Triangle Mystery Solved*, included many government documents such as U.S. Navy and U.S. Coast Guard documentation, Civil Aeronautics Board investigative reports, the U.S. Geological Survey's *National Atlas of the United States*, the Federal Aviation Administration's *Instrument Flying Handbook*, and *Merchant Vessels of the United States*.

---

### Limitations of FOIA

The Freedom of Information Act opens only federal executive agency files: Congress, the judiciary, and state and local agencies are not covered by the law. Many states and localities have passed their own freedom of information laws, however. The Freedom of Information Act pertains to agency files, not to published documents. Access to published documents is through depository libraries, the Government Printing Office, and other sources described in this text. While the current law has generally been interpreted to include access to computer files, many people seek an amended "electronic FOIA," which would guarantee access to newer record-keeping technologies.

## The Privacy Act

*At no time in the past has our government known so much about so many of its individual citizens. Government bureaucracies seem to thrive on collecting additional information. That information is now stored in over 7,000 government computers, and the names of over 150 million Americans are now in computer banks scattered across the country. In short, data banks affect nearly every man, woman and child in the United States today.* —Richard M. Nixon, 1974

The seeds of our "dossier society" were sown with those of government taxation and social welfare programs, making massive record-keeping a necessity for bureaucratic accountability.[12] Computers revolutionized federal record-keeping, making it possible for more agencies to keep tabs on "far more people at far less cost than ever was possible in the age of the manual file and the wizened file clerk."[13] Close to three decades ago Vance Packard was among those sounding an alarm about the government's "giant memory machines." In his 1964 book, *The Naked Society,* Packard wondered what the impact of computerized record-keeping would be in 1984, two decades hence: "If information is power, Americans should be uneasy about the amount of information the federal government is starting to file on its citizens in its blinking memory banks."[14]

Today the federal government is our nation's biggest record-keeper. Uncle Sam maintains some 3 billion files on individuals—an estimated twelve files per person. Most government agencies collect personal information in the course of their duties, from names and social security numbers to data on personal finances, health, and occupation. Uncle Sam maintains more than 2,000 computer systems of personal information, packed with details gathered from the subjects themselves, from federal, state, and local governments, and from third parties such as state motor vehicle departments, credit bureaus, and insurance companies.

*For the fish swimming in the ocean, the comprehension of wetness is impossible. Wet requires the contrast of dry. In the same way, it is hard for most Americans to appreciate the intricate layering of computerized networks that have been built up around each of our lives during the last twenty-five years. Abrupt violent changes, like the revolution in Iran, are easy to see. Incremental changes, stretching over decades, are harder to perceive.* —David Burnham, *The Rise of the Computer State*

Congressional concern about increased computer record-keeping led to the passage of the Privacy Act in 1974, requiring agencies to keep their records about individuals accurate, confidential, and within legal restrictions. The act allows citizens to find out what federal files are being kept about them, to see the files, and to correct them. Twelve years later, in a government study that made national headlines, Privacy Act protections were deemed eroded by use of new technologies for processing personal information.[15] New technologies not only complicate the public's ability to monitor and correct personal files, they also expedite interagency exchange of personal data and create possibilities undreamed of in the filing-cabinet era when the act was passed. The study acknowledged the existence of a de facto national database containing information on most Americans. This database emerged indirectly as a network of individual government databases and is searchable using what the report called a de facto electronic I.D., your social security number.[16] In the first substantial refinement of the Privacy Act since 1974, the Computer Matching and Privacy Protection Act of 1988 set rules for computer matching (electronic comparison of agency records about individuals, used to detect abuse, fraud, and waste). Comparing a list of Social Security recipients with a file of deceased Medicare recipients is an example (a computer-check that in 1981 identified 8,000 dead people to whom monthly Social Security checks were still being mailed).

*About one-half of the American public believes that computers are a threat to privacy, and that adequate safeguards to protect information about people are lacking.* —Congress's Office of Technology Assessment, 1986

Personal privacy is predicted to be a hot issue in the 1990s. Polls conducted in 1990 and 1991 found four out of five Americans concerned about threats to their privacy.[17] Concern about a computerized Big Brother may be reflected in anti-census sentiments springing up across the globe. Response to the 1990 American census was sluggish, and Holland hasn't had a census since 1971. West Germans boycotted their census for 17 years, partly from fear of government misuse of the computerized data. It didn't help that the Interior Minister announced a plan to issue each West German an identity card and a computer file. This prompted fears that detailed personal data would be transmitted to tax authorities, police, or other punitive government agencies.

### Government Files on You

When you fill out a student loan application, detail your finances to the IRS, register for the draft, or even rent a post office box, personal information is recorded about you. This information can be exchanged or used as the law allows. This is true not just for criminals, but for average, honest citizens. How might the average, honest citizen show up in CIA files, for example? Easily, on CIA lists such as:

- Authors of articles or books on intelligence (spying)
- Attorneys in private practice
- CIA employees with parking permits

- People writing to ask if the CIA has files on them (This catch-22 is also true for the FBI, which automatically starts a file on anyone asking whether she or he is in FBI files)

Even the postal service keeps files, at least seventy-five of them, including:

- People who have had their mail forwarded
- Members of carpools with postal service employees
- People who ask not to receive sexually oriented ads in the mail

## Using the Privacy Act

The Privacy Act allows you to know what government agency records are being kept about you; to read, correct, or append them; and to prevent their use for other than original purposes without your permission.

| FEDERAL FILES YOU MAY BE IN | |
|---|---|
| Agency | File |
| Education | Student loan recipients |
| IRS | Income tax filers |
| Social Security | Social security number holders |
| State Department | Passport holders |
| Transportation | Motorboat registrants |
| Veterans Affairs | Blood donors |

If this list piques your interest, you can read about thousands of other agency files kept about individuals in *Privacy Act Issuances Compilation* (AE 2.106/4: ). This biennial 5-volume set describes files, agency rules for requesting information from them, and how the records are used.

## The Laws in Action

*The cost of the Freedom of Information Act is the cost of carrying out a democratic government.*
—Katherine A. Meyer,
Director of the Freedom
of Information Clearinghouse

Government estimates set the yearly FOIA processing tab at $50 to $60 million. Although the cost is high, FOIA supporters point out that this price tag is less than the Pentagon's yearly marching band budget. Others argue that these are justifiable costs a free nation must pay for government accountability. FOIA requests total 500,000 yearly according to congressional estimates. Agencies like the FBI, CIA, and FDA have been deluged with FOIA requests. Along with legitimate requests, there are a sprinkling of kooky ones. A man from Allentown, Pennsylvania, calling himself "King Edward the Ninth" has repeatedly pestered the CIA for his personal

| PUBLIC ACCESS LAWS: SUMMARY | |
|---|---|
| Freedom of Information Act | Privacy Act |
| Covers federal executive agency records | Covers personal records maintained by federal executive agencies |
| Anyone can request | Any citizen or permanent resident alien can request information about himself or herself |
| Agency has ten working days to respond | No response time prescribed |
| Requester charged for searching and copying | Requester charged for copying |
| Exemptions: national security, internal personnel rules and practices, trade secrets, policy communications, personnel and medical files, law enforcement investigatory files, reports on regulation of financial institutions, geological and geophysical information | Exemptions: some CIA files, some federal law-enforcement files, national defense, solely statistical files, files that would reveal confidential sources |

file. A gentleman concerned about being followed by Martians asked the FBI for records of his correspondence with the agency regarding the alien pursuit.

## Using the Laws

Use of the Privacy Act to access personal files has been less than anticipated, in part due to public ignorance of Privacy Act rights, difficulties identifying records, and the time and cost of communicating with agencies (it has been estimated that seeing all your files would mean writing 5,800 separate letters and spending more than $1,600 on postage). Since there is no central clearinghouse to handle all requests, each must be sent to an individual agency holding files. The children of Julius and Ethel Rosenberg, for example, filed FOIA requests with more than eighteen agencies as part of their quest to clear their parents' names.

You must do your homework to file a FOIA or Privacy Act request. Research on agency missions and activities is often necessary to determine which agencies are likely to hold the information needed. Helpful sources are the *U.S. Government Manual*, with its descriptions of agency responsibilities and addresses, *Privacy Act Issuances Compilation*, the *Federal Register*, and *Code of Federal Regulations* (CFR). Search the *CFR Index and Finding Aids* volume (AE 2.106/3-2: ) under "Freedom of Information" to find agency announcements of rules for processing requests. The *Federal Register Index* publishes a quarterly listing of indexes to individual agency files, the

"Guide to Freedom of Information Indexes," describing each agency index's coverage and how to access it. Daily *Federal Register* issues also include agency FOIA rules. Scanning the *Federal Register* for notices of "Privacy Act: Systems of records" and "Privacy Act: Computer matching programs" is another way to monitor personal records systems. (See Chapter 9 for a detailed introduction to the *Federal Register*.) *Privacy Act Issuances* (AE 2.106/4: ) is a compilation of agency rules from the *Federal Register*.

## The Request Letter

*An unclassified document can be hidden just as deeply in a file drawer. . . as a classified document can. The Freedom of Information Act never even becomes relevant until someone knows enough to ask for an "identifiable" document.*
—Stanley Futterman, Associate Professor, New York University Law School

The FOIA requires requesters to "reasonably describe" the information sought. This means that requests for "everything" or "anything" on a subject are frowned upon. The more specific the request, the better. A proper request will identify the records sought using newspaper clippings, articles, citations to congressional reports, or citations to portions of the records that have already been released—anything to help the agency track the record within its filing system. For example, the American Library Association's FOIA request for details on the FBI's Library Awareness Program asked for "all records pertaining to FBI investigations [that] have thoroughly documented the many ways that specialized scientific and technical libraries have been used by the Soviet intelligence services, and all other documents pertaining to the Bureau's Library Awareness Program."[18] Remember that the Freedom of Information Act doesn't require the requester to reveal why the information is wanted or how it will be used.

To identify files kept on individuals, consult *Privacy Act Issuances Compilation* (AE 2.106/4: ). First identify the agency maintaining the records and then follow the agency's request procedures. Privacy Act requests must include the requester's full name and address, plus proof of identity—a photocopy of a document showing your signature or photograph, such as a passport. Requests should specify the type of list where the record is held plus any information required by the agency, such as dates, subject matter, and identifying numbers. Requests should be addressed to the official listed for the record system, and "Privacy Act Request" printed on the front of the envelope.

## THE FEDERAL INFORMATION CENTER

An automatic garage door mysteriously began opening by itself and emitting voices. The curious homeowner called the Federal Information Center (FIC), which relayed his question to the Federal Communications Commission. The FCC determined that the talking-door phenomenon was caused by a ham radio. A woman wanted to plant a tree in a national forest as a wedding gift. The FIC referred her to the U.S. Forest Service, and a tree was donated in honor of the happy couple.

The Federal Information Center is a clearinghouse for questions directed to the government. The federal government offers such a wide range of programs and services that people are sometimes confused about where to turn. The FIC can help identify which of hundreds of government offices to contact, avoiding a "merry-go-round of referrals." Calling or writing the Federal Information Center results in either an immediate answer or referral to a government expert. For FIC toll-free telephone numbers, consult the "U.S. Government" listing in your phone book or the *Federal Information Center* pamphlet (GS 1.2:F 31/year). If your area is not listed, call (301) 722-9098. Address letters to Federal Information Center, Box 600, Cumberland, MD 21502.

---

**Government Publications in Action**

In the closing chapters of *Roots*, Alex Haley described his quest to trace his family history. American and British Naval records helped Haley identify the ship which brought his ancestor, Kunta Kinte, to America in 1767. Poring through microfilmed census records from the 1800s, Haley found his great-aunt mentioned: "It was simply so uncanny sitting staring at those names actually right there in official U.S. Government records."

---

## FREE COPIES OF DOCUMENTS

*The golden age of government publications is over.*
—Nelson Fitton, head of the Department of Agriculture, Publications Division

While it's true that the "golden age" of documents has passed, we now enjoy the "zinc age," an era when patience, persistence, and knowledge of a few techniques can still lasso copies of publications and free information from the government. Although the techniques described below often bring results, they are not the quickest way to get materials and should be recommended to library users only with caution. Depository libraries and document purchases (described in chapters 3, 4, and 6) are more reliable sources of government information, but not nearly as much fun.

## Technique One: Write the Issuing Agency

Rising costs of maintaining mailing lists, postage, printing, and storing have forced more and more agencies to curtail free publication distribution. But even in tightfisted times, most agency missions or legal mandates dictate that they serve and inform the public. When you'd like a free copy of a specific document (preferably a recent one) you can try requesting a "single free copy" from the issuing agency. Contact the unit that issued the document or a local field office. The issuing unit can be ascertained from the document's bibliographic description in the *Monthly Catalog*, OCLC, or PRF, while agency addresses and telephone numbers, and field offices are listed in the *U.S. Government Manual*.

General requests for information about an agency's "products and services" often trigger a mailing of introductory brochures which can be very informative. These valuable sources alert requesters to other free materials, resource people, and useful telephone numbers. Many agencies will happily send general information brochures, copies of annual reports, publications lists, and computer database descriptions, and may add you to their mailing lists for free newsletters.

## Technique Two: Telephone Calls

Telephone calls are best when you have a specific question in mind, rather than for general information seeking. Agency personnel tend to be friendly and helpful, especially if you get the person most knowledgeable about your question. Back in 1979, Matthew Lesko described Washington as "the world's largest free public library," and started a research business based on the premise that "anything you want to know can be learned in Washington." Lesko relies upon telephone calls to track down Washington experts "on practically any topic."[19]

Initial tricks for successful calls are locating the unit's telephone number (the *Monthly Catalog* and *Government Reference Serials* list many agency telephone directories) and then getting past clerical gatekeepers, who often know little about agency subject specialties (and can be curtly nasty), to the experts. Once the appropriate person is found, she or he is invariably eager to help. It sometimes shocks the public to discover that so-called bureaucrats are real people like themselves: They pay taxes, enjoy sharing their knowledge, and occasionally wear mismatched socks.

## Technique Three: Contact Legislators

Senators and representatives can sometimes provide free copies of popular or special materials (such as laws or bills), and their local staffs may help track down materials. Senators and representatives also serve as links to the Congressional Research Service and are a source of free access to LEGIS, Congress's online legislative tracking system (see Chapter 8). Requesters should turn to legislators only for special problems or current materials—not for highly technical or scientific documents, retrospective titles, or repeated requests.

## Technique Four: Depository Libraries

Although depositories don't sell documents or give away free copies, they are still sources of cost-free access to government publications. They are equipped to provide comprehensive access to government-oriented indexes and abstracts, journals, and documents, some depositories boasting collections that span almost a century. Regular users of government information should get to know their local depository staff. Not only can staff assist in using their local collection, they can also refer requesters to other libraries and agencies and expedite interlibrary loan requests.

## ADDRESSES

Coalition on Government Information, American Library Association, Washington Office, 110 Maryland Ave., N.E., Suite 101, Washington, DC 20002; (202) 547-4440
  The Coalition focuses national attention on restricted access to government information and supports access enhancement.

The Freedom of Information Clearinghouse, Box 19367, Washington, DC 20036; (202) 785-3704
  Offers help in accessing government information through the Freedom of Information and Privacy Acts.

The National Security Archive, 1755 Massachusetts Ave., N.W., Washington, DC 20036; (202) 797-0882, fax (202) 387-6315
  A nonprofit library of declassified and unclassified government records, including materials released under FOIA.

## FREEBIES

From The Freedom of Information Clearinghouse, Box 19367, Washington, DC 20036; (202) 785-3704:

  "The Freedom of Information Act: A User's Guide:"

From OMB Watch, 1731 Connecticut Ave., N.W., Washington, DC 20009-1146; (202) 234-8494, fax (202) 234-8584:

  "Public Access to Government Information: Looking Ahead in 1991." A short, meaty flier describing the impact of OMB's Circular A- 130, along with a detailed summary of the 1985 document.

From U.S. Department of Justice, Office of Information Law and Policy, Washington, DC 20530:

  *Your Right to Federal Records: Questions and Answers on the Freedom of Information Act and the Privacy Act.*

The following pamphlets are sold for nominal fees:

  American Library Association. *Less Access to Less Information By and About the U.S. Government: A 1981-1987 Chronology* (indexed cumulation, $7; updated semiannually, $1; a new cumulation is expected in 1992). Prepaid with self-addressed mailing label from ALA, Washington Office, 110 Maryland Ave., N.E., Washington, DC 20002-5675; (202) 547-4440, fax (202) 547-7363.

  *Using the Freedom of Information Act: A Step by Step Guide* from the American Civil Liberties Union, 132 W. 43rd St.,

New York, NY 10036; (212) 944-9800, fax (212) 354-5290. $3. ISBN 0-86566-042-5.

*Using the Freedom of Information Act: A Step by Step Guide* is for sale from Center for National Security Studies, 122 Maryland Ave., N.E., Washington, DC 20002.

## REFERENCES

1. Donna A. Demac, *Keeping America Uninformed: Government Secrecy in the 1980s* (New York: Pilgrim Press, 1984), p. 4.

2. Fox Butterfield, *China: Alive in the Bitter Sea* (New York: Times Books, 1982), pp. 383-405.

3. Howell Raines, "Groans and Cheers in Britain for Secrets Plan," *New York Times* (June 30, 1988): A11.

4. "The KGB's Spies in America," *Newsweek* 98 (November 23, 1981), pp. 50-61; Senate, *Communist Bloc Intelligence Gathering Activities on Capitol Hill, Hearings before the Subcommittee on Security and Terrorism of the Committee on the Judiciary, 97th Congress, 2nd Session, May 12, 1982* (Serial No. J-97-116) (GPO, 1982). (Y 4.J 89/2:J-97-116).

5. "Pro and Con: Cut Access to Government Data?" *U.S. News and World Report* 92 (January 18, 1982): 69-70.

6. Kenneth C. Bass, "What Can the U.S. Do to Catch More Spies?" *Buffalo News* (June 29, 1986): F-15.

7. Senate, Committee on Governmental Affairs, *National Archives and Records Administration Act of 1983, Hearings before the Committee on Governmental Affairs, 98th Congress, First Session on S. 905 Entitled the National Archives and Records Administration Act of 1983, July 29, 1983* (S. Hrg. 98-488) (GPO, 1984), p. 38. (Y 4.G 74/9:S. Hrg. 98-488).

8. National Academy of Public Administration. *The Effects of Electronic Recordkeeping on the Historical Record of the U.S. Government: A Report for the National Archives and Records Administration.* NTIS, 1989. PB89-152219

9. Society of Professional Journalists, *Report from the FOIA Front: A Study of Journalists' Usage of the Freedom of Information Act* (The Society, 1989), p. 40.

10. John Horgan, "Civil Defense: The Military Loses a Fight for Control of Data—Or Does It?" *Scientific American* 258 (March 1988): 18, 20.

11. *Report from the FOIA Front.*

12. Arthur R. Miller, *The Assault on Privacy: Computers, Data Banks, and Dossiers* (Ann Arbor, MI: University of Michigan Press, 1971), p. 20.

13. David Burnham, *The Rise of the Computer State* (New York: Random House, 1983), p. 11.

14. Vance Packard, *The Naked Society* (New York: David McKay Co., 1964), pp. 41-42.

15. Congress, Office of Technology Assessment, *Electronic Record Systems and Individual Privacy* (OTA-CIT-296) (GPO, 1986), p. 3. (Y 3.T 22/2:2El 2/6).

16. Congress, pp. 10-33.

17. *The Equifax Report on Consumers in the Information Age* (Atlanta, GA: Equifax, Inc., 1990) (conducted by Louis Harris & Associates); *Harris-Equifax Consumer Privacy Survey 1991* (Atlanta, GA: Equifax, Inc., 1991).

18. Gerald R. Shields, "Point of View: Academic Libraries Must Oppose Federal Surveillance of Their Users," *The Chronicle of Higher Education* 34 (March 23, 1988): A48.

19. Leila Kigt and Matthew Lesko, "A Writer's Route to Government Information," in *The Writer's Resource Guide,* ed.

by Bernadine Clark (Cincinnati, OH: Writer's Digest Books, 1983), pp. 14-19.

## FURTHER READING

Babcock, Charles R. and Don Oberdorfer. "Computer Detective Found Crucial Data: Intern's High-Tech Sleuthing Led to Files." *The Washington Post* (February 28, 1987): A10 (LEXIS, Omni).

How a four-foot stack of secret Iran-Contra memos were coaxed from the White House computer by a Pentagon intern.

Burnham, David. *The Rise of the Computer State.* New York: Random House, 1983.

A thought-provoking review of the accidental and intentional misuse of computers and its impact on individual privacy.

Conable, Gordon. "The FBI and You." *American Libraries* 21 (March 1990):245-48.

The American Library Association's FOIA requests regarding the FBI's Library Awareness Program are described, along with sample Privacy Act requests.

Foerstel, Herbert N. *Surveillance in the Stacks: The FBI's Library Awareness Program.* New York: Greenwood Press, 1991.

A summary of the Federal Bureau of Investigation's counterintelligence activities in libraries.

Gross, Daniel. "Byting the Hand that Feeds Them: Information Vendors are Robbing the Government Blind." *The Washington Monthly* 23 (November 1991): 37-41.

The impact of privatizing public information.

Hernon, Peter and Charles R. McClure. *Federal Information Policies in the 1980's: Conflicts and Issues.* Norwood, NJ: Ablex Publishing Corp., 1987.

A thorough review of theoretical issues related to national information policy and public access to government information.

———. *Public Access to Government Information: Issues, Trends, and Strategies.* 2nd ed. Norwood, NJ: Ablex Publishing Corp., 1988.

An issue-oriented discussion of public access to government resources, collection development, and documents administration, presenting an excellent overview of government information of all kinds.

House Committee on Government Operations. *Citizen's Guide on Using the Freedom of Information Act and the Privacy Act of 1974 to Request Government Records.* (H.Rpt. 102-146). GPO, 1991 (Y 1.1/8:102-146).

A guide to rights under the laws, with details about how to request information.

*How to Use the Federal FOI Act.* 6th ed. Washington, DC: FOI Service Center, 1987.

A do-it-yourself guide to using the FOIA, amendments and court opinions affecting it, and detailed explanations of the exemptions.

Kaplan, Sheila. "Issue Splits Public-Interest Community: Libraries, Vendors at Odds Over Electronic Data." *Legal Times* 14 (July 15, 1991): 2.

What happens when private vendors serve as intermediaries for accessing public information.

McClure, Charles, Peter Hernon, and Harold C. Relyea. *United States Government Information Policies: Views and Perspectives.* Norwood, NJ: Ablex Publishing Corp., 1989.

An overview of information policy issues that guide federal government information management.

Riley, Tom and Harold C. Relyea, eds. *Freedom of Information Trends in the Information Age.* Totowa, NJ: Frank Cass, 1983.

A discussion of the historical development of FOIA and attempts to alter it, a review of other nations' FOIA protections, plus a fascinating list of FOIA disclosures announced in the press between 1972 and 1980.

Smith, Robert Ellis. *Compilation of State and Federal Privacy Laws, [year].* Washington, DC: Privacy Journal, annual.

State and federal laws related to confidentiality of personal information are described.

Spencer, Michael D. G. *Free Publications from U.S. Government Agencies: A Guide.* Englewood, CO: Libraries Unlimited, 1989.

A how-to manual for requesting free documents.

# CHAPTER 3
# GPO, The Mother Lode

*Printing is the other half, and in real utility the better half, of writing—both assist in communication between people.* —Abraham Lincoln

## WHAT

Although the Government Printing Office (GPO) is not the sole source of federal documents, it is the federal government's primary information reproducer and distributor.

## WHY

Title 44 of the *U.S. Code* requires that GPO fulfill the printing and binding needs of the federal government and distribute U.S. government publications to the public.

## HOW

GPO fulfills its distribution responsibility by preparing catalogs and indexes to government publications, distributing and selling government information products, and administering the federal depository library system. GPO's marketing program informs the public about what GPO has for sale and increases public awareness of depository libraries.

Congress's Joint Committee on Printing (JCP) administers and oversees GPO, acting as its board of directors. The JCP has authority over all government printing and binding, including microfiche, audiovisual productions, and electronic media.

## WHO

At GPO's helm is the Public Printer, nominated by the president and confirmed by the Senate. One of the Public Printer's subordinates is the Superintendent of Documents (SuDocs), who oversees depository libraries, sale of documents, and compilation of the *Monthly Catalog* and other bibliographic aids.

## WHEN

In 1991, GPO celebrated its 130th year. It opened for business in 1861, on the day President Lincoln was inaugurated.

## WHERE

GPO's central office is in Washington, DC, although not all GPO printing is done in the Capitol. More than three-quarters is contracted out to commercial printers, and some is done at GPO regional printing offices (all bear the GPO imprint, however). GPO's mail-order sales program operates from Washington, DC, with the assistance of twenty-three GPO bookstores nationwide, consigned federal agents like the Congressional Sales Office, and in cooperation with the Consumer Information Center distribution centers.

## PUBLICK PRINTING

At the outset our Congress had no permanent, official printer. For three-quarters of a century, government printing was assigned to a hodgepodge of private entrepreneurs called publick printers. Publick printing was an unstable vocation, with frequent turnover and heavy competition for contracts. Early printers tended to dawdle, and since printing was still in its infancy, even a diligent typesetter might complete only two or three pages before calling it a day. Many of these printing pioneers were slow, inaccurate, and messy, and were regularly fired by a disgruntled Congress. Early printers are also remembered for bribery, lost manuscripts, overcharging, and inspiring public scandals and congressional investigations.

The publick printers' steady stream of motley documents led to visions of an official government printer, but some factions argued against it. A Senate debate over printing led to a challenge to a duel in 1833, but the contest was mercifully halted by onlookers. One impassioned supporter of central government printing compared Congress's reliance on printed materials to people's need for food. "For ships you can wait; for guns you can generally wait," explained the congressman, "but you cannot be deprived of your printing for a single day without serious embarrassment and loss of time."[1]

*Printing created a new relationship between people and their governments, involving the individual to a far greater extent in his national destiny than ever before.*
—Robert E. Kling, Jr.,
*The Government Printing Office*

The dream of an official government printer languished for about forty years. Finally laws were passed to establish central government printing, which by 1860 evolved into the Government Printing Office, charged with federal printing and binding. GPO's creation ended printing corruption and favoritism and snatched public printing away from private printers and newspaper publishers. While GPO's original charge was solely printing, responsibility was added for sale and distribution in 1895, when Congress passed a comprehensive printing act which became Title 44 of the *U.S. Code*.

A new building was erected in Washington, complete with cupola, bell, and gilt eagle. The building was fully equipped for modern typesetting by hand, and boasted a boiler house, coal house, wagon shed, and stables (for which government issue included one black horse, a bobtail bay, and a delivery wagon). Passersby were sometimes pelted with discarded metal type tossed from GPO windows. The surrounding neighborhood was known as "Swampoodle" because of its swamp and puddles. Swampoodle bustled with geese, pigs, and goats, and was bordered by a creek characterized as an "indescribable cesspool."

GPO genealogy recounts how employees entered the new building on the morning Confederate guns opened fire on Fort Sumter. Soon after, they worked by gaslight to set type for the Emancipation Proclamation and, later, President Lincoln's eulogy. Today GPO presses continue to document America's triumphs, tragedies, and drudgeries by printing the laws, reports, and proclamations that shape the nation.

---

**This Is a Printing Office**

Crossroads of civilization
Refuge of all the arts against the ravages of time
Armory of fearless truth against whispering rumor
Incessant trumpet of trade
From this place words may fly abroad
Not to perish on waves of sound
Not to vary with the writer's hand
But fixed in time
Having been verified by proof
Friend, you stand on sacred ground
This is a printing office

*Beatrice L. Warde,*
from a bronze plaque
in the lobby of GPO

---

## GPO TODAY

*GPO is one of Washington's most neglected institutions.*
—Ralph Nader

As the primary information reproducer and distributor for the federal government, GPO's responsibilities include not only printing and binding, but also disseminating government information to the public. GPO facilitates public access to government publications by providing bibliographic control and physical access to them. Bibliographic control is achieved through compiling catalogs and indexes that cite these publications. Physical access is accomplished through the depository library system and by selling publications. The Superintendent of Documents fulfills GPO's dissemination role through distribution of documents to depository libraries (see Chapter 4), selling government publications, and compiling catalogs and indexes to them, including the *Monthly Catalog* and *Publications Reference File* (see Chapter 5). The Superintendent of Documents is also responsible for mailing documents.

Although Title 44 of the *U.S. Code* mandates that all government printing be funneled through GPO, loopholes allow smaller jobs to be printed elsewhere. Some agencies are granted waivers to do their own printing and distribution. These exceptions, coupled with a shift toward decentralized electronic and desktop publishing and private vendor-dissemination, have threatened GPO's command over government information. As a printing and distribution hub, GPO has been well situated to monitor government information products for inclusion in the *Monthly Catalog* and depository libraries. The electronic era threatens to aggravate the "fugitive" document problem by insulating GPO from a large portion of information production.

The name Government *Printing* Office may become an anachronism as traditional "ink-on-paper" printing is eclipsed by electronic formats. The Superintendent of Documents predicts that by the turn of the century GPO will have evolved from a traditional graphic printing plant to "an information-processing operation dominated by electronic information creation, replication, and dissemination." Currently the primary governmentwide sales outlet for paper publications, GPO is seeking a larger role in sales of electronic media. GPO sales items include database tapes and diskettes, including the *Congressional Record*, *Federal Register*, *Statistical Abstract*, and *Budget of the United States Government*. The free flier, "Electronic Information Products," lists GPO titles sold on magnetic tape or computer disks. GPO's first CD-ROM emerged in 1990 with EPA's *Toxic Release Inventory*, followed by the 1985 volume of the *Congressional Record* a year later. Now that the floodgates have opened, many more CD-ROMs will follow.

Although often called the "nation's biggest publisher," GPO is not a true publisher, but a printer. This distinction is made because GPO neither initiates nor editorially controls its publications. These responsibilities are shouldered by the agencies issuing the documents. As a service unit, GPO prints what agencies want printed, with no input regarding their content, titles, or even accuracy. The real publishers of government documents are the government issuing agencies responsible for their intellectual content.

---

**What's Wrong Here?**

A newspaper article attacked GPO for selling an outdated air force manual which advised pilots to repeat a mistake that had already caused ninety-two deaths in a plane crash.

*Answer:* GPO was innocent. The issuing agency, not GPO, is responsible for the content and accuracy of its publications printed by GPO.

---

## Sales

*We're not in business to make money. But sometimes we do.* —Carolyn Crout, GPO

Mail order is GPO's primary mode for selling government information products. As a matter of fact, GPO has been ranked among the top five mail-order houses in the country. While the bulk of GPO sales are to businesses, one-quarter of GPO customers are individuals. GPO prices are established by law at cost plus 50 percent, with the average document priced at around $8. Orders can be mailed, faxed, or telephoned in (see "Addresses" at the end of this chapter). Callers should be alerted that GPO uses a somewhat annoying telephone electronic voice-connect system. Customers may find it simpler to order through a GPO bookstore, using phone numbers given in each of the GPO promotional catalogs listed below.

GPO publishes several free current awareness publications to encourage sales. Each includes prices, stock numbers, and order forms. Remember that GPO sales catalogs are promotional tools meant to be scanned or browsed, not bibliographies or indexes equivalent to the *Monthly Catalog* or PRF. With their lack of indexes and limited coverage, *New Books, U.S. Government Books, Consumer Information Catalog,* and the subject bibliographies are not intended to serve as indexes to government documents.

---

**GPO Stock Numbers**

The GPO stock number configuration is: S/N 000-000-00000-0, often accompanied by the phrase "@GPO." A stock number with any other configuration is not for sale from GPO, but from another agency. The sales agency will be abbreviated after the @. Look for agency name in the *Monthly Catalog* or PRF bibliographic entry.

---

### Subject Bibliographies (GP 3.22/2: )

Subject bibliographies (SBs) are free lists of GPO sales documents on more than 300 topics. The subject bibliography index (SB-599) gives SB numbers for specific topics and is also free. These short bibliographies offer a quick starting point for documents literature searches by providing bibliographic information and some annotations. SBs are not comprehensive bibliographies of documents on a topic, but do list titles currently for sale from GPO.

While the subject bibliographies are free, the titles listed in them are not. Someone who doesn't care to buy documents can peruse many of them in a depository library, using the SuDocs number given in the subject bibliography as an access key.

### *U.S. Government Books* (GP 3.17/5: )

This is a free catalog of information products for sale from GPO (despite the "Books" in its title, this source covers various media). Titles range from popular to technical, in numerous subject areas and many formats—including books, journals, manuals, cloth decals, and posters. *U.S. Government Books* is embellished with illustrations and annotations, making it pleasant to browse. Although published quarterly, this sales catalog remains essentially unchanged with each reissue, with only a few new titles added each quarter. Since no mailing list is kept, each issue must be requested anew unless you bought something during the quarter.

Like the subject bibliographies, *U.S. Government Books* is not a comprehensive list of GPO sales titles, including only a handful for any subject. Since SuDocs numbers are usually noted, *U.S. Government Books* does serve as an access key to depository collections, where many of the documents may be used free of charge.

### *New Books* (GP 3.17/6: )

*New Books* is a free listing of new titles added to GPO's sales inventory during the last two months. Its newsprint format offers a sober roster of essential bibliographic details for ordering (or borrowing from a depository)—without annotations or frivolity. GPO keeps a mailing list for this publication, which arrives every other month.

### *Consumer Information Catalog* (GS 11.9: )

What comes to mind when you think of Pueblo, Colorado? Almost one in five Americans associates the city with government information for consumers.[2] Although the *Consumer Information Catalog* is issued by the General Services Administration, *Catalog* orders are processed by GPO, which operates GSA's Consumer Information Center in Pueblo, Colorado. The handy *Consumer Information Catalog* lists free and inexpensive pamphlets on popular topics and is aimed at the general public. If you watch late-night television you may see a thirty-second spot publicizing this free booklet or its cousin, *U.S. Government Books.* You may even have received a complimentary copy in the mail from your legislator.

When an agency agrees to pick up the tab for printing and distributing a publication, it is offered free in the *Catalog.* About 40 percent of the *Catalog's* titles are free. (The word "free" retains its 1980s flavor—you must enclose $1 when ordering freebies.) Priced booklets in the *Catalog* are GPO publications. In addition, there are some consumer-oriented pamphlets listed for fifty cents each, part of the Low Priced Publications Project, in which issuing agencies shoulder some of the costs usually assumed by GPO.

The *Consumer Information Catalog* is issued quarterly, and a Spanish version is available (*Lista de Publicaciones Federales en Español para el Consumidor*). Multiple copies for distribution giveaways can be requested by educators, libraries, and consumer and other nonprofit groups. The Consumer Information Center Bulletin Board is a source of press releases, radio scripts, consumer news, and publications announcements. Information is available from Consumer Information Specialist, General Services Administration, Consumer Information Center, Washington, DC 20405; (202) 501-1794.

### Government Periodicals and Subscription Services (GP 3.9:36/nos.)

Also known as Price List 36, this is a listing of government periodicals and loose-leaf subscriptions for sale from GPO. Brief bibliographic information, including SuDocs numbers, is included along with sales information and annotations. Available free, with automatic quarterly updates, Price List 36 is an asset at any reference desk (see "Appendix 4: A Documents Toolkit"). This is a handy source for quick verification of SuDocs number stems, or frequency and scope of GPO periodicals. Note: Unlike the *Monthly Catalog,* the bullets in Price List 36 indicate not depository status but subscription type.

## Catalogs and Indexes

GPO catalogs and indexes include the current awareness catalogs already described, along with major bibliographies such as the *Monthly Catalog* and *Publications Reference File* (PRF). It is important to recognize that these tools fall into two distinct categories: those limited to documents sold by GPO and those with broader scope. Many titles listed in the *Monthly Catalog,* for example, are not sold by GPO. Because GPO sells only a small portion of federal documents, GPO promotional catalogs, and even the PRF, are not comprehensive. Each of the GPO sales catalogs omits items sold by agencies other than GPO, out-of-print titles, and those not sold to the public. Because of their lack of comprehensiveness, the GPO

sales catalogs do not fully reflect the scope of depository library collections. (The Depository Library Program offers about ten times more publications than the GPO sales program.) The *Monthly Catalog* should be used for a more comprehensive search, along with special-subject indexes as appropriate.

| GPO CATALOGS | | |
|---|---|---|
| **Title** | **Scope** | **GPO Sales Only** |
| *Monthly Catalog* | Attempts to list all federal publications | |
| *New Books* | New GPO sales publications for the past two months | x |
| PRF | Titles currently in stock at GPO, plus some from ERIC and other agencies | |
| Price List 36 | Periodicals and other subscriptions sold by GPO | x |
| Subject Bibliographies | GPO sales titles on particular topics | x |
| *U.S. Government Books* | Quarterly listing of popular GPO sales items | x |

## Government Bookstores

*The Government Printing Office publishes the proverbial something for everyone.*

—Betsy Pisik,
*The Washington Times*

A disadvantage of mail order is the anxious mailbox vigil, coupled with the "pig in a poke" factor—not knowing exactly what the document will be like until you receive it. Imagine the thrill of examining documents before you buy and browsing through hundreds of new, crisp documents in a bookstore atmosphere. GPO operates twenty-three walk-in bookstores where you can browse, ask questions, buy documents, and take them home immediately, plus order GPO titles not in stock (fewer than one-quarter of available titles are stocked in the bookstores).

Formerly cloistered in federal buildings, the GPO bookstores of the 1990s have been relocated and refurbished—transferred to shopping malls and key downtown sites. A complete list of locations, telephone numbers, and addresses can be found in *New Books, U.S. Government Books,* Price List 36, and the *Monthly Catalog* (see Figure 3.1). GPO also lists bookstores in the telephone yellow pages of each bookstore city, under "Book Dealers - Retail".

**FIGURE 3.1: GPO Bookstore Locations.**

## Locations of Your U.S. Government Bookstores

### Your U.S. Government Bookstores

*GPO operates U.S. Government bookstores all around the country where you can browse through the shelves and take your books home with you. Naturally, these stores can't stock all of the more than 12,000 titles in our inventory, but they do carry the ones you're most likely to be looking for. And they'll be happy to order any Government book currently offered for sale and have it sent directly to you. All of our bookstores accept VISA, MasterCard, and Superintendent of Documents deposit account orders. For more information, please write to your nearest U.S. Government Bookstore.*

**Atlanta**
275 Peachtree Street, NE
Room 100
PO Box 56445
Atlanta, GA 30343
TEL: (404) 331-6947
FAX: (404) 331-1787

**Birmingham**
O'Neill Building
2021 Third Ave., North
Birmingham, AL 35203
TEL: (205) 731-1056
FAX: (205) 731-3444

**Boston**
Thomas P. O'Neill Building
Room 169
10 Causeway Street
Boston, MA 02222
TEL: (617) 720-4180
FAX: (617) 720-5753

**Chicago**
One Congress Center
401 South State Street, Suite 124
Chicago, IL 60605
TEL: (312) 353-5133
FAX: (312) 353-1590

**Cleveland**
Room 1653, Federal Building
1240 E. 9th Street
Cleveland, OH 44199
TEL: (216) 522-4922
FAX: (216) 522-4714

**Columbus**
Room 207, Federal Building
200 N. High Street
Columbus, OH 43215
TEL: (614) 469-6956
FAX: (614) 469-5374

**Dallas**
Room IC50, Federal Building
1100 Commerce Street
Dallas, TX 75242
TEL: (214) 767-0076
FAX: (214) 767-3239

**Denver**
Room 117, Federal Building
1961 Stout Street
Denver, CO 80294
TEL: (303) 844-3964
FAX: (303) 844-4000

**Detroit**
Suite 160, Federal Building
477 Michigan Avenue
Detroit, MI 48226
TEL: (313) 226-7816
FAX: (313) 226-4698

**Houston**
Texas Crude Building,
801 Travis Street, Suite 120
Houston, TX 77002
TEL: (713) 228-1187
FAX: (713) 228-1186

**Jacksonville**
100 West Bay Street
Suite 100
Jacksonville, FL 32202
TEL: (904) 353-0569
FAX: (904) 353-1280

**Kansas City**
120 Bannister Mall
5600 E. Bannister Road
Kansas City, MO 64137
TEL: (816) 765-2256
FAX: (816) 767-8233

**Laurel**
U.S. Government Printing Office
Warehouse Sales Outlet
8660 Cherry Lane
Laurel, MD 20707
TEL: (301) 953-7974
TEL: (301) 792-0262
FAX: (301) 498-9107

**Los Angeles**
ARCO Plaza, C-Level
505 South Flower Street
Los Angeles, CA 90071
TEL: (213) 239-9844
FAX: (213) 239-9848

**Milwaukee**
Room 190, Federal Building
517 E. Wisconsin Avenue
Milwaukee, WI 53202
TEL: (414) 297-1304
FAX: (414) 297-1300

**New York**
Room 110, Federal Building
26 Federal Plaza
New York, NY 10278
TEL: (212) 264-3825
FAX: (212) 264-9318

**Philadelphia**
Robert Morris Building
100 North 17th Street
Philadelphia, PA 19103
TEL: (215) 597-0677
FAX: (215) 597-4548

**Pittsburgh**
Room 118, Federal Building
1000 Liberty Avenue
Pittsburgh, PA 15222
TEL: (412) 644-2721
FAX: (412) 644-4547

**Portland**
1305 SW First Avenue
Portland, OR 97201-5801
TEL: (503) 221-6217
FAX: (503) 225-0563

**Pueblo**
World Savings Building
720 North Main Street
Pueblo, CO 81003
TEL: (719) 544-3142
FAX: (719) 544-6719

**San Francisco**
Room 1023, Federal Building
450 Golden Gate Avenue
San Francisco, CA 94102
TEL: (415) 252-5334
FAX: (415) 252-5339

**Seattle**
Room 194, Federal Building
915 Second Avenue
Seattle, WA 98174
TEL: (206) 553-4270
FAX: (206) 553-6717

**Washington, DC**
U.S. Government Printing Office
710 N. Capitol Street, NW
Washington, DC 20401
TEL: (202) 512-0132
FAX: (202) 512-1355

1510 H Street, NW
Washington, DC 20005
TEL: (202) 653-5075
FAX: (202) 376-5055

*All stores are open Monday through Friday with the exception of Kansas City, which is open 7 days a week.*

Source: *U.S. Government Books*, 1992

## Publications Reference File (PRF)

GPO's comprehensive microfiche catalog of sales titles is the *GPO Sales Publications Reference File* (PRF). No paper equivalent is available. The PRF functions as a "*GPO Books in Print*," listing documents currently for sale by the Government Printing Office. It also lists forthcoming and recently out-of-stock publications.

---

**GPO All-Time Best-Sellers***

1. *Infant Care*
2. *Metric Conversion Card* (wallet-size)
3. *Federal Benefits for Veterans and Dependents*
4. *United States Government Manual*
5. *Occupational Outlook Handbook*
6. *Adult Physical Fitness*
7. *Economic Report of the President*
8. *Constitution of the United States*

---

*Sales as of 10/91 for titles still in the GPO inventory.

The PRF is useful for identifying bibliographic information about GPO documents for sale, and for verifying current prices and stock numbers for ordering. The PRF may also be used to find out what GPO has printed on a particular subject and to identify documents that may be available in depository libraries. Tips for searching the PRF are given in Chapter 5.

### Standing Orders

Many recurring GPO publications and series can be received automatically on standing order. The free GPO flier, "Standing Order Item List by Titles in Alphabetical Order," lists series and titles available on standing order.

## SUPERINTENDENT OF DOCUMENTS CLASSIFICATION SCHEME

Library classification systems allow arrangement of materials by shelving books on the same subject together. Most people are familiar with the Dewey Decimal and Library of Congress classification systems, which group books within major classes of knowledge. Identifying the classification number, or call number, leads the searcher to the shelves, where other books on the same topic await. Such a system facilitates browsing by eliminating the need for title-by-title searching of the catalog. The Superintendent of Documents (SuDocs) Classification Scheme is not like this.

Unlike the Dewey and Library of Congress schemes, the SuDocs system is based not on the subject of a work, but rather on provenance, or source of origin—the agency which issued it. This means that titles are shelved together according to their issuing agencies, not their subject matter.

A SuDocs number is an alphanumeric notation designating the issuing unit, type of series, and individual book number of a document. Since full bibliographic information is available elsewhere (in the *Monthly Catalog*, for example), being able to decode these elements within a SuDocs number is not imperative. Just as you needn't understand electronics to use your television set, to use SuDocs class numbers you need not understand their derivation beyond a few simple rules. (If you are determined to torture yourself, however, consult the references at the end of this chapter.[3]) Ability to recognize SuDocs numbers is a handy skill: The knowledgeable person will be surprised how often others confidently identify another number (a GPO stock number, for instance) as a SuDocs number.

A SuDocs notation denotes the document's issuing agency and its subunits using letters and numbers, periods, slashes, and dashes. Each SuDocs number has two distinguishing elements: a letter or letters at the beginning, and a colon in the middle. SuDocs classification numbers begin with a letter or letters to designate the agency issuing the document:

LC, for the Library of Congress,
A, for the Department of Agriculture, or
NAS, for NASA

The part of the SuDocs number through the colon is called the class stem. The addition of an individual book number following the colon makes each SuDocs number unique. For example, the SuDocs class stem for each *Department of Agriculture Yearbook* is identical:

A 1.10:

The addition to the stem of three digits indicating the year distinguishes between different editions and creates a unique class number for each:

A 1.10:948 (1948 edition)
A 1.10:992 (1992 edition)

Similar techniques frequently designate revised editions of numbered publications:

A 1.35:381 (original edition)
A 1.35:381/2 (first revision)
A 1.35:381/986 (1986 edition)

This straightforward practice can expedite bibliographic searching in reference sources with SuDocs number indexes. When a SuDocs stem is known, it can be quickly searched in the PRF, the semiannual and annual *Monthly Catalog* indexes, or OCLC to identify the most recent edition or other bibliographic information.

## The SuDocs Scheme in Action

In collections arranged by SuDocs classification, SuDocs numbers can serve as a link between bibliographies and indexes and the documents collection. SuDocs numbers are noted in many major documents reference tools, including the *Monthly Catalog*, PRF, and *CIS/Index*. These sources can function as subject indexes to documents collections, with the SuDocs number used like a call number to retrieve many documents from shelves or microfiche cabinets.

The *Daily Depository Shipping List* (GP 3.16/3: ), an invoice accompanying each shipment of depository documents, lists SuDocs numbers for depository titles. This simplifies processing in libraries using the SuDocs scheme, since the SuDocs number can be quickly transferred to the document for immediate shelving. Because depository shipments should be processed and shelved quickly, a document may reach the shelves before a bibliographic source such as the *Monthly Catalog* can list it. There it may languish, with potential users unaware of its existence until bibliographic tools catch up. Knowledge of SuDocs number stems can help overcome these indexing time lags. When the stem of the notation remains unchanged, new editions can be retrieved without bibliographic verification. For example, knowing that the stem for the *Agriculture Yearbook* is

A 1.10:

allows you to locate the most recent edition on the shelves without waiting for it to be listed in the PRF or *Monthly Catalog*. Remember that when the year is part of a SuDocs number, the initial digit is dropped: 1992 becomes /992.

The *List of Classes of United States Government Publications Available for Selection by Depository Libraries* (GP 3.24: ) is an aid to quick identification of SuDocs number stems (see Figure 3.2). It lists all categories of depository publications by SuDocs number stems, and allows quick referral from SuDocs stems to their issuing agencies and documents series (or vice versa). The *Monthly Catalog* and PRF both have SuDocs number indexes, and the SuDocs number is one of the search keys for accessing OCLC (see Chapter 5). When the stem or complete SuDocs number is known, a SuDocs number search is usually faster than an author or title search.

Because of its usefulness, the SuDocs number should be included whenever a government document is cited. Citations lacking SuDocs numbers are incomplete and a nuisance for the person wishing to locate cited titles. Since the documents seeker often needs a SuDocs number to locate documents within a depository collection (about 70 percent are arranged by SuDocs numbers), he or she will be forced to complete the bibliographic work neglected by the citing author.

---

**Tip: Finding Documents on the Shelves**

In SuDocs class numbers, the numbers following periods are integers, not decimals. Thus, A 1.9: precedes A 1.88: just as 9 precedes 88 when counting. In a decimal system like the Library of Congress Classification, .88 would be shelved before .9, since 88/100 precedes 90/ 100. For an easy practice sequencing SuDocs numbers, review the *List of Classes* or *Monthly Catalog*, both of which are arranged in SuDocs number order.

---

## Disadvantages of the SuDocs Scheme

### Browsers Beware

The SuDocs scheme does not guarantee successful browsing. Users in the habit of scanning library shelves to find interesting titles should remember that this technique relies upon subject arrangement of materials. The SuDocs scheme arranges by issuing agency, not subject content. While documents browsing may provide some successful finds (after all, agency missions restrict them to certain topics and concerns), browsing alone should never be relied upon to locate documents. Guessing which agencies might publish on a topic is not recommended either. Browsing is impeded not only by arrangement according to provenance, but also by the predominance of depository documents in microfiche. Microfiche titles will be overlooked by someone scanning the bookshelves. Because of browsing limitations,

**FIGURE 3.2:** *List of Classes.*

---

**LIST OF CLASSES OF UNITED STATES GOVERNMENT PUBLICATIONS
AVAILABLE FOR SELECTION BY DEPOSITORY LIBRARIES**

REVISED DECEMBER 02, 1985

*Office of the Assistant Public Printer (Superintendent of Documents),
U.S. Government Printing Office, Washington, D.C. 20402*

(CLASS: GP 3.24:985/4)                          (INCLUDES SURVEY 85-010)

---

NOTE.—Numbers following class titles are depository item numbers. The MF or P in parentheses indicates whether the class is distributed in microfiche or paper format. Decisions have not been made for all classes, and all decisions are subject to change. Agencies marked with an asterisk (*) have been reorganized, and current classes will be established when publications are received.

**AGRICULTURE DEPARTMENT**

| | | | | |
|---|---|---|---|---|
| A 1.1: | Annual Report (non-GPO) (P) 0006 | | A 1.82: | Marketing Research Reports (MF) 0013-B |
| A 1.1/3: | Semiannual Report, Office of Inspector General (P) 0006-G | | A 1.84: | Production Research Reports (numbered) (MF) 0013-C |
| A 1.2: | General Publications 0010 | | A 1.87: | Home Economics Research Reports (numbered) (MF) 0011-B |
| A 1.9: | Farmers' Bulletins (P) 0009 | | | |
| A 1.i0: | Yearbook (P) 0017 | | A 1.88: | Utilization Research Reports (MF) 0016-A |
| A 1.10/a: | Yearbook (separates) 0017 | | | |
| A 1.11/3: | Handbooks, Manuals, Guides (P) 0011-C | | A 1.89: | Telephone Directory (P) 0080-E |
| A 1.32: | Posters and Maps (P) 0080-H | | A 1.89/3: | Directories (P) 0080-E |
| A 1.34: | Statistical Bulletins (MF) 0015 | | A 1.89/4: | Telephone Directory, Alphabetical Listing (semiannual) (P) 0080-E |
| A 1.34/2: | Federal Milk Order Market Statistics (annual) (MF) 0015 | | A 1.93: | Budget Estimates for the United States Department of Agriculture for Fiscal Year ... (P) 0006-H |
| A 1.35: | Leaflets (P) 00¹2 | | | |
| A 1.36: | Technical Bulletins (MF) 0016 | | A 1.95: | Marketing Bulletins (numbered) (P) 0013-G |
| A 1.38: | Miscellaneous Publications (MF) 0013-A | | | |
| A 1.47: | Agricultural Statistics (P) 0001 | | A 1.100: | Picture Story (irregular) (P) 0012-A |
| A 1.58/a: | Agriculture Decisions (monthly) (P) 0002 | | A 1.107: | Agricultural Economics Reports (MF) 0042-C |
| A 1.60/3: | Bibliographies and Literature of Agriculture BLA (series) (P) 0032-B-01 | | A 1.114: | Conservation Research Reports (numbered) (MF) 0025-D |
| A 1.68: | PA (Program Aid) Series (P) 0014-A | | A 1.116: | Rural Telephone Bank (P) 0002 |
| A 1.75: | Agriculture Information Bulletin (AIB series) (P) 0004 | | A 1.121: | Agriculture Fact Sheets AFS (series) (P) 0090-B |
| A 1.76: | Agriculture Handbooks (P) 0003 | | A 1.127: | Agriculture and the Environment (annual) (MF) 0006-F |
| A 1.77: | Home and Garden Bulletins (P) 0011 | | A 1.128: | Land Use Notes (irregular) (P) 0014-C |

---

The *List of Classes* is a handy guide to 1) SuDocs number stems, 2) the issuing agency associated with a SuDocs number, and 3) the document series represented by a SuDocs number.

knowledge of bibliographic tools such as the *Monthly Catalog* and PRF is essential for the documents seeker.

### Government Musical Chairs

The federal government is constantly in flux, with departments merging, dissolving, and changing names, sometimes altering agency SuDocs numbers in the process. For example, when the Education Division was a subagency of the Department of Health, Education, and Welfare (HEW), the division's publications were issued under a SuDocs number beginning with HE. Since 1979, when a separate Department of Education was established, the SuDocs number for the Education Department has begun with the prefix ED instead of HE.

There are two approaches to handling shelving problems caused by government reorganization: reclassifying older documents to conform with the new number, or allowing both class numbers to remain, leaving related titles physically separated. (This is another reason documents browsing is inefficient.)

## ADDRESSES

Superintendent of Documents, U.S. Government Printing Office, Washington, DC 20402. Mail orders to: Superintendent of Documents, Box 371594, Pittsburgh, PA 15250-7954; or the nearest GPO bookstore. Telephone: (202) 783-3238, FAX: (202) 783-3238. Payment: Advance payment is required. Checks or money orders should be made out to the Superintendent of Documents. Orders may be charged to MasterCard or VISA (include expiration date), or to a prepaid $50-minimum deposit account. Handy order forms are included in each of the GPO sales catalogs or the *Monthly Catalog.*

Online ordering: DIALOG's DIALORDER allows computerized ordering of titles in the PRF at a slightly higher cost. Standing Order Service: U.S. Government Printing Office, Superintendent of Documents, Stop: SSOP, Washington, DC 20402-9328

## FREEBIES

The following Subject Bibliographies are available free from U.S. Government Printing Office, Superintendent of Documents, Washington, DC 20402:

    77.   Printing and Graphic Arts

    244.   U.S. Government Printing Office Publications

Also free from GPO:

*Customer Information* (information for ordering)

*Electronic Information* Products

*New Books* - U.S. Government Printing Office, Superintendent of Documents, Stop: SSOM, Washington, DC 20402-9328

Price List 36 - U.S. Government Printing Office, Superintendent of Documents, Stop: SSOP, Washington, DC 20402-9328

*Subject Bibliography Index* (SB-599) - U.S. Government Printing Office, Superintendent of Documents, Stop: SSOP, Washington, DC 20402-9328

*U.S. Government Books* - write to Free Catalog, Box 37000, Washington, DC 20013

*U.S. Government Books for Business Professionals*: documents about business, import/export, patents and trademarks, accounting, taxes, law, labor relations, statistics, and selling to the federal government.

For your free copy of *Consumer Information Catalog* or to be added to the bulk mailing list, write to Consumer Information Center, Pueblo, CO 81009.

## REFERENCES

1. Government Printing Office, *100 GPO Years, 1861-1961, History of United States Public Printing,* by Harry Schecter (GPO, 1961), p. x. (GP 1.2:G 74/7/861-961)

2. Judith Waldrop, "Educating the Customer," *American Demographics* 13 (September 1991):46.

3. Superintendent of Documents, Depository Administration Branch, *An Explanation of the Superintendent of Documents Classification System* (GPO, 1990). (GP 3.2:C 56/8/990:) Many explanations of SuDocs number intricacies are excerpted directly from this source; Government Printing Office. Library Programs Service, *A Practical Guide to the Superintendent of Documents Classification System* (GPO, 1986-.) (GP 3.29:Pr 88) A detailed description of the SuDocs scheme for catalogers and other professionals.

4. R. R. Bowker, "Women in the Library Profession," *Library Journal* 45 (August 1920): 635-40.

## FURTHER READING

Government Printing Office. *Annual Report.* GPO, Annual. (GP 1.1: )
    GPO's annual reports provide a quick overview of government printing, trends, and statistics.

House of Representatives. *The Government Printing Office Improvement Act of 1990. Hearings before the Subcommittee on Procurement and Printing of the Committee on House Administration, House of Representatives, 101-2, on H. R. 3849 to Amend Title 44, United States Code, To Reform the Public Information Functions of the Public Printer and the Superintendent of Documents, March 7 and 8, 1990.* GPO, 1990. (Y4.H 81/3:G 74)
    An overview of GPO operations, with a summary and interpretation of OTA's *Informing the Nation,* pp. 27-41.

House of Representatives. *Oversight of the U.S. Government Printing Office General Sales Program: Hearings Held Before the Subcommittee on Procurement and Printing of the Committee on House Administration, U.S. House of Representatives, 100-2, July 26 and 27, 1990.* GPO, 1991. (Y 4.H 81/3:Sa 1)
    A look behind the scenes at GPO (and NTIS) sales programs.

Kling, Robert E., Jr. *The Government Printing Office.* New York: Praeger, 1970.
    A history of GPO, from its beginnings into the twentieth century.

Nelson, Gail K. and John V. Richardson, Jr. "Adelaide Hasse and the Early History of the U.S. Superintendent of Documents Classification Scheme." *Government Publications Review* 13 (January-February 1986): 79-96.
    A profile of the woman who devised the SuDocs classification scheme and her work at GPO.

Shiflett, Lee. "Measurement of Subject Scatter in the Superintendent of Documents Classification." Summarized in *Annual Review of OCLC Research* July 1987-June 1988.
    Reclassification of documents from SuDoc to LC results in significant dispersion of documents because there is little relationship between LC and SuDoc shelf placements.

U.S. Government Printing Office. *GPO/2001: Vision for a New Millennium.* GPO, 1991. (GP 1.2:V 82)
    GPO's strategic plan for the electronic information age.

## EXERCISES

1.  What is the SuDocs number for the *Congressional Record*? (Use one of the GPO promotional catalogs for a quick answer.)
2.  Sequencing SuDocs Numbers: Arrange the following SuDocs numbers in shelf order.

    J 21.22:1
    D 101.2:N 56
    LC 3.4/2:62/991
    J 21.2/10:988
    Y 3.T 22/2:2 C 73/13/v.2/pt.2/charac
    LC 3.4/2:62 a
    I 19.81:40121-B 3-TF-024/991
    Pr 41.8:P 96
    Y 3.T 22/2:2 T 22/24/v.2/pt.2/China
    D 101.2.A8
    PrEx 2.2:C 86

# CHAPTER 4
# Depository Libraries: Federal Information Safety Net

## WHAT

In return for receiving federal publications free "on deposit," depository libraries accept responsibility for making them available to the public. There are two kinds of depositories: selective (or partial) depositories, which collect only those documents that meet the needs of their clientele, and regionals, which take all depository titles and keep them permanently.

## WHY

Federal depository libraries exist to make federal government information accessible to the public. Depositories ensure free access to information about government, make government publications widely available to anyone wanting to use them, and ensure their preservation for future generations. Depositories do not sell government publications but rather loan or allow on-site use of them.

## WHEN

Among the oldest right-to-know statutes, the laws establishing the depository library system date back to the late 1850s. Key legislation that solidified the system as we now know it can be found in the Printing Act of 1895 and the Depository Library Act of 1962.

## WHERE

Depository libraries are located in each state and congressional district, in the Canal Zone, Guam, Micronesia, Puerto Rico, and the Virgin Islands. About 1,400 depositories are dispersed throughout the United States and its territories, in academic, public, state, and other types of libraries.

## WHO

Since each depository is required to open its collection for the free use of the general public, anyone may use a depository anywhere. Depositories serve not only the library's indigenous clientele, but also any member of the public. Each week about 167,000 people across the nation use depository libraries.

## HOW

The Depository Library Program is administered by GPO's Superintendent of Documents, at an estimated yearly cost of about ten cents per person in the United States. The fifteen-member Depository Library Council serves as an advisory board to the Public Printer, and meets each spring and fall. The authority for the Depository Library Program (DLP) is in Title 44, Chapter 19 of the *United States Code* (44 USC 1901 et seq.).

## ONE OF AMERICA'S BEST-KEPT SECRETS

*More people know the closest star than are aware of depository libraries.*
—Ralph E. Kennickell, Jr., Public Printer

The federal depository library system has been characterized as both "the nation's collective memory," and "one of America's best-kept secrets."[1] Although depository libraries exist to make government information accessible to the public, the fact is that many Americans have no idea what depositories have to offer. Heisser found that three-quarters of a group of forty-six people interviewed had never heard of depository libraries, and Hernon discovered that GPO bookstore customers were unaware of depository collections[2] (see Figure 4.1). When asked to define a "federal depository library," people asked at random in Buffalo, New York, offered the following definitions: a library book drop; a library for government personnel; a bank; where Lee Harvey Oswald shot President Kennedy; a storehouse for old federal books; and a library that gets all government documents. None of these responses was correct.

**FIGURE 4.1: Depository Library Program Logo.**

When shown the depository eagle logo, people incorrectly guessed that it designated the U.S. Post Office; censorship (an eagle guarding a book); or an airline. The logo became a registered trademark in 1992.

## DESIGNATION

Depository libraries are designated by law or by members of Congress. Depository law specifies that certain types of libraries—accredited law school libraries and state libraries, for example—are automatically eligible to be depositories. Additional depository locations in each state are determined according to provisions allowing for two in each congressional district (designated by U.S. representatives) and two within each state (designated by U.S. senators). Additional provisions allow depository status for land-grant colleges and state libraries. Chances are your nearest depository is in an academic library, since about two-thirds are. Public libraries are the second most common sites, housing about two out of every ten depositories. The remainder are in many other types of libraries, including state, court, federal, historical, and medical libraries.

To locate nearby depository libraries, consult the free *Directory of U.S. Government Depository Libraries* (Y 4.P 93/1-10: ), available from the Superintendent of Documents, Washington, DC 20402. This annual directory lists depositories by state and city, their addresses, and telephone, FAX, and E-mail numbers. A list of regional depositories is also included in *Monthly Catalog* issues and in the GPO sales catalogs, such as *U.S. Government Books.*

A librarian needn't work in a depository to help people find government information. Reference specialists in both depository and nondepository libraries should acquaint themselves with the addresses, telephone numbers, and scope of nearby depositories, and be ready to refer patrons to them. Blind referrals can be avoided by telephoning ahead to verify whether the material sought is available, and to alert the depository staff to the patron's needs. For the names of depository librarians, consult the *Directory of Government Documents Collections and Librarians*, published by the Congressional Information Service. Reference specialists in nondepository libraries can expedite referral by familiarizing themselves with the twenty core titles that will be found in every depository collection (see list under "Selective Depositories" in this chapter).

## RESPONSIBILITIES

The Federal Depository Library Program (FDLP) is a partnership between government and libraries to link the public with government information. The federal government subsidizes creating, reproducing, and distributing information to depositories, while the cost of processing, housing, staffing, and servicing the depository collection comes from the library's budget. The library also picks up the tab for supplementing the collection with commercial access tools such as *CIS/Index*, and plugging collection gaps. For every government dollar invested, depository libraries contribute at least $10. Brown University, for example—a selective depository—spends some $175,000 annually to maintain its depository.

To fulfill its obligation to serve the general public, a depository must:

1. Make depository materials available for the free use of the community at large, including the disabled, retired, culturally deprived, disadvantaged, other libraries, and educational agencies
2. Establish focal points for inquiries and help, including use of the collection, identification of other local resources, and interlibrary loan requests
3. Establish circulation policies for depository materials
4. Facilitate use of materials within the library, including provision of photocopiers and microform readers
5. Publicize the collection
6. Provide reference assistance

As a "library within a library," a depository's operations parallel the functions of its host library. The depository's accommodations should be of equal quality, with decent lighting, temperature, ventilation, and noise control. The collection should be open during the same hours as other major library departments. Shipments of depository documents should processed quickly.

Although GPO dictates free access to depository collections "without impediments," circulation policies are determined by each individual depository. Some elect not to loan materials for use outside the library. All, however, are required to open their collections for on-site use, and many allow documents to be borrowed.[3]

## ORGANIZATION

Depository materials are not required to be housed together as a special collection. They may be kept separate or integrated with other library materials. Another option is a partially integrated collection, with government information housed in both a special documents department and within other library departments. Since many government publications are valuable reference or bibliographic tools, some may be transferred to a non-circulating reference collection. Others may be shelved with magazines, finding their way into the library's periodicals collection. Government pamphlets may be sent to the vertical file. Wherever depository materials are housed, however, they remain government, not library, property. The documents department often maintains a shelf list in SuDocs number order, showing locations of all depository documents.

Thus, in a single library, depository materials may be scattered to facilitate access. This physical dispersion may result in documents being shelved according to various classification schemes. The Superintendent of Documents system may be used in the documents department, while documents shelved with the regular book collection may be assigned Library of Congress or Dewey Decimal numbers. This is not as confusing as it seems.

## Locating Depository Documents

### A Good Rule of Thumb for Locating Documents: Ask

Librarians in the documents department or at the reference desk should be able to recommend the best approach for locating documents in their library. Today, with documents cataloging records available through OCLC and other vendors, more and more depositories are "mainstreaming" documents by listing holdings in their library online catalogs. Many libraries, however, continue to own many more documents than are represented in their public catalogs. Both library users and librarians should be alerted that some library catalogs are poor sources for identifying documents, since they may list only those titles shelved with the regular collection.

Depository access is sometimes thwarted by the GPO cataloging backlog, which has delayed bibliographic

records for up to a year and a half for some documents. When a title is too new to be verified in either the *Monthly Catalog* or PRF, the librarian may be able to identify its SuDocs number using the *Daily Depository Shipping List* (GP 3.16/3: ), an inventory that accompanies every depository shipment from GPO (see Figure 4.2).

Since more than half of depository documents are received in microfiche, many will be in microfiche cabinets rather than on bookshelves. The same is true for Readex microfiche collections of depository and nondepository titles. Titles in electronic formats, such as CD-ROMs, floppy disks, and online databases, may be in yet another location.

## LOOPHOLES

*During [the last] 100 years, there is probably not one moment when the [depository library] system was ever perfect.*
—Jeanne Isacco, Readex Microprint Corporation

Some types of government documents are never sent to depositories: those perceived to be without public interest or educational value, wholly administrative or operational titles, classified materials, and "cooperative" publications, which must be sold to be self-sustaining (the *National Union Catalog* is an example). Although Title 44 of the *U.S. Code* mandates that all agency publications of public interest or educational value be submitted to GPO for depository distribution, as many as one-third never reach depository shelves.[4] These lost titles are known as "fugitive documents": government information products eligible for, but missed by, the Depository Library Program (a subset has been dubbed "depository not distributed," or DNDs).

Depository copies are culled automatically when GPO prints for an agency, with GPO picking up the tab for the extras. Fugitives often emerge when products are created independently of the GPO machinery. Although the law mandates that all government printing be funneled through GPO, a loophole allows smaller jobs to be contracted out to commercial printers when JCP waives 44 USC 501 requirements. Born in agency field offices, on floppy disks or CD-ROMs, within electronic bulletin boards, or through private vendor contracts, many information products escape GPO's dragnet. The emergence of fugitives is attributed more to agency neglect than to legal loopholes, however. Although agencies are mandated to pay for supplying depository copies even when they publish independently of GPO, noncompliance is common.

The Library of Congress's Documents Expediting Project (Doc Ex) is a vehicle for obtaining government publications not designated for depositories and sold neither by GPO nor the issuing agency. Doc Ex is a cooperative effort between the Library of Congress and a subscribing membership consisting of university, public, and special libraries. In addition to providing members with nondepository titles and congressional committee documents, the project enjoys a special arrangement with the CIA for acquiring *CIA Reference Aids* (this series may be subscribed to by nonmembers of Doc Ex).

Another source of nondepository titles is the Readex microfiche collection, containing the full text of every depository and nondepository publication cited in the *Monthly Catalog* since 1953. Since 1981 the collection has been sold on microfiche rather than microprint. Libraries subscribing to the Readex collection arrange their microfiche in either SuDocs number or *Monthly Catalog* entry number order.

## A TWO-TIER SYSTEM

The federal depository system comprises two types of depositories: selective and regional. Selective depositories select which publications to receive from more than 3,800 categories and must keep them for at least five years. Regional depositories agree to receive all depository documents and to keep them permanently.

## Selective Depositories

Selectives are not required to collect every depository document, although they may opt to receive all of them. They are called selective, or partial, depositories because they select only those classes of documents meeting the needs of their clientele. In recent years, tight budgets have forced many depositories to reduce the percentage of item numbers they elect to receive. With selectives taking anywhere from 10 to 90 percent of all depository documents (about 40 percent select less than 25 percent), each selective's collection is unique, and every depository document will not necessarily be available in every collection. All depositories are expected, however, to own the following core collection:

*Budget of the United States Government*
*Catalog of Federal Domestic Assistance*

**FIGURE 4.2: Daily Depository Shipping List.**

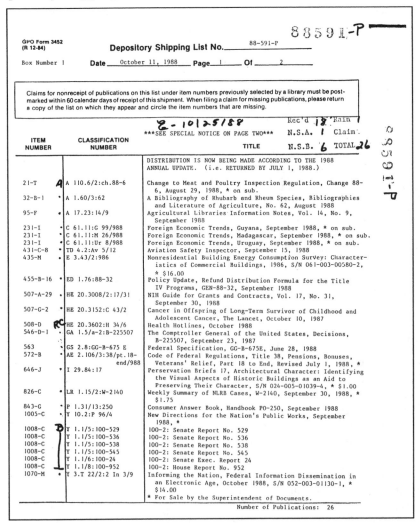

*Informing the Nation* and its Sudocs number appeared on the depository shipping list of October 11, 1988, but was not listed in the *Monthly Catalog* until 3 months later, in January 1989. Note that titles on the DSL that are for sale from GPO are supplemented with price and GPO stock number.

*Census Catalog and Guide*
Census of Population and Housing (for state of
   depository only)
*Code of Federal Regulations*
*Congressional Directory*
*Congressional Record*
*County and City Data Book*
*Federal Register*
*Historical Statistics of the United States*
*Monthly Catalog*
*Publications Reference File*
Slip Laws (public)
*Statistical Abstract*
*Statutes at Large*
Subject Bibliographies
*U.S. Code*
*U.S. Government Manual*
*United States Reports*
*Weekly Compilation of Presidential Documents*

## Regional Depositories

Regionals have many responsibilities beyond those of selectives. They automatically receive all depository titles and must keep them permanently, serving as archival collections for their states. The presence of a comprehensive collection in a regional depository makes it possible for selectives to discard older materials (with the regional's supervision). The regional must also provide interlibrary loan and reference service to both depository and nondepository libraries in the region served as well as coordinate workshops, training, and consultations.

Designation as regional requires approval by the state library and a majority of the local selectives before it can be enacted by one of the state's U.S. senators. Only selective depositories can be candidates for regional status. Nearly two-thirds of the 53 regionals are academic libraries (61 percent), with almost a third (29 percent) located in state agencies and 10 percent in public libraries. A regional may serve two or more states or may share regional responsibilities with another library. Regional status is voluntary, and there is no requirement that each state have a regional depository, although all fifty states are currently served by regionals.

> *We do not want the best public information system that money can buy because we will not be able to afford it.*
> —Representative Jim Bates, Chair of the House Subcommittee on Procurement and Printing

Although two regional depositories are allowed in each state, most states have only one. That's because living up to regional responsibilities is expensive. Neither selectives nor regionals receive government subsidies to operate their depositories—the host library picks up the tab. In exchange for receiving about $100,000 worth of free materials yearly, each regional invests anywhere from one-half to three-quarters of a million dollars each year. Because they must collect all depository documents, regionals often face storage problems.

## Nitty-Gritties of Selection

A depository collection begins when the library assumes depository status, with no retrospective materials provided. If the library wants earlier titles it must purchase them, just as a nondepository does. Instead of selecting title-by-title, selective depositories choose categories (called "classes") of documents which are sent automatically from then on. (Titles in the news, like the "Plum Book," are automatically sent to all depositories, even those not selecting that class.) Each depository class is assigned an item number (example: Item 0017), the key to determining which documents are available to depositories. Item numbers are noted in the PRF, *Monthly Catalog* (usually accompanied by a black bullet), OCLC (field 074), and in numerous bibliographies, indexes, and abstracts.

The *List of Classes of United States Government Publications Available for Selection by Depository Libraries* (GP 3.24: ) is a catalog of publication categories available to depositories, listed in SuDocs stem order, with the item number and a short title listed for each class (see Figure 3.2). The quarterly *List of Classes* serves as a handy guide to depository titles, allowing referral from SuDocs number stem to issuing agency and class title. The list is helpful not only to depository staff but also to any librarian or documents user wanting a source of quick verification of depository status or SuDocs number stem. Updates to the *List of Classes* are published irregularly in *Administrative Notes*. Another source of information about depository item classes is the microfiche and magnetic tape *GPO Depository Union List of Item Selections* (GP 3.32/2: ), which describes the various depository classes and notes the depositories receiving them.

## Bulletin Board Link with GPO

The Federal Bulletin Board (FDLP/BBS) is available to depository libraries and the Depository Library Council.[5] FDLP/BBS is currently used for E-mail (electronic mail) and access to federal electronic information.

## The *Daily Depository Shipping List* (GP 3.16/3: )

The *Daily Depository Shipping List* (DSL) is an inventory accompanying each depository shipment. Each shipping list is individually numbered, with an E, M, or P suffix to indicate a shipment in electronic, microfiche, or paper. Shipping lists for electronic media note accompanying paper documentation.

## Disposal of Documents

Examine a depository document and you'll see a notice of government ownership, probably on the cover.

Depository documents never belong to the library housing them, but remain U.S. government property. As such, they cannot be discarded without adherence to strict regulations. A selective depository served by a regional may discard documents, but only after keeping them for five years. Even then it is not a matter of tossing the document into a wastebasket—the regional must supervise weeding. The selective begins by asking the regional's permission to discard, submitting a list of the candidates for disposal. Since the regional serves as a state backup collection with responsibility for interlibrary loan, it may claim some of the discards to fill gaps in its own collection. Regionals' 100-percent collections are fairly new, many established in the early 1960s, so their retrospective holdings are not necessarily complete. The selective is required to offer the remaining discards to other depositories, then to nondepository libraries, and finally may sell the leftovers, with the profits going to the Superintendent of Documents.

Discarding after five years is a privilege granted by the regional, not a right of the selective. Thus, selectives not served by a regional may not discard, even after five years. They must keep all depository materials permanently, since they cannot resort to a backup regional collection. Certain types of documents may be discarded automatically, however. These include superseded publications and those replaced by bound volumes or microfiche copies. (See Appendix C of *Instructions to Depository Libraries* "List of Superseded Depository Documents [that may be discarded]." A revised Superseded List was published separately in summer 1992.)

## Archival Backup Collection

The most complete collection of federal documents is in the National Archives, designated as Record Group 287, "Publications of the U.S. Government." The core of the collection is the former Public Documents Library begun in the 1890s, with recent materials regularly transferred from GPO's custody to the National Archives and Records Administration (NARA). Record Group 287 serves as a "resource of last resort" for depository libraries, which may request photocopies of materials. The *Cumulative Title Index to United States Public Documents, 1789-1975* (Historical Documents Institute) is a guide to retrospective titles in the former GPO collection. For information about specific publications, contact NARA's Center for Legislative Archives at (202) 523-4185.

## Inspections

Just as becoming a depository is voluntary, a depository may voluntarily relinquish its status (six did so in 1990). The privilege may also be withdrawn by the Superintendent of Documents if the library fails a periodic inspection. In 1990, depository inspectors placed fourteen libraries on probation and removed one from the program for failing to meet depository responsibilities. Each depository is inspected at least once every seven years. These are not surprise inspections—the libraries are notified, usually several months in advance. The inspectors are professional librarians who provide advice and a channel for communication between depository staff and the Superintendent of Documents. Inspectors verify whether depository responsibilities are being fulfilled, especially accessibility of the collection to the public. A library neglecting its responsibilities receives a warning and six months to correct deficiencies. If it does not, it may be stripped of depository status by the Superintendent of Documents.

## FORMATS

GPO and the Joint Committee on Printing maintain that any informational matter produced for public dissemination, regardless of format, is depository fodder. Depositories are entitled to agency maps, atlases, charts, posters, photographs, materials printed in braille, microfiche, CD-ROMs, floppy disks, and multimedia kits.[6] Before 1962, depositories received only GPO imprints, which accounted for only half of all government printing. The Depository Library Act of 1962 rectified this weakness by broadening the definition of a government publication to "informational matter which is published as an individual document at government expense, or as required by law." GPO's General Counsel has recently interpreted "publish" as "disseminate to the public," noting that in 1962 all government publications were ink on paper.

## Depository Microfiche

The depository microfiche saga began in 1977, when GPO mounted its depository micropublishing program to mass-produce fugitive titles. Before 1977, the bulk of documents in microformat had been NTIS technical reports. GPO's depository micropublishing program began by converting non-GPO, limited-quantity, and bulky or costly publications to microfiche—expanding the range of publications available to depositories while saving space, money, and distribution time. GPO offers a choice of either hard copy or microfiche for many titles, called "dual distribution." ("Mixed distribution" occurs when microfiche is substituted for paper after hard-copy supplies are exhausted.)

Today, microfiche is GPO's preferred depository format. About 60 percent of depository titles arrive on microfiche, including reference and heavy-demand titles, issues of magazines, maps, and loose-leaf updates. Microfiche predominates because it is cheaper to produce (usually through GPO contracts with private producers), and easier to store. Microfiche has its problems, however. It is unpopular with users, and has a limited shelf life—diazo microfiche may begin to deteriorate after a single decade. GPO's depository microfiche program has also been troubled by contractor defaults, time lags, distribution gaps, and quality control problems. GPO's major microfiche contractor defaulted in 1987, strangulating the flow of depository microfiche for more than a year. At one point more than 12,000 depository titles awaited microfiche conversion, a backlog that caused distribution delays of up to two years. Microfiche that finally emerged from the microfiche production bottleneck entered the cataloging backlog—resulting in further access delays.

## Electronic Formats

*If these databases are not made available in some fashion, then the whole depository library program will be undermined.*
—Glenn English, Chair of the House Subcommittee on Government Information, Justice, and Agriculture

The electronic era has broadened the scope of government information media beyond print and microfiche. Government agencies are "publishing" electronically through bulletin boards, online databases, floppy disks, and CD-ROMs (sometimes called "electronic microfiche"). To ensure public access to government information, depository library collections must include all informational formats, including the new technologies. In 1984, an ad hoc congressional committee recommended that electronic information be provided to depository libraries and made available free to the public. The committee recommended a pilot program to test the feasibility and cost of such access. By 1991, GPO had completed five electronic pilot tests, and teamed up with the General Accounting Office to analyze the results. Final assessment is due in 1992. The pilot projects tested three CD-ROM products (the full text of the 1985 *Congressional Record*, a census test disk, and the Environmental Protection Agency's Toxic Release Inventory) and two online databases (the Commerce Department Economic Bulletin Board and a Department of Energy bibliographic database).

Defining depository "publications" as not only print, but any format, GPO's General Counsel maintains that Title 44 of the *United States Code* mandates that depository libraries receive electronic publications even when no paper counterpart exists (still valid is a 1982 opinion by the previous General Counsel that GPO was not required to provide free depository access to unpublished computer databases, but it is interpreted to mean that depository distribution is not limited to printed publications). The Joint Committee on Printing issued a similar decision in 1988, but in reference to electronic products published as either "a complement to or as a substitute for conventionally printed material."

Although the Superintendent of Documents is committed to integrating electronic formats into the depository library program, many federal agencies balk at

sending depository copies of their electronic products to GPO. The cost of providing multiple copies, coupled with the need for user support are seen as "disincentives" for agencies. Since there is no governmentwide consensus that agencies "are *required* to go through GPO or provide depository copies, 500 or 800 or 1400 copies is an expense they can avoid."[7] And, because tackling electronic products is more complex than using paper or microfiche, public distribution heightens the demand for agencies to provide adequate indexing, software, user manuals, staff training, and user assistance to support their electronic products. In practice, some agency CD-ROMs sent to depositories have been problematic because of weaknesses in support materials or software.

In 1988, a long-awaited report from Congress's Office of Technology Assessment, *Informing the Nation: Federal Information Dissemination in an Electronic Age* (Y 3.T 22/2:2 In 3/9) analyzed the nation's collection, processing, and dissemination of information, especially in electronic formats. Assessing the implications of electronic technology for GPO, the Superintendent of Documents, and depository libraries, OTA called for legislation to resolve urgent federal information dissemination issues and set the nation's future course. The report emphasized that the government is at a crossroads where opportunities and challenges abound, and acknowledged two key problems: equity of public access and the dissemination roles of government and the private sector.

More and more depository titles are available electronically in full text. When government information is stored only in electronic format, however, its public accessibility may be endangered. The number of federal databases is burgeoning, with agencies sometimes providing public access directly or through database vendors. The prevalence of databases makes depository library access to government information in electronic data files vitally important. It is expected that eventually depository libraries will be linked to government online databases, using GPO as a gateway. The GPO WINDO bill, introduced during the 102nd Congress, proposed that GPO be a central conduit to hundreds of federal databases and information systems, accessible to both subscribers and depository libraries.

During the 101th Congress, the "Bates bill" raised the possibility of "cost sharing"—charging users and depository libraries for database searching. This controversial issue also arose during the electronic pilot projects. The GPO General Counsel later ruled that depositories cannot charge the public to use depository information, and that depositories themselves cannot legally be asked to pay to access depository information.[8]

## RESTRUCTURING THE DEPOSITORY SYSTEM

Recent financial and technological challenges have led to proposals for restructuring the Depository Library

Program. The Association of Research Libraries (ARL) has called the depository library system "a program in crisis" because of diminishing public access to government information. The ARL cited fugitive documents, delays in depository receipts, and omission of new formats such as electronic media from the program as weaknesses in the DLP as we now know it.

## DEPOSITORY LEGISLATION

The General Printing Act of 1895 combined several unrelated laws governing printing and distribution of government publications; made GPO's Superintendent of Documents responsible for the depository library system; and provided for one depository per congressional district, but not the disposal of documents—they had to be kept permanently.

The Depository Library Act of 1962, the first major revision of depository law since 1895, allowed two depositories per district and established regionals and a system for disposal of unwanted documents by selectives. To provide for receipt of documents not printed by GPO, the law defined government publications as "informational matter which is published . . . at Government expense, or as required by law." Because the 1895 and 1962 laws did not spell out requirements for depository access to (then unforeseen) electronic media, many factions are pushing for modernization of the depository laws.

In 1978, libraries of accredited law schools were allowed depository status with the enactment of Public Law 95-261.

## OTHER DEPOSITORIES

The federal depository program is only one of numerous government deposit arrangements. Some federal agencies operate their own depository systems: The Patent and Trademark Office and the Census Bureau are two examples. There are also depositories maintained by state and local governments and for foreign and international organizations, such as the United Nations.

---

### The Documents Prayer

Our Father who art in Washington,
SuDoc be thy name,
thy Depository come,
thy Publication be done,
in Microform as in Hard Copy.
Give us this day our Daily Shipment.
And forgive us our Class Numbers,
as we forgive those who number against us.
And lead us not into non-Depository status,
but deliver us from the Post Office.
For thine is the Census, and the Patents
and the Monthly Catalog, forever.

Amen
—*Hal Hall*, 1976

---

## ADDRESSES

Doc Ex: Documents Expediting Project, Exchange and Gift Division, Library of Congress, Washington, DC 20540; (202) 707-9527.

## FREEBIES

The following subject bibliographies are available free from U.S. Government Printing Office, Superintendent of Documents, Washington, DC 20402:

150. Libraries and Library Collections
244. U.S. Government Publications

## REFERENCES

1. Donna A. Demac, *Keeping America Uninformed: Government Secrecy in the 1980's* (New York: Pilgrim Press, 1984), p. 136; GPO, the agency responsible for administering the Federal Depository Program, acknowledged that the program has long been "one of America's best-kept secrets." Government Printing Office, *Annual Report: Fiscal Year 1984* (GPO, 1985), p. 5.

2. David C. R. Heisser, "Marketing U.S. Government Depository Libraries," *Government Publications Review* 13 (January-February 1986): 55-65; Peter Hernon, "Use of GPO Bookstores," *Government Publications Review* 7A (1980): 362.

3. Three sources detail depository responsibilities: *Instructions to Depository Libraries* (GPO, 1988) GP 3.26:D 44/988 (the official rules and regulations of the Federal Depository Library Program); *Guidelines for the Depository Library System* (GPO, 1978) GP 1.23/4:D 44/978 (recommended standards); and *Federal Depository Library Manual* (GPO, 1985-. Loose-leaf) GP 3.29:D 44 (supplements and expands on *Instructions* but procedures described are not mandatory).

4. General Accounting Office, *Government Printing Office's Depository Library Program* (GAO/AFMD-85-19) (GAO, 1984), p. 2. Free from GAO, Document Handling and Information Services Facility, P.O. Box 6015, Gaithersburg, MD 20760; (202) 275-6241; Cynthia Bower, "Federal Fugitives, DNDs and Other Aberrants: A Cosmology," *Documents to the People* 17 (September 1989):120-26.

5. "The FDLP Bulletin Board and How to Use It," *Administrative Notes* 12 (August 15, 1991):12-15. (GP 3.16/3-2:12/19); "New Look for the Bulletin Board," *Administrative Notes* 13 (September 15, 1992): 3-9.

6. Government Printing Office. Circular Letter 320, "Guidelines for the Provision of Government Publications for Depository Library Distribution" (GPO, 1990).

7. Jane Bartlett, "Information Technology Program Update," *Administrative Notes* 12 (May 31, 1991), p. 22. (GP 3.16/3-2:12/12.)

8. "'Cost Sharing' for the Dissemination of Government Information in Electronic Formats," *Administrative Notes* 12 (August 15, 1991):16-21. (GP 3.16/3-2:12/19)

## FURTHER READING

Congress. *Government Information as a Public Asset.* Hearing before the Joint Committee on Printing, 102-2, April 25, 1991. (S. Hrg. 102-114) GPO, 1991. (Y 4.P 93/1:G 74/12)

A treatise on fugitive documents and how they hinder depository access to government information.

Hale, Barbara and Sandra McAninch. "The Plight of U.S. Government Regional Depository Libraries in the 1980s: Life in a Pressure Cooker." *Government Publications Review* 16 (July/August 1989):387-95.

A look at the special challenges facing regional depositories.

Hernon, Peter and Charles R. McClure. *Public Access to Government Information: Issues, Trends, and Strategies.* 2nd ed. Norwood, NJ: Ablex Publishing Corp.,1988.

Covers collection development; documents administration, planning, and evaluation; physical facilities; processing depository items; and resource sharing.

Hernon, Peter, Charles R. McClure, and Gary R. Purcell. *GPO's Depository Library Program: A Descriptive Analysis.* Norwood, NJ: Ablex Publishing Corp., 1985.

A key source of history and statistics about depository libraries.

Kerze, Naomi V. "Separate vs. Integrated: The Disappearing Debate over the Organization of United States Government Publications in Depository Libraries." *Government Publications Review* 16 (September/October 1989): 439-45.

Kovacs, Diane K. "Government Printing Office Dissemination of Government Documents on CD-ROM: Report from the GovDoc-L Discussion List." *Laserdisk Professional* 4 (July 1991):36+. (LEXIS, Current)

A summary of librarians' E-mail discussions of depository documents on CD-ROM.

McClure, Charles R. and Peter Hernon. *Improving the Quality of Reference Service for Government Publications* (ALA Studies in Librarianship no. 10) Chicago: American Library Association, 1983.

Results of the authors' unobtrusive study of library reference service for government information questions suggest that the public has problems accessing some depository collections and that both documents and reference staff are unable to answer many of the test questions. LeRoy C. Schwarzkopf's review of the study in *Public Documents Highlights* 63 (September 1983): 364-65 (GP 3.27/2:63/1) questions the validity of some of the conclusions, the test questions used, and administration of the test.

——. *Users of Academic and Public GPO Depository Libraries.* GPO, 1989. (GP 3.2:Us 2)

This landmark study is the first national analysis of academic and public depository library users.

Mooney, Margaret T. "GPO Cataloging: Is It a Viable Current Access Tool for U.S. Documents?" *Government Publications Review* 16 (May/June 1989):259-70.

The time lag between receipt of depository documents and their appearance in the *Monthly Catalog* and library online catalogs averaged about six months, while a few had not been listed after two years.

Morton, Bruce. "The Depository Library System: A Costly Anachronism." *Library Journal* 112 (September 15, 1987):52-54; Hernon, Peter and Charles R. McClure. "GPO's Depository Library Program: Building for the Future." *Library Journal* 113 (April 1, 1988): 52-56.

Opposing appraisals of the state of the DLP.

Sanchez, Lisa. "Dissemination of United States Federal Government Information on CD-ROM: An Issues Primer." *Government Publications Review* 16 (March/April 1989):133-44.

A review of the space needs, costs, access points, durability, user acceptance, standardization, advantages, and disadvantages of depository CD-ROMs.

Sears, Jean L. and Margaret A. Lewis. "Currency of Selected U.S. Federal Government Agency Annual Reports Received by Depository Libraries." *Government Publications Review* 15 (July/August 1988):323-41.

About half of 440 annual reports checked were missing from depository libraries because of publication delays, discontinuations or consolidations, loopholes in the depository system, or microfiche conversion delays.

Smith, Diane H. "Depository Libraries in the 1990s: *Whither*, or *Wither* Depositories?" *Government Publications Review* 17 (July/August 1990):301-24.

An examination of the viability of "electronic depositories."

Snowhill, Louise. "Privatization and the Availability of Federal Information in Microform: The Reagan Years." *Microform Review* 18 (Fall 1989):203-09.

A review of the impact of microform on depository library collections during the 1980s.

Superintendent of Documents. Library Programs Service. *Administrative Notes.* GPO, 1985- . Irregular. (GP 3.16/3-2: )

A newsletter for depository libraries with information about depositories, government publications, and GPO. AN issued a cumulated table of contents for 1980-1989 (vol.11, January 1, 1990 (GP 3.16/3-2:11/1); also available on the Federal Bulletin Board, and distributed to depository libraries on floppy disk. Includes "The E-Report: Status of Federal Electronic Information," an irregular status report on the availability of electronic products to depositories.

Watts, Carol. "The Depository Library Inspection Program." *Reference Services Review* 10 (Summer 1982): 55-62.

A detailed discussion of how and why federal depositories are periodically inspected.

## EXERCISES

1. Is *General Information Concerning Patents* a depository title? (Use sources discussed in this chapter to answer this question.)

2. How many other strategies could be used to determine whether *General Information Concerning Patents* is a depository title?

# CHAPTER 5
# Bibliographies and Indexes

## WHAT

The *Monthly Catalog* is the most comprehensive list of federal publications, including both depository and nondepository documents from all federal agencies. The *Monthly Catalog* does not list all government publications and information resources, however. The *Publications Reference File* (PRF) lists titles for sale from GPO, providing basic bibliographic information and some annotations. Neither PRF nor *Monthly Catalog* indexes the contents of government periodicals, a role partially fulfilled by several commercially published indexes discussed in this chapter.

## WHERE

You should find the *Monthly Catalog* and PRF in any depository library and in many nondepositories, the *Monthly Catalog* in hard copy or microfiche from GPO, or on CD-ROM from commercial publishers. The *Monthly Catalog*, PRF, and most of the commercial indexes discussed in this chapter may also be searched online, and *Monthly Catalog* entries may be accessed using the OCLC database.

## WHEN

The *Monthly Catalog* is issued monthly (but you guessed that), with retrospective volumes going back to 1895 under various titles. Computer and CD-ROM searches of the *Monthly Catalog* can go back to July 1976. Each bimonthly issue of the PRF is cumulative and supersedes previous issues. A PRF for out-of-print GPO sales publications is retrospective to 1972.

## THE KEYS TO THE KINGDOM: THE *MONTHLY CATALOG*

If you were to learn about only one search tool for government publications, it should probably be the *Monthly Catalog*. Its formal title is *Monthly Catalog of United States Government Publications* (GP 3.8:), but friends call it MoCat. Why is the *Monthly Catalog* so valuable? Because, although it falls short of its goal of listing all unclassified government publications, it is the most comprehensive bibliography of federal publications. It has been characterized both as the national bibliography of federal government publications and as a *Cumulative Book Index* for documents. As such, it provides an archival record of federal agency documents, including those no longer in print.

## The Electronic MoCat

In July 1976, the *Monthly Catalog* entered the electronic age with its conversion to machine-readable MARC format. The repercussions of that modernization are being enjoyed today, allowing online searches of the *Monthly Catalog* (through BRS, DIALOG, and on OCLC), and cumulations from private publishers on CD-ROM. As a government publication, the *Monthly Catalog* is free of copyright restrictions, allowing commercial companies to reproduce their own versions of it. By 1990, fifteen *Monthly Catalog* incarnations in varied formats were available from both government and commercial sources.[1] With so many format options available, GPO is weighing the feasibility and cost/benefits of publishing the government version of *Monthly Catalog* in paper, microfiche, computer tapes, CD-ROM, or online.

In libraries where the GPO *Monthly Catalog* cataloging database has been loaded into the local online catalog, federal publications join other materials in the "bibliographic mainstream." They can be identified through author, title, or subject searches of the online catalog, counteracting the disadvantages of their frequent physical segregation into a separate library department. *Monthly Catalog* computer tapes may be purchased from the Library of Congress or from commercial vendors like OCLC (GOVDOC Service) or MARCIVE, which offer enhanced versions. The records may then be added to online, CD-ROM, COM, or traditional card catalogs.

The *Monthly Catalog*'s electronic era ushered in a format change and enhanced bibliographic documentation. Since July 1976 the *Monthly Catalog* has used Library of Congress subject headings, followed Anglo-American Cataloging Rules, incorporated MARC format, and participated in the OCLC cataloging network. As a result, the MoCat provides full bibliographic information for documents, is easy to use, and can be searched using the same subject headings as library catalogs. Since 1976 *Monthly Catalog* entries have resembled traditional library catalog records—and look as familiar as your own driver's license photo.

By comparison, the old-format *Monthly Catalog* may seem sluggish and troublesome, but it can be conquered by adjusting to its idiosyncrasies. Searching the MoCat before 1976 requires an understanding of the differences between its old and new formats. The old format used keywords instead of Library of Congress subject headings (LCSH), had minimal information in each entry, and fewer special indexes. Figure 5.1 shows the differences between old and new format entries for the same document.

**FIGURE 5.1: Old- and New-Format *Monthly Catalog* Entries.**

Both provide 1) SuDocs number and 2) an indicator of depository status, but the new format entry also gives 3) a bibliographic history, 4) LC subject headings, 5) LC classification number, 6) LC card number, 7) OCLC number. The price and availability of information given in either entry should be verified in PRF before attempting to order.

## Using the *Monthly Catalog*

It's important to remember that while various incarnations of the *Monthly Catalog* are essentially the same, each commercial version has been uniquely en-

hanced, giving each a distinct personality. Thorough searching requires familiarity with the protocols for the version being used. The descriptions that follow are based on the GPO hard-copy *Monthly Catalog*.

The *Monthly Catalog* is conveniently arranged: Index entries list a short title and refer to the full bibliographic information by means of an "entry number." Since mid-1976, entry numbers have included a prefix indicating the year, making each entry number unique. Previously without year prefixes, the same entry numbers were reused each year.

The *Monthly Catalog*'s indexes offer several approaches to searching, including the traditional author, title, or subject options, plus a title keyword approach. MoCat can also be searched by series/report numbers and names, contract numbers, GPO stock numbers (S/N), and, in the semiannual and annual index cumulations, by SuDocs numbers. The title and subject indexes provide not only a short title and entry number but also SuDocs number and author, making referral to the full bibliographic entry unnecessary if the SuDocs number is the only information sought. Searching can be streamlined by using any of several cumulations, available both from GPO and from commercial publishers. Its editors rightfully call the *Monthly Catalog* "an evolving publication," and enhancements are regularly added.

**Search Tip**
Commercial versions of the *Monthly Catalog* are not identical, since each has been uniquely enhanced. Thorough searching requires familiarity with the protocols of the version being used.

In addition to bibliographic information, the GPO hard-copy *Monthly Catalog* provides an indicator of depository status (look for the word "Item," usually preceded by a black bullet) and gives SuDocs numbers. In a library where documents are shelved according to the SuDocs classification system, one can often go directly from the *Monthly Catalog* to the shelves or microfiche cabinets to retrieve a depository document. The *Monthly*

*Catalog* also serves as an index to Readex full-text microfiche collections, which are arranged either in SuDocs number or *Monthly Catalog* entry number order.[2]

| THE *MONTHLY CATALOG* | |
|---|---|
| **Old Format** | **New Format** |
| Keywords | LC subject headings |
| Entry numbers reused each year | Unique entry numbers |
| Author, title, and subject indexes | Adds series/report, title keywords, S/N, contract number indexes; SuDocs number indexes in the semiannual and annual cumulations; bill number index in the Serial Set Catalog; cataloged according to AACR II, with MARC format; entries are added to the OCLC database; full cataloging information including LC and Dewey class numbers, OCLC number, and tracings |

## Subject Searches

Both the subject and title keyword indexes may be used for subject searching. Note an essential difference between these: The subject index is based on a controlled vocabulary (Library of Congress subject headings), while the title keyword index is derived from document titles. This difference affects search strategy.

Before searching the *Monthly Catalog* subject index, *Library of Congress Subject Headings* (LCSH) should be consulted to determine the terminology used for a topic. LCSH is available in book format and in CD-ROM (CDMARC Subjects). Subject headings can also be identified once any useful document is discovered, by checking the subject headings for that document in the *Monthly Catalog*, OCLC, or the Cataloging in Publication (CIP) information on the verso of the title page of the document itself. Figures 5.1 and 5.2 show the location of subject headings in a *Monthly Catalog* entry and in the CIP information inside the document itself.

**FIGURE 5.2: Sample CIP Form.**

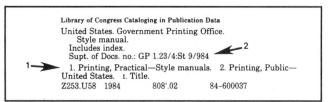

The Cataloging in Publication information located on the verso (back) of the document title page usually notes the 1) subject headings and 2) SuDocs number for the document. Each can be helpful in bibliographic searching.

Popular, current, and synonymous terms are often easily traced using the title keyword index. Remember that this is a permuted title index derived from words in document titles: If a searched word is not in a title, the keyword index will not locate that document. Searching the subject index using Library of Congress subject headings, on the other hand, provides a comprehensive subject search independent of document titles—and therefore less dependent upon luck. For example, searching for materials on preschool education in the keyword index would miss the unrevealing title *Even Start*. A subject search, on the other hand, would identify that same title under the LCSH "Education, Preschool—United States—Periodicals."

To locate a document about eradicating bedbugs, either a keyword or subject search could be used. Keyword searching offers the advantage of harnessing popular terminology, and is quicker because it bypasses an LCSH lookup. If "bedbugs" appeared in any document title, a match is found. A successful subject search, on the other hand, must be preceded by identification of exact terminology: either in LCSH or in the OCLC or CIP record within a useful document.

---

**Search Tip: Keyword vs. Subject Searching**

Never guess at subject headings. The Library of Congress subject heading for *How to Control Bed Bugs* (1976), for example, is "Beetles—Control—United States," an unlikely candidate for a lucky guess. Keyword searches depend upon an exact title-word match. A keyword search of the 1976 *Monthly Catalog* for "bedbugs" does not retrieve *How to Control Bed Bugs*, a title we already know exists. Why? Because the title words are "bed bugs," not the single-word "bedbugs," which would appear in a different filing sequence.

---

In its old format the *Monthly Catalog* had a subject index, but no title keyword index. Since Library of Congress subject headings were not the authority for the old format, terms used in a pre- and post-July 1976 search may differ. In 1992, for example, materials on the U.S.S.R. were indexed under the subject heading "Soviet Union," while in 1974 the heading used was "Union of Soviet Socialist Republics." Because the *Monthly Catalog* provides no see references from new terminology to old, searchers must be alerted that subject headings may vary in the old and new formats. The same caution applies when searching across different indexes: Subject terms that are productive in the *Monthly Catalog* are not necessarily those used in other indexes.

Carrollton Press has published two cumulative subject indexes to the *Monthly Catalog*, covering 1895 to 1971: *Cumulative Subject Index to the Monthly Catalog of U.S. Government Publications, 1895-1899*, and *Cumulative Subject Index to the Monthly Catalog of U.S. Government Publications, 1900-1971*. These serve as subject indexes to the defunct *Document Catalog* and to the *Monthly Catalog* through 1971. In addition to the ease of subject searching they offer, the two cumulations provide SuDocs numbers for pre-1925 *Monthly Catalog* entries, something the *Monthly Catalog* itself didn't do. For this reason these two subject cumulations are called the "Classes Added" editions.

**Cumulative Indexes**

In addition to its semiannual and annual *Monthly Catalog* indexes, GPO issues decennial (every ten years) and quinquennial (every five years) index cumulations. For searches spanning several years, the cumulations offer an alternative to searching annual indexes one by one, and are therefore great time savers. Unlike the cumulative indexes between 1941 and 1976, the cumulations for 1976-1980, 1981-1985, and 1986-1990 were issued in microfiche rather than paper.

In addition to the commercially published subject cumulations already discussed, Pierian Press offers the *Cumulative Personal Author Indexes to the Monthly Catalog of U.S. Government Publications, 1941-1970*, and the Historical Documents Institute has published a *Cumulative Title Index to United States Public Documents, 1789-1976*. The author cumulation is especially helpful for access to mid-1946 to 1962 issues, when the MoCat itself had no personal author index. By indexing all personal names associated with each title, the Pierian Press cumulation solves another problem, since between 1941-1946 and 1963-1975 MoCat indexed only the first personal author. The Historical Documents Institute's title cumulation is not restricted to *Monthly Catalog* listings, but represents titles in the GPO collection now housed in the National Archives. Another retrospective index is Kanely's *Cumulative Index to Hickcox's Monthly Catalog of United States Government Publications, 1885-1894* (Carrollton Press).

Commercial CD-ROM cumulations offer a single compilation of all *Monthly Catalog* entries since July 1976, making searches of multiple cumulations unnecessary. Each pocket-sized CD-ROM holds the equivalent of 330,000 typed pages or 1,841 single-sided floppy disks. Because the CD-ROM versions of *Monthly Catalog* cumulate the contents of dozens of printed MoCat issues, they offer one-stop searches which can harness the advantages of Boolean logic, and can also be printed or downloaded.

Commercial CD-ROM versions do not always bear the *Monthly Catalog* moniker, substituting names like Government Publications Index, GPO CAT/PAC, IMPACT, and GPO on SilverPlatter. The enhanced CD-ROM versions may not even acknowledge *Monthly Catalog* in their scope descriptions. MARCIVE's GPO CAT/PAC, for example, describes itself as a CD-ROM index to the "U.S. Government Printing Office database of government publications since 1976." The clue that the MARCIVE product is *Monthly Catalog* rather than PRF (also a GPO database) is the 1976 date: the year *Monthly Catalog* was converted to machine-readable form. Hernon

and McClure have warned that librarians' growing dependence upon technology has not been balanced by technological insight: not understanding, for instance, that a CD-ROM index to government titles is the equivalent of *Monthly Catalog*.[3] CD-ROM searchers should begin by clarifying the scope and protocols of the source being used. Lack of understanding can lead to time-consuming search duplications: searching the same *Monthly Catalog* in two formats, for example.

## Periodicals Supplement (GP 3.8/5: )

An annual issue of the *Monthly Catalog* called the Periodicals Supplement usually appears as the first issue of the year. The Periodicals Supplement lists government periodicals ("magazines," in layperson's terms) issued at least three times yearly. There are separate sections listing "Title Changes," "Discontinued Periodicals," and "Classification Changes" in the Periodicals Supplement preliminary pages.

Except for its specialized coverage, the Periodicals Supplement is like any other MoCat issue, with entry numbers, indexes, and full bibliographic information. A Periodicals Supplement bonus is the addition of notes telling where some government magazines are indexed and which titles are self-indexed (see Figure 5.3). The difference between the Periodicals Supplement and Price List 36 (see Figure 5.4) parallels differences between the *Monthly Catalog* and PRF (discussed below). Price List 36 lists only serials sold by GPO, while the more comprehensive Periodicals Supplement lists serials for sale from GPO and from other government agencies (see Figures 5.3 and 5.4).

## Loopholes

Although the *Monthly Catalog* is the most comprehensive listing of federal documents, it has omissions which should be noted. The MoCat does not index individual articles in government periodicals, provide abstracts, index federal specifications, or comprehensively document government audiovisuals, databases, technical reports, and certain agency special publications, such as those of NASA or the Department of Defense. Nor are cooperative publications, which must be sold to be self-sustaining, included in the *Monthly Catalog*.

> *If the only tool you have is a hammer, you treat everything like a nail.*   —Abraham Maslow

One particular danger of becoming overly fond of the *Monthly Catalog* is forgetting its poor coverage of technical reports. Overlap between the *Monthly Catalog* and NTIS's *Government Reports Announcements and Index* (GRA & I), the most comprehensive bibliography of technical reports, is only 10 percent (primarily depository titles).[4] When McClure, Hernon, and Purcell unobtrusively tested twelve libraries by asking NTIS-oriented reference questions, only about four out of every ten questions were answered correctly, even though the libraries owned the NTIS titles required.[5] One reason for the low accuracy rate was the mistaken assumption that *Monthly Catalog* listed all government documents and that GPO was the sole distributor of government publications. Reading Chapter 6 will help documents users learn clues that steer a search away from the *Monthly Catalog* and toward GRA & I or the NTIS Bibliographic Database.

## OCLC

Since 1976, GPO has created machine readable MARC records to produce the *Monthly Catalog*, allowing documents cataloging records to be input into OCLC, an international online bibliographic database. The resulting computer tapes are used to compile the *Monthly Catalog*. Although sometimes overlooked as a source of documents bibliographic verification, OCLC serves this function well. OCLC offers two especially useful approaches to documents searching—by title or by SuDocs number—both of which are simple and quick. The SuDocs number search key is

gn:

followed by one or two letters, plus up to ten numbers of the SuDocs number. For example, the SuDocs number E 1.28:TID-28163 may be searched as follows:

gn:e12828163

The OCLC title search key for government documents is the same as for other materials. For instance, the *Handbook of Labor Statistics* is searched as:

han,of,la,s

Searchers also have the option of using an entry command of PRSMGOVT to limit the OCLC search to government publications and related materials (for example, *CIS/Index:* not a government publication, but given a government tag in the database).

When a title's publication date is unknown, an OCLC title search is often easier than a *Monthly Catalog* search. Even when the publication date is known, OCLC offers speedier searching than the hard-copy *Monthly Catalog*, because the *Monthly Catalog* time lag (from two months to two years or more after the issue date) often necessitates searching through numerous individual issues.[6] The currency of *Monthly Catalog* coverage of various document types is affected by GPO's cataloging priorities. Congressional documents are the first to be cataloged, followed by (in priority order): titles in the news, GPO sales titles, presidential documents, legislative branch documents (except technical reports), executive and judicial branch documents (except technical reports), technical reports, and, finally, nondepository documents. Access to low-priority titles is speeded up through abridged cataloging, but there is still a considerable cataloging backlog.

### FIGURE 5.3: *Monthly Catalog* Periodicals Supplement Sample Entry for *Federal Register.*

**86-2285**

**AE 2.106:(v.nos.&nos.)**

Federal register. [Washington, D.C. : Office of the Federal Register, National Archives and Records Service, General Services Administration : Supt. of Docs., U.S. G.P.O., distributor, Supt. of Docs., U.S. Govt. Print. Off., Washington, D.C. 20402

v. ; 28 cm.

Daily (except Saturday, Sunday, and official Federal holidays)

$300 (U.S.) $375 [illegible]) $1.50 (single copy, U.S.) $1.88 (single copy, foreign)

Began with v. 1, no. [illegible] 14, 1936. Previously classed: AE 2.7: and GS 4.107: [illegible]tion based on: Vol. 49, no. 64 (Apr. 2, 1979); title from cover. Indexed by: Hospital literature index ISSN 0018-5736 Indexed by: Coal abstracts ISSN 0309-4979 Indexed by: Chemical abstracts ISSN 0009-2258 Indexed by: Energy information abstracts ISSN 0147-6521 Indexed by: Environment abstracts ISSN 0093-3287 Vols. for (1985-) distributed to some depository libraries in microfiche. Indices: Indexed by: Federal register index, (July 1976- ); and by: CIS Federal register index, 1984- ●Item 573-C, 573-D (microfiche) S/N 722-004-00000-1 ISSN 0097-6326 Related records: Federal register index ISSN 0364-1406 Related records: Regulatory Information Service Center (U.S.). Calendar of federal regulations

1. Administrative law — United States — Periodicals. 2. Delegated legislation — United States — Periodicals. I. United States. Office of the Federal Register. II. United States. National Archives. OCLC 01768512

The Periodicals Supplement entry for *Federal Register* notes government and commercial indexes that index the title, 1986.

### FIGURE 5.4: Price List 36 Sample Entry for *Federal Register.*

**FEDERAL REGISTER. (Daily Monday through Friday, except on a legal holiday.)** Provides a uniform system for making available to the public regulations and legal notices issued by Federal agencies. These include Presidential proclamations and Executive orders and Federal agency documents having general applicability and legal effect, documents required to be published by Act of Congress and other Federal agency documents of public interest.

*Discounts are not allowed on subscription or single copy sales.*

**Please Note:** Subscribers to this service will automatically receive copies of the *Federal Register Index*, and the *Code of Federal Regulations, LSA List of CFR Sections Affected*, which is listed in this Price List, at no additional cost.

►Paperback. Subscription price: Domestic—**$340.00** a year; Foreign—**$425.00** a year. Single copy price: Domestic—$1.50 a copy; Foreign—$1.88 a copy [85].
[*FR*] AE 2.106:
(File Code 3A) S/N 722-004-00000-1

**NOTE: A special six-month subscription to the *Federal Register paper edition* is available at Domestic—$170.00; Foreign—$212.50.**

►Microfiche (24X). Subscription price: Domestic—**$188.00** a year; Foreign—**$235.00** a year. Single copy price: Domestic—$1.50 a copy; Foreign—$1.88 a copy [Current calendar year plus previous year].
[*MFFR*] AE 2.107:
(File Code 3A) S/N 722-003-00000-4

**NOTE: A special six-month subscription to the *Federal Register Microfiche Edition* is available at Domestic—$94.00; Foreign—$117.50.**

The Price List 36 listing for *Federal Register* includes an annotation and more availability information than the *Monthly Catalog* but less bibliographic information, 1987.

Verifying a title on OCLC offers the added advantage of identifying it as government-issued. This prevents one of the pitfalls of a futile library catalog search—incorrectly assuming the library does not own a document because it is not listed in the catalog. Verification in OCLC can alert the searcher to the fact that the title is government-issued, redirecting the search toward the government documents collection. And because OCLC entries often give SuDocs numbers (field 086) and note depository status (field 074 gives item number), the searcher may be able to go directly to the shelves or microfiche cabinets to retrieve the document (see Figure 5.5).

## GPO Sales Publications Reference File (GP 3.22/3: )

Known as the "Books in Print" for GPO sales documents, the *Publications Reference File* (PRF) lists publications for sale from GPO. Issued bimonthly with monthly supplements, the PRF is on microfiche (no hard-copy edition is available) and is computer-searchable on DIALOG and Knowledge-Index, with the capability of online ordering. The complete PRF master file can also be purchased on magnetic tape.

| OCLC Fields | |
|---|---|
| 001 | *Monthly Catalog* entry number |
| 010 | LC control number |
| 020 | ISBN |
| 022 | ISSN |
| 027; 088 | Technical report number |
| 035 | OCLC number |
| 037 | GPO stock number or agency accession numbers (ERIC, NTIS, etc.) Note: For older cites, price and S/N (stock number) require verification in PRF |
| 074 | Depository item number |
| 086; 099 | SuDocs number |
| 260 | Publisher, date |
| 500 | Notes; if nondepository, may include the note, "Not distributed to depository libraries" |
| 650 | Subject headings |

**FIGURE 5.5 Sample OCLC Entry**

The OCLC record shows 1) SuDocs number, 2) depository status (because the title was receiving media coverage, it was automatically sent to all depositories), and 3) subject headings. Another clue that this was a depository item is given in line 18, where the depository shipping list number is noted. (OCLC Record 1859428 is used with OCLC's permission.)

## Fear Not Fiche

Familiarity with the PRF often leads to love, so don't be intimidated by the PRF's microfiche format. This source is easy to use, and many prefer it to the *Monthly Catalog* for searching current GPO titles (see Figures 5.6 and 5.7). The PRF is useful for finding bibliographic information about GPO sales titles and verifying current prices and stock numbers for ordering from GPO. This step is a must when a title has been found in an older issue of the *Monthly Catalog* and the searcher wants to buy a copy. Verification in the PRF ensures that the title is still for sale and confirms its current price. The PRF may also be used to determine what's available from GPO on a topic and to identify titles available to depository libraries (look for the word "Item" *without* a black bullet) (see Figure 5.8). Because the PRF tends to be more current than the *Monthly Catalog*, it often lists new depository titles not yet be listed in the MoCat. Remember that titles hot off the press may be too new to be listed in either the *Monthly Catalog*, OCLC, or PRF. Access to depository publications can be thwarted by the chronic GPO cataloging backlog, which can delay appearance of bibliographic records in the *Monthly Catalog* and OCLC for up to a year and a half. A librarian may be able to identify a SuDocs number for a backlogged title using the *Daily Depository Shipping List*.

It is important to realize that a document's absence from the PRF does not mean it does not exist, or even that it's no longer in print or for sale. Absence from the PRF does indicate that the title is not currently sold by GPO. A futile PRF search should be followed up with a search of the more comprehensive *Monthly Catalog*.

Like the *Monthly Catalog*, the PRF can be searched using numerous approaches. It is divided into three sections, searchable by:

Section 1. GPO stock numbers (includes ISBNs)
Section 2. SuDocs numbers
Section 3. Alphabetically interfiled: Report numbers, subjects, keywords and phrases, authors, titles, agency series

### FIGURE 5.7: Sample *Monthly Catalog* Entry.

> 89-3747
> Y 3.T 22/2:2 In 3/9
> Informing the nation : federal information dissemination in an electronic age. — Washington, DC : U.S. Congress, Office of Technology Assessment : For sale by the Supt. of Docs., U.S. G.P.O. [1988]
> xi, 333 p. : ill. ; 26 cm. Shipping list no.: 88-591-P. "October 1988"—P. [4] of cover. Bibliography: p. 331. "OTA-CIT-396"—P. [4] of cover. ●Item All libraries S/N 052-003-01130-1 @ GPO $14.00
> 1. Electronic publishing — Government policy — United States. 2. Government information — United States. 3. Federal government — United States — Information services. 4. United States. Government Printing Office. 5. Libraries, Depository — United States. 6. Information storage and retrieval systems — Government publications. I. United States. Congress. Office of Technology Assessment. II. Title: Federal information dissemination in an electronic age. OCLC 18595428

Monthly Catalog entries include information omitted from the PRF, including: 1) LC subject headings, 2) OCLC number, and 3) a bullet identifying the item number.

NewsBank/Readex sells the *Popular Government Publications File* (PGP), a CD-ROM index to PRF, with the full text of popular government titles (those most frequently purchased from GPO) available on microfiche. The collection is customized according to library type and size. The PGP Index and microfiche are updated quarterly.

| PRF/*MONTHLY CATALOG* COMPARISON | |
|---|---|
| **PRF** | **MoCat** |
| Primarily GPO publications | GPO, plus many other issuing agencies |
| Sales publications only | For-sale, out-of-print, and not-for-general-distribution titles |
| Current price | Prices may be out of date |
| Keywords (no authority list) | LCSH |
| Searchable online | Searchable online |
| Available free to depository libraries | Available free to depository libraries |
| Not input into OCLC | Input into OCLC |

Because each bimonthly PRF cumulation completely supersedes the last, many libraries discard their old sets. A library or reference department without easy access to

### FIGURE 5.6: Sample PRF Entry.

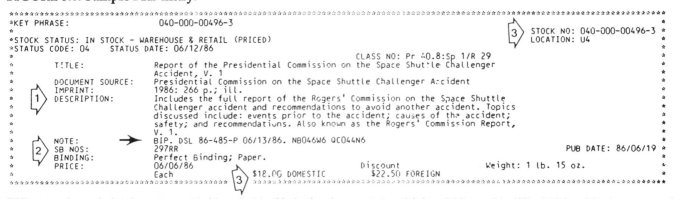

```
*KEY PHRASE:              040-000-00496-3                                                          STOCK NO: 040-000-00496-3
*                                                                                                  LOCATION: U4
*STOCK STATUS: IN STOCK - WAREHOUSE & RETAIL (PRICED)
*STATUS CODE: 04     STATUS DATE: 06/12/86
*                                                                  CLASS NO: Pr 40.8:Sp 1/R 29
*        TITLE:          Report of the Presidential Commission on the Space Shuttle Challenger
*                        Accident, V. 1
*        DOCUMENT SOURCE: Presidential Commission on the Space Shuttle Challenger Accident
*        IMPRINT:        1986: 266 p.; ill.
*        DESCRIPTION:    Includes the full report of the Rogers' Commission on the Space Shuttle
*                        Challenger accident and recommendations to avoid another accident. Topics
*                        discussed include: events prior to the accident; causes of the accident;
*                        safety; and recommendations. Also known as the Rogers' Commission Report,
*                        V. 1.
*        NOTE:           BIP. DSL 86-485-P 06/13/86. NB046W6 QC044N6
*        SB NOS:         297RR                                                       PUB DATE: 86/06/19
*        BINDING:        Perfect Binding; Paper.
*        PRICE:          06/06/86                       Discount          Weight: 1 lb. 15 oz.
*                        Each            $18.00 DOMESTIC   $22.50 FOREIGN
```

PRF entries often include information omitted from the *Monthly Catalog*: 1) an annotation, 2) Subject Bibliographies (SB) which listed the document, and 3) current price and GPO stock number (*Monthly Catalog* price may be out of date). Although no item number is noted in this entry, the Depository Shipping List (DSL) number (black arrow) indicates the document was sent to depository libraries.

the PRF may be able to find a depository library willing to donate superseded microfiche.

The *Out-of-Print GPO Sales Publications Reference File* (OPRF) is a cumulative listing of out-of-stock GPO sales titles (GP 3.22/3-3: ). There have been two six-year cumulations: the *Exhausted GPO Sales Publications Reference File, 1980* (EPRF), covering 1972-1978, and the OPRF 1986, covering 1979-1984. The 1986 OPRF has been supplemented with cumulations issued in 1989 and 1990. In 1992, a third six-year cumulation will supersede all but the 1980 and 1986 cumulations. Since the six-year cumulations do not supersede the earlier files, all should be kept for a complete record of out-of-stock titles between 1972 and 1988.

| Search Strategy: *Monthly Catalog*, PRF, OCLC | |
|---|---|
| **If you know:** | Search: |
| **Author** | MC Author Index |
| | PRF |
| | OCLC [4,3,1] |
| **Title** | MC Title Index |
| | PRF |
| | OCLC [3,2,2,1] |
| **Part of title** | MC Keyword Index |
| | PRF |
| **Issuing agency** | MC Author Index |
| | PRF |
| **Subject** | MC Subject Index |
| | [LCSH] |
| | PRF |
| **GPO stock number** | MC S/N Index |
| | PRF |
| **SuDocs number** | MC SuDocs number |
| | Index (annual or |
| | semiannual issues only) |
| | PRF |
| | OCLC [gn: ] |
| **ERIC ED number** | MC S/N Index |
| | PRF (S/N sequence) |
| **NTIS accession number** | MC Series/Report Index |
| | MC S/N Index |
| **Series title** | MC Series/Report Index |
| | PRF |
| **Conference title** | MC Author Index |
| | PRF |

**FIGURE 5.8: Sample PRF Entry with SuDocs Number and Depository Item Number Noted.**

There has been growing interest in a government-wide, comprehensive information index ever since the Commission on Federal Paperwork proposed the idea in 1977. The Paperwork Reduction Act tapped the Office of Management and Budget to pursue this ideal, and the preliminary result was the Federal Information Locator System (FILS), an index to agency information collection programs approved by OMB. Although available on microfiche in depository libraries (PrEx 2.14/2:989), and through NTIS on magnetic tape, FILS is cumbersome to use and is slated for further development.[7]

## DECLASSIFIED DOCUMENTS

*The Declassified Documents Catalog*, (Research Publications), lists declassified post-World War II documents formerly classified as Top Secret, Secret, or Confidential, plus materials declassified under the Freedom of Information Act. Most are CIA, State Department, and Department of Defense materials. The quarterly catalog with abstracts is part of the Declassified Documents Reference System, which also includes a cumulative annual subject index (referring to citations and abstracts in the quarterly catalog) and microfiche containing the full text of the declassified documents. Since titles are indexed after they are declassified, issue dates and indexing dates do not correspond.

## HISTORICAL SOURCES

Poor Benjamin Poore. In the early 1880s he and his staff faced an awesome, pioneering task. For a century, the nation's publications had eluded bibliographic control. The handful of indexes that did exist were unsatisfactory, leaving knowledge "virtually hidden, the benefits of the labors of the best minds of the country were diminished, and the lights of experience were obscured."[8] To fill the void, Congress commissioned a catalog of all government publications issued since the birth of the nation, and assigned its compilation to Ben Poore, the Senate's Clerk of Printing Records.

Ben Poore surveyed the task before him, feeling like "Christopher Columbus when he steered westward on his voyage of discovery, confident that a new world existed, but having no knowledge of its distance or the direction in which it lay. No one could estimate how many publications were to be cataloged, where they were to be found, how long it would take . . . or . . . the probable cost."[9]

Despite the obstacles, it took Poore only two years to compile the catalog known today as Poore's Catalogue, the *Descriptive Catalog of the Government Publications of the United States, September 5, 1774-March 4, 1881* (Senate Miscellaneous Document 67, 48th Congress, 2nd Session, Serial Number 2268; also available as a reprint from Johnson Reprint Corporation). Poore's Catalogue has its weaknesses—many departmental publications were omitted and the index is troublesome—but it is the sole documentation for many of the titles it lists. Its brief entries and annotations comprise more than a retrospective bibliography—they sketch the nation's early history in entries like the one below:

> *Treaty with the Cherokee Indians The whites not to settle on Indian hunting-grounds; The hatchet to be forever buried. (p. 17)*

In the decades that followed, several more catalogs were compiled, some documenting only congressional publications, others covering all branches of government. These have been summarized in the adjoining table. Thorough descriptions of these and other retrospective titles are provided in Schmeckebier and Eastin's *Government Publications and Their Use*, pp. 6-64. "Modern" documentation began in the late 1890s with the emergence of the biennial *Document Catalog* (GP 3.6: or Serial Set), which recorded federal publications issued between 1893 and 1940, until it was eclipsed in 1947 by the *Monthly Catalog*. Historical searchers should not overlook the CIS indexes to congressional hearings, committee prints, and the Serial Set (described in Chapter 8), which are easy to use and retrospective to the 1700s and 1800s (see table). In *Using Government Publications*, Sears and Moody recommend using these CIS indexes rather than Greeley's *Public Documents of the First Fourteen Congresses, 1789-1817*, and the *Tables and Index*, which are "older, much less sophisticated indexes."[10] The Congressional Information Service's CD-ROM *Congressional Masterfile 1* streamlines historical searching between 1789 and 1969 by merging CIS indexes to the Serial Set, published and unpublished committee hearings, committee prints, and Senate Executive Documents & Reports. Purchasers may select all or some indexes for inclusion on their CD-ROM.

## TRADE BIBLIOGRAPHIES

Although none offers comprehensive coverage, some trade bibliographies offer partial coverage of government publications. Most notable is Bowker's *Books in Print* (BIP). Bowker cooperates with GPO to list many

| RETROSPECTIVE SOURCES | |
|---|---|
| **Title** | **Coverage** |
| **General:** | |
| Poore's Catalogue | All three branches of government; covers 1774-1881 |
| Ames, John. *Comprehensive Index to the Publications of the United States Government, 1881-1893* (known as Ames's Index; Serial no. 4745-4746; reprinted by Johnson Reprint Corporation) | Ames continued where Poore left off, covering all three branches of government; some departmental publications were omitted; covers 1881-1893 |
| *Document Catalog* (Catalog of the Public Documents of the [53rd to 76th] Congress and of all Departments of the United States) | The first systematic record of federal publications, covering 1893-1940; continued Ames' Index |
| *Monthly Catalog* | Published since 1895 under various titles. Before 1925 no SuDocs numbers were given; Research Publications' cumulative subject indexes include them |
| Hickcox's Monthly Catalog (*United States Government Publications. A Monthly Catalog*, John Hickcox, editor) | Covers 1885-1894; not a government document, reprinted by Research Publications |
| **Congressional:** | |
| CIS Serial Set Index | Lists Serial Set volumes for 1789-1969; continued by *CIS/Index* |
| CIS U.S. Congressional Committee Prints Index | Covers 1830-1969; continued by *CIS/Index* |
| CIS U.S. Congressional Committee Hearings Index | Covers 1833-1969; continued by *CIS/Index* |

GPO sales titles, including high-demand publications in the news like the Tower Commission report or the Space Shuttle *Challenger* investigative report. GPO submits bibliographic information and GPO price and stock number (S/N) for inclusion in *Books in Print*, but depository status and SuDocs numbers are omitted.

In general, however, *Books in Print, Ulrich's International Periodicals Directory*, and other mainstream bibliographies that include federal publications are most useful for alerting uninitiated searchers to the availability of government titles. Seasoned documents users will find government sources such as PRF and the *Monthly Catalog* more comprehensive. And since trade bibliographies focus on sales, they usually omit any notice of free access in depository libraries or SuDocs numbers, frequently the keys to depository access.

## PERIODICAL INDEXES

Traditional periodical indexes offer only sketchy coverage of government periodicals.[11] The 1992 *Reader's*

*Guide to Periodical Literature* indexed only four of the titles covered by the defunct *Index to U.S. Government Periodicals*; PAIS covered three. Nor can one turn to the *Monthly Catalog*, because although it provides bibliographic information about government periodicals, it does not index their contents.

## Index to U.S. Government Periodicals

Until 1987, the role of "documents *Reader's Guide*" was served by the quarterly *Index to U.S. Government Periodicals*, sometimes ponderously abbreviated as IUSGP, or IGP. This source indexed federal government periodicals only, making it a key resource for identifying government periodical articles. Unfortunately, this source has been quiescent for some time. The Congressional Information Service is expected to launch a government periodicals index, however.

## American Statistics Index

Another index to government periodicals is the Congressional Information Service's *American Statistics Index* (ASI), a master guide to federal government statistics. The ASI editorial staff promises to scan every type of federal publication: "If it contains statistics, it is indexed and described in ASI." It is important to realize that the usefulness of ASI goes beyond statistics. When a federal periodical publishes statistical information on a topic, those statistics are often embedded in an article on the same topic. This allows ASI to indirectly serve as an index to government periodical articles.

ASI provides SuDocs numbers for the periodicals indexed, notes depository status, and includes prices and ordering information. ASI offers the added advantage of detailed abstracts which can help users determine the scope of the document in which the statistics appeared. ASI is searchable online through DIALOG and SDC, and available on CD-ROM from CIS as part of the *Statistical Masterfile*.

## PAIS International

> *PAIS is like the nice little grandmother who used to give you cookies and tea and is now into nouvelle cuisine.*
> —PAIS Executive Director
> Barbara M. Preschel

In 1991 *PAIS International in Print* incorporated the former *PAIS Bulletin* and *PAIS Foreign Language Index*. PAIS (Public Affairs Information Service, Inc.) selectively indexes literature about business, economic and social conditions, public administration, and international relations. While including federal documents, PAIS also covers journal articles, books, serials, pamphlets, public and private organization reports, and state and foreign government publications. The only federal documents indexed are public policy-related titles that emphasize facts and statistics. Federal coverage is most thorough for congressional hearings and committee prints, agency reports, and studies. Congressional committee reports, appropriations documents, and annual reports are generally excluded (see Chapter 8).

PAIS provides abstracts and thorough bibliographic information for the documents cited, including report number, SuDocs number (identified as "SD cat. no."), and source of purchase (titles available free are identified also). Since no indication of depository status is given, searchers should be reminded that federal publications may be available for free use in depository libraries.

PAIS is available online as *PAIS International Online*, searchable through DIALOG, BRS, OCLC First Search, Data-Star and on CD-ROM as *PAIS on CD-ROM*. (Note that although the PAIS accession number provided in online and CD-ROM records resembles a *Monthly Catalog* entry number, it is not.) Searching PAIS print and online indexes is streamlined by using *PAIS Subject Headings*, a thesaurus of PAIS index terms.

## ERIC

The Educational Resources Information Center (ERIC) is an information system specializing in the literature of educational research and practice. ERIC's sixteen subject clearinghouses collect and analyze education literature, which is then indexed, abstracted, and added to the ERIC database. While most of the titles cited in ERIC's database and indexes are not government documents, ERIC itself is sponsored by the U.S. Department of Education's Office of Educational Research and Improvement (OERI).

ERIC publications are either privately funded or federally funded (distributed to depository libraries, ED 1.310/2:nos.). ERIC's major abstract journals are *Resources in Education* (ED 1.310: and from The Oryx Press) and *Current Index to Journals in Education* (ED 1.310/4: and from Oryx Press). *Resources in Education*, also called RIE, announces research reports, books, syllabi, manuals, bibliographies, and numerous other documents, each assigned an ED number. *Current Index to Journals in Education* (CIJE) announces journal articles, which are assigned EJ numbers. Paper or microfiche copies of documents cited in RIE may be found in many depository collections (ED 1.310/2: ), in libraries owning the ERIC microfiche collection, or purchased from the ERIC Document Reproduction Service. Journal articles announced in CIJE may be found in public or academic library journal collections, borrowed through interlibrary loan, or (if indicated in CIJE) purchased from University Microfilms International or the Institute for Scientific Information.

Both RIE and CIJE are searchable online using the ERIC database, one of the most heavily used databases in the world. It is available through BRS, DIALOG, and

OCLC, and through service centers identifiable through the biennial *Directory of ERIC Information Service Providers* (ED 1.30/2:Ed 8/, also available online through the ERIC database). ERIC magnetic tapes may also be purchased. ERIC on CD-ROM is available through DIALOG, and SilverPlatter. Searches of ERIC indexes or the database are facilitated by using the *Thesaurus of ERIC Descriptors* (ED 1.310/3: on microfiche, and from Oryx Press), a controlled vocabulary of educational terms used to index documents in the ERIC system.

---

**Access Tip**

*Monthly Catalog* or OCLC entries with SuDocs number ED 1.310/2: are ERIC documents. The number following the colon is the ED number. Example: ED 1.310/2:249504 = ED 249504. These titles are in many depository collections, in libraries owning the ERIC microfiche collection, or may be ordered from ERIC Document Reproduction Service.

---

## Periodical Pitfalls

Ideally, indexes covering government periodicals should be used in tandem with traditional periodical indexes to ensure a thorough search of the thousands of topics covered by federal publications. Without a librarian's guidance, however, government periodical indexes are easily overlooked. The problem is exacerbated when the indexes covering government periodicals are located in a separate documents department. Duplicate copies of government indexes in the general reference collection or physical proximity of reference and documents departments are desirable, but proximity alone will not solve the problem of user unfamiliarity. Direction and instruction from knowledgeable librarians is a must.

Another difficulty of tandem searches of traditional and government-oriented indexes is locating desired periodicals on the library shelves: In many depository collections, government periodicals may be shelved by SuDocs numbers, separated from the mainstream periodical collection. In such situations, users will need guidance to find the government periodicals they need.

## ADDRESSES

ACCESS ERIC, 1600 Research Blvd., Rockville, MD 20850-3172; (800) LET-ERIC, FAX (301) 251-5212.

Questions should be referred to ACCESS ERIC at (800) LET-ERIC or to the appropriate ERIC clearinghouse.

## FREEBIES

The following subject bibliographies are available free from U.S. Government Printing Office, Superintendent of Documents, Washington, DC 20402:

244. United States Government Printing Office Publications

From ACCESS ERIC (see address and telephone number above under "Addresses"):

"All About ERIC" (ED 1.302:Ed 8/2/990)

"The ERIC Review" (ED 1.331: )

"A Pocket Guide to ERIC" (ED 1.308:Ed 8/6/yr)

## REFERENCES

1. Jim Walsh and Mallory Stark, "The *Monthly Catalog of United States Government Publications:* One Title, Many Versions," *Government Information Quarterly* 7/3 (1990):359-70: A must-read summary of the various *Monthly Catalog* versions on the market; Plum, Terry and Hans Raum, "*Monthly Catalog* on CD-ROM" *Choice* 27 (September 1989):59-60: A critique of five *Monthly Catalog* CD-ROMs.

2. Readex Microprint Corp., *Readex U.S. Government Document Collection: Depository Publications 1956-1980; Non-Depository Publications 1953-1980* (microprint), and *Readex Comprehensive Collection: Depository and Non-Depository, 1981-present* (microfiche): These collections include the full text of all documents, both depository and nondepository, cited in the *Monthly Catalog.* Since 1981, they have been published in microfiche rather than microprint.

3. Peter Hernon and Charles R. McClure, *Public Access to Government Information: Issues, Trends, and Strategies*, 2nd ed. Norwood, NJ: Ablex Publishing Corp., 1988, p. 168.

4. Charles R. McClure, Peter Hernon, and Gary R. Purcell, *Linking the U.S. National Technical Information Service with Academic and Public Libraries* (Norwood, NJ: Ablex Publishing Co., 1986), p. 117.

5. McClure, Hernon, and Purcell, pp. 77-88.

6. U.S. General Accounting Office, *Government Printing Office's Depository Library Program* (GAO/AFMD-85-19) (GAO, 1984), p. 10. Free from GAO, Document Handling and Information Services Facility, P.O. Box 6015, Gaithersburg, MD 20760; (202) 275-6241; Margaret T. Mooney, "GPO Cataloging: Is It a Viable Current Access Tool for U.S. Documents?" *Government Publications Review* 16 (May/June 1989):259-70: The time lag between receipt of depository documents and their appearance in the *Monthly Catalog* or availability for library online catalogs averaged about six months, while a few had not been listed after two years.

7. Gary D. Bass and David Plocher, "Finding Government Information: The Federal Information Locator System (FILS)," *Government Information Quarterly* 8 (January, 1991):11-32: A review of the "ill-fated" history of FILS, and a description of its potential; Charles R. McClure, et. al. *Federal Information Inventory/Locator Systems: From Burden to Benefit, Final Report to General Services Administration and Office of Management and Budget.* (Syracuse, NY: School of Information Studies, 1990) ED 326247: A study commissioned by OMB of the feasibility, costs, and potential structure of a comprehensive FILS.

8. Senate, *Descriptive Catalog of the Government Publications of the United States, September 5, 1774-March 4, 1881 by Ben Perley Poore.* (Senate Miscellaneous Doc. 67, 48th Congress, 2nd Session, Serial No. 2268), III.

9. Senate, p. III.

10. Jean L. Sears and Marilyn K. Moody, *Using Government Publications. Vol. 2: Finding Statistics and Using Special Techniques* (Phoenix, AZ: Oryx Press, 1986), p. 149.

11. Judith Gilligan and Susan Hajdas, "A Checklist of Indexed Federal Periodicals," *Government Publications Review* 13 (July/August 1986):507-18; Peter Hernon and Clayton A. Shepherd, "Government Publications Represented in the *Social Sciences Citation Index:* An Exploratory Study," *Government Publications Review* 10 (March/April 1983): 227-44; Charles R. McClure, "Indexing U.S. Government Periodicals: Analysis and Comments," *Government Publications Review* 5 (1978): 409-21; and Steven D. Zink, "The Impending Crisis in Government Publications Reference Service," *Microform Review* 11 (Spring 1982):106-11.

## FURTHER READING

Atkinson, Richard C. and Gregg B. Jackson, eds. *Research and Education Reform: Roles for the Office of Educational Research and Improvement.* Washington, DC: National Academy Press, 1992.
> A report from the National Research Council on the status of the government's role in educational research and development.

Cornwell, Gary. "GPO Cataloging Records: Background and Issues." *Documents to the People* 17 (June 1989):83-85.
> An overview of issues related to GPO OCLC cataloging and MARCIVE.

Heinzkill, Richard. *Reading the OCLC Screen.* Eugene, OR: John Richard Heinzkill, 1989.
> A quick reference guide for deciphering codes and abbreviations in OCLC records.

Lang, Elizabeth. "Government Periodicals and the Reference Librarian: Obstacles and Accommodations." *The Reference Librarian* no. 27-28 (1989):305-12.
> Suggestions for incorporating government periodicals into the reference librarian's repertoire.

Murphy, Cynthia E. "A Comparison of Manual and Online Searching of Government Document Indexes." *Government Information Quarterly* 2 (May 1985):169-81.
> Print and online versions of the *Monthly Catalog* are compared for search costs, recall, precision, overlap, and effort.

Sears, Jean L. and Marilyn K. Moody. *Using Government Publications. Vol. 2: Finding Statistics and Using Special Techniques.* Phoenix, AZ: Oryx Press, 1986.
> Chapter 18, "Historical Searches," discusses strategies for historical searching, describes sources, and explains ways to identify SuDocs numbers when they have been omitted from retrospective indexes.

Superintendent of Documents. *PRF User's Manual: A Guide to Using the GPO Sales Publications Reference File.* GPO, 1981. (GP 3.22/3: Manual/981)
> A concise, helpful guide to using the PRF.

Tyckoson, David. "Format, Usage, and Patron Preference for Information Sources." *Technicalities* 8 (August 1988):5-7.
> Use comparisons of the *Monthly Catalog* in paper, CD-ROM, PAC, and other formats at Iowa State University.

## EXERCISES

1. In the first national analysis of academic and public depository library users, Charles R. McClure and Peter Hernon estimated that at least 167,000 people used depository libraries weekly. Academic depositories were more heavily used than public, and users tended to be highly educated students, professionals, or managers. Identify Hernon and McClure's 1989 report.

2. As part of its Library Awareness Program, the FBI asked librarians to alert them to "foreigners" seeking sensitive but unclassified information in libraries. After a flurry of unfavorable media attention, congressional hearings explored possible conflicts between the FBI program and individual privacy rights. Identify the hearing on FBI "counter-intelligence visits to libraries" which occurred in the late 1980s.

3. Cite any USDA "Farmers' Bulletins" issued before 1976, noting SuDocs number and depository status.

4. Thomas Jefferson sold his personal library to Congress after the British burned Washington in the War of 1812. When Jefferson's books were loaded onto wagons for the trip from Monticello to Washington, he tucked his own handwritten catalog of his collection in with them. Long lost, a copy of the Jefferson catalog was recently rediscovered and published by the Library of Congress in 1989. Identify it bibliographically.

5. A magazine article about the FBI's Library Awareness Program mentions an FBI report called *The KGB and the Library Target, 1962 - Present.* No additional information about the report was given in the article. Identify it bibliographically.

6. Identify full bibliographic information (including depository status and SuDocs number) for any of the core titles held in every depository library, listed on pp. 30–31 of Chapter 4.

# CHAPTER 6
# Scientific Information

## WHAT

Scientific and technical information collected by or for government is an important subset of all government information. The federal government takes science very seriously, spending about $65 billion yearly to support research and development.

## WHY

Science and technology have been heralded as "pervasive determinants of modern life," instrumental in advancing our understanding of nature, achieving national goals, and solving societal problems.[1] Government-generated scientific literature is useful not only to scholars and researchers, but also to businesspeople, students, hobbyists, homeowners, medical patients, and other members of the public who use sci/tech research results in their daily lives, sometimes without realizing it.

## HOW

As the nation's central clearinghouse for unclassified technical reports of government-sponsored research, the National Technical Information Service indexes, abstracts, and sells U.S. and foreign technical reports and federal government databases and software. Required by law to be self-supporting, NTIS recovers its costs through product sales.

Numerous other agencies announce and disseminate sci/tech information through special subject indexes and abstracts, databases, electronic bulletin boards, clearinghouses, and information analysis centers. A small percentage of scientific literature is funneled through GPO and federal depository libraries.

## WHO

The federal government performs only about 10 percent of its own research. The rest is contracted out to industry, universities, and nonprofit organizations. Four agencies support about 90 percent of government research: Health and Human Services accounts for about one-third, followed by the Department of Defense, NASA, and the Department of Energy.

## SCIENTIFIC LITERACY

Although Americans are interested in science, they have little understanding of it.[2] Fewer than half, for example, realize that the earth revolves around the sun once a year. A 1980 U.S. Department of Education report warned that Americans were heading toward "virtual scientific and technological illiteracy."[3] Today it is estimated that "at least nine out of ten citizens lack the scientific literacy to understand and participate in the formulation of public policy on a very important segment of their national political agendas."[4] Or, expressed another way: "Do you want these people deciding where to stash leftover plutonium?"[5]

## TECHNICAL REPORTS

They are called "technical" because they are often aimed at experts within a discipline. They are called "reports" because they report to sponsoring organizations about the progress of funded research. National, state, and foreign governments, international organizations, and research institutions all sponsor research, and therefore generate technical reports. Most U.S. government research is conducted by corporations and universities under contract to government agencies that require reports for accountability. Some are brief progress reports of a few typewritten pages, while others are bulky volumes crammed with details. More frequently than journal articles, technical reports document unsuccessful as well as successful research. They may be informally photocopied or typed, with most never passing through the Government Printing Office either for printing or bibliographic control. Instead they are channeled through a bibliographic control system independent of GPO: the National Technical Information Service (NTIS), the government's central clearinghouse for technical reports.

Before World War II, most scientific research was privately funded and then reported in scientific journals. The federal government did not assume a major role in research until World War II. Technical reports evolved after a flood of World War II government research money necessitated new ways to report research results. The versatile technical report could be quickly and cheaply reproduced and easily classified, and partly eclipsed journal articles and books as conduits for scientific communication after World War II.

Technical reports have been characterized as "science right now," the leading edge of research disclosing the newest sci/tech findings.[6] As primary information sources, technical reports are raw rather than polished. Quickly released, they bypass traditional publication channels, including peer review and editing. As a result, new technical reports are more current than either books or journal articles (although some technical reports themselves are published in books or journal articles). Technical reports are unbound, interim, and ephemeral, usually in a numbered series. They enjoy minimal use initially, and that diminishes quickly. They are often categorized as "unpublished," and many never appear in any nonreport format. If information seekers overlook national report collections and their announcement bulletins, they may miss key documents untraceable using traditional bibliographic searches.

*No one reads the literature.*
—Dr. Rustum Roy,
Pennsylvania State University

Government technical reports are underused. In fact, most U. S. scientists fail to survey the literature, even in their own research specialties.[7] Underuse stems partly from a sci/tech dissemination system that "is passive, fragmented, and unfocused."[8] The nation's sci/tech infrastructure is decentralized and electronic, spanning multiple disciplines and research areas, but with no central, comprehensive sci/tech databank. Many agencies rely heavily on electronic dissemination of sci/tech data, increasing the percentage of fugitives that elude the NTIS and GPO dragnets. Dissemination of sci/tech information is shifting toward media like electronic mail and bulletin boards, floppy disks, and CD-ROMs, with concomitant displacement of paper and microfiche.

## Technical Report Citations

Technical reports are tagged with multiple numbers, any of which may function as access points for bibliographic searching. Besides title, author, and agency information, a single technical report may boast contract numbers, grant numbers, accession numbers, report series codes, report numbers, project and task numbers, and SuDocs numbers. Although often not identified as

such on the report itself, a standard technical report number (STRN) or nonstandard technical report number may be included in the report's cataloging record (OCLC fields 027 and 088). Occasionally, a report sports a Report Documentation Cover Page, which specifies the STRN in the "Report No." box. Unfortunately, many authors cite technical reports sloppily, creating trauma for the poor souls who later try to track down references.

One of the more common designators of technical reports is the NTIS accession number, which doubles as an ordering number. NTIS accession numbers begin with alphabetical prefixes designating the origin or processing source of the document, followed by numbers (example: PB85-232650). Some of the more common alpha prefixes are:

PB, for NTIS-processed reports
AD or ATI, for Defense Department documents
ED or EJ, for ERIC documents
TT, for technical translations
PR, for free brochures describing NTIS products and services

NTIS accession numbers function as order numbers and should be provided when ordering documents from NTIS. They are also computer search keys within the NTIS Bibliographic Database. The *Dictionary of Report Series Codes* (1973) and its update, *Report Series Codes Dictionary* (1986), are helpful for identifying report/accession numbers, contract/grant numbers, and corporate authors.

## Obtaining Technical Reports

Thousands of technical reports are for sale from NTIS, with others sold by GPO or scientific issuing agencies. In addition, some may be in library technical-report collections, while a small percentage are sent to federal depository libraries. Various libraries shelve technical reports differently, often by either report numbers or SuDocs numbers. To familiarize yourself with technical-report arrangement in a library, ask at the reference desk. To determine whether a particular title was sent to federal depository libraries, search the *Monthly Catalog's* title or report number index, do an OCLC title-search (check field 074, depository item number), or ask at the depository reference desk.

The Library of Congress's Science and Technology Division maintains the world's largest, most accessible collection of technical reports, primarily on microfiche. The division's Technical Reports and Standards Collection includes reports from some sixty nations. The division also collects information on all aspects of science and technology except technical agriculture and clinical medicine (covered by the National Agricultural Library and the National Library of Medicine). A collection of historical materials includes first editions of Copernicus and Newton and the personal papers of the Wright brothers and Alexander Graham Bell. Inquiries flow into the division from all over the world in the form of letters, telephone calls, and walk-in visits. Researchers are welcome in the division's reading room, which houses a reference collection that includes technical dictionaries, encyclopedias, handbooks, directories, standard scientific texts, journals, and indexes and abstracts. A guide to on-site use of the collection is free from Library of Congress, Science and Technology Division, Washington, DC 20540.

The division's *LC Science Tracer Bullet* (LC 33.10:) is a series of free literature guides or "pathfinders" pointing library users to information resources on both popular and technical scientific topics. New Tracer Bullets are announced in the *Library of Congress Information Bulletin* (LC 1.18:). Individual Tracer Bullets and a list of all Tracer Bullet titles are free from LC's Science and Technology Division.

## NATIONAL TECHNICAL INFORMATION SERVICE

NTIS began after World War II with a collection of captured German documents and was formally established by President Truman's 1945 executive order. Today's NTIS has evolved into the broker for much of the federal government's scientific and technical information. Its coverage includes both the "hard" and "soft" sciences, including disciplines like management, information technology, history, law, personnel, psychology, and sociology. NTIS emphasizes two types of information products: (1) research reports and (2) federally generated bibliographic and numeric databases and computer programs. NTIS is also the central source for licensing U.S.-government-owned patents.

Each month some 6,000 new reports join the NTIS inventory. With more than two million reports, it is the largest publicly available research pool in the world. These technical reports emanate from the sponsored research of more than 350 federal agencies, in addition to state, local, and foreign governments, and some nongovernment organizations. The bulk of the NTIS collection pours out of three agencies: NASA and the Departments of Defense and Energy, although many other agencies are represented.

Despite its vast collection, NTIS does not have all technical reports. Because agency submissions are voluntary rather than legally mandated, one-third to one-half of federal technical reports never reach NTIS. A recent technical report held neither by NTIS nor by other government clearinghouses (ERIC, for example) may sometimes be available from the sponsoring agency or contractor.

NTIS is the central, permanent source of specialized scientific, business, economic, and social information, primarily from federal agencies. Summaries of these U.S. and foreign research reports are published regularly by NTIS in a variety of weekly newsletters, indexes, and subscriptions. Paper and microfiche copies of NTIS announcement titles have been declining, however, in deference to NTIS's fastest growing product line: computer products, including bibliographic databases. The reports themselves are sold in paper or microfiche. With two-thirds of its documents sold in microfiche, NTIS is one of the nation's major microform producers and distributors. Copies are made on demand from the NTIS archival collection, allowing titles to remain perpetually in print. Reports can be ordered online, by mail, or purchased on-site in Springfield, Virginia, at the NTIS bookstore.

> **Search Tip**
> Searches in the old-format *Monthly Catalog* may retrieve citations that declare availability from the Clearinghouse for Federal Scientific and Technical Information, CFSTI, Publication Board, Technical Services Office, or OTS. All are former names of NTIS. Because NTIS publications remain perpetually in print, older titles cited in *Monthly Catalog* can still be purchased (although at today's prices).

In early 1987, the Office of Management and Budget pushed to privatize NTIS, ordering it contracted out to the private sector. This controversial proposal was derided in Congress as "a triumph of ideology over common sense," because NTIS is fully self-supporting. The costs of running NTIS are paid by the sale of its products, and the agency is "at least as cost-effective as private firms." House and Senate hearings, a Department of Commerce analysis, and public comments all documented opposition to privatization, which was viewed as costly and risky for the government, NTIS customers, and the information industry. The conflict was resolved by a merger between NTIS and the Commerce Department's new Technology Administration. NTIS's future will emphasize modernization and joint ventures.

> **The Genesis of NTIS**
> During the denouement of World War II, Allied teams scrambled to capture Nazi war secrets before they could be destroyed. Many Germans had ignored Hitler's dying orders to scuttle all equipment and documentation, instead secreting them away. In dynamited mountain caves, mine shafts, factories, labs, and hideaways, Allied search squads ferreted out tons of scientific documentation, German patents, Himmler's papers, machines, and even scientists themselves.
>
> To process the flood of Nazi military, scientific, and industrial secrets, President Truman established the Office of the Publication Board. Each week some one thousand enemy documents were translated, abstracted, announced in the *Bibliography of Scientific and Industrial Research Reports*, and then sold without copyright restrictions at the cost of microfilm reproduction. The Russians reportedly bought everything, while American entrepreneurs "practically park[ed] on the . . . doorstep,"

vying to get a jump on production secrets for medicines, chemistry, aviation, plastics, textiles, synthetic rubber, synthetic fuel, rockets, insect replants, and fire extinguishers.[9]

The Office of the Publication Board later became NTIS (but is remembered in the PB-prefix of NTIS accession numbers); its *Bibliography of Scientific and Industrial Research Reports* evolved into GRA & I; and technical reports became the predominant method for communicating research results.

## BIBLIOGRAPHIC SEARCHING

Computerized databases are handy for identifying technical reports because of the searching versatility they offer. Any of several bibliographic elements—author, title, numbers—can quickly retrieve a specific citation from a database. Manual searching of specialized print indexes is another option. Many indexing and abstracting services list technical reports and many are searchable online or in CD-ROM cumulations.

Technical report searches should begin with the most comprehensive source, *Government Reports Announcements and Index* or its database counterpart, followed by searches of special scientific subject indexes and their database equivalents, and finally the *Monthly Catalog*, as appropriate.

### *Government Reports Announcements and Index(C 51.9/3: )*

Abstracts of the research reports received by NTIS are published biweekly in the comprehensive *Government Reports Announcements and Index* (GRA & I). The index itself is available to depository libraries, but most of the publications cited in it are not. The index is also sold on subscription through NTIS. Both the biweekly and annual GRA & I indexes are searchable by subject, personal and corporate authors, contract/grant numbers, and NTIS order/accession numbers. The annual index cumulates the twenty-four GRA & I bimonthly issues.

### GRA & I Search Tips

To find the abstract for an index entry listed in pre-1980 issues, first locate the subject field and group numbers within the abstract section, and then find the report number in alphanumeric sequence within the subject field. A sample citation from the 1976 GRA & I annual index shows how these components were indicated:

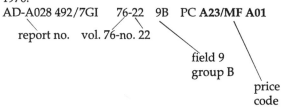

Between 1980 and 1983, the annual indexes referred to a GRA & I issue and page where the abstract would be found under NTIS order number, in alphanumeric sequence:

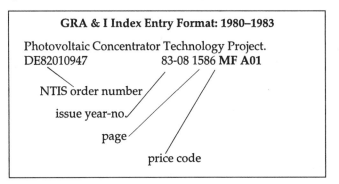

Since 1984, the indexes have referred to an abstract number within a particular biweekly issue:

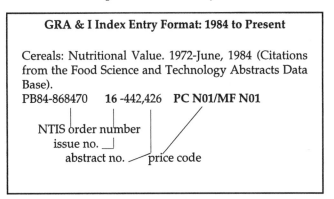

## Title Searches

Amazingly, neither the biweekly GRA & I nor its annual index allows for title searches. This has created a demand for the separately published, microfiche *NTIS Current Title Index.* Quarterly issues list new publications, with cumulations every two years. The Retrospective Package of the NTIS Title Index provides a cumulation since 1964, regularly updated by two-year supplements. Both the retrospective and current title indexes can be searched by title keywords, author, and report/accession numbers.

---

<table>
<tr><td>

**GRA & I Search Tip**

GRA & I and the NTIS Bibliographic Database cite journal articles, identified by NTIS accession numbers and sold by NTIS. Purchase is unnecessary, however, if the journal is owned locally or the article is available through interlibrary loan. An entry for a journal article will cite the journal immediately preceding the abstract—for example: "Pub. in Jnl. of Laboratory and Clinical Medicine, v108 n2 p121-132 Aug 86."

</td></tr>
</table>

## Other Search Tools

The annual *Corporate Author Authority List* standardizes corporate author names for NTIS documents (C 51.18:). *NTIS Library Reference Files 1943–1971* offers access to older NTIS reports, with indexes to report/ accession numbers, subjects, personal and corporate authors, and contract numbers.

## NTIS Bibliographic Database

The NTIS Bibliographic Database, the computerized counterpart to GRA & I, is one of the most heavily searched databases in the world. It cites and abstracts every title added to the NTIS collection since mid-1964, including U.S. and foreign technical reports, periodicals, government patents and patent applications, federally generated data files and databases, and software programs, with an increasing proportion of citations to unpublished foreign material.

The NTIS Database is searchable by title, personal and corporate authors, accession number, contract number, and subjects. There are four electronic access options: online, CD-ROM, lease from NTIS, and on-demand batch searches from NERAC. Online access is available through BRS, CISTI (in Canada), DATA-STAR, DIALOG, ORBIT, and STN International. Free search guides are available for each online service (see "Freebies" at the end of this chapter). A database HELP desk links searchers with NTIS staff to answer questions: (703) 487-4640, between 8:00 A.M. and 5:00 P.M. EST. CD-ROM versions of the NTIS Bibliographic Database are available from DIALOG, OCLC, and SilverPlatter, offering coverage from the early 1980s.

### Subject Searching

Because numerous disciplines are represented in the NTIS collection, several thesauri and reference aids are used to select subject terms (descriptors) describing the content of reports. Since most of the NTIS collection comes from the Departments of Defense and Energy, and NASA, it makes sense that the three principal thesauri used are the *NASA Thesaurus* (NAS 1.21: and supplement, NAS 1.21:7064/), *Energy Information Database: Subject Thesaurus* (E 1.55:), and *DDC Retrieval and Indexing Terminology*. Reports from agencies such as the Environmental Protection Agency and the Departments of Commerce, Transportation, and Housing and Urban Development are indexed by NTIS using the *Thesaurus of Engineering and Scientific Terms*, published by the Engineers Joint Council. "Microthesauri" are used to select terminology in energy, environment, health care, highways and motor vehicle safety, and water resources.[10]

After a useful NTIS document is identified, noting its descriptors and identifiers will help to locate similar titles. NTIS Database citations include a "descriptors" field, with asterisks indicating major descriptors. Keywords in the "identifiers" field are subject terms not in the thesauri, such as chemical compounds, city names, biological species, and computer-program names. Unfortunately, recent GRA & I citations have omitted the descriptor and identifier fields, making descriptors and identifiers available only through a search of the database or CD-ROM.

NTIS Published Searches are prepackaged bibliographies on high-interest topics. Often cheaper than customized online searches, Published Searches are selected bibliographies with abstracts, culled from the NTIS Bibliographic Database and numerous other databases, including some from the United Kingdom and Western Europe. The free *Published Search Master Catalog* (PR-186, updated by PR-824, *Published Search Mini Catalog*) describes more than 3,000 published searches, each costing about $60, plus handling. Published Searches are also announced in the NTIS Bibliographic Database, GRA & I, and in the biweekly *NTIS Alert* for Library and Information Sciences.

### Monthly Catalog

Because the roles of NTIS and GPO overlap, GPO's *Monthly Catalog* offers partial coverage of technical reports, listing some that are available to depository libraries. Some technical-report series, including those from the Environmental Protection Agency and the Nuclear Regulatory Commission, are printed at GPO, sent to depositories, and listed in the *Monthly Catalog*. Overlap is hardly comprehensive, however: One comparison found that for every twenty EPA titles in the NTIS Database, only one was listed in the *Monthly Catalog*.[11] Some reports are listed in both *Monthly Catalog*, GRA & I, and their electronic counterparts; are for sale from both GPO and NTIS; and are available in depository libraries. Occasionally documents go out of print at GPO only to be picked up by NTIS, which continues to sell them, although often at a higher price.

During the 1980s, the cost of NTIS paper reports increased 180 percent. Prices in both the NTIS database and GRA & I are listed not as dollar amounts but as price codes. To translate a price code, consult the price code table in a recent issue of GRA & I or request a free copy from NTIS (PR-360). NTIS prices tend to exceed GPO's because NTIS enjoys fewer economies of scale in printing and sales. GPO sales titles, averaging about $8 apiece, can be selected for their high sales potential, lowering the unit cost per copy. Meanwhile, the average NTIS title sells only 5-10 copies, but must be permanently archived regardless of its sales potential. In fact, one-quarter to one-third of NTIS titles never sell any copies.

As illustrated in the table below, the GPO price is often lower.

| PRICE COMPARISON: GPO AND NTIS* | | |
|---|---|---|
| | GPO | NTIS |
| *Compilation of Air Pollutant Emission Factors* | $8 | $23 |
| *Infection Control File* | $12 | $16 |
| *Metropolitan Statistical Areas, 1990* | $5.50 | $17 |
| *National List of Plant Species That Occur in Wetlands: Northeast* | $12 | $23 |
| *RCRA Orientation Manual* | $12 | $23 |
| *Short-Term Methods for Estimating the Chronic Toxicity of Effluents and Receiving Waters to Freshwater Organisms* | $13 | $31 |
| *Short-Term Methods for Estimating the Chronic Toxicity of Effluents and Receiving Waters to Marine and Estuarine Organisms* | $13 | $45 |
| *Test Methods for Evaluating Solid Waste Physical/Chemical Methods* | $319 | $73 |
| *U.S. Industrial Outlook, 1991* | $28 | $28 |
| *World Factbook, 1990* | $23 | $39 |

*Titles on NTIS's "100 Best Seller List" 1974-1991, also for sale from GPO (February 1991)

GRA & I notes a title's availability from GPO or ERIC, but omits notation of depository status, a source of free access and an alternative to purchase, or SuDocs numbers. Throughout the years, *Monthly Catalog* and GRA & I have been inconsistent about alerting searchers to a duplicate citation in the other source or dual availability from GPO/NTIS (see Figure 6.1). GRA & I does offer the advantage of listing titles about half a year earlier than *Monthly Catalog,* however.[12] After all, two-thirds of GPO's cataloging backlog is technical reports, which are near the bottom of the priority list. Because technical-report cataloging lags behind depository shipments, technical reports in depositories may languish for months without recognition in the *Monthly Catalog* or online library catalog. Some technical reports receive abridged OCLC records to speed the bibliographic process.

The *Monthly Catalog* offers the added advantage of listing SuDocs numbers, which are needed to locate technical reports in many depository collections. Often when a technical report is identified in GRA & I or the NTIS Bibliographic Database, it must be searched again in the *Monthly Catalog* or OCLC to identify its SuDocs number for retrieval from a depository collection. Overlap with GRA & I is 10 percent for the *Monthly Catalog* (depository documents only), and 30 percent for OCLC

**FIGURE 6.1: Sample GRA & I Entry.**

Compare this GRA & I entry with the *Monthly Catalog* entry in Chapter 5 (Figure 5.7). Although availability from GPO is noted, price and stock number are omitted, there is no hint that copies were sent to depository libraries, and no SuDocs number. A person wishing to identify the SuDocs number would be forced to search *Monthly Catalog,* PRF, or OCLC. Similarly, the *Monthly Catalog* and OCLC entries for the same title (Figures 5.5 & 5.7, Chapter 5) omit any mention of availability from NTIS or PB number.

(two-thirds are nondepository documents).[13] McClure, Hernon, and Purcell recommend title searches as the best strategy for locating NTIS publications in the *Monthly Catalog,* as well as in OCLC.[14]

GRA & I and the *Monthly Catalog* often use different, even contradictory, subject terms to describe document contents. The Library of Congress subject headings used in the MoCat tend to be more general, while GRA & I leans toward more technical descriptors.

| OCLC Fields | |
|---|---|
| 027 | Standard technical report number |
| 037 | NTIS accession number; price (may need updating) or price codes |
| 074 | Depository item number |
| 086; 099 | SuDocs number |
| 088 | Nonstandard technical report number |
| 260 | Publisher, date |
| 500 | Notes; if nondepository, may include the note "Not distributed to depository libraries" |
| 650 | Subject headings |

## NTIS Alerts

These current awareness bulletins provide summaries of research, software and data files in special subject fields, or in customized Alerts covering any of 190 topics.

Each NTIS Alert gives full bibliographic citations, abstracts, and order forms for purchasing full text. Many have annual subject indexes. The NTIS Alerts flier (PR-797) is free from NTIS. The subjects are:

Agriculture and Food
Astronomy and Astrophysics
Biomedical Technology and Human Factors
    Engineering
Building Industry Technology
Business and Economics
Civil Engineering
Combustion, Engines and Propellants
Communication
Computers, Control and Information Theory
Detection and Countermeasures
Electrotechnology
Energy
Environmental Pollution and Control
Foreign Technology
Government Inventions for Licensing
Health Care
Library and Information Sciences
Manufacturing Technology
Materials Sciences
Mathematical Sciences
Ocean Technology and Engineering
Ordnance
Photography and Recording Devices
Regional and Urban Planning and Technology
Transportation

## NTIS and Libraries

When McClure, Hernon, and Purcell tested how well libraries linked users with NTIS, they found NTIS resources to be largely untapped. The six public and six academic libraries studied were ineffectual in alerting their users to NTIS products and services. Unobtrusive reference questions garnered an accuracy rate of about 42 percent, even though the libraries owned the NTIS answer sources and housed federal depository collections.[15] (Academic libraries fared better than public, tallying about 53 and 30 percent correct answers, respectively).

*If the assumptions are wrong, the conclusions aren't likely to be very good.*
    —Robert E. Machol, operations researcher

Clues in the unobtrusive test questions that should have telegraphed the need for NTIS sources were ignored, and staff failed to associate PB numbers with NTIS, or to consult GRA & I to verify technical report citations. Some staff mistakenly assumed GPO to be the only distributor of government publications, or that the *Monthly Catalog* would list all government titles.

*Academic Library Use of NTIS: Suggestions for Services and Core Collection* (PB86-228871) is a handbook created to familiarize information professionals with NTIS. Academic libraries may request a free copy from NTIS.

NTIS's Library Liaison Network serves as a communication vehicle between NTIS and its users. Individuals from libraries, library schools, and professional organizations volunteer to serve as NTIS liaisons, receiving the free *Liaison Letter* and other announcements. To participate, contact Director, Office of Customer Services, NTIS.

## Specialized Subject Sources

The Department of Defense, NASA, and the Department of Energy have their own technical information centers that serve their agency personnel and contractors: Energy's Office of Scientific and Technical Information (OSTI), the Defense Technical Information Center (DTIC), and NASA's Scientific and Technical Information Facility (STIF). Each uses NTIS to supply its reports to the public.

### Defense Technical Information Center

The Defense Technical Information Center (DTIC, pronounced "dee-tick") is the central point within the Department of Defense (DoD) for handling scientific and technical information. Topics of interest to the Defense Department span the sciences: not only aeronautics, missile and space technology, navigation, and nuclear science, but also biology, chemistry, energy, environmental sciences, oceanography, computer sciences, sociology, and human factors engineering. The DTIC collection supports these diverse interests with technical reports, research summaries, a referral database, World War II documents, and DoD patents.

Many of these resources are searchable through DTIC's online database and *Technical Reports Awareness Circular* (TRAC), both accessible only to DoD, its contractors, and other registered users. The general public is allowed access only to DoD's unclassified, unlimited technical reports, which are funneled through NTIS. In 1987, the monthly TRAC replaced *Technical Abstract Bulletin* (TAB). TRAC is an unclassified publication which announces DTIC's newly accessioned reports (accession number series AD-xxx xxx), including those unclassified/unlimited reports announced to the general public through NTIS.

### NASA

NASA's *Scientific and Technical Aerospace Reports* (STAR) indexes and abstracts worldwide unclassified technical reports on aeronautics, space, and related physics, chemistry, mathematics, and life sciences. STAR (NAS 1.9/4:) lists reports, translations in report form, patents, and dissertations emanating from NASA, other government agencies, universities, industry, and research organizations worldwide. STAR can be searched by subject, corporate source, author, report number, or contract number. An annual cumulated index is published separately (NAS 1.9/5:). Both STAR and its indexes are available free to depository libraries, and NASA distributes microfiche titles to depositories. STAR's report/accession number index refers from SuDocs numbers (NAS 1.[no.]:) to STAR accession numbers indicating where the STAR abstract can be found. The SuDocs number is also noted in the abstract itself. The STAR abstract indicates availability for sale from GPO with the abbreviation SOD or GPO (see Figure 6.2). When the same document is listed in GRA & I (see Figure 6.1), the SuDocs number (beginning with NAS) is listed in the abstract and in the NTIS order/report number index as an order/report number. There is considerable overlap between GRA & I and STAR.

While STAR concentrates on world report literature, a companion journal, *International Aerospace Abstracts* (IAA) announces non-NASA literature in NASA's database. IAA indexes and abstracts books, journal articles, conference proceedings, journal translations, and

**FIGURE 6.2: Sample Entry from Scientific and Technical Aerospace Reports.**

**16** SPACE TRANSPORTATION

Includes passenger and cargo space transportation, e.g., shuttle operations; and rescue techniques.
For related information see also *03 Air Transportation and Safety* and *85 Urban Technology and Transportation*.

N86-24726# Presidential Commission on the Space Shuttle Challenger Accident, Washington, D.C.
REPORT OF THE PRESIDENTIAL COMMISSION ON THE SPACE SHUTTLE CHALLENGER ACCIDENT, VOLUME 1
William P. Rogers, Neil A. Armstrong, David C. Acheson, Eugene E. Covert, Richard P. Feynman, Robert B. Hotz, Donald J. Kutyna, Sally K. Ride, Robert W. Rummel, Joseph F. Sutter et al 6 Jun. 1986 260 p refs Original contains color illustrations 5 Vol.
Avail: NTIS MF A01; also available GPO HC $18.00. ←

The findings of the Commission regarding the circumstances surrounding the Challenger accident are reported and recommendations for corrective action are outlined. All available mission data, subsequent tests, and wreckage analyses were reviewed and specific failure scenarios were developed. The Commission concluded that the cause of the Mission 51-L accident was the failure of the pressure seal in the aft field joint of the right solid rocket motor. The failure was due to a faulty design unacceptably sensitive to a number of factors. These factors were the effects of temperature, physical dimensions, the character of materials, the effects of reuse, processing, and the reaction of the joint to dynamic loading. In addition to analyzing the material causes of the accident, the Commission examined the chain of decisions that culminated in approval of the launch. It concluded that the decision making process was flawed in several ways including (1) failure in communication resulting in a launch decision based on incomplete and misleading information, (2) a conflict between engineering data and management judgements, and (3) a NASA management structure that permitted flight safety problems to bypass key Shuttle managers. M.G.

Although availability from GPO and GPO price are noted, the PRF should be checked to verify current GPO availability and price before an attempt to purchase. Since no indicator of depository status or SuDocs number is given, a person wanting to use the document in a depository library would need to search the PRF, *Monthly Catalog*, or OCLC looking for depository item number and SuDocs number.

selected foreign dissertations. Because IAA is not a government publication (it is sponsored by NASA, but privately published by the American Institute of Aero-

nautics and Astronautics), it is not sent to depository libraries.

Entries from STAR and IAA can be retrieved through DIALOG and NASA/RECON, NASA's internal online service. NASA/RECON searches provide access to the NASA STI Database, including STAR and IAA, plus other scientific and technical databases. Access is limited to government agencies, contractors, and organizations with aerospace-related grants, contracts, or programs of interest to NASA. Government and commercial databases can also be searched at NASA Applications Centers. Users of NASA information resources should consult the *NASA Thesaurus* (NAS 1.21: and supplement NAS 1.21:7064/), the controlled vocabulary used to index NASA documents.

## Energy Literature

*Energy Research Abstracts* (E 1.17:) cites energy-related reports from DOE, other government agencies, and private sources, both U.S. and foreign. There is considerable overlap between ERA and GRA & I. Materials abstracted and indexed in ERA include technical reports, patent applications, theses, conference papers and proceedings, audiovisuals, electronic media, and engineering drawings (see Figure 6.3). Since 1991, ERA has been limited to literature in report form. ERA notes availability from NTIS and includes NTIS accession/order numbers. Availability in depository libraries is also noted (GPO Dep.), but SuDoc numbers are omitted.

ERA's online equivalent is the DOE Energy Science and Technology Database (EDB). EDB is searchable through DIALOG, STN International, NERAC, Inc. (batch searches), and leasable on magnetic tape from the National Technical Information Service (NTIS). The Integrated Technical Information System (ITIS) is DOE's online database of more than a year of *Energy Research Abstracts*, plus ten other databases. ITIS was the subject of one of the depository library electronic pilot projects, providing online access to a year's worth of EDB citations in ITIS and a computer "gateway" for access to older DOE bibliographic files held by commercial vendors. The pilot also tested electronic full text delivery of DOE reports.

Many Department of Energy reports may be identified only through *Energy Research Abstracts* or EDB. Under a cooperative agreement between GPO and the Department of Energy, however, retrospective DOE reports are available to depositories on microfiche (E 1.28:), and unlimited-distribution DOE reports in *Energy Research Abstracts* are sent to depository libraries (E 1.99:). DOE also publishes nineteen announcement journals in its Current Awareness series, listing publications related to conservation, fossil energy, renewable

**FIGURE 6.3: Sample Entry from *Energy Research Abstracts*.**

> **33543**   **(DOE/BP—2) Passive solar design handbook.**
> Baker, M.S. (USDOE Bonneville Power Administration,
> Portland, OR; Western Solar Utilization Network, Portland,
> OR (USA)). Apr 1985. 28p. NTIS, PC A03/MF A01; GPO   ←
> Dep. File Number DE85014263.
>     A basic introduction to solar energy is provided in this
> manual. The most common passive solar heating designs are de-
> scribed very briefly. The designs presented fall under three passive
> heating classifications: direct gain, indirect gain, and isolated gain.
> Design considerations for buildings are included along with consid-
> erations for: thermal storage walls, thermal storage roofs, attached
> sunspaces, and convective loops. A glossary of solar energy related
> terms is included. (BCS)

This ERA entry notes availability of the document from NTIS and in depository libraries (GPO Dep.). The File Number that immediately follows the GPO Dep. indicator is not the SuDocs number, but is used for ordering from NTIS. To identify the SuDocs number needed to access the document in many depository libraries requires a search of *Monthly Catalog*, PRF, or OCLC.

energy, reactor technology, and radioactive waste. For a list of titles, all sold by NTIS, request the DOE periodicals brochure from OSTI.

The Department of Energy's Energy Information Administration (EIA) provides energy information to the public through statistical and analytical publications. *EIA Publications Directory, 1977-1989 [DOE/EIA-0149(77-89)]*, supplemented by the annual *EIA Publications Directory* (E 3.27:), contains abstracts of Energy Information Administration publications, with information on EIA data files and modeling programs, and is free from EIA. EIA also sells data files and software models on magnetic tape and floppy disks through NTIS and GPO. The data files contain survey data from energy producers and consumers and include data appearing in EIA publications. Some of the EIA data files on floppy disk are sent to depository libraries. The software models are those used by EIA to perform projections. A free booklet, "Energy Datafiles" (PR-712), is available from NTIS.

Timely statistical reports from the Energy Information Administration are available through the EIA electronic bulletin board: EPUB, Electronic Publishing System. Instructions are in "Electronic Publishing System (EPUB) Quick Start Users Guide" (E 3.8:El 2), which is free from EIA. The pocket-sized *Energy Facts* (E 3.49:) is an annual synopsis of U.S. and international energy data, organized by energy source.

EIA's National Energy Information Center (NEIC) is a source of information about energy sources, reserves, production, consumption, distribution, imports, exports, and related economic and statistical information and forecasts. Requests are accepted by letter, telephone, and from visitors to the NEIC Reading Room.

### Environmental Literature

Although EPA is attempting to reverse the trend, many EPA publications have traditionally slipped through the depository library net. This has been attrib-

uted to EPA's decentralization and reliance upon contractors, a common antecedent of fugitive documents. The Environmental Protection Agency did participate in the depository library electronic pilot projects by making its Toxic Release Inventory (TRI) available to depositories on CD-ROM. Mandated by law, TRI includes information about toxic chemicals released into the environment. It can be purchased from GPO or NTIS, or searched on MEDLINE as TOXNET. EPA's User Support Program provides free floppy disks of data for any state and will perform MEDLINE searches of TRI: (202) 382-3531. A TRI hotline provides user assistance: (800) 535-0202. Two useful guides are *Directory of Public Libraries: Toxic Chemical Release Inventory*, which lists public libraries with microfiche copies of TRI, and *Federal Depository Libraries: Your Source for the Toxic Release Inventory*, both free from the EPA.

*EPA Publications Bibliography: Quarterly Abstract Bulletin* (EP 1.21/7:) lists Environmental Protection Agency technical reports and journal articles in the NTIS collection (the information is duplicated in GRA & I and the NTIS Bibliographic Database). Cumulations are available for 1984-1990, 1977-1983, and 1970-1976 (EP 1.21/7-2:). While all *EPA Publications Bibliography* listings are for sale from NTIS and cited in GRA & I and the NTIS Database, some are also available in depository libraries and co-listed in the *Monthly Catalog*. Since neither GRA & I nor *EPA Publications Bibliography* notes SuDocs numbers for EPA depository publications, the *EPA Index: A Key to U.S. Environmental Protection Agency Reports and Superintendent of Documents and NTIS Numbers* (Oryx Press) serves as a handy guide to SuDocs numbers when either the EPA report number or title is known.

The ACCESS EPA series (EP 1.8/13:Ac 2/) provides annual directories to EPA information resources for Public Information Tools; Clearinghouses and Hotlines; Major EPA Environmental Databases; State Environmental Libraries; Major EPA Dockets; Records Management Programs; and Library and Information Sources. Titles in the series are available individually, and also consolidated into one volume in *ACCESS EPA* (EP 1.8/13:Ac 2). Therefore, ACCESS EPA indicates both the series of seven titles, and the consolidated edition.

The EPA Library Network maintains a computerized union catalog, the Online Library System, which is accessible to the public through NTIS: (703) 487-4807. The *ACCESS EPA Library and Information Sources* pamphlet (EP 1.8/13:Ac 2/library) describes the special collections of EPA libraries and information centers.

| SCIENTIFIC SEARCH SCORECARD | | |
|---|---|---|
| **Title** | **Strengths** | **Limitations** |
| GRA & I | Most comprehensive coverage of technical reports; includes abstracts; searchable online on NTIS Bibliographic Database | Except for NASA documents (NAS), omits SuDocs numbers needed for retrieval in depository collections; emphasizes sales, omitting indication of free access through depository libraries; does not list subject descriptors |
| NTIS Bibliographic Database | Comprehensive technical report coverage; includes abstracts and subject descriptors | Usually omits SuDocs numbers; gives no indication of depository status |
| MoCat | Gives SuDocs numbers; searchable by numerous access points, including report numbers; searchable online; citations give full bibliographic information and are input into OCLC | No abstracts; slower than GRA & I to list technical reports; limited technical report coverage |
| OCLC | Quickly searched; gives SuDocs numbers and notes depository status; full bibliographic information | Cannot be searched by report numbers; no abstracts |
| ERA | Notes depository status and SuDocs numbers for DOE reports sent to depository libraries, and availability from NTIS, with NTIS price code and order number; abstracts; searchable online through EDB | Subject scope limited |
| STAR | Abstracts; notes depository status, with SuDocs numbers given in abstracts; notes NTIS and GPO for-sale status with prices | Subject scope limited |

# NATIONAL LIBRARY OF MEDICINE

*It is simply the best medical library on earth.*
—Andy Rooney,
television commentator and
newspaper columnist

The world's largest medical research library, the National Library of Medicine (NLM), has an exhaustive health sciences collection and selective holdings in such areas as chemistry, physics, botany, zoology, and veterinary medicine (NLM and the National Agricultural Library cooperate to collect veterinary science information). Its collections include books, journals, technical reports, theses, microfilm, pictorial and audiovisual materials, and the nation's largest medical-history collection, spanning the eleventh to mid-nineteenth centuries.

NLM's computerized literature retrieval system, MEDLARS, is searchable through a nationwide network of universities, medical schools, hospitals, and government agencies, and through numerous online services, including DIALOG and BRS, and on CD-ROM from several vendors. MEDLARS is a family of about twenty online databases, including MEDLINE, "the most sought-after database in medicine." MEDLINE is essentially *Index Medicus* online, with citations to the world's biomedical journal articles since 1966, including *International Nursing Index* and *Index to Dental Literature*. MEDLINE is searchable through numerous online services, including DIALOG and BRS, and is available on CD-ROM.

MEDLARS is used to produce printed indexes and bibliographies, including *Index Medicus*, the monthly subject/author guide to current articles from about 2,500 of the world's biomedical journals (HE 20.3612:). *Abridged Index Medicus* (HE 20.3612/2:), designed to meet the needs of small hospitals and clinics, is a monthly bibliography based on articles from more than 100 English-language journals. The *National Library of Medicine Current Catalog* (HE 20.3609/2: and its annual cumulation, HE 20.3609/3:) is a bibliography of publications cataloged by NLM.

*Medical Subject Headings* (MeSH) should be consulted before constructing MEDLINE subject searches (HE 20.3612/3-4:yr.). NLM offers short courses on rudimentary MEDLINE search techniques. Training information is available from the Regional Online Training and Information Centers serving each geographic area. Self-paced training for using MeSH and searching MEDLINE is available in the workbook *The Basics of Searching MEDLINE*, for sale from NTIS (PB89-146179) and MEDTUTOR (PB89-780027), a microcomputer training package. NLM's Unified Medical Language System, an ongoing project to link diverse medical vocabularies, has produced the UMLS METATHESAURUS, Meta-1.1 (1991 version).

GRATEFUL MED is a user-friendly software interface for searching MEDLINE using a personal computer. The GRATEFUL MED floppy disk guides searchers inexperienced with formal NLM search language. The system calls up the NLM computers, logs on, enters queries, retrieves citations, logs off, and downloads search results for leisurely review. Full-text articles can be ordered through Loansome Doc, GRATEFUL MED's document ordering feature. GRATEFUL MED is for sale from NTIS for about $30. Information is available by calling (703) 487-4807. A GRATEFUL MED Fact Sheet is free from NLM, and a GRATEFUL MED tutorial is available from NTIS (PB89-16779).

MiniMEDLINE is a user-friendly search system developed at the Georgetown University Medical Center. The database is a subset of MEDLINE designed for searching by students, medical residents, and faculty seeking quick answers to questions that do not justify a more expensive, less convenient MEDLINE search. MiniMEDLINE is obtained through Georgetown University and then loaded into local library catalogs. The customized database subset includes only citations to journals owned by the subscribing library.

| SAMPLING OF MEDLARS DATABASES* | |
|---|---|
| **Bibliographic:** | |
| MEDLINE | Worldwide journal articles |
| AVLINE | Audiovisual teaching packages |
| BIOETHICSLINE | Documents discussing ethical questions in health care or biomedical research |
| CANCERLIT | Worldwide cancer literature |
| CATLINE | Books and serials cataloged at NLM |
| HISTLINE | History of medicine citations from NLM's Bibliography of the History of Medicine |
| POPLINE | Citations to world literature on population and family planning |
| SERLINE | NLM serials |
| **Nonbibliographic:** | |
| CHEMLINE | An online chemical dictionary of chemical names, synonyms, CAS Registry Numbers, molecular formulas, and limited ring information |
| DIRLINE | A directory of private and public organizations providing information on health and disease |
| PDQ | Cancer treatment and referral information |
| TOXLINE | Toxicology information online, covering the pharmacological, biochemical, physiological, environmental, and toxicological effects of drugs and chemicals |

*Descriptions of MEDLARS databases are given in the free pamphlet *MEDLARS, The World of Medicine at Your Fingertips*. A personal-computer disk is available to demonstrate the content and capabilities of five chemical and toxicological files: CHEMLINE, TOXLINE, RTECS (Registry of Toxic Effects of Chemical Substances), HSDB (Hazardous Substances Data Bank), and CCRIS (Chemical Carcinogenesis Research Information System). The cost is under $20 from NTIS (PB87-143327). Additional information is available from Specialized Information Services Division, NLM; (301) 496-1131.

**Profile: Dr. John Shaw Billings**
**Pioneering Medical Librarian**

A century and a quarter ago, twenty-seven-year-old Dr. John Shaw Billings was assigned to spend his spare time overseeing the Surgeon General's fledgling library of medical books. Billings began by selecting books and journals for the library's collection, eventually devoting over a quarter of a century to developing the collection into today's National Library of Medicine, the world's largest medical library. As an admirer in a later century explained, John Shaw Billings *"was the library between 1865 and 1895."*

Through letters, personal charm, and an army of volunteer "book scouts," Billings garnered book and journal donations to fill gaps in the library's collections. Within a decade he had transformed a small reference collection into the best medical library in the world and had begun a journal-indexing project that was the genesis of NLM's *Index-Catalogue* and *Index Medicus*.

A student of chemistry, poetry, literature, fungi, crania, and vital and medical statistics, Billings was praised as "virtually an all-around superman, who has certainly had no equal." His impact was felt beyond the NLM: It was Billings who suggested a census-tabulating machine to Herman Hollerith, and Billings who wooed Adelaide Hasse (creator of the SuDocs classification scheme) from government service to the New York Public Library, where he was director.

## OTHER HEALTH RESOURCES

### Clearinghouses

When you think patient education and professional health education, think CHID: the Public Health Service's Combined Health Information Database. CHID combines information from various producers to serve as a central hub for information from PHS divisions, including the Centers for Disease Control, NIH, and the Office of Disease Prevention and Health Promotion. Coverage includes AIDS; aging; heart, lung, and blood; veterans; diabetes, digestive, and kidney disease; arthritis and skin diseases; eyes; and chronic disease prevention. Searchable through BRS, CHID is intended to compliment MEDLARS, focusing on hard-to-find information resources from hospitals, voluntary health associations, government, pharmaceutical companies, and specialized health publishers, plus citations to selected journal articles.

ODPHP, the Office of Disease Prevention and Health Promotion, maintains a referral database of organizations with information about diseases, health statistics, health education materials, health promotion, nutrition, exercise, and other general health topics. The ODPHP National Health Information Center is a health information switching center, referring people with health questions to organizations with answers. The Center's online directory includes government and nongovernment organizations and is publicly accessible through the National Library of Medicine's DIRLINE. *Health Information Resources in the Federal Government* (HE 20.37:990) and its companion database (from ODPHP National Health Information Center) describe federal government biomedical and health information resources. The Center's library is open by appointment.

## MEDOC

MEDOC is a bibliography of U.S. government publications in the biomedical sciences. Because of its focus on government publications, MEDOC compliments MEDLINE and *Index Medicus*, which concentrate on biomedical journal articles. Although its coverage overlaps with the *Monthly Catalog*, MEDOC offers the advantages of subject specialization, plus a four- to six-month lead over *Monthly Catalog* in currency of listings. MEDOC lists documents in the medical and health sciences, plus related topics such as environmental health, occupational and consumer safety, patient education, health care financing, hospital administration, medical education, behavioral sciences, and vital statistics.

Produced by the University of Utah Health Sciences Library, MEDOC may be searched by title, author, MeSH subject headings, and SuDocs and report numbers. Entries give bibliographic information, including depository status (GPOD, designating "GPO depository," and item numbers). Readex's *U.S. Medical Publications on Microfiche* offers the full text of technical reports and monographs cited in MEDOC as a microfiche subscription service, arranged by SuDocs numbers.

### Index to Health Information (IHI)

The Congressional Information Service's *Index to Health Information: A Guide to Statistical and Congressional Publications on Public Health* consolidates health-related citations and abstracts from *American Statistics Index*, *Statistical Reference Index*, *Index to International Statistics*, and *CIS/Index*.

### Dentistry

*Dental Literature Index* is published by the American Dental Association, with the cooperation of the National Library of Medicine. It is not a government document, but the journal articles listed in the index are gleaned from MEDLARS.

The National Institute of Dental Research (NIDR) operates an electronic bulletin board called NIDR ONLINE. The bulletin board offers access to news about NIDR research, conference schedules, directories, and announcements of funding opportunities; lists NIDR publications and films; and allows online ordering. Access is through many dental libraries or through NIDR Research Data and Management Information Section.

NIDR's brief newsletter, *NIDR Research News*, is free from NIDR, Information Office.

| BIOMEDICAL SEARCH SCORECARD | | |
|---|---|---|
| **Title** | **Strengths** | **Limitations** |
| MEDLARS | Numerous databases, including MEDLINE | Cost |
| MEDLINE | *Index Medicus* online, world biomedical journal articles | Cost |
| MiniMEDLINE | User-friendly, quick, free use in subscribing libraries, customized to local library journal holdings | Subset of MEDLINE |
| *Index Medicus* | World biomedical journal articles since 1966 | Manual search |
| MEDOC | More current than *Monthly Catalog* | Government documents only |
| *Index to Health Information* (IHI) | Statistical and congressional federal documents; one-stop searching of ASI, SRI, IIS, and *CIS/Index* | Primarily government documents |

## NATIONAL AGRICULTURAL LIBRARY (NAL)

The National Agricultural Library is the world's foremost agricultural library. On its forty-eight miles of bookshelves are 2.1 million volumes not only about agriculture but also veterinary science, entomology, botany, forestry, soil science, food and nutrition, rural sociology, economics, physics, chemistry, biology, natural history, wildlife, ecology, genetics, natural resources, energy, meteorology, and fisheries. Bibliographic access to NAL's vast collections is available through the *Bibliography of Agriculture* (Oryx Press) and the AGRICOLA database.

The *Bibliography of Agriculture* is an index to worldwide agriculture research and general periodical literature. AGRICOLA (AGRICultural Online Access) comprehensively covers worldwide agriculture-related literature, focusing on journal articles. It may be searched online through DIALOG or BRS, batch-searched through NERAC, Inc., and through NAL itself (for USDA personnel and federal, state, or county agencies), or purchased or leased from NTIS. AGRICOLA is available on CD-ROM from SilverPlatter, OCLC, and Quanta Press. Search tips are given in the *AGRICOLA User's Guide* (A 17.22:Ag 8; PB85-100618). Subject searching is based on the *CAB Thesaurus*, compiled by CAB International in cooperation with NAL.

NAL is the U.S. input center for AGRIS, a decentralized United Nations database maintained by the United Nations' Food and Agriculture Organization. The AGRIS database and its print counterpart, *Agrindex*, emanate from the International Information System for Agricultural Science and Technology, a cooperative system for collecting and disseminating world agricultural literature. More than one hundred national and multinational centers contribute to AGRIS, which does not duplicate citations listed in AGRICOLA. AGRIS emphasizes literature unavailable commercially and contains many citations not included in any other database. AGRIS may be leased from NTIS or searched online through DIALOG.

NAL's twelve information centers include specialties in youth development, agricultural trade and marketing, alternative farming, animal welfare, aquaculture, biotechnology, food and nutrition, plant genome, rural development, technology transfer, and water quality.

NAL's electronic bulletin board, ALF, provides news about NAL products and services, policies, programs, workshops, job vacancies, and general interest reference materials. Information and a free user's guide are available from the National Agricultural Library.

The Department of Agriculture's Computerized Information Delivery Service (CIDS) is an electronic bulletin board covering "barnyards to boardrooms."[16] Containing research bulletins, data, and policy reports from the USDA, the State Department, and the Commodity Futures Trading Commission, CIDS is available on subscription through Martin Marietta Corporation, but is not free through depository libraries.

The USDA's "The National CD-ROM Sampler: An Extension Reference Library" contains 75 major collections and handbooks for use in USDA field offices but is also sold to the public. The sampler has graphics, audio (such as bird songs), and text, and can be ordered from Interactive Design and Development, Virginia Tech, Plaza I, Bldg. D, Blacksburg, VA 24061-0524.

## OCCUPATIONAL SAFETY AND HEALTH

The National Institute for Occupational Safety and Health Technical Information Center Database (NIOSHTIC) indexes all aspects of occupational safety and health, covering literature dating back to 1973, with some key references from as early as the nineteenth century. Much of the literature indexed and abstracted in NIOSHTIC is from sources outside the core occupational safety or health journals. References in the following subject areas are included: toxicology, epidemiology, occupational medicine, pathology, histology, physiology, metabolism, sampling and analytical methods, chemistry, industrial hygiene, health physics, control technology, engineering, behavioral sciences, ergonomics, safety, hazardous wastes, education, and training. The

NIOSHTIC Database may be leased from NTIS, searched online through DIALOG and ORBIT, or on CD-ROM through SilverPlatter, with batch searching available from NERAC.

## WATER RESOURCES

The U.S. Geological Survey's Selected Water Resources Abstracts (SWRA) Database comprehensively covers water-related literature in the life, physical, and social sciences, along with the engineering and legal aspects of water conservation, control, use, and management. Its companion index, the monthly *Selected Water Resources Abstracts* (I 1.94/2:), ceased in 1991. The database contains abstracts of journal articles, monographs, reports, patents, conference proceedings, and court cases related to water research. Material has been submitted by organizations pursuing water research, state water-resources research institutes, and federal agencies. The database may be leased from NTIS or searched online through DIALOG, with batch searching available from NERAC, Inc. CD-ROM versions are sold by NISC (National Information Services Corporation), SilverPlatter, and OCLC.

## RESEARCH IN PROGRESS

Ongoing research-information systems bridge the prepublication gap by alerting scientists to projects recently funded, in progress, or recently completed. Because up-to-date information is vital, research-in-progress information systems are frequently computerized. Such systems tell what research is being performed, where, and by whom, and identify funding sources, beginning and ending dates, and sources of additional information. They can be used to avoid duplication, identify funding sources, stimulate ideas, or locate subject specialists.

The United States pioneered monitoring ongoing research during the 1950s, sparking the creation of the Smithsonian Science Information Exchange, a national registry for scientific research in progress. When SSIE succumbed to budget cuts and was phased out in 1981, some of its functions were assumed by NTIS, which created the FEDRIP (Federal Research In Progress) database. NTIS has characterized FEDRIP as "one of the government's best kept secrets," a cache of federally funded research summaries in the physical and life sciences and engineering. Particularly strong in health and medicine, FEDRIP includes research summaries contributed by the National Science Foundation, Departments of Energy (CRISP is FEDRIP's largest subfile), and Agriculture, Transportation Research Board, NASA, National Institute for Occupational Safety and Health, National Institutes of Health, National Institute for Standards and Technology, U.S. Geological Survey, and Veterans Affairs.

FEDRIP users should remember that many federal R & D agencies are not represented in the database, including DoD, a key funder of research, and EPA (although plans to add EPA are in the works). FEDRIP may be accessed through DIALOG, Knowledge Express Data Systems, and offline batch processing from NERAC, Inc. A free DIALOG search guide can be requested from NTIS (PR-847).

Numerous agencies maintain their own research-in-progress databases and may generate publications from them. Some must be searched directly through the agency, while others are accessible through commercial database vendors.

| A SAMPLING OF AGENCY RIP SERVICES | |
|---|---|
| Agriculture and Forestry | CRIS, from USDA; DIALOG and on CD-ROM from OCLC |
| Child Abuse | Child Abuse and Neglect Database; through the National Center on Child Abuse and Neglect or DIALOG |
| Criminal Justice | Federal Criminal Justice Research Database, National Criminal Justice Reference Service; DIALOG, free searches from NCJRS |
| Dentistry | DENTALPROJ, from National Institute of Dental Research; MEDLINE |
| Energy | DOE Office of Scientific and Technical Information, Energy Research-in-Progress file; FEDRIP on DIALOG; also CRISP; *Biomedical Index to PHS Supported Research* (HE 20.3013/2: ), CRISP Thesaurus |
| Occupational Safety and Health | NIOSHTIC, National Institute for Occupational Safety and Health; leased through NTIS, DIALOG, ORBIT, and SilverPlatter CD-ROM |
| Smoking | Office on Smoking and Health, Public Health Service Smoking and Health Bulletin; DIALOG |
| Transportation | TRIS, from Transportation Research Information System (TRIS), Transportation Research Board; DIALOG and *HRIS Abstracts* |

## FOREIGN SCIENTIFIC INFORMATION

*The person who knows three languages is trilingual; two languages, bilingual; one language, American.*
—German graffiti

In the 1950s and 1960s, the United States generated three-quarters of the world's research and development but today is responsible for only about one-third. That makes access to the work of foreign scientists crucial.

Unfortunately, many U.S. researchers "do not sense the need to consider foreign STI, and do not have the skills needed to do so even if they wanted."[17]

About one-quarter of the NTIS collection is foreign reports and translations, including many from Japan and Western Europe. The Japanese Technical Literature Act of 1986 requires NTIS to monitor Japanese technical activity and collect and translate Japanese technical reports. NTIS provides online access to some Japanese databases and oversees Japanese literature translation and exchange. NTIS's *Directory of Japanese Technical Resources* lists businesses and government agencies that collect, abstract, translate, or disseminate Japanese technical literature, and cites translations of Japanese technical documents available through NTIS or the National Translations Center.

---

**GRA & I Search Tip**

Many GRA & I citations are to non-English publications. Foreign-language titles can be identified by the note, "In [language]" or by a non-English title, followed by an English translation.

---

NTIS sells foreign reports and translations and lists them in the NTIS Bibliographic Database, GRA & I, and the weekly *NTIS Foreign Technology Abstract Newsletter*, a selective dissemination of information source for foreign technology news. NTIS announces about 1,500 translations yearly, which are indexed with the keyword "Translations." NTIS identifiers indicate the foreign country producing a report: The code format is NTISFNxx, with xx being the country code. Examples:

Japan      NTISFNJA
U.S.S.R.   NTISFNUR

An NTIS citation identifier code also indicates the language of non-English reports: NTISLNxxx, with xxx being the first three letters of the language. Examples:

French     NTISLNFRE
Spanish    NTISLNSPA

Some foreign documents are in English when received by NTIS. Others have been translated, like those from the Joint Publications Research Service (PrEx 7.14: through PrEx 7.23:) and from the Foreign Broadcast Information Service (PrEx 6.2:). Both the Joint Publications Research Service (JPRS) and Foreign Broadcast Information Service (FBIS) are units of the Central Intelligence Agency. JPRS is the nation's translator, commissioning translations of sci/tech and social science materials from around the globe. Although "no single index" lists all JPRS translations, many may be identified using Bell and Howell's microfiche *Transdex Index*, GRA & I, the NTIS Bibliographic Database, or the *Monthly Catalog*.[18] The Foreign Broadcast Information Service issues daily reports of news, commentaries, and government statements gleaned from foreign broadcasts and news media. Reports can be identified using GRA & I, the NTIS Bibliographic Database, the *Monthly Catalog*, or the Readex/NewsBank FBIS Index on CD-ROM. Both JPRS and FBIS reports are sold by NTIS, sent to depository libraries, and may be purchased from NewsBank/Readex.

Another source of translations is the National Translations Center (NTC), recently transferred from the John Crerar Library in Chicago to the Library of Congress. NTC is an international depository and referral center for unpublished translations in the natural, physical, medical, and social sciences (the Center itself does not perform translations). Copies of translations may be purchased for about $35.

Until 1986, NTC translations were indexed in the *Translations Register-Index*. They are now included in the *World Translations Index*, published by the International Translations Centre in the Netherlands. An index to the NTC collection may be consulted on-site in the Science Reading Room of the Library of Congress. NTC also distributes copies of its translations database to many government and private online systems.

Numerous databases incorporate foreign sci/tech information. The National Library of Medicine's *Index Medicus* and MEDLINE cite non-English articles in biomedical journals and include English abstracts when available. NLM's CANCERLIT database of worldwide literature on cancer provides English abstracts for all references. Almost two-thirds of the National Agricultural Library collection is non-English. NAL also has a translation collection that is indexed in AGRICOLA. Copies of translations may be borrowed through landgrant university libraries or purchased from NTIS or the National Translations Center. Foreign literature coverage in the *Bibliography of Agriculture* has been eclipsed by *Agrindex*, published by the Food and Agriculture Organization of the United Nations. The Energy Database, from the Department of Energy, lists energy literature worldwide, including translations and foreign technical reports.

## REFERRAL: EXPERTS AND SPECIAL FACILITIES

Federally funded R & D centers are government supported but administered by industry, universities, or other nonprofit organizations. Most focus on basic research in a single area, and many provide major, unique, research facilities for national use. NTIS's biennial *Directory of Federal Laboratory and Technology Resources: A Guide to Services, Facilities, and Expertise* (4th ed PB90-104480; C 51.2:T 22/3/) lists federal facilities willing to share their expertise, equipment, and, sometimes, their facilities to aid researchers. It includes descriptions of Technical Information Centers offering expertise in areas such as fuels, cold regions, concrete, fisheries, toxicology, pesticides, and plastics. The directory may be searched online through BRS.

Information analysis centers (IACs) repackage information for their clients, providing reference service and creating compilations, digests, state-of-the-art reviews, newsletters, and announcement services. IAC products are designed to be current and authoritative, and to review, summarize, and analyze information. Federally supported IACs fall primarily into science and technological disciplines, with IAC publications sold through typical sources like NTIS and GPO, and cited in their publications catalogs. To identify IACs, consult *A Directory of Scientific and Technical Information Programs of the U.S. Government* (PB91-180216), or *Government Research Directory* (Gale Research Company).

Although budget reductions caused the closing of the National Referral Center in 1986, the NRC database is maintained within the Library of Congress. The database allows referral to organizations, institutions, groups, or individuals with specialized knowledge in the sciences, medicine, social sciences, engineering, and humanities. This service is not intended to answer reference questions or provide bibliographic citations but rather to identify sources of expertise. The National Referral Master File (NRCM) is searchable on-site at the Library of Congress using LOCIS and through the National Library of Medicine's DIRLINE (Directory of Information Resources OnLINE) database. Questions that cannot be satisfied through other channels can be forwarded to General Reading Rooms Division, Library of Congress, Washington, DC 20540.

Directory of Biotechnology Information Resources (DBIR), an online directory of biotechnological referral information, is searchable through MEDLINE. Included are descriptions of databases, networks, publications, organizations, collections, contact people, and repositories of cells and subcellular elements.

## STANDARDS AND SPECIFICATIONS

Standards and specifications for materials, products, or services are set by government, trade, learned, technical, consumer, labor, and other organizations. They set minimum performance, quality levels, optimal conditions, or methodology by standardizing dimensions, ratings, terminology and symbols, test methods, and performance and safety specifications. American National Standards are voluntary, unless adopted or referenced by government.

The National Institute of Standards and Technology (NIST, formerly the National Bureau of Standards) operates the National Center for Standards and Certification Information (NCSCI), the central inquiry point for standards and certification information. The Center provides information about United States, foreign, and international voluntary standards by responding to inquiries, maintaining a reference library, and serving as the U.S. switching center for information to and from foreign countries. The Center does not provide copies of standards, but refers requesters to the appropriate standards organization.

The Library of Congress's Science and Technology Division collects standards and specifications from some sixty nations in its Technical Reports and Standards Collection. The collection includes extensive holdings of current American National Standards and other domestic industrial engineering standards from numerous organizations. The division's Science Reading Room is open to the public.

Several government agencies issue standards and specifications, both mandatory and voluntary. *The Department of Defense Index of Specifications and Standards* (D 1.76:), available in both paper and microfiche, lists unclassified federal, military, and departmental standards and specifications. Army, navy, and air force specifications are available from Naval Publications and Forms Center, 5801 Tabor Avenue, Philadelphia, PA 19120, which also provides standardization documents to Department of Defense contractors and federal or military establishments. The Office of Federal Supply and Services issues the annual *Index of Federal Specifications and Standards and Commercial Item Descriptions* (GS 2.8/2:), which lists federal specifications and standards and handbooks and identifies qualified products. Copies of current federal standards and specifications needed by businesses for bidding and contracting are free from GSA Business Service Centers (listed in SB-231). The *Code of Federal Regulations* lists many mandatory agency standards, while the *Monthly Catalog* cites standards and standards-related publications.

The American National Standards Institute (ANSI) is the private, nonprofit coordinating organization for America's federated national standards system. The National Standards Association offers several print, database, and on-demand services for tracing and obtaining standards.

## ADDRESSES

### Agriculture

National Agricultural Library, 10301 Baltimore Blvd., Beltsville, MD 20705-2351; (301) 504-5755. The DC Branch Reading Room is in Room 1052, South Agriculture Bldg., 14th Street and Independence Avenue, S.W., Washington, DC 20250; (202) 720-3434.

ALF (NAL's electronic bulletin board): For information and a free user's guide, write to National Agricultural Library, Public Services Division, Room 100, ATTN: ALF, 10301 Baltimore Blvd., Beltsville, MD 20705-2351.

### Child Abuse

Clearinghouse on Child Abuse and Neglect Information, Health and Human Services, P.O. Box 1182, Washington, DC 20013; (202) 245-2856, (703) 558-8222 (search-line number)

### Criminal Justice

The Federal Criminal Justice Research Database, National Institute of Justice/NCJRS, Department AFL, Box 6000, Rockville, MD 20850; (800) 851-3420

### Dentistry

NIDR ONLINE, NIDR Research Data and Management Information Section, Office of Planning, Evaluation and Communications, Westwood Bldg., 5333 Westbard Ave., Room 535, Bethesda, MD 20892; (301) 496-7843. *NIDR Research News* is from NIDR, Information Office, Bldg. 31, Room 2C-35, 9000 Rockville Pike, Bethesda, MD 20892; (301) 496-6621

### Energy

National Energy Information Center, Energy Information Administration, Forrestal Bldg., 1F-048, 1000 Independence Ave., SW, Washington, DC 20585; (202) 586-8800

Office of Scientific and Technical Information (OSTI), U.S. Department of Energy, P. O. Box 62, Oak Ridge, TN 37831; (615) 576-1301.
OSTI is an energy information clearinghouse.

### Environmental Protection Agency

EPA, Public Information Center, PM-211B, 401 M Street, S.W., Washington, DC 20460; (202) 475-7751, FAX (202) 382-7883. For referral and general, nontechnical environmental information and popular publications.

### Highways

Transportation Research Information System, Transportation Research Board, 2101 Constitution Ave., N.W., Washington, DC 20418; (202) 334-3250, FAX (202) 334-2527

### Medicine

National Library of Medicine, 8600 Rockville Pike, Bethesda, MD 20894; (800) 272-4787 (general information); (800) 638-8480 (online search training)

MiniMEDLINE: Dahlgren Memorial Library, Georgetown University Medical Center, Library Information System, 3900 Reservoir Rd., N.W., Washington, DC 20007; (202) 687-1305

Readex Microprint Corporation, ATTN: Medical Documents Department, 58 Pine St., New Canaan, CT 06840-5408; (800) 762-8182, (813) 263-6004; FAX (813) 263-3004

*Regional Medical Libraries:* Each Regional Medical Library coordinates NLM's online searching and interlibrary loan for a geographic region. Each offers document delivery, reference service, local bibliographic locator help, and online access to the databases in MEDLARS. The three designated with asterisks* also coordinate online training for their regions.

*The New York Academy of Medicine, New York; (212) 876-8763

University of Maryland, Health Sciences Library, Baltimore; (301) 328-2855

University of Illinois at Chicago, Library of the Health Sciences; (312) 996-2464

*University of Nebraska Medical Center Library, Omaha; (402) 559-4326

Houston Academy of Medicine-Texas Medical Center Library; (713) 790-7053

University of Washington, Health Sciences Center Library, Seattle; (206) 543-8262

*UCLA Biomedical Library, Los Angeles; (213) 825-1200

University of Connecticut Health Center, Stowe Library; (203) 679-4500

## NTIS

National Technical Information Service, 5285 Port Royal Rd., Springfield, VA 22161; (703) 487-4650, RUSH service (800) 553-NTIS, FAX (703) 321-8547. NTIS deposit-account customers and DIALOG, OCLC, ORBIT, and STN users may order online.

## Standards

National Center for Standards and Certification Information, National Institute of Standards and Technology, Administration Bldg., Room A629, Gaithersburg, MD 20899; (301) 975-4040, 975-4038, or 975-4036; FAX (301) 963-2871.

## Translations

The Library of Congress, National Translations Center, Washington, DC 20541; (202) 707-0100; FAX (202) 707-6147.

## FREEBIES

The following subject bibliographies are free from the U.S. Government Printing Office, Superintendent of Documents, Washington, DC 20402. Many others on sci/tech topics are listed in the free SB Index (SB-599).

22. Dentistry
133. National Bureau of Standards Handbooks and Monographs
139. National Standard Reference Data Series
162. Agricultural Research, Statistics, and Economic Reports
231. Where Can You Obtain Government Specifications, Federal Standards, Drawings, and the Indexes Which List These Specifications?
257. NASA Scientific and Technical Publications
271. National Bureau of Standards Special Publications

## Agriculture

From Public Affairs Office, Room 204, National Agricultural Library, 10301 Baltimore Blvd., Beltsville, MD 20705-2351; (301) 504-6778:

*Agricultural Libraries Information Notes, ALIN* (Monthly) (A 17.23:)

"Guide to Services of the National Agricultural Library" (enclose a pre-addressed mailing label)

"How to Get Information from the United States Department of Agriculture." (A 107.2:In 3/yr)

"Information Alert" (NAL press releases)

"Learning to Search AGRICOLA on SilverPlatter CD-ROM" (A 17.2:Ag 8/4)

*List of Journals Indexed in AGRICOLA* (A 17.18/5:) gives NAL call number, ISSN, publisher, and indexing coverage; copies free with a self-addressed label from Indexing Branch, Room 011, Attn: LJI991, National Agricultural Library, 10301 Baltimore Blvd., Beltsville, MD 20705-2351

[Additional free NAL publications are listed in *Bibliographic Series, Current Titles Listing* (A 17.18/7: ]

From Food and Nutrition Information Center, National Agricultural Library, Room 304, Beltsville, MD 20705 (301) 344-3719:

"Publications List"

Send a self-addressed label to NAL, Reference Branch, Room 111, 10301 Baltimore Blvd., Beltsville, MD 20705 for:

"Agri-Topics" and the "Quick Bibliography" series (QB's) are bibliographies culled from AGRICOLA; Special Reference Briefs (S.R.B) are copies of custom bibliographies

## Energy

From National Energy Information Center, EI-231, Energy Information Administration, Forrestal Bldg, Washington, DC 20585 (202) 586-8800:

*EIA Publications Directory* (E 3.27:)

*EIA New Releases* (E 3.27/4:)

"Electronic Publishing System (EPUB) Quick Start Users Guide" (E 3.8:El 2)

*Energy Information Directory* (E 3.33:)

## Environmental Protection Agency

From the Office of Pesticides and Toxic Substances, 401 M Street, S.W., Washington, DC 20460:

*Federal Depository Libraries: Your Source for the Toxic Release Inventory; Directory of Public Libraries: Toxic Chemical Release Inventory.* A list of EPA datafiles from NTIS: PR-758.

## Health

From ODPHP National Health Information Center, Box 1133, Washington, DC 20013-1133; (800) 336-4797; in Washington, DC and Maryland (301) 565-4167:

"Federal Health Information Clearinghouses"
(Healthfinder)

"Online Health Information" (Healthfinder) lists databases, software and services, and electronic bulletin boards

"Toll-Free Numbers for Health Information"

## National Library of Medicine

From the Office of Inquiries and Publications Management, National Library of Medicine, 8600 Rockville Pike, Bethesda, MD 20894:

"Factsheets": NLM Online Databases; Medical Subject Headings, DIRLINE: Directory of Information Resources Online

*National Library of Medicine News* (HE 20.3619:)
A free newsletter covering NLM and health sciences in general. It announces new publications, database products, and free materials. To be added to the mailing list write to Editor, NLM News, Office of Public Information

"A Catalog of Publications, Audiovisuals, and Software Produced by the National Library of Medicine"
An annual supplement to *National Library of Medicine News*, lists new titles and prices.

"Searching Tools"
A list of manuals and training packages for NLM databases

## Library of Congress

From Science Reference Section, Science and Technology Division, Library of Congress, 10 First St., S.E., Washington, DC 20540; (202) 707-5580:
Individual Tracer Bullets and a list of all Tracer Bullet titles

## NTIS

From NTIS, 5285 Port Royal Rd., Springfield, VA 22161:
*Newsline*, a quarterly newsletter announcing NTIS activities and new products (PR-660)

*NTIS Online Alert* discusses database updates, search techniques, training opportunities (PR-862).

Published Search Master Catalog (PR-186)

NTIS Products and Services Catalog (PR-827)

Search Guide to FEDRIP Database on DIALOG (PR-847)

Search Guide to the NTIS Bibliographic Database: on BRS (PR-831); on DIALOG (PR-829); on ORBIT (PR-830); on STN (PR-837); on DATA-STAR (in preparation)

## REFERENCES

1. National Science Board, *Science Indicators: The 1985 Report* (GPO, 1985), p. xiii. (NS 1.28/2:985)

2. John R. Durant, Geoffrey A. Evans, and Geoffrey P. Thomas, "The Public Understanding of Science," *Nature* 340 (July 6, 1989):11-14.

3. National Science Foundation and the U.S. Department of Education, *Science & Engineering Education for the 1980s & Beyond* (GPO, 1980):3. (NS 1.2:Ed 8/20)

4. "Scientific Illiteracy," *Society* 27 (July/August 1990):3.

5. Judith Stone, "Ignorance on Parade," *Discover* 10 (July, 1989): 102.

6. John Sullivan, "What's Going on in Sci-Tech," *LC Information Bulletin* 42 (January 17, 1983): 18.

7. House. Committee on Science, Space, and Technology, OTA Report, "Federally Funded Research: Decisions for a Decade" *Hearing before the Subcommittee on Science of the Committee on Science, Space, and Technology, 102-1, March 20, 1991 (GPO, 1991)*, pp. 79, 97. (Y 4.Sci 2:102/7)

8. Thomas E. Pinelli and Madeline M. Henderson, "Access to Federal Scientific and Technical Information Through U.S. Government Technical Reports," in McClure, Charles R. and Peter Hernon, eds. U. S. *Scientific and Technical Information (STI) Policies: Views and Perspectives* (Norwood, NJ: Ablex Publishing Corp., 1989), p. 110.

9. C. Lester Walker, "Secrets by the Thousands," *Harper's Magazine* (October 1946): 336. Related articles are Groff Conklin, "The Publication Board—World's Biggest Publishing Project." *Publisher's Weekly* (August 10, 1946): 581-83; Julius C. Edelstein, "Science as Reparations," *Physics Today* 1 (December 1948): 6-14.

10. NTIS, *A Reference Guide to the NTIS Bibliographic Database* (NTIS, 1980), pp. 15-16. (PR-253); Charles R. McClure and Peter Hernon, *Academic Library Use of NTIS: Suggestions for Services and Core Collections* (NTIS, 1986), pp. 22-26. (PB86-228871)

11. An unpublished study by Steve Hayes was described in *Government Information as a Public Asset Hearing before the Joint Committee on Printing, 102-2, April 25, 1991.* (S. Hrg. 102-114) GPO, 1991, p. 18 (Y 4.P 93/1:G 74/12)

12. Charles R. McClure, Peter Hernon, and Gary R. Purcell, *Linking the U.S. National Technical Information Service with Academic and Public Libraries* (Norwood, NJ: Ablex Publishing Co., 1986), p. 117.

13. McClure, Hernon, and Purcell, pp. 116-17.

14. McClure, Hernon, and Purcell, p. 116.

15. McClure, Hernon, and Purcell, pp. 78-88.

16. Florence Olsen, "CIDS Runs Gamut from Barnyards to Boardrooms," *Government Computer News* 10 (July 22, 1991) p. 38.

17. Congress. Office of Technology Assessment, *Helping America Compete: The Role of Federal Scientific & Technical Information* (OTA-CIT-454) (GPO, 1990), p. 55. (Y 3.T22/2:2 Am 3/2)

18. Debra Hassig, "U.S. Joint Publications Research Service Translations: A User's Manual," *Government Publications Review* 14 (September/October 1987):559-72.

## FURTHER READING

Chitty, Mary Glen. *Federal Information Sources in Health and Medicine: A Selected Annotated Bibliography.* New York: Greenwood Press, 1988.
An annotated bibliography of government and commercial biomedical publications and databases.

Day, Melvin S. *Federal Health Information Resources.* Arlington, VA: Information Resources Press, 1987.

A guide to federal government biomedical and health information resources.

Defense Technical Information Center. *How to Get It: A Guide to Defense-Related Information Resources* (AD-A201 600). Alexandria, VA: DTIC, 1988. (D 7.15/2:89/1)
A guide to identifying and obtaining government publications, maps, patents, specifications, and standards.

Gimbel, John. *Science, Technology, and Reparations: Exploitation and Plunder in Postwar Germany.* Stanford, CA: Stanford University Press, 1990.
The story behind the allies' "intellectual reparations" program to exploit Nazi know-how.

Hernon, Peter and Charles R. McClure. *Public Access to Government Information: Issues, Trends, and Strategies.* 2nd ed. Norwood, NJ: Ablex Publishing Corp., 1988.
See Gary R. Purcell's chapter on "Technical Report Literature."

McClure, Charles R. and Peter Hernon. *Academic Library Use of NTIS: Suggestions for Services and Core Collections.* NTIS, 1986. (PB86-228871). Free to academic libraries by calling (703) 487-4929.
A manual of practical suggestions for making NTIS products and services available in libraries, with an annotated bibliography of "core" NTIS collections for specific subject areas.

McClure, Charles R. and Peter Hernon, eds. *U.S. Scientific and Technical Information (STI) Policies: Views and Perspectives.* Norwood, NJ: Ablex Publishing Corp., 1989.
An overview of key sci/tech information policies and issues; a companion volume to *U.S. Government Information Policies: Views and Perspectives and Federal Information Policies in the 1980s: Conflicts and Issues.*

Murphy, Cynthia E. "A Comparison of Manual and Online Searching of Government Document Indexes." *Government Information Quarterly* 2 (May 1985): 169-81.
A comparison of GRA & I online and print versions.

Phillips, Zlata Fuss. "The Availability and Use of Joint Publications Research Service Translations in U.S. GPO Depository Libraries in New York State." *Government Publications Review* 14 (July/August 1987):449-63.
Includes a history and description of JPRS, plus an introduction to finding aids.

Subramanyam, K. "Standards and Specifications," in *A Guide to U.S. Government Scientific & Technical Resources* by Rao Aluri and Judith Schiek Robinson. Littleton, CO: Libraries Unlimited, Inc., 1983, pp. 119-35.
An introduction to standards and specifications and sources of information about them.

## EXERCISES

1. Bibliographically verify any of the following titles using GRA & I or the NTIS Bibliographic Database. Use varied access points to increase the value of your practice.
   a. *How to Get It: A Guide to Defense-Related Information Sources* (Defense Department)
   b. *The KGB and the Library Target, 1962 - Present* (FBI)
   c. *AGRICOLA User's Guide* PB85-100618
   d. *The Effects of Electronic Recordkeeping on the Historical Record of the U.S. Government: A Report for the National Archives and Records Administration,* a study by the National Academy of Public Administration
   e. *Protection of Personal Privacy Interests Under the Freedom of Information Act* by T. J. Hasty
   f. *Managing Federal Information Resources: Annual Report (1st) Under the Paperwork Reduction Act of 1980* (OMB)
   g. *Federal Government Information Technology: Electronic Record Systems and Individual Privacy* OTA-CIT-296 (1986)

2. Use STAR to identify the first volume of the report on the space shuttle *Challenger* accident, issued in 1986.

3. How can you get the video *NTIS—The Competitive Edge* PR-858?

# CHAPTER 7
# Patents, Trademarks, and Copyrights

*The Patent System added the fuel of interest to the fire of genius.* —Abraham Lincoln

## WHAT

Patents, trademarks, and copyrights are known as "intellectual property." Although some people confuse them, the protection granted for each is completely different, and each serves a different purpose. Patents relate to inventions; trademarks to product names or symbols; and copyright to literary or creative works. Both patents and copyrights grant exclusive rights for a limited time, after which the work, process, or invention enters the public domain. Utility and plant patents protect for seventeen years (if periodic maintenance fees are paid); design patents, for fourteen. Copyright protects for the author's lifetime plus fifty years, while trademarks may be renewed indefinitely as long as they are being used.

## WHERE

The Patent and Trademark Office (PTO) of the Department of Commerce grants patents, issues trademarks, and administers patent and trademark laws. Copyrights are registered by the Register of Copyrights within the Library of Congress. Protection for each is granted in the United States only—protection in other countries is granted by individual governments according to their laws.

## WHY

The basis for patents and copyrights is embedded in the Constitution, which granted Congress the power to "promote the Progress of Science and useful Arts" by giving authors and inventors exclusive rights to their own writings and discoveries for a limited time. Trademark protection is based on the commerce clause of the Constitution.

## WHEN

In 1990, the United States celebrated the bicentennial of its patent and copyright laws. Patents have been granted since 1790, when the first patent law was signed by George Washington and three patents were issued. The first copyright law was enacted the same year. Trademark protection was enacted in 1905.

## WHO

Anyone may obtain a U.S. patent, trademark, or copyright, regardless of age or nationality.

## PATENTS

*We said, "What is it that makes the United States such a great nation?" And we investigated and found that it was patents, and we will have patents.*
—Japanese official visiting the United States in 1900

A patent holder receives exclusive rights to make, use, or sell an invention, design, or plant. To be issued a United States patent, the patentee must file a detailed description of the invention, which is then published by the government. The result is a mutually beneficial system that allows individuals to profit from their ideas while the nation accumulates one of the world's greatest repositories of scientific information. The public disclosure of inventions in published patents forms a reservoir of technical information that has been called "the depository of genius of the country." (Sometimes the public-disclosure requirement deters companies from seeking patents because they wish to protect secrets. The formulas for Coca Cola and Silly Putty are two examples of such "trade secrets," kept private to maintain a company's competitive advantage.)

Because U.S. patents are the world's greatest repository of technical information, they offer a means both of keeping abreast of the latest technology and reviewing technological history. By definition, patents report new ideas, since a patentable invention must be new, useful, and nonobvious. Patents also appear before other publication formats, with fully 80 percent never republished anywhere else, not even in journals.

## Utility Patents

Most patents are utility patents, granted for a product, process, apparatus, or composition of matter. Utility patents chronicle the nation's technological growth: Alexander Graham Bell's telephone (no. 174,465), Thomas Edison's electric lamp (no. 223,898), the Wright brothers' flying machine (no. 821,393), television (no. 1,773,980), oral contraceptives (no. 2,744,122), and the artificial heart (no. 3,641,591). Standing shoulder-to-shoulder with these noble inventions is an army of more whimsical notions: the alarm clock bed (no. 1,293,102), a means to detect life from the grave (no. 1,436,757), a coat for two (no. 2,636,176), a shoe that makes backward footprints (no. 3,823,494), and a urinal target for men (no. 4,044,405).[1] A thousand and one uses and all are documented in United States patent literature.

---

**Living Patents**

In 1980, a landmark Supreme Court decision ruled that a living microorganism could be patented, making life forms other than plants patentable for the first time. Ground was again broken when Harvard was issued a patent for a "higher" animal: their laboratory mouse. The "Harvard mouse," genetically engineered to be cancer-prone, illustrates the PTO's requirements for patentable animals: It is human-engineered, not found in nature, and nonhuman (the PTO won't patent people). Animal patents are utility patents.

\* \* \* \* \*

John Moore was a victim of a rare form of leukemia. Without Moore's knowledge, his doctors cultured his unusual spleen cells, obtained a patent on the cell line, and sold it for use in cancer and AIDS research. Although Moore's unique cells are expected to earn millions, Moore will not share the profits: He lost his suit for "royalties" from the sale of his cells.

---

## Plant Patents

Until the Plant Patent Act passed in 1930, there were few plant breeders in the country. Since breeders couldn't keep others from reproducing or selling their discoveries, there was little incentive for horticultural experimentation. After Thomas Edison urged Congress to "give the plant breeder the same status as the mechanical and chemical inventors now have through patent law," protection for new plants was granted. The plant patent law allowed new varieties of asexually reproducible plants to join the list of patentable items. (Asexual reproduction is by means other than seed, such as rooting cuttings, layering, budding, or grafting). Eligible plants include roses, fruit, conifers, broadleaf trees, shrubs, vines, and flowers (see Figure 7.1). Tuber-propagated plants—the Irish potato and Jerusalem artichoke—are not protected. Other types of plants, seeds, and plant parts may be patented under general patent laws, as long as they are "nonnaturally occurring . . . a product of human ingenuity."

## Design Patents

The appearance of ornamental products can be protected by design patents, which protect the "look" of an object rather than how it works or the way it is made. Offering the same legal protection as utility patents, design patents protect the appearance of objects like furniture, containers, games, toys, food, guns, and pet supplies (see Figure 7.2).

## Classification

Patents are classed within the U.S. Patent Classification System (USPC), the world's most comprehensive system for categorizing patented technology. Each patent is assigned first to broad classes and then to narrower subclasses, grouping inventions under about 112,000 categories of technology. Class and subclass numbers can be used as access points for searching. The Design Patent Classification System has thirty-seven classes and more than 3,800 subclasses. Plant patents are classified under about eighty-nine subclasses. The Patent and Trademark Office sells lists of patents or of cross-referenced patents contained in subclasses.

## Patent Numbers

Every patent is assigned a unique number. Since 1836, when number one was issued, the total has swelled to more than 4.5 million. Design patent numbers are in a different number series, and are often preceded by the letter D or Des. (Example: Des. 270,936).

## Patent Searches

Patents are identified through manual, online, or CD-ROM searches, and examined in either of two formats: the patent summary in the *Official Gazette* or a full text copy of the patent itself. The *Official Gazette* is available in many federal depository libraries and in Patent Depository Libraries, or may be purchased from the Government Printing Office. Copies of patents can be purchased from the Commissioner of Patents and Trademarks, examined in Patent Depository Libraries, or extracted from full-text online databases.

**FIGURE 7.1: Plant Patent.**

April 5, 1932.   L. BURBANK   Plant Pat. 15

PEACH

Filed Dec. 23, 1930

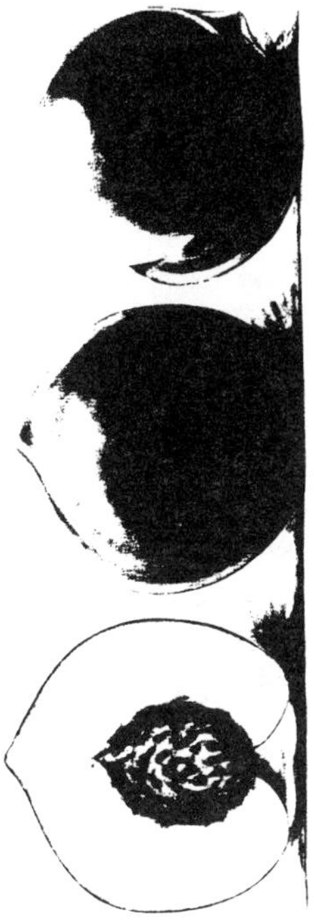

Patented Apr. 5, 1932

**Plant Pat. 15**

# UNITED STATES PATENT OFFICE

LUTHER BURBANK, DECEASED, LATE OF SANTA ROSA, CALIFORNIA, BY ELIZABETH WATERS BURBANK, EXECUTRIX, OF SANTA ROSA, CALIFORNIA, ASSIGNOR TO STARK BRO'S NURSERIES & ORCHARDS COMPANY, OF LOUISIANA, MISSOURI

PEACH

Application filed December 23, 1930. Serial No. 504,399.

This invention relates to a new and distinct variety of peach.

This new variety of peach has resulted from years of experimenting with a definite objective in view, that is, to produce a satisfactory yellow freestone peach which ripens half way between the ripening periods of the known varieties, the June Elberta and the Early Elberta. It is similar to the Hale peach except that it has a large pit. Its blood and seed are similar to the Muir, but the fruit is more golden in color. It is a stronger growing tree than the Valient and is not subject to peach curl and disease (Bacteria impruni) as is the last named variety. This new variety produces a very large fruit which averages about one-half pound. Its golden color with maroon shadings modified by a grayish pubescence, adds to its effectiveness in size. Although the skin of the fruit is thin and tender, tests have proven it to be a remarkable shipper; coupled with its great size, impressive coloring, excellent quality, and being a freestone, it represents an outstanding commercial peach. When cut in half, a pleasing modified apricot yellow flesh is disclosed which has a peach red tinge near the pit.

The following specifications and attached drawing show the distinctions and general characteristics of this new variety which has been asexually reproduced.

### Tree

*Tree.*—The tree, being of vigorous growth, is larger than other varieties of the same age. Its branches are stout, with strong, well knit forks, of divergent habit, with an average angle of 45° to 60°. The bark on the trunk of the young tree forms scales, curling in rather thin flakes, transversely around the trunk. The color is russet brown, modified by light olive gray scarfskin, which, on younger branches has a silvery gloss.

*Twigs.*—The new growth twigs are vigorous and stout, varying to rather slender on lower branches and becoming drooping as growth progresses. The color of the bark of the twigs is glossy courge green minutely dotted with lighter green and shaded vandyke red on exposed side, changing to buckthorn brown on earliest growth of the season. The internodes are short to medium. The dormant fruit buds are medium to large, prominent, free, and dull red-brown with grayish pubescence. The leaf buds are rather small and appressed.

*Foliage.*—The foliage is abundant. The leaves are medium to large, strongly incurved. The texture is thick, soft, and almost velvety. The base is tapering and acute. The blade is flat to distinctly folded, and wrinkled along the midrib. The margin is wavy with a crenate edge having minute reddish points strongly forward. The apex is acuminate to lanceolate. The upper surface is smooth, dull, with slight sun very sheen on oldest leaves. The color is hellebore to courge green. The undersurface is smooth and deep grape green in color.

*Glands.*—There are from two to four large reniform glands, often with additional rudimentary glands on the base of the blade.

*Petiole.*—The petiole is rather short, and is stout. Its color is clear dull green-yellow, extending to midrib and often extensively tinged vandyke red as on the twigs. The upper side is deeply grooved.

### Fruit

*Form.*—The form is globular with rather broad base and prominent apex producing a broad cordate outline in the longitudinal cross-section. The size is large and uniform, being about three inches axial diameter and three inches largest transverse diameter, and two and three quarters inches smallest transverse diameter, the sides being unequal. The stem is short and moderately stout. The cavity is wide and of medium depth. The suture begins in the cavity, being rather deep at first, becoming a line over the side of the fruit, again more distinct and deep, and ending at the apex which is prominent acute to mammiform.

*Color.*—The color is light orange yellow to capucine orange, largely tinged with minute dots of peach red shading to nopal red and maroon on exposed cheek. The general color

E. W. BURBANK
Executrix of
Luther Burbank, Deceased

By Robert Cobb

ATTORNEYS

Luther Burbank, who died four years before the passage of the Plant Patent Act of 1930, was awarded sixteen plant patents posthumously. His Plant Patent 15, Peach, earned him entry into the National Inventors Hall of Fame.

**FIGURE 7.2: Design Patent.**

---

# United States Patent [19]

### Everson

[11]   **Des. 270,936**

[45]   ★★ **Oct. 11, 1983**

[54]   **COMBINED TOILET TANK AND AQUARIUM**

[76]   Inventor:   **D. Randall Everson,** 18615 Loree Ave., Cupertino, Calif. 95014

[**]   Term:   **14 Years**

[21]   Appl. No.:   **227,164**

[22]   Filed:   **Jan. 22, 1981**

[51]   **Int. Cl.** ................................................ **D23—02**

[52]   **U.S. Cl.** .................................... **D23/49; D23/66; D30/11**

[58]   **Field of Search** ............................ D23/49, 65–67; D30/11; 4/353, 661; 119/5

[56]   **References Cited**

#### U.S. PATENT DOCUMENTS

| | | | |
|---|---|---|---|
| D. 101,441 | 10/1936 | Dreyfuss | D23/65 |
| D. 179,484 | 1/1957 | Lampkins | D30/11 |
| D. 199,729 | 12/1964 | Kaiser | D23/66 |
| D. 229,766 | 1/1971 | Kephart | D30/11 |
| 830,286 | 9/1906 | Alexander | D23/66 X |
| 918,456 | 4/1909 | Marcellus | D23/66 X |
| 2,238,699 | 4/1941 | Levine | 4/353 |
| 3,968,525 | 7/1976 | Alexander | D23/66 X |
| 4,364,132 | 12/1982 | Robinson | 4/661 X |

*Primary Examiner*—James R. Largen
*Attorney, Agent, or Firm*—Thomas E. Schatzel

[57]   **CLAIM**

The ornamental design for a combined toilet tank and aquarium, as shown and described.

#### DESCRIPTION

FIG. **1** is a perspective view taken from the top, front and left side of a combined toilet tank and aquarium showing my new design;
FIG. **2** is a front elevational view thereof;
FIG. **3** is a top plan view thereof;
FIG. **4** is a bottom plan view thereof;
FIG. **5** is a left side elevational view thereof;
FIG. **6** is a right side elevational view thereof; and
FIG. **7** is a rear elevational view thereof.
The broken line representation of plants and gravel in FIGS. **1** and **2**, a toilet bowl in FIG. **1** and plumbing hardware in FIG. **7** is for purposes of illustration only and form no part of the claimed design.

---

The ornamental design for a combined toilet tank and aquarium is protected by Des. 270,936, reproduced in its entirety on these two pages. Since design patents don't deal with how an invention works, the patent drawings need only hint at the answer to an obvious question: How do you prevent flushing the fish?

**FIGURE 7.2: Design Patent (continued).**

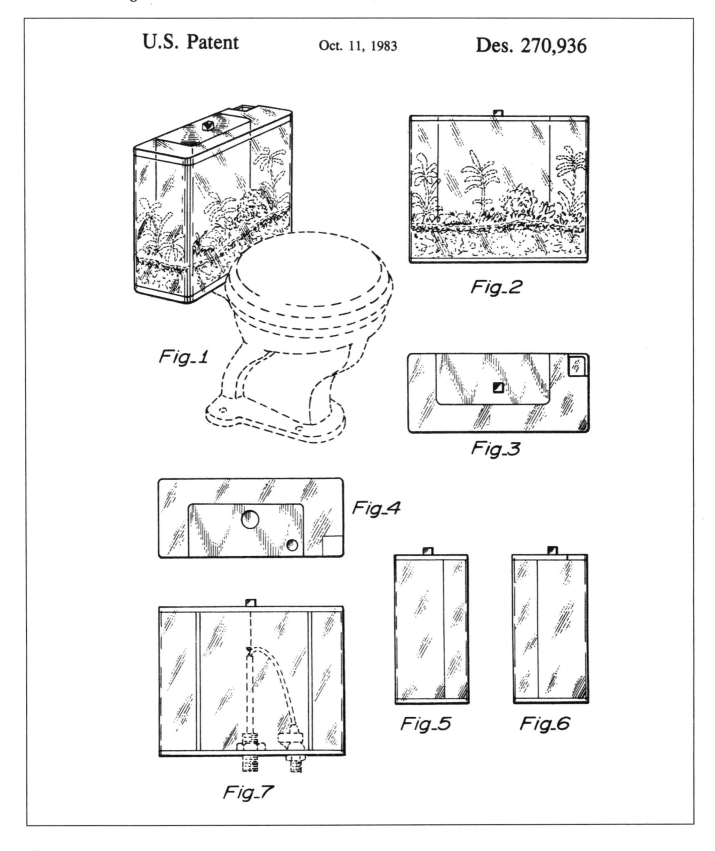

U.S. Patent     Oct. 11, 1983     Des. 270,936

Fig. 1

Fig. 2

Fig. 3

Fig. 4

Fig. 5

Fig. 6

Fig. 7

## Patent Depository Libraries

Patent Depository Libraries (PDLs) across the country provide public access to at least twenty years of patents. With some seventy-two PDLs scattered coast to coast and about three added yearly, almost half of all Americans are within commuting distance of a patent collection. Patent libraries offer access to CASSIS, a CD-ROM index to U.S. patents that helps define a "field of search" and identify specific patents within that field. The patents identified can then be reviewed in the PDL's paper or microfilm patent collection. CASSIS can be purchased from PTO. Patent Depository Library addresses are listed in issues of the *Official Gazette*, in *General Information Concerning Patents* (C 21.26/2: ), or obtained from the PDL Program Office in Washington.

---

### The Patent Office Building

When the British burned Washington in 1814, the U.S. Patent Office building was the only government structure to survive. In a conflagration cliff-hanger, torch-wielding British troops were dissuaded by the chief of patents himself, William Thornton, who threw himself before the building shouting, "Are you Englishmen or vandals?" Thornton warned that burning the U.S. patent depository would be as barbarous as burning the Alexandrian Library, "for which the Turks have been ever since condemned by all enlightened nations." Persuaded by the plucky stranger, the marauders doused their torches and spared the building.

Within forty years the Patent Office occupied a new building which attracted thousands of visitors to see displays of patent models in its exhibition halls. Patent models were a major Washington tourist attraction until 1877, when a disastrous fire consumed the building and many models, including such treasures as Robert Fulton's original drawings for his steamboat. The loss was considered a national tragedy.

Today's Washington visitors may view the renovated remains of the Old Patent Office, which now houses two Smithsonian museums: the National Portrait Gallery and the National Museum of American Art.

---

## Search Aids

Patent language is not like everyday language. Descriptions of patents seek to technically describe the invention's use, function, or effect. In the world of patents, chewing gum becomes "food or edible material processes, compositions and products normally nondigestible chewable material" (Class 426/Subclass 3). The familiar pencil is transformed into "coating implements with material supply, solid material for rubbing contact or support therefor" (Class 401/Subclass 49); and lipstick becomes "drug, bio-affecting and body treating compositions, live skin colorant containing, lip" (Class 424/Subclass 64). This illustrates the need to use the *Index to U.S. Patent Classification* to construct a search according to "patent language" rather than everyday language.

## Translating Patent Language: The *Index to U.S. Patent Classification*

The *Index to U.S. Patent Classification* (C 21.12/2: ) is a gateway into the language of patents and is especially helpful for novices or those unfamiliar with a technology. The *Index* is an alphabetical list referring from keywords to patent classes and subclasses. If, for example, a searcher wanted to locate patents for mousetraps, he or she could search the index under **"MOUSE, Traps"** and be referred to Class 43 and Subclass 58+. (The + designates class 58 and all subclasses indented under it.) The *Index* can be searched in hard copy or on CASSIS. CASSIS also identifies classifications by searching for words in class titles and patent abstracts.

## Classes and Subclasses

The *Manual of Classification* (C 21.12:) lists the descriptive titles of each class and subclass (see Figure 7.3). Design-patent classes are listed in the last volume of the *Manual* and listed alphabetically in the *Index to U.S. Patent Classification*. Plant patent classification is also given in the *Manual* and the *Index*. The *Manual of Classification* can be searched in print or scanned using CASSIS.

## Classification Definitions

More detailed definitions for classes and subclasses are given in *Classification Definitions* (microfiche, C 21.3/2:), which differentiates between similar classes and clarifies inclusions and exclusions. Regarding what most of us call a mousetrap, for example, *Classification Definitions* distinguishes between traps and vermin destroyers. The explanation is not always simple (or savory): Traps "lure animals not domesticated or take advantage of some habit of the same and which by reason of some voluntary action on the part of the said animals catch or wound or paralyze or kill the same or in general render them helpless, that man may work his will on them." Vermin destroyers, on the other hand entice vermin to approach of their "own free will, whether impelled by curiosity, hunger or habit" and (in the best tradition of Greek tragedy) forces them "in spite of themselves, to destruction." *Classification Definitions* can be searched on CASSIS.

## Patent Summaries

The *Official Gazette: Patents* (C 21.5:) contains summaries and drawings for all patents issued during the previous week. Published weekly since 1872, the *Official Gazette* (OG) does not reproduce the entire patent, only the patent abstract and one drawing (see Figure 7.4), except for plant patents, which are not illustrated. OG

**FIGURE 7.3: Sample Page from *Manual of Classification*.**

```
43-2
            CLASS 43   FISHING, TRAPPING AND VERMIN DESTROYING                    DECEMBER 1984

            FISHING                                  100    .Fish
            .Line-attached bodies, hooks and rigs    101    ..Weirs
            ..Selectively free sliding or fixed on   102    ..Elevatable cage
                line                                 103    ..Portable or floating
   44.88    ...Line strain or motion actuated, e.g., 104    ...Towable
                strike or pole tip released          105    ..Foldable or collapsible
   44.89    ..Bendable or deformable material for    106    ..Porpoise
                line connection, e.g., split shot    107    .Insect
   44.9     ..With line passing through center of    108    ..Tree trunk
                body                                 109    ..Furniture
   44.91    ...With line-gripping means             110    ..Operator-controlled
   44.92    ..With relatively movable parts and/or   111    ..Mechanically operated
                resilient construction for           112    ..Electrocuting
                attachment to line                   113    ..Illuminated
   44.93    ...Movable wedge or collect ring type   114    ..Adhesive
   44.94    ...Spiral or pigtail line holder wrapped 115    ...Flypaper holders
                around stem                          116    ...Flexible with drawable section
   44.95    ...Resiliently biased or elastic line   117    ...Upright perch slidable receptacle
                clamping means                       118    ..Reticulate fabric
   44.96    ..Sinkers with ground-engaging means,   119    ..Window screen or door
                e.g., trolley or surf anchors        120    ..Garbage can
   44.97    ..Sinkers with guards or retrieving     121    ..Crawling insect type
                features                             122    ..Fly vases
   44.98    .Lines and/or leaders                    123    ..Bedbug type
   44.99    .Bait distributors, e.g., chumming       124    VERMIN DESTROYING
                devices                              125    .Fumigators
   53.5     .Disgorgers and gags                     126    ..Tree apparatus
   54.1     .Holder                                  127    ..Smokers
   55       ..Catch and natural bait                 128    ...Bee type
   56       ..Minnow buckets                         129    ..Vaporizers
   57       ...Aerating pump                         130    ...Steam
   57.1     ..Hook                                   131    .Poison holders
   57.2     ...Holder for snelled hook under tension 132.1  .Insect
   57.3     ..Trotline holder                        133    ..Catchers
   58       TRAPS                                     134    ...Implements
   59       .Burglar                                 135    ....Spring-operated
   60       .Imprisoning                             136    ....Adhesive
   61       ..Swinging or sliding closure            137    ....Swatters
   62       ..Falling encaging member                138    ...Machines
   63       ..Jaw cage type                          139    ....Suction
   64       .Self and ever set                       140    .....Traveling
   65       ..Nonreturn entrance                     141    ....Blast
   66       ...Victim-opened                         142    ....Rotated agitator
   67       ...Victim-closed                         143    ....Oscillated agitator
   68       ..Sinking compartment                    144    ..Burners
   69       ..Tiltable platform
   70       ...Trigger-released                             CROSS-REFERENCE ART COLLECTION
   71       ..Rotatable platform
   72       ...Trigger-released                      900    LIQUID INSECTICIDE SPRAYER
   73       .Self-reset
   74       ..Rotating door or platform
   75       ..Smiting
   76       .Victim-reset
   77       .Impaling or smiting
   78       ..Rectilinear striker movement
   79       ...Impaling
   80       ....Burrow type
   81       ..Swinging striker
   81.5     ...Auxiliary striker holder
   82       ...Direct engaging latch
   83       ....Automatic catch
   83.5     ...Automatic set
   84       .Explosive
   85       .Choking or squeezing
   86       ..Movable loops
   87       ..Constricting noose
   88       .Jaw
   89       ..Suspended
   90       ..Modified jaw
   91       ...Parallel oscillating
   92       ..Modified trigger mechanism
   93       ...Direct engagement
   94       ....Wedge or toggle
   95       ...Automatic catch
   96       ..Attachments
   97       ...Setting
   98       .Electrocuting
   99       ..Body-removing or concealing
```

To locate mousetraps in the manual, the searcher must know the class. In Class 43, Fishing, Trapping and Vermin Destroying, Subclass 58, Traps, we find numerous types of mousetraps. The dots in the manual show levels of subclassification, with each level providing greater detail.

**FIGURE 7.4: Patent from *Official Gazette*.**

2,026,082
**BOARD GAME APPARATUS**
Charles B. Darrow, Philadelphia, Pa., assignor to
Parker Brothers, Inc., Salem, Mass., a corpora-
tion of Maine
Application August 31, 1935, Serial No. 38,757
9 Claims. (Cl. 273—134)

1. In a board game apparatus a board acting as
a playing-field having marked spaces constituting
a path or course extending about the board, said
path affording a continuous track for the purpose
of continuity of play, certain of said spaces being
designated as by position or color so as to constitute a distinguishable group, there being a plu-
rality of such groups each differing from the
others and each having its spaces adjacent on
the same side of the board, the apparatus having
indications of the rentals required for the use and
occupancy, by opponent players, of spaces of one
or more such groups, which rentals are subject
to increase by the acquisition of an additional
space or spaces of the same group by the same
individual player, thereby making it possible for
the possessor to exact greater payments or penal-
ties from any opponent resting or trespassing
thereon.

The patent abstract and one drawing for a board game called
MONOPOLY appeared in the December 31, 1935, *Official Gazette*.

patent summaries are arranged in patent number sequence and indexed by class and subclass numbers and
by patentees (with separate indexes for utility, design,
and plant patents). Plant patents precede utility patents
in the *Gazette*; design patents follow. An annual separate
issue, *Index of Patents* (C21.5/2:), serves as a cumulative
index to each year's *Official Gazette*, allowing searches by
names of patentees and assignees, by patent class and
subclass numbers, and by class titles. OG can be searched
online or on CD-ROM in several commercial packages
(descriptions can be found in sources like *Computer-
Readable Databases*).

---

**Search Tip**

To determine the OG issue where a particular patent
number appears, consult the table in Part II of the annual
*Index of Patents*, "List of Patent, Design, Plant Patent,
Reissue and Defensive Publication Numbers Appearing
in the Individual Issues of the Official Gazette for [year]."

---

| PATENT SEARCHES* | | |
|---|---|---|
| **Information Known** | **Search** | **To Locate** |
| Patent number | *Official Gazette* | Patent summary |
| | Patent Depository Library | Complete patent |
| | *U.S. Patent Classification Subclass and Numeric Listing* | Classification |
| | CASSIS | Classification |
| | Write PTO | Purchase copy of complete patent |
| Inventor's name | *Index of Patents* | Patent number |
| | *Official Gazette* | Patent number |
| | CASSIS | Bibliographic information |
| | *Patentee/Assignee Index* (microfiche) C 21.27: | Patent number |
| Keywords | *Index to the U.S. Patent Classification* | Class/Subclass |
| | ASIST (CD-ROM complement to CASSIS) | *Index to the U.S. Patent Classification* on CD-ROM |
| | CASSIS | Classification, patent numbers: *Manual of Patent Examining Procedure* online |
| Classification | *Manual of Classification* | Descriptive title of class and subclass |
| | *Index of Patents* | Patent numbers |
| | CASSIS | Patent numbers, titles, and subclasses; *Manual of Classification* on CD-ROM |
| | *U.S. Patent Classification Subclass Listing* | Patent numbers |
| | PTO Information Resource Branch | Patent numbers in selected subclasses |

*Commercial database services are omitted.

## Government Patents

Federal agencies have patented more than 24,000 inventions. About two-thirds are health-related; another quarter deal with agriculture and forestry. All U.S. government patent applications are publicly available through the National Technical Information Service (NTIS). Because NTIS licenses businesses to use government inventions, cooperating government agencies notify NTIS of new inventions, which are then included in the NTIS Bibliographic Database and GRA & I (no privately owned patents are listed). This has made NTIS the central source of information about government patents and pending patent applications. Government inventions such as an AIDS test kit, nonpolluting insecticides, a blood coagulant for hemophilia patients, high-speed centrifuges, and diagnostic tests for cancer are available for licensing through NTIS's Center for Utilization of Federal Technology (CUFT).

NTIS does not grant licenses for government patents from NASA, the Department of Energy, or the Department of Defense, which handle their own patent licensing. The indexes and databases of the Department of Defense, Department of Energy, and NASA list government-owned patents and patent applications. These include DoD's TRAC, DOE's *Energy Research Abstracts* and Energy Science and Technology Data Base (EDB), and NASA's *Scientific and Technical Aerospace Reports* (see Chapter 6).

NTIS accession numbers for patents and patent applications have a PAT or PAT-APPL (pronounced "pat-apple") alpha prefix, followed by the patent or application number granted by the Patent and Trademark Office. Government patents may be searched on the NTIS database using the keywords "Patents" or "Patent Applications" combined with the NTIS subject category 90. (Omit NTIS subject category 90 to retrieve foreign patents along with U.S. patents). NTIS sells copies of government patent applications; copies of patents themselves must be purchased from PTO.

Government-owned patents are announced in the weekly *Government Inventions for Licensing Abstract Newsletter*, which contains patent abstracts and drawings arranged under general subject areas. Notices of patents available for license or sale appear in the annual *Catalog of Government Inventions Available for Licensing* (C 51.16/2: ), the *Federal Register*, and OG (in the PTO notices section). Early notification is available through NTIS's free Patent Licensing Bulletin Board (PLBB), with online searches available through the Federal Applied Technology Database, produced by CUFT. Patent bibliographies and abstracts are included in NTIS's *Published Search Master Catalog*, serving as quick guides to patent information on a technology.

## Searching the Complete Patent

For peripatetic searchers, the Patent and Trademark Office in Arlington, Virginia, is considered "the greatest technical library in the world" and the best place to conduct a patent search. The PTO's Public Search Room has copies of patents granted since 1836, arranged by subject matter in classes and subclasses, and public access to APS, the Automated Patent System full text searching developed for patent examiners. The PTO patent files are a source of technical information or, alternatively, can help determine whether an invention has already been patented. The PTO also opens its scientific library and record room to the public. The scientific library collections include scientific and technical books in numerous languages, scientific journals, the official patent journals of foreign countries, and copies of foreign patents. The record room provides for public inspection of patent records and files, as well as other open records. Copies of patents may be purchased by mail from PTO for $1.50.

Patent Depository Libraries are another place to examine the full patent. About seventy of these libraries are scattered across the country, each receiving a copy of every current patent issued. Since the breadth of their retrospective collections varies, not all patent depository libraries have patents back to number one, but all have at least a twenty-year backfile. Unlike the collection at the Patent and Trademark Office, all but one of these collections are arranged in patent-number order, with many patents on microfilm rather than paper. People wishing to search a specific technology will find this arrangement less convenient, but may identify patent numbers in specific classes and subclasses using CASSIS or the microfilm *United States Patent Classification Subclass Listing* (Research Publications). PDLs receive supplemental aids from the Patent and Trademark Office that are not publicly available anywhere else. PDL staff can answer questions and help patent seekers construct a search strategy.

### Computer Searching

Patents can be searched online and on CD-ROM through numerous commercial vendors. In 1990, there were some 80 patent/trademark databases (descriptions can be found in sources like *Computer-Readable Databases*). In addition to CASSIS, available free at Patent Depository Libraries, the Patent and Trademark Office is pilot-testing provision of free public access to the Automated Patent System (APS) full text searching in fourteen PDLs during 1992. This experiment is expected to lay the groundwork for provision of APS in every Patent Depository Library.

The Patent and Trademark Office's Technology Assessment and Forecast Program (TAF) is a source of statistics on patent activity. TAF calculations show that almost half of U.S. patent applications are from foreign nationals, for example (the Japanese are the most active, with Californians ranking as the most productive U.S. inventors). TAF prepares statistical analyses showing patent activity by elements such as year, state, country, SIC, and patent class. TAF will also perform custom reports on a cost-reimbursable basis.

## Components of the Patent

A typical patent includes drawings, a brief "abstract" or summary, plus the patent "specification," a detailed description of how to make or use the invention. Every patent cover page provides similar information, as shown in Figure 7.5. The numbers in brackets, called INID Codes, are part of an international system that allows elements on the patent cover page to be identified even when written in an unfamiliar language.

## Claims

Claims are formally written phrases that precisely define the invention. Patent claims have been likened to land deeds, outlining the boundaries of the claimed invention. "Crossing [a claims] boundary without the owner's permission is a trespass or, in intellectual property terms, an infringement."[2]

---

**Patent Models**

Until 1880, each patent application was accompanied by a miniature working model. Thousands of the models were destroyed in the Patent Office fire of 1877, with even more lost during a clumsy PTO relocation or from being stored in a leaky tunnel. The neglected collection was finally auctioned off by President Coolidge for $1,550. As many as 100,000 models may have survived, and Invent America! is working to recover, restore, and display them in the Smithsonian Institution.

Although the model requirement was rescinded in 1880, patent models remain part of the American psyche. Gordon Gould's 28-year legal battle for the laser patent resulted partly from a patent model misunderstanding. Assuming he needed a working model, Gould postponed filing for two years. Meanwhile, Charles Townes scooped up the laser patent, became known as the father of the laser, and won a Nobel Prize.

---

## Foreign Patents

Patents provide protection only in their country of issue. Almost half of U.S. patents are granted to foreign nationals to protect their inventions in this country. Likewise, Americans may seek not only a U.S. patent, but also patents in other nations. To protect an invention in any of about 120 countries offering patent protection, an inventor must file in each country under that country's laws.

International treaties such as the Paris Convention and the Patent Cooperation Treaty (PCT) provide reciprocal protection and filing rights in member countries. The United Nations' World Intellectual Property Organization, in Geneva, Switzerland, administers the Paris Convention and PCT and publishes the International Patent Classification. Some countries are served by a regional patent office like the European Patent Office, where a single application can be simultaneously registered in any member nation. Timing is important since most countries grant a patent to the first person filing an application (the United States is unusual in granting the patent to the original inventor, the "first-to-invent," rather than the first-to-file).

### Foreign Patent Searching

A "patent family" is created when an inventor applies for multiple national patents. It includes all the applications and patents for the same invention from various nations. These are differentiated in patent databases as the "basic patent" (the first entered in the database, not necessarily the first published), and "equivalent patents," subsequent database entries for the same invention.

Online patent family (or patent equivalent) searches are useful when an English-language version of a non-English patent is sought, or for translating from a U.S. application number to a patent granted from another nation. Because non-U.S. patents and gazettes are difficult to locate in the U.S., it helps to identify the U.S. equivalent of a foreign patent. While United States patent applications remain secret until a patent is granted, European applications are often available before the U.S. counterpart is granted.

Numerous online database services offer U.S. and foreign patent searching, including INPADOC (International Patent Documentation Center) available on ORBIT (the print companion is the *INPADOC Patent Gazette*), and Derwent's World Patents Index database (WPI) available through DIALOG, ORBIT, and QUESTEL. The *Concordance: United States Patent Classification to International Patent Classification* (C 21.14/2:C 74/990) is a guide for relating the U.S. patent classification system to the International Patent Classification System (IPC) from WIPO. The International Patent Classification number is listed on U.S. patents, designated by the INID Code [51].

Most countries publish an official patent journal similar to our *Official Gazette*, many of which may be consulted in the Patent and Trademark Office's collection of official foreign patent-office journals. Helpful guides to foreign patent documentation include *A Guide to Official Gazettes and Their Contents* (1985) issued by the Library of Congress's Law Library, *Patents Throughout the World*, a digest of national patent laws, and J. W. Baxter's *World Patent Law and Practice*. The *NTIS Foreign Technology Abstract Newsletter* includes a section on "For-

**FIGURE 7.5: Cover Page of Patent.**

## Patent Front Pages

This brief explanation of the information available from a U.S. Patent is designed for the person unfamiliar with patents.

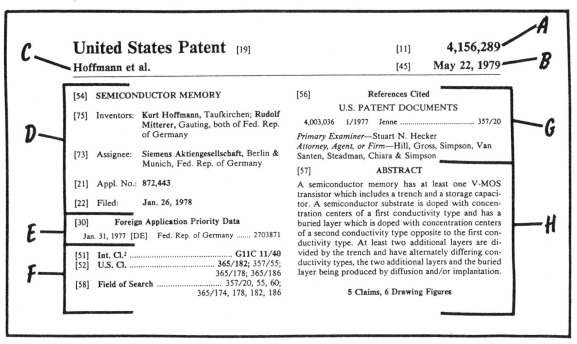

A.    4,156,289 is the U.S. Patent number.

B.    **May 22, 1979** is the issue date.

C.    **Hoffmann** is the last name of the inventor who is listed first.

C.    **et al** indicates that there are other inventors.

D.    **Semiconductor Memory** is the title describing the claimed invention.

D.    The patent shows the name and city of residence of each of the **Inventors.** Unassigned patents show the full address of the Inventors.

D.    **Assignee** refers to a company, organization or individual to which the inventors' rights to a patent are assigned. The name and city are shown.

D.    872,443 is the serial number given to the application, which was filed on **Jan. 26, 1978.**

E.    **Foreign Application Priority Data** indicates corresponding applications which were filed in other countries, gives the filing date and foreign application number. By fulfilling certain requirements, an applicant filing in the U.S. may be entitled to the benefit of the filing date of a prior application in a foreign country.

F.    **Int. Cl...G11C 11/40** is the International Patent Classification.

F.    **U.S. Cl...365/182, 357/55, 365/178 and 365/186** are the four U.S. Classifications listed for this patent: Class 365, subclass 182, Class 357, subclass 55, Class 365, subclass 178 and Class 365, subclass 186. The classification listed in boldface on the patent is called the original classification (OR). The others are the cross-reference classifications (XR). Every patent has one and only one original classification. If the disclosure of the patent falls into more than one subclass, additional copies of the patent are placed in those subclasses as cross-reference classifications.

F.    The **Field of Search...** refers to the U.S. Classification where the Patent Examiner searched to compare the claimed subject matter to that disclosed in previous patents and articles.

G.    **References Cited** refers to references which may be cited by the examiner and applicant to show the state-of-the-art or to indicate the prior art most closely related to the invention which is claimed in the application.

H.    The Patent and Trademark Office (PTO) requires that the patent application include a brief **Abstract** of the technical disclosure in the specification. The purpose of the abstract is to enable the PTO and the public to determine quickly the nature and gist of the technical disclosure.

H.    The front page also lists the number of **Claims** and the number of **Drawing Figures** in the patent. When appropriate, a representative drawing is also included on the front page of the patent.

Source: *Patent Profiles. Microelectronics - II.* GPO, 1983. (C 21.25:M 58/v. 2)

eign government-owned inventions for licensing," with abstracts and U.S. patent numbers.

The Patent and Trademark Scientific Library maintains a foreign patent collection from which photocopies may be made, and the Patent and Trademark Office sells copies of some foreign patents. Some PDLs also collect foreign patents. Several commercial publishers and online services offer subscriptions to foreign patents and gazettes.

---

### Patent Glossary

**Digest**—(Dig.) a collection of cross-reference patents assembled to streamline patent examiner searches; now called Cross-Reference art collections (X-art)

**Field of search**—cross-referenced patent classes (OR and XR) examined when searching for similar patents

**File wrappers**—the documentation and cited art associated with a patent

**Interference**—a proceeding to determine the original inventor of a contested invention

**MPEP**—*Manual of Patent Examining Procedure*, the "patent examiner's bible" (C 21.15: )

**Name and Date Patents**—unnumbered patents issued between 1790 and 1836; some have been placed in the classified files with an x- prefix and called the X-Numbered Patents; indexed in *Early Unnumbered United States Patents 1790-1836: Index and Guide to the Microfilm Edition* (Research Publications)

**OR**—a patent's primary [original] classification assignment; noted on the patent in bold type under **[52] U.S.Cl.**, but not in OG

**Patent family**—all patents and patent applications for the same invention in various countries; sometimes called "patent equivalents"

**Patent number equivalents**—the U.S. equivalent of a foreign patent

**Prior art**—the technology related to an invention; searched to determine the novelty of a patent application

**Reclassification**—a change in class or subclass to reflect a new technology; when a new number is created, previous patents may be reclassified

**Reissue patent**—a patent that corrects and replaces an unexpired patent reexamined by PTO for invalid claims

**Shoes**—PTO patent files; descendants of the original shoe boxes in which patents were stored

**SIR**—Statutory Invention Registration; a defensive patent that prohibits a similar patent, but does not prevent others from making, using, or selling the invention

**UX**—unofficial cross-references, related patents consulted by the examiner

**X-art collections (cross-reference art collections)**—cross-reference patents in a class; listed in the *Manual* at the end of a class in numerical sequence, in the *Index* denoted with an asterisk

**X-Numbered Patents**—unnumbered Name and Date Patents (issued 1790–1836) placed in the classified files with an x-prefix

**XR**—cross-reference, or additional, classifications; noted on the patent under **[52] U.S.Cl.**, but not in OG

---

## Computer Searches

*We are missing more documents than most federal agencies have.*        —Gerald Mossinghoff,
                        Patent and Trademark Office, 1984

Hobbled by manual search techniques acknowledged to be among the slowest on the planet, PTO began automating its patent examination process in the early 1980s. Throughout PTO's two centuries of business, searching had been by hand through millions of sheaves of paper. PTO officials readily admitted that some seven percent of their 25 million documents are always missing or misfiled. With manual patent examinations averaging about two years and 3,500 new applications arriving weekly, Congress ordered PTO to automate.

After a troubled start, the $600 million Automated Patent System (APS) has rebounded and should be fully operational by 2002. Eventually millions of United States and foreign patents will be converted to digitized images, and searchable on terminals in the PTO Public Search Room by the general public. The system will allow searching of both text and drawings, including English-language abstracts of Japanese and Chinese patents. The mammoth project has made PTO the government's pioneer in optical-disc storage technology.

## TRADEMARKS

Trademarks are words, names, symbols, or devices used to identify and distinguish goods. Even colors, smells, and sounds can occasionally be registered as trademarks—Owens-Corning has a lock on the color pink for home insulation, the sounds of the NBC chimes and the MGM lion are protected, as is the smell of Clarke Company's perfumed embroidery thread.

How many trademarks will you encounter today? If you are an average American, as many as 1,500. These ubiquitous words and pictures are so much a part of our lives that we are not always conscious of them. Take the case of the American airport crew told to remove billboards to convince a hijacker he was landing in Russia: As the plane descended, the hijacker panicked and returned skyward—the ground crew had forgotten to remove a Coca-Cola sign. It was so familiar, it was invisible.[3]

Some trademarks are engraved in the public consciousness (see Figure 7.6). Colonel Sanders died in 1980, but his face continues to identify products of the Kentucky Fried Chicken Corporation. The canine model for Nipper, the RCA dog, has been dead for more than ninety years, but his image remains one of America's best-loved trademarks.

### Genericide

Have you ever "xeroxed" an article? The Xerox Corporation begs to differ: Actually you "photocopied"

**FIGURE 7.6: The Morton Salt Umbrella Girl.**

|  |  |  |  |  |  |
|---|---|---|---|---|---|
| 1914 | 1921 | 1933 | 1941 | 1956 | 1968 |

The Umbrella Girl design is a registered trademark of Morton International, Inc. No one modeled for the Morton Salt umbrella girl's picture, designed in 1911 for the first national advertising campaign for salt. The original slogan under the picture was "Even in rainy weather, it flows freely." Both the revised slogan, "When it rains it pours," and the umbrella girl are protected by registered trademarks, and the round blue Morton Salt container sports a patented pouring spout. *Courtesy Morton International, Morton Salt Division.*

it. The distinction may seem unimportant to ordinary people, but company lawyers who see their trademark used as a verb or noun are likely to dash off a letter to offenders asking them not to repeat the error. It's called "genericide"—the loss of a trademark too often used generically. When the courts decide a trademark has become associated with a type of product rather than a specific brand, the trademark enters the public domain for anyone's use.

| Trademark Graveyard Former Trademarks Now in the Public Domain | |
|---|---|
| aspirin | malted milk |
| brassiere | milk of magnesia |
| cellophane | mimeograph |
| celluloid | mineral oil |
| corn flakes | nylon |
| cube steak | phonograph |
| dry ice | pocket book |
| escalator | shredded wheat |
| harmonica | thermos |
| kerosene | trampoline |
| lanolin | vanilla |
| linoleum | yo-yo |

Aspirin lost its trademark protection because its owner used it as a noun ("Buy aspirin") instead of an adjective ("Buy ASPIRIN brand analgesic"). Corn flakes, escalator, harmonica, malted milk, trampoline, and yo-yo are all former trademarks now in the public domain. A trademark can lose its registration in one country, but not all. Aspirin is still a Bayer trademark in South America and Canada. Thermos is generic in the United States, but

remains a registered trademark in Britain. The trademark graveyard's most recent entry is Monopoly, now in the public domain after a Parker Brothers lost a legal battle with a rival game named Anti-Monopoly. Companies designate their trademarks with an ® or ™ in superscript\*, and also capital letters, followed by the generic name of the product in smaller type (JELL-O brand gelatin dessert; BAND-AID brand adhesive bandages).

## Trademark Searching

The weekly *Official Gazette: Trademarks* (C21.5/4:) lists and illustrates trademarks and has an index of registrants (the companies, organizations, and people owning the trademarks). The *Index of Trademarks* (C21.5/3:), an annual index to the *Gazette*, is arranged alphabetically by registrants' names, with address and registration information. For all practical purposes, though, "the government has no real index to trademarks."[4] Until PTO trademark examination files are fully automated and opened to the public, the best alternatives are commercial sources like the Compu-Mark (in print, online, and on CD-ROM) and TRADEMARKSCAN (online and on CD-ROM) which list trademark registrations and applications, and commercially published references such as *The Trademark Register of the United States, The Trademark Design Register,* and *The Directory of U.S. Trademarks.*

The most thorough trademark searches are conducted at the Patent and Trademark Office, where the search library of Trademark Examining Operations maintains digests of both pending applications and registered

---

\*® indicates the trademark has been registered with the U.S. Patent and Trademark Office, while ™ protects unregistered trademarks.

marks. Registered word marks are arranged alphabetically, and symbol marks (birds, stars, flowers, etc.) are arranged according to trademark classification.

**Computer Searches**

In its $600 million quest to fully automate its examination procedures, PTO embarked upon automating its trademark examination files in the early 1980s. Unfortunately, early trials on the newly automated T-Search system took four minutes longer than the average manual search and were riddled with inaccuracies. More controversial were PTO's attempts to cut costs through an exchange agreement with three commercial companies (Compu-Mark, Thomson & Thomson, and TCR) which created the trademark database in exchange for exclusive access rights to it until the mid-1990s. In 1989, after the General Accounting Office challenged the exclusivity arrangement, PTO terminated it. T-Search is available to the public in the PTO public search rooms and is expected to be replaced with a new system by the mid-1990s. In 1991, Patent Depository Libraries received a pilot TRADE-MARKS CD-ROM containing the text of some 800,000 pending and registered trademarks, for the free use of the public. Continued enhancements of trademark searching in PDLs are expected.

Online trademark searches are available through commercial vendors such as Thomson & Thomson, which offers TRADEMARKSCAN and Compu-Mark. Thomson & Thomson's Compu-Mark and TRADEMARKSCAN are computerized databases of the PTO records, containing all trademark registrations and applications since 1884. They also include state trademarks and *SHEPARD'S Citations* of litigated trademarks. Searching is through Compu-Mark; for TRADEMARKSCAN, searching is available through DIALOG or Thomson & Thomson.

---

**The Trademark Wars
Trademark Infringement Cases**

McDonald's Corp. vs. McTeddy (teddy bears)
Toys R Us vs. Phones R Us
NutraSweet vs. Stadt Corp. (blue sugar-substitute packets)
Tinker Toys vs. Thinker Toys (the first are toys; the second, electronic components and circuit boards)
Godiva Chocolates vs. Dogiva dog biscuits
Jordache vs. Lardashe (both are jeans; Lardashe jeans are for "full-figured" women)

---

# COPYRIGHT

Copyright protects authors, artists, and others from theft of their intellectual property, including books, music, plays, choreography, photographs, game boards and rules, art, motion pictures, sound recordings, computer programs, architectural blueprints, advertisements, labels, and maps (see Figure 7.7). Copyright protects the way a work was expressed but not the ideas, systems, or facts conveyed through the work. Protection cannot be granted for slogans, processes, procedures, ideas, standard calendars, blank forms, U.S. government publications, names, short phrases, expressions, or titles (this book, for example, could legally have been titled *Gone with the Wind*).

Soon after Noah Webster (of dictionary fame) lobbied for the U.S. copyright protection that would safeguard his *American Spelling Book,* Congress enacted the 1790 copyright law. Since then, the Library of Congress has been in the copyright business, registering U.S. copyrights while accumulating free materials for its collections. To register a copyright, the creator pays a $20 fee and deposits two copies of the work with the Library of Congress.[5]

Libraries of copyright deposit have been likened to collections of botanical specimens which hold definitive examples of classified plants. Copyright deposit has allowed the Library of Congress's collections to reflect a century of America's creative products. The results reveal themselves in the library's unparalleled collections: The world's greatest Civil War and Old West photograph collection and the only surviving copies of some nineteenth-century dance music, ballads, minstrel songs, and ragtime are examples.

The United States and other nations enjoy reciprocal copyright protection as members of the Universal Copyright Convention (UCC) and the Berne Convention for the Protection of Literary and Artistic Works. Member nations honor each other's copyrights and allow infringement suits to cross national borders. A list of nations maintaining copyright relations with the United States is given in the free Copyright Office Circular 38a, "International Copyright Relations of the United States."

## Copyright Searches

The free Copyright Office Circular 22, "How to Investigate the Copyright Status of a Work," is the best starting point for a copyright search. The Copyright Office suggests three approaches for determining whether a work is protected: looking for the copyright notice on a copy of the work; searching Copyright Office records; or paying the Copyright Office to search for you. (The Copyright Office also cautions that a combination of the three methods may be needed, and that even then results may be inconclusive.) Commercial vendors such as Thomson & Thomson also offer copyright search services.

The microfiche *Catalog of Copyright Entries* (LC 3.6/6:) lists copyright registrations and is divided into eight parts according to formats. Since 1979, CCE has been available only in microfiche. Copyright registrations and renewals since 1978 are also computer-searchable by author's and claimant's names, titles, and registration numbers on the Library of Congress's online database, SCORPIO. Citations include the name of author and copyright claimant, title of the work, dates of creation and deposit, and related works. Unfortunately, SCORPIO is publicly searchable only on-site at the Library of Congress. This and other copyright records are open to the public at the Copyright Office. Individuals planning to search at the Library of Congress should consult the free Copyright Office Circular 23, "The Copyright Card Catalog and the Online Files of the Copyright Office."

**FIGURE 7.7: Copyrightable Works.**

## OVERLAPPING PROTECTION

Some works may be eligible for both copyright and patent protection: Computer programs, designs for objects that are simultaneously functional and aesthetic, and games are good examples (see Figure 7.8). A single game, for instance, may have patent protection for the game apparatus; copyright for the board, box, and game-piece design and the written rules; and trademark registration for the name (although Parker Brothers lost the trademark for the name "Monopoly," they still hold a copyright on the game). Other examples of overlapping protection are the Rolls-Royce hood ornament, which is

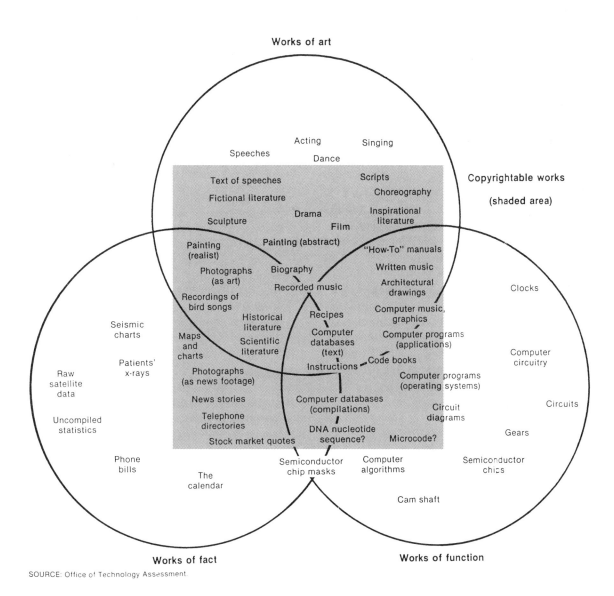

SOURCE: Office of Technology Assessment

Congress's Office of Technology Assessment has identified three types of copyrightable works: works of art, of fact, and of function. Those deemed suitable for copyright protection are shown in the shaded area. Source: *Intellectual Property Rights in an Age of Electronics and Information.* GPO, 1986. (Y 3.T22/2:2 In 8/3)

protected by copyright (as sculpture), a design patent, and a trademark, and the Coca-Cola bottle, which enjoys both patent and trademark protection.

**FIGURE 7.8: Ghostbusters.**

The GHOSTBUSTERS logo is protected both by trademark registration and copyright. Courtesy Columbia Pictures Industries, Inc.

## THE COURTS

Patent infringement disputes and patentability appeals are heard first by U.S. district courts and then by the Court of Appeals for the Federal Circuit (formerly two separate courts: the courts of Claims and of Customs and Patent Appeals), with the cases searchable on LEXIS and WESTLAW. BNA's *United States Patents Quarterly* reports patent, trademark, and copyright cases, Patent Office tribunals, and Supreme Court opinions related to patents, trademarks, or copyrights. *Patent, Trademark & Copyright Journal*, published by BNA and searchable on LEXIS and WESTLAW, reports intellectual property developments in the courts, Congress, the executive branch, PTO, and professional associations.

*Decisions of the United States Courts Involving Copyright and Literary Property (1789-1909) with an Analytical Index* (LC 3.3/3:13-16) contains judicial and administrative decisions before July 1, 1909. This title is continued by the annual *Decisions of the United States Courts Involving Copyright* (LC 3.3/3:), covering cases decided by the federal and state courts. *Shepard's United States Citations: Patents and Trademarks* lists citations to litigated patents, trademarks, and copyrights.

## ADDRESSES

### Copyright

Copyright Office staff will perform copyright searches for $20 an hour (1992 cost). The free Circular 22, "How to Investigate the Copyright Status of a Work" (see "Freebies" below), describes the information that should be furnished with search requests. Send requests to Reference and Bibliography Section, LM-451, Copyright Office, Library of Congress, Washington, DC 20559; (202) 707-6850.

Individuals may search copyright records at the Copyright Office, Library of Congress, James Madison Memorial Bldg., 101 Independence Ave., S.E., Washington, DC 20559.

## Patents and Trademarks

CASSIS can be purchased by contacting Office of Electronic Information Products and Services, Crystal Mall Bldg. 2, Room 304, Washington, DC 20231; (703) 557-5652.

The Commissioner of Patents and Trademarks, Patent Office, U.S. Department of Commerce, Washington, DC 20231 sells copies of any patent (identified by patent number). Prices are $1.50 for utility and design patents and trademarks; $10.00 for plant patents (which include a color photograph) and foreign patents. General patent or trademark information: (703) 305-HELP.

NTIS's free Patent Licensing Bulletin Board—for information and a user's manual, contact: Director, Center for the Utilization of Federal Technology, Box 1423, Springfield, VA 22151; (703) 487-4738; PLBB dial-up: (703) 487-4061.

The Patent and Trademark Office and its Scientific Library, Search Room, and Record Room are located at Crystal Plaza, 2021 Jefferson Davis Hwy., Arlington, VA 22202.

The Patent Depository Library Program Office will answer questions about PDLs and CASSIS: Office of Patent Depository Library Programs, Crystal Mall Bldg. 2, Room 306, U.S. Patent and Trademark Office, Washington, DC 20231; (703) 308-3924.

Technology Assessment and Forecast Program, U.S. Patent and Trademark Office, CM2-304, Washington, DC 20231; (703) 557-5652.

The PTO Information Resources Branch will answer questions about patent classification orders, definitions, addenda, and the *Manual of Classification*. They also sell inexpensive subclass listings showing patent numbers in selected subclasses; (703) 557-5100.

The United States Trademark Association, a non-profit organization dedicated to protecting trademarks and their owners' interests, provides a free list of companies that conduct searches of U.S., state, foreign, and other trademarks. The list gives addresses, telephone numbers, and a brief description of services. Contact USTA, 6 E. 45th St., New York, NY 10017; (212) 986-5880; FAX (212) 687-8267.

## FREEBIES

The following subject bibliographies are free from the U.S. Government Printing Office, Superintendent of Documents, Washington, DC 20402:

21.  Patents and Trademarks
126.  Copyrights

### Copyright

From Publications Section, LM-455, Copyright Office, Library of Congress, Washington, DC 20559 or by calling the twenty-four-hour Copyright Office Hotline and leaving a recorded request; (202) 707-9100:

Circular 1, "Copyright Basics" (LC 3.4/2:1/991)

Circular 2, "Publications on Copyright" (LC 3.4/2:2/987)

Circular 2b, "Selected Bibliographies on Copyright" (LC 3.4/2:2b/7)

Circular 3, "Copyright Notice" (LC 3.4/2:3)

Circular 21, "Reproduction of Copyrighted Works by Educators and Librarians" (LC 3.4/2:21/988)

Circular 22, "How to Investigate the Copyright Status of a Work" (LC 3.4/2:22/3)

Circular 93, "Highlights of U.S. Adherence to the Berne Convention" (LC 3.4/2:93)

Circular 93a, "The United States Joins the Berne Union" (LC 3.4/2:93a)

Copyright applications are available from the Register of Copyrights, Copyright Office, Library of Congress, Washington, DC 20559 or by calling the Copyright Office Hotline; (202) 707-9100. Specify type of work to be registered—poem, music, etc.

## Patents

From the European Patent Office (EPO), Dept. 4.5.2 (Distribution), Erhardtstrasse 27, D-8000 Munich 2:

"How to Get a European Patent"

"Protecting Inventions in Europe"

From the World Intellectual Property Organization (WIPO), UN Liaison Office, 2 United Nations Plaza, Room 560, New York, NY 10017; (212) 963-6813:

"General Information," publication no. 401 (E)

## REFERENCES

1. Thanks to Charles Wilt, Patent Depository librarian in Philadelphia, who compiled a list of "crazy patents."

2. Sidney B. Williams, "Protections of Plant Varieties and Parts as Intellectual Property," *Science* 225 (July 6, 1984):19.

3. Anthony Haden-Guest, *The Paradise Program: Travels through Muzak, Hilton, Coca-Cola, Texaco, Walt Disney, and Other World Empires* (New York: William Morrow & Co., 1973), p. 97.

4. Dorothy Solomon, "The Patent Depository Library System," *The Bookmark* 44 (Summer 1986): 215.

5. Copyright protection is enhanced by including an optional but recommended copyright notice in the publication, and by registration with the Copyright Office. For details, consult Circular 3, "Copyright Notice," and Circular 1, "Copyright Basics," free from from the Copyright Office (see address above).

## FURTHER READING

Ardis, Susan B. *An Introduction to U.S. Patent Searching: The Process.* Englewood, CO: Libraries Unlimited, Inc., 1991.
Details on patents and how to find them, with chapters on online searching and foreign patents.

Caney, Steven. *The Invention Book.* New York: Workman Publishing, 1985.
A fascinating cavalcade of now-familiar inventions (the drinking straw, Frisbees, Band-Aids) and the stories behind them.

Hambleton, Ronald. *The Branding of America: From Levi Strauss to Chrysler, from Westinghouse to Gillette, the Forgotten Fathers of*

*America's Best-Known Brand Names.* Dublin, NH: Yankee Books, 1987.
The stories behind famous brand names.

House of Representatives. *Patents and the Constitution: Transgenic Animals. Hearings before the Subcommittee on Courts, Civil Liberties, and the Administration of Justice of the Committee on the Judiciary, House of Representatives, 100-1, June 11, July 22, August 21, and November 5, 1987.* (Serial No. 23) Y4.J89/1:100-23
Congress explores the pros and cons of allowing genetically altered plants and animals to be patented.

Kaback, Stuart M. "Access All the Information in Patents." *Chemtech* 15 (March 1985): 146-51.
An introduction to chemical patents.

Lawless, Benjamin. "Working with Working Models." *American Heritage of Invention and Technology* 1 (Fall 1985):10-17.
A look back at patent models, a mandatory component of every patent application until 1880.

Leaffer, Marshall A., ed. *International Treaties on Intellectual Property.* Washington, DC: Bureau of National Affairs, 1990.
Full text of worldwide treaties on patents, trademarks, and copyrights, including proposed treaties.

Lubar, Steven. "'New, Useful, and Unobvious'." *American Heritage of Invention & Technology* 6 (Spring/Summer 1990): 9-16.
The rocky history of determining the patentability of an invention.

Morgan, Hal. *Symbols of America.* New York: Viking, 1986.
An illustrated compendium of trademark life stories.

*The Old Patent Office Building and the Act of 1836: Cornerstones of the American Patent System.* Washington, DC: Intellectual Property Owners, Inc., n.d.

Patent and Trademark Office. *Basic Facts About Trademarks.* GPO, 1989. (C21.2:T 67/4/989)
A brief introduction to trademarks and trademark applications.

———. *General Information Concerning Patents.* GPO, 1922– . Annual. (C21.26/2: )
An overview of patents and how to apply for them.

———. *Patents and Inventions: An Information Aid for Inventors.* GPO, 1980. (C21.2:P 27/10/980)

———. *Q & A about Patents: Answers to Questions Frequently Asked about Patents.* PTO, 1979. (C21.2:P 27/9/979)

———. *Q and A about Plant Patents: Answers to Questions Frequently Asked about Plant Patents.* PTO, 1969.

———. *Q & A about Trademarks: Answers to Questions Frequently Asked about Trademarks.* PTO, 1985. (C 21.2:T 67/2/985)

———. *The Story of the U.S. Patent and Trademark Office.* GPO, 1988. (C21.2:P 27/3/988)
A history of inventions, inventors, and the patent system in America.

———. Office of Technology Assessment and Forecast. *Design Patents.* GPO, 1983. (C21.24:D 46/983)
An overview of design patents, plus trends and statistics about design patents granted between 1977 and 1982.

———. Office of Technology Assessment and Forecast. *Patent Profiles.* GPO, 1979- . Irregular. (C21.25: )
A series of reports on patent activity in particular fields.

Peltz, James F. "Bright Lights, Big Money." *Discover* 9 (March 1988):78-79, 81.

> The story of Gordon Gould's 28-year fight for the patent rights to the laser.

Pressman, David. *Patent It Yourself.* 3rd ed. Berkeley, CA: Nolo Press, 1991.

> A manual of patent information and search techniques.

Stone, Judith. "Cells for Sale." *Discover* 9(August 1988): 33-39.

> An account of the legal battle for rights to patented cells from leukemia patient John Moore's spleen.

Weinstein, David A. *How to Protect Your Creative Work: All You Need to Know About Copyright.* New York: Wiley, 1987.

> A clearly written guide to the basics and details of copyright protection.

Wildman, Iris J. and Rhonda Carlson. *Researching Copyright Renewal: A Guide to Information and Procedure.* Littleton, CO: Fred B. Rothman & Co., 1989.

> Detailed strategy for researching copyright renewals, including format and details of the *Catalog of Copyright Entries.*

## EXERCISES

1.  Patent number search
    Locate something with a patent number and identify the patent summary.

2.  Patent name search
    Locate and cite the patent for any of the following:
    a.  David Golde and Shirley Quan, cells from leukemia patient John Moore's spleen, 1984
    b.  Gordon Gould, laser, 1987
    c.  Philip Leder and Timothy Stewart, the "Harvard mouse," 1988
    d.  Richard James, SLINKY (toy), 1947
    e.  Herman Hollerith, early computer, 1889
    f.  Ananda Chakrabarty, living microorganism, 1981

3.  What's wrong with this description of how *Bartlett's Familiar Quotations* protected its title:
    "As other editors took over, it became necessary to patent `Bartlett' as a trademark protected by law, something that would have shocked its creator."[1]

---

1. Peter Gorner. "From the Mouths of History—'Bartlett' Notes the Quotables." *Chicago Tribune* (October 16, 1980): Sect. 2, pp.1, 4.

# CHAPTER 8
# Legislative Information Sources

*The United States is the greatest law factory the world has ever known.* —Chief Supreme Court Justice Charles Evans Hughes

## WHAT

The chief function of Congress is lawmaking.

## WHY

The United States Constitution grants all legislative powers to "a Congress of the United States, which shall consist of a Senate and House of Representatives."

## WHEN

Nineteen eighty-nine was the U.S. Congress's 200th anniversary. A term of Congress lasts two years, and is made up of a first and second session, each lasting one year. Congresses are numbered consecutively: For example, in 1993, the 103rd Congress is in its first of two one-year sessions (103-1).

## HOW

The United States Congress is bicameral, comprising the Senate, with 100 members (two from each state), and the House of Representatives, with a membership of 435, apportioned according to state populations.

## WHO

A member of the House is referred to as representative, congressman, or congresswoman; a member of the Senate, as senator. A U.S. senator must be at least thirty years old, a resident of the state represented, and a U.S. citizen for at least nine years. A representative must be at least twenty-five years old, a resident of the state represented, and a U.S. citizen for at least seven years.

## WHERE

Most legislation may be introduced in either the House or Senate, except revenue measures, which must originate in the House. The bulk of Congress's legislative work takes place in committees. There are twenty-two standing committees in the House and sixteen in the Senate.

## TYPES OF LEGISLATION

*Congress is disorganized, overworked, and very little of what it does becomes law.* —Andy Rooney, *A Few Minutes with Andy Rooney*

Bills, joint resolutions, concurrent resolutions, and simple resolutions are the four types of U.S. legislation.

Bills are the usual form in which legislation is proposed. Although thousands of bills may be introduced during a congressional session, few are enacted into law, and most never receive serious consideration. If not enacted into law, both bills and resolutions die at the end of a Congress—the fate of about 95 percent of those introduced.

Basically the same as bills, joint resolutions usually pertain to more limited matters and are used for constitutional amendments and money measures. To become law, both bills and joint resolutions must pass both chambers and be approved by the president (except for constitutional amendments). If vetoed by the president, passage by a two-thirds majority of both houses of Congress is required to override the veto and enact the legislation. Copies of bills and joint resolutions are available in depository libraries (often on microfiche rather than hard copy, Y 1.4/[no.]: ) and sold both by the Government Printing Office and in microfiche collections from the Congressional Information Service. Single copies of current bills are often free from members of Congress.

Concurrent resolutions are used to express facts, opinions, principles, or purposes shared by the House and Senate. Examples include fixing the time for adjournment of Congress, appointing joint committees, or sending a congratulatory message to a foreign country. Concurrent resolutions must be passed by both chambers. If approved, concurrent resolutions are published in the *Statutes at Large*.

A simple resolution (or resolution) is considered only by the body in which it was introduced and is used largely for procedural matters and rules. During the 100th Congress, the House of Representatives amended its rules to allow members to refer to the Senate by its name instead of as "the other body." The change was accomplished through a House resolution.

| TYPES OF LEGISLATION | | |
|---|---|---|
| **Legislation** | **Final Result** | **Numbering** |
| Bill | Law | H.R. + number<br>S. + number |
| Joint Resolution | Law | H.J. Res + number<br>S.J. Res + number |
| Concurrent Resolution | Formal statement issued from both houses | H. Con. Res. + number<br>S. Con. Res. + number |
| Resolution | Formal statement from either house (but not both) | H. Res. + number<br>S. Res. + number |

## Public and Private Bills

Unlike public bills, which pertain to the general public or classes of citizens, private bills affect only specific individuals or organizations, not the public at large. Examples are claims against the government, land titles, and immigration or naturalization cases. When passed, public bills become public laws; private bills become private laws. Public and private laws are numbered in separate sequences and are printed in separate sections of the *Statutes at Large*.

| A SAMPLING OF PRIVATE LAWS | |
|---|---|
| 110-10 | Grant of citizenship to Tracey McFarlane |
| 100-15 | Compensation of injuries from a dog attack suffered by postal worker Marsha D. Christopher while delivering mail |
| 94-5 | Discharging the liability of postal clerk Raymond Monroe of Overland Park, Kansas, for a $5,445 loss resulting from his error in setting a postage meter |
| 96-77 | $625,000 to James Thornwell of Oakland, California, for permanent injuries inflicted in Army LSD experiments conducted without his knowledge |

## THE LEGISLATIVE PROCESS

The Congressional Research Service reports that few Americans clearly understand how Congress executes its legislative responsibilities.[1] Knowledge of the legislative process is essential to tracing legislation and identifying the documents generated at each step (see Figure 8.1). These documents deal with much more than Congress itself: They span the breadth of congressional legislation and oversight from apples to zoos, and are often the most current sources of information on a topic. The researcher who overlooks congressional publications may be missing definitive primary information.

The knowledgeable observer also recognizes that because of undocumented political activities interwoven at every stage, the formal legislative process offers only a glimpse of what really happens in Congress. Eric Redman, junior staffer for a senior senator, described his personal research on the Senate: "The books I read seemed to describe a wholly different institution from the one I worked in and had come to know."[2]

## Introduction and Preliminary Deliberations

*Congress in its committee rooms is Congress at work.*
—Woodrow Wilson

A bill may be introduced by one or more legislators (called sponsors and cosponsors). Preliminary deliberations occur in committee or subcommittee, where Congress's most important work is transacted. Congressional committees have been called the nerve endings of Congress: collecting information, sifting alternatives, refining legislation. To assess proposed legislation, a committee may hold hearings and may commission a study called a committee print. Hearings, committee prints, and reports are the three basic types of congressional committee publications.

In their oversight role, congressional committees are "watchdogs of the executive branch," overseeing the execution of laws and conducting investigations for fact-finding or to uncover incompetence or wrongdoing. Since the first congressional inquiry in 1792, a cavalcade of investigations has touched almost every conceivable subject, from "un-American activities" to Watergate and Iran-Contra. Committees also consider executive communications, presidential nominations and treaties, and execute the congressional budget process.

## FIGURE 8.1: How a Bill Becomes Law.

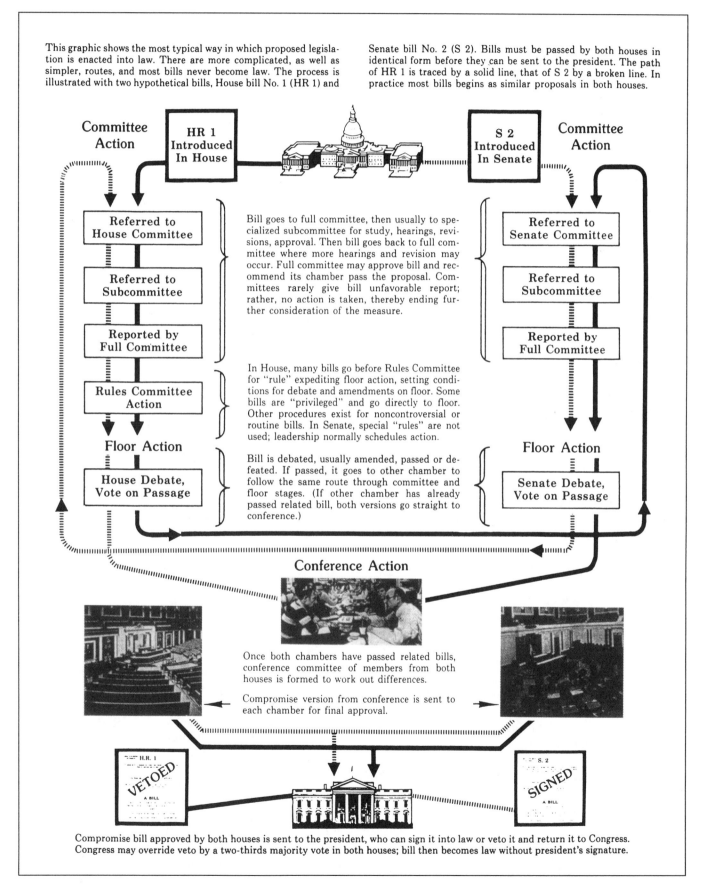

This graphic shows the most typical way in which proposed legislation is enacted into law. There are more complicated, as well as simpler, routes, and most bills never become law. The process is illustrated with two hypothetical bills, House bill No. 1 (HR 1) and Senate bill No. 2 (S 2). Bills must be passed by both houses in identical form before they can be sent to the president. The path of HR 1 is traced by a solid line, that of S 2 by a broken line. In practice most bills begins as similar proposals in both houses.

Committee Action

HR 1 Introduced In House

S 2 Introduced In Senate

Committee Action

Referred to House Committee

Referred to Subcommittee

Reported by Full Committee

Rules Committee Action

Floor Action

House Debate, Vote on Passage

Bill goes to full committee, then usually to specialized subcommittee for study, hearings, revisions, approval. Then bill goes back to full committee where more hearings and revision may occur. Full committee may approve bill and recommend its chamber pass the proposal. Committees rarely give bill unfavorable report; rather, no action is taken, thereby ending further consideration of the measure.

In House, many bills go before Rules Committee for "rule" expediting floor action, setting conditions for debate and amendments on floor. Some bills are "privileged" and go directly to floor. Other procedures exist for noncontroversial or routine bills. In Senate, special "rules" are not used; leadership normally schedules action.

Bill is debated, usually amended, passed or defeated. If passed, it goes to other chamber to follow the same route through committee and floor stages. (If other chamber has already passed related bill, both versions go straight to conference.)

Referred to Senate Committee

Referred to Subcommittee

Reported by Full Committee

Floor Action

Senate Debate, Vote on Passage

### Conference Action

Once both chambers have passed related bills, conference committee of members from both houses is formed to work out differences.

Compromise version from conference is sent to each chamber for final approval.

H.R. 1 VETOED A BILL

S. 2 SIGNED A BILL

Compromise bill approved by both houses is sent to the president, who can sign it into law or veto it and return it to Congress. Congress may override veto by a two-thirds majority vote in both houses; bill then becomes law without president's signature.

Reprinted from *CQ Guide to Current American Government*, Spring 1992, with permission of Congressional Quarterly, Inc.

---

| Sources of Information on Committee Membership* |
|---|

*CIS/Index* (by members' names)
*Congressional Staff Directory*
*Congressional Yellow Book*
*Congressional Index*
*Calendars of the House of Representatives* (conference committees)
*U.S. Code Congressional and Administrative News*
*Congressional Directory*
*Politics in America*

*Arranged with the most current first

## Hearings

You have probably seen snippets of congressional hearings on the evening news. A witness sits before a committee panel and delivers a statement or answers questions. The witness may be a government official, outside expert, scholar, special-interest group spokesperson, celebrity, sports figure, or concerned citizen. Witnesses' words are transcribed and compiled into hearings documents. The Senate has a system for numbering its hearings; the House does not. These publications provide a transcript of testimony, questions from committee members, discussion, and any supplementary material inserted into the record such as exhibits, related reports, statistics, letters, magazine articles. For example, the FBI's *The KGB and the Library Target, 1962 - Present,* which OCLC notes as available from NTIS, was inserted into the House hearings, *FBI Counterintelligence Visits to Libraries* (Y 4.J89/1: 100/123).

Hearing transcripts are not necessarily verbatim— both members and witnesses are granted editing privileges, "smoothing" the verbatim record to correct grammar and syntax. Off-the-record statements are not included, and testimony about confidential matters discussed in closed sessions is noted but not divulged.

There are numerous reasons a committee might hold hearings, including fact-finding and political motivations. A common objective is gathering background information for legislation or congressional oversight. Other motivations may be to garner public opinion, provide an outlet for citizen frustration, foster support for a bill, work toward compromise, or delay action on a bill. Executive hearings (also called executive sessions) are the opposite of public hearings—they are closed to the public and rarely printed.

Public release of hearing transcripts is at the committee's discretion. Although most transcripts are available to the public—directly from the committee, through depository libraries, or on microfiche sold by the Congressional Information Service—others are never mass produced for public distribution. The printing run for most hearings is small: about one-thousand copies, which are often quickly snapped up by journalists, lobby-

ists, and other eager readers. After that, requesters are referred to GPO or the Congressional Sales Office in Washington, DC, where copies can be purchased. Hearings are heavily used in depository libraries: In one study of academic library circulation statistics, they accounted for one-third of documents circulated.[3]

The *CIS Index to Unpublished U.S. Senate Committee Hearings* and *CIS Index to Unpublished U.S. House of Representatives Committee Hearings* identify "long-buried" hearings from the mid-1800s through the 1960s. CIS's *Congressional Masterfile 1* on CD-ROM includes citations to these unpublished House and Senate hearings. Full text of the unpublished hearings is sold on microfiche by the Congressional Information Service.

| Identifying Hearings Documents* |
|---|

LEGIS
*Congressional Index*
*CIS/Index*
*PAIS*
*Monthly Catalog*
*CIS U.S. Congressional Committee Hearings Index* (1833-1969)

*Arranged with the most current first

Each published hearing includes a table of contents identifying witnesses, but no index. The *Monthly Catalog* lists but does not abstract hearings. The keys to the contents of hearings are the *CIS/Index* and its electronic counterparts. The Congressional Information Service (CIS) sells full texts of each indexed hearing and expedites requesting copies from depository libraries or committees by listing SuDocs numbers and committee information in the CIS bibliographic citation. Focusing on aspects of hearings not covered by *CIS/Index*, the *Congressional Hearings Calendar*, published by Hein (biennial with quarterly updates), indexes hearings by date held, committee and subcommittee names, chairperson, and title.

## Committee Prints

A committee may commission a special research report for background information about proposed legislation, called a committee print. Prepared by committee research staffs, the Congressional Research Service, or outside consultants, committee prints frequently provide highly valuable situation reports, statistics, historical background, and legislative analyses.

Although committee prints are often published, they can be difficult to learn about or obtain. They have been characterized by the Congressional Information Service as "once the most private of public documents," because of their inconsistent distribution, limited printings, and frequent unavailability to the public. Some are not labeled "committee print" on their covers, and many are not identified by committee serial numbers. The

Senate has a numbering system for its general distribution committee prints; the House does not.

A key index for retrospective committee prints is the *CIS U.S. Congressional Committee Prints Index*, covering prints issued from the mid-1800s through 1969 (also included in CIS's *Congressional Masterfile 1* on CD-ROM). Most committee prints since 1970 can be identified using *CIS/Index* or the *Monthly Catalog*. Committee prints are sold by CIS on microfiche; some are available in depository library collections or from the congressional issuing committee. Officially, committee prints are not available free, but are for sale from GPO or the Congressional Sales Office.

---

**Identifying Committee Prints***

*Congressional Index*
*CIS/Index*
*PAIS*
*Monthly Catalog*
*CIS U.S. Congressional Committee Prints Index* (1833-1969)

---

*Arranged with the most current first

## Reporting from Committee

The committee has several options for the disposition of a bill. It may fail to report the bill, causing it to "die" in committee (colorfully described as "sleeping the sleep of death"). About 85 percent of bills die in committee. Occasionally, an unfavorable report may be issued, in which the committee recommends against the bill's passage. Most often, though, if a bill is "reported from committee" for consideration by the larger body, the report is favorable. The reported bill is sent to the chamber floor along with a written explanation called a report, which describes the bill, summarizes committee opinion, and discusses issues. The bill may remain exactly as originally introduced or it may have been amended or completely rewritten in committee ("marked up").

The committee report can be a meaty and important document, containing much more than the proposed legislation. It often includes detailed analysis, committee rationale, issues disclosed in hearings, cost projections, and sometimes minority or supplemental views of individual committee members. Changes are noted by typographical comparison, with amendments explained at the beginning of the report. The results of any committee roll-call votes on reporting the bill are also given (their inclusion is noted on the report's cover). Recorded committee votes are also noted in the annual index to *CQ Weekly Report* (usually appearing in January of the following year).

The report's immediate function is to inform the larger body so members can evaluate the bill, but later the judicial and executive branches may consult it to determine "legislative intent." The courts may refer to the committee report to help interpret the law, while executive agencies responsible for executing and enforcing laws may consult it when writing regulations emanating from the law.

Each committee report is designated as "H." for House or "S." for Senate, and sequentially numbered by Congress (for example, "102" for the 102nd Congress) followed by the individual report accession number:

H. Rpt. 102-342
S. Rpt. 102-16

Committee reports can be purchased from GPO or CIS (microfiche), and are sometimes free from the issuing committee. They are also available in depository libraries in paper or microfiche (Y 1.1/5: [Senate] and Y 1.1/8: [House]). They are noted in the *Monthly Catalog* and *CIS/Index*, which also abstracts their content. Issues of *U.S. Code Congressional and Administrative News* reprint portions of key committee and conference reports, both of which are also included in the serial set.

---

**Identifying Reports***

LEGIS
*Congressional Index*
*Calendars of the House of Representatives*
*Congressional Record Index*
*CIS/Index*
*Monthly Catalog*
*CIS Serial Set Index* (1789-1969)

---

*Arranged with the most current first

The reported bill is placed on a calendar and given a chronological calendar number. This number is for internal control and does not mean that the bill will be called in calendar number order. The weekly *Calendars of the House of Representatives* (Y 1.2/2: ) is a cumulative record of the status of reported bills from both the House and Senate.[4] Its frequency (weekly), price (free to depository libraries), and cumulative, detailed information combine to make the House *Calendars* a key resource for tracing the status of legislation in either chamber. Its title is plural because the House maintains five calendars for various types of legislation.[5] (The Senate has only one calendar for legislation reported from committee.) The weekly Monday issues include an index and a history of bills and resolutions section, which gives a complete chronological legislative history for all legislation reported out of committee in both the House and the Senate. Hearings and committee prints are omitted, however. The final issue of the first session is a permanent reference until the second-session final issue, which cumulates information on bills acted upon in both houses during the two-year Congress.

## Floor Action

### Debates and Amendments

*It doesn't work efficiently . . . It's a messy, untidy spectacle to watch. But I think it is vital to the nation.*
—Senator J. Bennett Honston,
describing Senate debate

A bill brought to the floor for consideration may be debated, with amendments proposed, debated, and voted upon. Floor action may take several days, although most legislation is not controversial enough to warrant more than half an hour's debate. Zwirn notes that although "the ideal functions of floor debate are to inform and persuade," most legislators have already made up their minds about the bill.[6] In these cases, debate often takes the form of prepared statements.

---

#### The Heat of Debate

The floors of Congress are safer than they used to be. Until the Civil War, it was common for legislators to be armed: During one House debate, thirty members drew pistols. Early floor action was punctuated by fistfights, spitting, toupee-snatchings, and pummelings. Such behavior has always been considered unparliamentary. Today, standards of unparliamentary behavior prescribe that profanity, obscenities, and disparaging remarks about colleagues be stricken from the *Congressional Record*. Only those watching the live proceedings from the galleries or on C-Span witness the full spectacle of floor action.

---

#### Identifying Dates of Floor Action*

LEGIS
*Congressional Record Index*
*CIS/Index* Legislative Histories annual
Journals of the House and Senate
Slip law
*Statutes at Large*

---

*Arranged with the most current first

### Voting

Votes are taken in several ways: some providing only a final tally, others documenting how individuals voted. A member has the option of voting for or against, or being recorded either as present but not voting, absent, or pairing. Pairing is done in coordination with another member who wants to vote the opposite way, so that the two votes cancel each other.

Unrecorded methods of voting that provide only an overall count are the voice vote, the division vote, and the unrecorded teller vote. In the untabulated voice vote, those in favor shout "Aye," followed by the shout of "No" by those opposed. This is sort of an "applause meter" vote, difficult to determine if results are close. In the division vote, those voting "Aye" and "No" are asked to stand (or raise hands) and be counted. The House also allows an unrecorded teller vote which tallies responses electronically. Results show totals for and against the measure but not how individuals voted.

| VOTING RECORDS* | |
|---|---|
| **Final Tallies** | **Roll-Call Votes** |
| LEGIS | *Congressional Record* |
| House and Senate Journals | *Congressional Roll Call* |
| *Congressional Record* | *Congressional Quarterly Weekly Report* |
| | *CQ Almanac* |
| | *Congressional Index* |

*Arranged with the most current first

Roll calls record how each member voted. These can be tallied electronically in the House (the Senate does not have an electric voting system), where voting is done at consoles by inserting a plastic card and pressing a button for "Aye" or "No." A system of lights, bells, and buzzers alert members to roll calls, quorum calls, and other events. Members have fifteen minutes to answer an electronic voting call. Roll-call votes are numbered consecutively throughout each session.

### Action in Second Chamber

After a bill passes it is conveyed to the other chamber, and thereafter may be called an "act," rather than a bill. Additional documentation is generated in the second chamber, as the act follows the same route as in the first house: (1) assignment to committee; (2) possible hearings, committee prints; (3) report from committee; and (4) floor action. The act may be accepted as is, rejected, amended, or ignored while the second chamber pursues its own version (called a companion, similar, identical, or related bill). Companion bills are often introduced simultaneously, with different bill numbers, in the two chambers. Often one is allowed to die while the other continues through legislative channels. The House *Calendars* note this in the "History of Bills and Resolutions" by recording that one bill was "laid on table," and the companion bill "passed in lieu."

### *Congressional Record* (X/a.Cong.-sess.: )

*For a long time I have argued, unsuccessfully, for permission to enter the* Congressional Record *in the fiction category of the National Book Award and Pulitzer prizes.*
—Joe Morehead,
library educator and documents specialist

On October 18, 1972, Hale Boggs of Louisiana stood to address the House of Representatives, praising his colleagues' legislative accomplishments in a thirty-four-page speech. Or so it seems from reading the *Congressional Record*. On the day of his speech Mr. Boggs had actually been dead for forty-eight hours, victim of a plane crash on October 16. Hale Boggs's speech has become a classic metaphor for the paradoxical character of the *Congressional Record*, a publication mistakenly assumed by many Americans to include a verbatim transcript of congressional debates.

Characterized over the years as an "oratorical shell game," a "comic book," a "vanity press," a "fraud," and a "sham," the *Congressional Record* has stood firm as an enigma of government documentation. Although mandated to be "substantially a verbatim" account of congressional proceedings, the *Record* is in fact legally altered every day. Under the guise of correcting transcription errors, some legislators change, omit, or add remarks, creating a fascinating, and often indistinguishable, blend of truth and fiction. The transformation begins when each participant in debates is given a transcript of his or her remarks as recorded by official reporters. These remarks are allowed to be edited—theoretically to correct grammar or mistakes, but actually in almost any way imaginable.

---

### The $2-Million Comma

The *Book of Lists* recounts the error of a congressional clerk who was supposed to transcribe the words "All foreign fruit-plants are free from duty," but wrote instead, "All foreign fruit, plants are free from duty." It cost the government $2 million before a new session of Congress could correct the error.

---

Members may change the meaning of their remarks: for example, changing "My conscience demands that I vote against this measure," to "My conscience demands that I vote for this measure." Legislators experiencing second thoughts may withdraw remarks actually spoken, excising a characterization of a distinguished colleague as a blathering idiot, for example. And finally, members can appear to be speaking when no speech was actually delivered. This technique, called inserting remarks, allowed Hale Boggs to file the text of his "speech" before leaving for vacation.

The weaknesses of such a system have not been overlooked. As an official record of the deliberations behind lawmaking, used by the courts and executive agencies to interpret legislative intent, the *Record* has its flaws. In 1984, three House members actually took the *Congressional Record* to court, contending that it was unconstitutionally depriving them of their First Amendment right to a truthful record of congressional debates. Both the U.S. District Court and the U.S. Court of Appeals for the District of Columbia dismissed the case, however.

> *There simply is no first amendment right to receive a verbatim transcript of the proceedings of Congress.*
> —Gregg v. Barrett,
> 771 F.2d 539 (D.C. Cir 1985)

To combat the *Record*'s documentary weaknesses, a major reform was enacted in 1978 when the beginning and end of inserted speeches were tagged with black bullets. While the Senate continues to use bullets, the House has incorporated a different typeface to identify statements not actually delivered on the floor. Although both chambers have tightened rules about inserting undelivered remarks, a senator can still avoid bullets by delivering as little as one sentence of the speech. The bullet is also omitted by special request, even if none of the text was actually uttered on the floor. Even in the wake of the 1978 reform, it was estimated that fully half of the words in the *Record* were never spoken.[7]

---

### No Bullets for VIP Legislators?

In *Running in Place,* James A. Miller notes Howard Baker's habit of inserting poems into the *Congressional Record* at the beginning of Monday sessions. Although Baker did not actually read the poems on the Senate floor, they were not designated with the customary bullets. Miller explains it this way: "Baker and Byrd never have dots next to their names because chief printing clerk Russell Walker believes they are too busy and too important to be saddled with dots. Maybe decades, centuries, or eons from now, historians will assume that Howard Baker stood before the Senate and recited poetry."[8]

---

The *Congressional Record* and its predecessors (the *Annals of Congress, Register of Debates,* and *Congressional Globe*) have been published since 1789. The *Record* is available from GPO on subscription in paper or microfiche, from CIS on microfiche, online from several vendors, and in many depository collections. Each senator may earmark fifty subscriptions of the *Record* to be mailed free to constituents; representatives are allotted thirty-four. Senators and representatives may also send reprints from the *Record* to constituents as free, franked mail. This explains much of the "down-home" content in the "Extensions of Remarks," discussed below.

There are four sections in the *Congressional Record,* each with a different character and veracity: the proceedings of (1) the House and (2) the Senate; (3) extensions of remarks; and (4) the Daily Digest. The House and Senate proceedings offer more than edited debates—they include records of votes and legislative actions, and full texts of many bills. The Extensions of Remarks are undelivered texts that members ask to have appended to the record. These range from speeches and book or magazine excerpts to poems, recipes, and songs, and must be examined to be appreciated (at a cost of about $500 a *Congressional Record* page, this hodgepodge of Americana might be deemed extravagant by some readers).

The Daily Digest, a summary of daily activities, is a concise factual record of committee and floor proceedings, including action on bills, votes, hearings, meetings, bill status, and, at week's end, the agenda for the following week. At the start of each month, the digest offers statistics on the number of days Congress has been in session, the number of pages in the *Congressional Record*, bills enacted into law, measures reported from committee, reports, quorum calls, votes taken, vetoed bills, and executive nominations. At session's end the Daily Digest is issued as a separate part of the *Congressional Record*, with a subject index and a table of bills enacted into public law.

The *Congressional Record Index* (X/a.Cong.-sess.:nos./ind.) provides biweekly access to the contents of daily *Records*, plus a "History of Bills and Resolutions" detailing the status of legislation acted upon during the previous two weeks, citing *Congressional Record* pages where action occurred. Legislative histories are chronicled from introduction through enactment (but omit hearings and committee prints). Unfortunately, the "History of Bills and Resolutions" is not cumulative until the bound end-of-session edition (see Figure 8.2, which compares the legislative history for H.R. 3570 as it appears in the *Congressional Record Index* and the House *Calendars*).

At year's end, a permanent, bound final *Congressional Record* for the entire annual session is published. It is this bound *Congressional Record*, not the daily issues, that is considered authoritative, used to interpret legislative intent. There is a separate index to the permanent, bound *Congressional Record* which includes Daily Digest volumes. In the bound annual edition, the Extensions of Remarks are inserted into the body of the text. The *Congressional Record* annual cumulations do not always reproduce every word that appeared in the daily issues.[9] Because of differences between the daily issues and the annual compilation, the bound index cannot be used with the daily issues, and vice versa.

Since 1983, the bound *Congressional Record* has been distributed to depositories only in microfiche, except for the Index and Daily Digest volumes, which are available in either paper or microfiche. A printing and funding backlog for the bound *Congressional Record* has dogged depository libraries for years. It wasn't until 1990 that all depositories received the 1985 annual *Congressional Record*, Index, and Daily Digest, and then only because full text of the *Record* on CD-ROM was tested as a depository electronic pilot project. (To say the pilot CD-ROM was not well liked would be putting it lightly. One librarian called it the worst mess she had ever seen: unmanageable, illogical, complicated, and user unfriendly.) Some depositories may be missing daily or final issues since 1986 because of funding and printing delays.[10] Printed volumes for 1985-1988 will be sent to regional depositories. Decisions about future formats of the *Congressional Record* are on hold until the CD-ROM test has been evaluated, but there have been rumblings about discontinuing the paper version altogether in favor of microfiche or CD-ROM versions. The full text of *Congressional Record* is available from several commercial vendors, including LEGI-SLATE, WESTLAW and Congressional Quarterly's Washington Alert database.

### Federal Index

The monthly *Federal Index* from National Standards Association indexes all information in the *Congressional Record* as well as in the *Federal Register* and *Weekly Compilation of Presidential Documents*. *Congressional Record Abstracts*, also from NSA, summarizes and cites all congressional actions, organized by subject, and is searchable online through DIALOG.

## Congressional Television

*I was impressed by the fact that it's a little more boring than you would actually think the House would be.*
—Citizen viewer

The House began live radio and television broadcasts of chamber proceedings in 1979, followed by a hesitant Senate seven years later, in 1986. Senate television coverage, initially proposed thirty-nine years earlier, was preceded by heated debate (one senator cautioned that floor proceedings were "not a pretty thing to watch") and a two-month pilot test.

C-Span broadcasts live, gavel-to-gavel coverage of House and Senate proceedings, while the major television networks show only vignettes. Video- and audiotapes of chamber proceedings may be purchased through the House or Senate clerks (videotapes are erased every two months and reused). Audio- and videotapes of chamber action are kept permanently in the Library of Congress, the National Archives, the Public Affairs Video Archives at Purdue University, and can be bought from C-Span. The existence of complete, unedited audio and video recordings of floor action creates dual records of congressional proceedings: the verbatim tapes and the printed *Congressional Record*, "a record of what we wish we would have said, if only we had said it right."[11]

## House and Senate *Journals*

Actually, the *Congressional Record* was never intended to be the official record of congressional proceedings. The official records are the annual legislative logs of each chamber, covering the first or second congressional session. As mandated by the Constitution, the House *Journal* (XJH) and Senate *Journal* (XJS) record minutes of daily sessions, plus a concise record of legislative action, including motions and votes. The journals do not include the text of floor debate. For tracing action in either

**FIGURE 8.2: Legislative History: House *Calendars* and *Congressional Record Index*.**

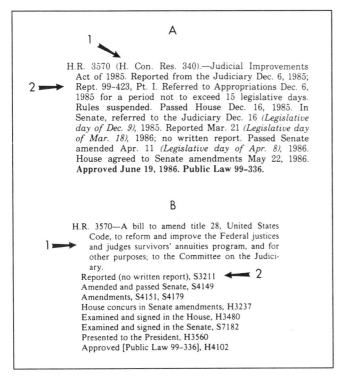

Compare the legislative history for H.R. 3570 from A, the House *Calendars* (October 14, 1986), and B, the *Congressional Record Index* (June 16–26, 1986). The *Calendars* identify (1) a related piece of legislation and (2) the House Report number, and dates when action occurred. The *Congressional Record Index* provides (1) a short title of the bill and (2) *Congressional Record* pages where action on the bill was documented, without dates.

chamber, the concise journals are more easily searched than the voluminous *Congressional Record Index*. Each has a "History of Bills and Resolutions" section arranged by bill number, with name, title, and subject indexes. CIS sells microfiche collections of the House and Senate journals since the first Congress in 1789. The *National State Papers of the United States, 1789-1817* (M. Glazier, publisher) reprints the Journals of the first fourteen Congresses.

## Bicameral Action

*A bronco is something that kicks and bucks, twists and turns, and very seldom goes in one direction. We have one of those things here in Washington—it's called the Congress.* —Gerald R. Ford

Before an act can be forwarded to the president, the House and Senate versions must be identical. When different versions emerge from the two bodies, one chamber may simply accept the other's amendments. If not, differences may be resolved through a conference committee. The conference committee, composed of representatives from each chamber, reconciles the two versions so that an identical bill can be approved by each.

The House *Calendars* include information on the status and membership of conference committees in two tables: "Bills in Conference" and "Bills Through Conference," which also notes presidential action and public law number, where appropriate.

The conference committee's report is called, logically, a conference report, containing the text of the compromise legislation and background information. It cannot be amended and must be accepted in its entirety by both the House and Senate, or the legislation dies. Approval of the conference report means approval of the compromise bill. Conference reports are numbered and designated in the same way as other committee reports. They are listed in the *Monthly Catalog* and indexed and abstracted in *CIS/Index*. Like other congressional reports, conference reports are available in depository libraries, from their issuing committee, in full text on microfiche from the Congressional Information Service, and frequently reprinted in *U.S. Code Congressional and Administrative News*.

### CIS/Index

*CIS/Index to Publications of the U.S. Congress* and its CD-ROM and online equivalents index and abstract the working papers of Congress since 1970. Widely respected as the most comprehensive index of congressional publications, *CIS/Index* covers committee reports, hearings, committee prints, and House and Senate documents (but not the *Congressional Record* ). Note that "Supplementary Material" in hearings is not individually indexed. For example, the FBI's *The KGB and the Library Target, 1962 - Present* was inserted on pages 244-78 in the House Committee on the Judiciary's 1989 *FBI Counterintelligence Visits to Libraries, Hearings* (Y 4.J89/1: 100/123). But because it was lumped amid supplementary material in the hearing it cannot be identified by title in *CIS/Index* or *Congressional Masterfile 2*.

The annual Legislative History volumes of *CIS/Index* include what has been lauded as "probably the most complete status table summary of an act's legislative history."[12] *CIS/Index* provides availability information for every congressional publication cited: All may be purchased on microfiche from the Congressional Information Service; many are sold by GPO or available for free use in depository libraries (the CIS abstract includes SuDocs and Item numbers); and some may be requested from issuing committees. *CIS/Index* is available in print, on CD-ROM (as the *Congressional Masterfile 2*), and also searchable online through DIALOG and SDC.

### Legislative Summaries

*Major Legislation of the Congress* (LC 14.18: ), from the Congressional Research Service, summarizes congressional issues and pending legislation. Arranged by subjects, MLC can be searched by title or bill and public law numbers. Issued irregularly, the final issue for a Congress is designed to serve as a permanent reference.

---

**Congressional Glossary**

**Congressional Edition** - the Serial Set
**Executive document (Ex. Doc.)**—a executive branch communication to Congress, printed as a House or Senate document (and in the Serial Set)
**Executive session**—a congressional committee meeting closed to the public and press; the Senate frequently dissolves into executive session when considering presidential nominations and treaties
**Legislative day**—the span of time before adjournment; the House tends to adjourn daily, but a Senate legislative day may last for several calendar days
**LOCIS (Library of Congress Information System)**—a legislative history database searchable at the Library of Congress
**Long title of a bill**—preamble
**Pamphlet print**—slip law
**Unanimous consent**—enactment of a bill without debate in both chambers, usually with a voice vote

---

## PRESIDENTIAL ACTION

The president has ten days (excluding Sundays) to either sign or veto a bill. In either case the president often issues a statement, which is published in the *Weekly Compilation of Presidential Documents* and usually incorporated in the Serial Set as a House or Senate document. When Congress is in session, the president may opt not to act, allowing the bill to automatically become law after ten days, or to die on his desk—called a "pocket veto"—if Congress adjourns before the ten-day time limit. About four out of every ten presidential vetoes are pocket vetoes.

---

**Presidential Action\***

**Text of statements:**
*Congressional Record*
*CQ Weekly Report*
*Weekly Compilation of Presidential Documents*
House and Senate Journals
*Public Papers of the Presidents*
Serial Set

**References to text:**
LEGIS
*Congressional Record Index*
House *Calendars*
*CIS/Index*
Slip law
*Monthly Catalog*
*Statutes at Large*
*CIS Serial Set Index* (through 1969)

---

*\*Arranged with the most current first*

If Congress takes no action on a vetoed bill, it dies. To override a veto requires two-thirds majority vote in both the House and Senate. This is rare: Overrides have occurred for only about seven percent of presidential vetoes since George Washington's administration. In the case of a pocket veto, the bill is dead, with no opportunity for an override. For a comprehensive list of presidential vetoes from the 1st to 94th Congress, consult *Presidential Vetoes, 1789-1976* (Y 1.3:V 2/789-976) and *Presidential Vetoes: 1977-1984* (Y 1.3:S.pub.99-5), covering through Ronald Reagan's first term. Arranged chronologically by Congress and bill number, with name and subject indexes, these tabulations of vetoes note any congressional action following the veto, and cite the *Congressional Record*. If a bill becomes law, the veto is part of its legislative history.

---

**Congressional Votes on Vetoes\***

LEGIS
*Congressional Record*
*Congressional Index*
*CQ Weekly Report*
*CQ Almanac*
*Congressional Roll Call*
House and Senate Journals

---

*\*Arranged with the most current first*

## LAW

Slip law → *Statutes at Large* → *U.S. Code*

A new law, or statute, is identified by a public or private law number, composed of the number of the Congress in which it passed, followed by a chronological number. It becomes effective on its enactment date unless a different effective date is specified in the law. Figure 8.3 shows the components of a public law in slip-law form (and in the *Statutes at Large*).

Individual public and private laws are published separately in pamphlet form as slip laws a few days after enactment, and are available in depository libraries (AE 2.110: ), free from the House or Senate Document Rooms while supplies last, and are sold by GPO. The public (but not private) slip laws include a citation to their future location in the *Statutes at Large,* marginal notes, citations to the *U.S. Code,* and a brief legislative history. Later, individual slip laws join other laws: first in the *Statutes at Large,* where they are bound in chronological order for each session of Congress, then later by subject arrangement in the *U.S. Code.*

### United States Statutes at Large (AE 2.111: )

Following each congressional session, slip laws are compiled chronologically in the *Statutes at Large,* which contains the complete text of all public and private laws

**FIGURE 8.3: 92 STAT. 199.**

 PUBLIC LAW 95-261—APR. 17, 1978     92 STAT. 199

Public Law 95-261
95th Congress

## An Act

To amend title 44, United States Code, to provide for the designation of libraries of accredited law schools as depository libraries of Government publications.

Apr. 17, 1978
[H.R. 8358]

*Be it enacted by the Senate and House of Representatives of the United States of America in Congress assembled,* That chapter 19 of title 44, United States Code, is amended by adding at the end thereof the following new section:

Depository libraries, designation.

 "**§ 1916. Designation of libraries of accredited law schools as depository libraries**

44 USC 1916.

"(a) Upon the request of any accredited law school, the Public Printer shall designate the library of such law school as a depository library. The Public Printer may not make such designation unless he determines that the library involved meets the requirements of this chapter, other than those requirements of the first undesignated paragraph of section 1909 of this title which relate to the location of such library.

"(b) For purposes of this section, the term 'accredited law school' means any law school which is accredited by a nationally recognized accrediting agency or association approved by the Commissioner of Education for such purpose or accredited by the highest appellate court of the State in which the law school is located.".

"Accredited law school."

. SEC. 2. The table of sections for chapter 19 of title 44, United States Code, is amended by adding at the end thereof the following new item:

"1916. Designation of libraries of accredited law schools as depository libraries."

SEC. 3. The amendments made by this Act shall take effect on October 1, 1978.

Effective date.
44 USC 1916 note.

**Approved April 17, 1978.**

---

**LEGISLATIVE HISTORY:**

HOUSE REPORT No. 95-650 (Comm. on House Administration).
SENATE REPORT No. 95-670 (Comm. on Rules and Administration).
CONGRESSIONAL RECORD:
    Vol. 123 (1977): Oct. 25, considered and passed House.
    Vol. 124 (1978): Mar. 6, considered and passed Senate, amended.
        Apr. 4, House agreed to Senate amendments.

The slip law in the *Statutes at Large* shows (1) Public Law number and date of enactment, (2) *Statutes* citation where the slip law would be reprinted, (3) the original bill from which this law emerged, (4) the *U.S. Code* citation where this amendment would be placed, (5) effective date (in this case, different from enactment date), (6) legislative history showing the House and Senate committees that considered the bill and their report numbers plus dates when action was documented in the *Congressional Record*, and (7) the text of the amendment.

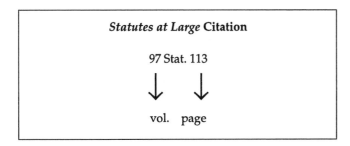

*Statutes at Large* **Citation**

97 Stat. 113

↓    ↓

vol.   page

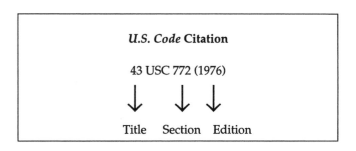

*U.S. Code* **Citation**

43 USC 772 (1976)

↓   ↓   ↓

Title   Section   Edition

and concurrent resolutions passed during the year. Like the slip laws it holds, the *Statutes at Large* gives citations to the *U.S. Code* plus a brief legislative history. The *Statutes* volumes are sometimes called session laws because they hold the laws enacted in a single congressional session, arranged chronologically by enactment date. The volumes also include reorganization plans, proposed and ratified Constitutional amendments, and presidential proclamations. Finding aids for *Statutes* volumes include a subject index and Laws Affected tables.

During each yearly session, laws are also compiled in the commercially published *U.S. Code Congressional and Administrative News,* a monthly which offers quicker access to laws than the official *Statutes at Large.* USCCAN provides the full text of every newly enacted public slip law, with the text of selected documents in its legislative history, such as committee and conference reports and statements in the *Congressional Record.* A legislative summary gives quick access to dates of consideration and passage and to report numbers, plus a subject index and list of acts by popular names. USCCAN updates *United States Code Annotated,* which annually codifies the same material.

## United States Code (Y 1.2/5: )

The official compilation of general and permanent laws in force, the *U.S. Code,* offers a subject arrangement of public laws under fifty "titles" or subject categories. It codifies the laws, consolidating similar topics, incorporating amendments, and deleting repealed text. Private or temporary laws are not included. The *Code* contains subject, name, and popular name indexes, along with conversion tables to translate *Statutes at Large,* Revised Statutes, Public Laws, Executive Orders, and Proclamations citations into *United States Code* citations. Unlike the *Statutes at Large,* the *U.S. Code* does not summarize legislative history, but cites the *Statutes,* where legislative histories are included. Figures 8.3 and 8.4 compare a public law as it appears in the *Statutes at Large* and the *U.S. Code.*

The *Code* is updated every six years, with annual cumulative supplements in the meantime. The annual supplements contain all changes to the general and permanent laws since the last edition, accessible through the same indexes and tables. The full text of the *U.S. Code* is available through several vendors, including LEGISLATE, LEXIS, and WESTLAW, and from GPO on CD-ROM.

## Annotated Codes

Unofficial, annotated codes note relevant court decisions after each code section, with citations to regulations in the CFR. These are *United States Code Annotated* (USCA) and *United States Code Service* (USCS). Both USCA and USCS offer speedier updating than the official version, plus simpler supplements using pocket parts (annual paperback addendums inserted into a slit in the back cover) and periodic pamphlet supplements. The two are differentiated by the fact that "the USCA purports to include all annotations, so that a single volume may encompass only two or three Code sections; while the USCS provides more selective but more detailed annotations, and also includes references to some law review articles."[13] Before being codified in USCA, session laws are compiled in the companion publication, *United States Code Congressional and Administrative News.* USCA is available in print and through WESTLAW.

A short pamphlet entitled *How to Find U.S. Statutes and U.S. Code Citations* (GS 4.102:St 2/980) shows how to quickly locate current and accurate *Statutes* and *U.S. Code* citations from typical references that require further citing. These include references to the Revised Statutes section; date, name, or number of the law; *Statutes* citation; or *Code* citation. Tables for translating *Statute* citations into *U.S. Code* citations are included in the USC, USCA, and USCS.

## LEGISLATIVE HISTORY

A law's legislative history comprises the documents generated during the legislative process. These documents permanently record legislative intent, Congress's rationale for enacting the law. Legislative histories are important for both judicial and administrative interpretation in executing the law.

Bill or public-law numbers are keys to reconstructing legislative history. When the bill or law number is unknown, it may be identified through subject, name, or other indexes provided in *Statutes at Large, U.S. Code,* the annotated codes, *CIS/Index,* or *Shepard's Acts and Cases by Popular Names.*

*Digest of Public General Bills and Resolutions* (LC 14.6: ) summarizes all public legislation, with greatest detail for those reported out of committee. The "bill

**FIGURE 8.4: 44 USC 1916.**

**§ 1912. Regional depositories; designation; functions; disposal of publications**

Not more than two depository libraries in each State and the Commonwealth of Puerto Rico may be designated as regional depositories, and shall receive from the Superintendent of Documents copies of all new and revised Government publications authorized for distribution to depository libraries. Designation of regional depository libraries may be made by a Senator or the Resident Commissioner from Puerto Rico within the areas served by them, after approval by the head of the library authority of the State or the Commonwealth of Puerto Rico, as the case may be, who shall first ascertain from the head of the library to be so designated that the library will, in addition to fulfilling the requirements for depository libraries, retain at least one copy of all Government publications either in printed or microfacsimile form (except those authorized to be discarded by the Superintendent of Documents); and within the region served will provide interlibrary loan, reference service, and assistance for depository libraries in the disposal of unwanted Government publications. The agreement to function as a regional depository library shall be transmitted to the Superintendent of Documents by the Senator or the Resident Commissioner from Puerto Rico when the designation is made.

The libraries designated as regional depositories may permit depository libraries, within the areas served by them, to dispose of Government publications which they have retained for five years after first offering them to other depository libraries within their area, then to other libraries.

(Pub. L. 90-620, Oct. 22, 1968, 82 Stat. 1286).

HISTORICAL AND REVISION NOTES

Based on 44 U.S. Code, 1964 ed., § 84a (Pub. L. 87-579, § 9, Aug. 9, 1962, 76 Stat. 355).

SECTION REFERRED TO IN OTHER SECTIONS

This section is referred to in section 1911 of this title.

**§ 1913. Appropriations for supplying depository libraries; restriction**

Appropriations available for the Office of Superintendent of Documents may not be used to supply depository libraries documents, books, or other printed matter not requested by them, and their requests shall be subject to approval by the Superintendent of Documents.

(Pub. L. 90-620, Oct. 22, 1968, 82 Stat. 1286.)

HISTORICAL AND REVISION NOTES

Based on 44 U.S. Code, 1964 ed., § 85a (June 27, 1956, ch. 453, § 101, 70 Stat. 369).

**§ 1914. Implementation of depository library program by Public Printer**

The Public Printer, with the approval of the Joint Committee on Printing, as provided by section 103 of this title, may use any measures he considers necessary for the economical and practical implementation of this chapter.

(Pub. L. 90-620, Oct. 22, 1968, 82 Stat. 1287.)

HISTORICAL AND REVISION NOTES

Based on 44 U.S. Code, 1964 ed., § 81c (Pub. L. 87-579, § 10, Aug. 9, 1962, 76 Stat. 356).

**§ 1915. Highest State appellate court libraries as depository libraries**

Upon the request of the highest appellate court of a State, the Public Printer is authorized to designate the library of that court as a depository library. The provisions of section 1911 of this title shall not apply to any library so designated.

(Added Pub. L. 92-368, § 1(a), Aug. 10, 1972, 86 Stat. 507.)

**§ 1916. Designation of libraries of accredited law schools as depository libraries**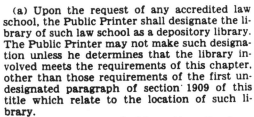

(a) Upon the request of any accredited law school, the Public Printer shall designate the library of such law school as a depository library. The Public Printer may not make such designation unless he determines that the library involved meets the requirements of this chapter, other than those requirements of the first undesignated paragraph of section 1909 of this title which relate to the location of such library.

(b) For purposes of this section, the term "accredited law school" means any law school which is accredited by a nationally recognized accrediting agency or association approved by the Commissioner of Education for such purpose or accredited by the highest appellate court of the State in which the law school is located.

(Added Pub. L. 95-261, § 1, Apr. 17, 1978, 92 Stat. 199.)

EFFECTIVE DATE

Section 3 of Pub. L. 95-261 provided that: "The amendments made by this Act [enacting this section] shall take effect on October 1, 1978."

TRANSFER OF FUNCTIONS

The functions of the Commissioner of Education were transferred to the Secretary of Education pursuant to section 3441(a)(1) of Title 20, Education.

CHAPTER 21—ARCHIVAL ADMINISTRATION

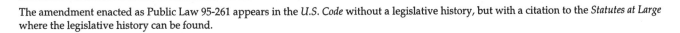

The amendment enacted as Public Law 95-261 appears in the *U.S. Code* without a legislative history, but with a citation to the *Statutes at Large* where the legislative history can be found.

digest" describes public bills and resolutions, noting committee and floor action, sponsors, identical bills, and short titles. This source is published in cumulative issues about five times during each session and can be searched by sponsors, subjects, bill titles, and identical bills. A cumulative final edition is meant for permanent retention at each session's end. The Library of Congress's SCORPIO database includes status information about federal legislation in an online version of the *Digest*. Unfortunately, the system is available to the public only on-site at the Library. Retrospective legislative histories may be traced with the help of Eugene Nabors' *Legislative Reference Checklist: The Key to Legislative Histories from 1789-1903* (Rothman).

| SOURCES FOR TRACING LEGISLATIVE HISTORY AND BILL STATUS | |
|---|---|
| **Title** | **Access Points** |
| LEGIS | Bill and law numbers, words and subjects |
| *U.S. Code Congressional and Administrative News* | Keywords in public law titles, subjects, public law numbers, and popular names |
| *CIS/Index; CIS/Annual* (Legislative Histories volume), CIS online, *Congressional Masterfile 1* on CD-ROM | Title, bill number (only those reported from committee), Report number, Document number, Senate hearing numbers, Senate print number, names of committee and subcommittee chairs, public law number, SuDocs number |
| Slip law | The text concludes with a concise legislative history that cites presidential remarks in the *Weekly Compilation of Presidential Documents* |
| House *Calendars* | Bill numbers in "History of Bills and Resolutions," law numbers in "Public Laws" and "Private Laws" sections, subjects and names in the index. Covers only bills reported from committee |
| *Congressional Record Index* | Subjects and names in the index; bill numbers in "History of Bills and Resolutions." Biweekly issues cover only bills acted upon during the previous two weeks; end-of-session issue is cumulative. |
| *Digest of Public General Bills and Resolutions* | Public law number, bill number, sponsor, subject, bill title, companion bills |
| *Statutes at Large* | Number of bill or law; reprints the slip law's concise legislative history with *Weekly Compilation* cites |
| *CQ Almanac* | Public law number |

## Computer Access

The House of Representatives operates LEGIS, a computerized system for tracking House and Senate legislation. The database contains status information such as bill and law numbers, sponsors, introduction date, content, committee referral, and action taken. All information is current through the previous day. LEGIS is available to the public through telephone or written inquiries. The LEGIS staff in the Office of Legislative Information will answer status questions by phone, or will send a computer printout (twenty cents a page, $5 minimum, as of 1992). Printout charges are waived if the constituent's request is channeled through a member of Congress.

The addresses of several commercial vendors offering congressional information databases, full text of congressional documents, and alert services are given in Appendix I. They are Congressional Quarterly's Washington Alert, Commerce Clearing House's Electronic Legislative Search System (ELSS), LEGI-SLATE, and Washington On-Line's Congressional Tracking System.

## Compiled Legislative Histories

The GAO Legislative History Collection is considered the most comprehensive set of legislative histories of public laws enacted since 1921. Although compiled by the General Accounting Office, the full-text collection is sold through Information on Demand, Inc. including initial and companion bills, amendments, hearings, committee reports, and discussion recorded in the *Congressional Record*.

The Congressional Information Service sells selected legislative histories for significant legislation. Offering overnight service for many laws, CIS Legislative Histories on Demand are available in paper or microfiche, the microfiche version being the more comprehensive of the two. A free list of the legislative histories available for sale may be requested from CIS.

## BIOGRAPHICAL SOURCES

*The first six months it's How did I get here? The next six months it's How did they get here?*
—Senator Robert Dole, Kansas

The *Congressional Directory* (Y 4.P 93/1:1/cong) presents short official biographies of House and Senate members, along with their committee memberships, terms of service, addresses, and telephone numbers. Also functioning as a general directory to the government similar to the *U.S. Government Manual*, the *Congressional Directory* lists government agency addresses and phone numbers, state and territorial governors, foreign diplomats, and news media personnel, plus maps of congressional districts. Brief biographical sketches are also given in *Congressional Index* and Congressional Quarterly's online Washington Alert.

For retrospective biographies, refer to the *Biographical Directory of the American Congress, 1774-1989* (Y 1.1/3:100-34) which includes members since the Continental Congress, plus executive branch officers since the administration of George Washington. *Women in Congress, 1917-1976* (Y 4.B47:W 84) provides biographies and photographs of women senators and representatives through 1976.

When a photo is needed, turn to the pocket-sized *Congressional Pictorial Directory* (Y 4.P 93/1:1 p/cong), which offers small black-and-white photographs of House and Senate members, officials of the Capitol, chaplains, the president, and vice president. Photos of members are also presented in the *Congressional Yellow Book* and *Congressional Staff Directory*.

Congressional staff far outnumber senators and representatives on Capitol Hill. Legions of anonymous staffers do much of Congress's daily, behind-the-scenes work. The *Congressional Directory* helps to identify some of these aides by listing administrative assistants and secretaries of members of Congress. Other sources are the *Congressional Staff Directory* published by Staff Directories Limited, and *Congressional Yellow Book* from the Washington Monitor.

## CONGRESSIONAL DISTRICTS

*One of a congressman's small pleasures is reading an angry letter from a person who says he'll never vote for you again—and then seeing from the address that the writer lives in another district.*
—Rep. Gilbert Gude, Maryland

To identify senators and representatives and their addresses and telephone numbers, use the *Congressional Directory*, the commercially published *Congressional Staff Directory, Congressional Yellow Book,* CQ's *Politics in America,* or call the Federal Information Center (check the "U.S. Government" section in your telephone book).

---

**Writing Senators and Representatives**

Senators: The Honorable Robert/Roberta Slone
U.S. Senate
The Capitol
Washington, DC 20510
Dear Senator Slone:

Representatives: The Honorable Robert/Roberta Slone
U.S. House of Representatives
The Capitol
Washington, DC 20515
Dear Mr./Ms. Slone:

---

Facts about congressional districts are available in the *Congressional Directory,* the *Congressional District Atlas,* and the *Congressional District Data Book,* a component of the Census of Population and Housing, as well as in numerous privately published reference sources. The *Atlas* (C 3.62/5: ) provides district maps and refers from county and incorporated municipality to the proper district. The *Data Book* gives population, housing, and election statistics for districts, and was PHC-80-4 of the 1980 Census of Population and Housing (*Population and Housing Census, 1980,* volume 4).

## THE LIBRARY OF CONGRESS

*The Library of Congress is the world's greatest single repository of human memory and thought.*
—James H. Billington,
Librarian of Congress

The Library of Congress, the world's largest library, began in 1800 as a parliamentary reference library. When the British burned Washington fourteen years later, British soldiers used the Library's books for kindling. After the collection was reduced to ashes, Thomas Jefferson offered his personal library of 6,700 volumes to rebuild it. Jefferson's library, considered one of the country's finest, was purchased by Congress for $23,950 in 1815 to seed the Library of Congress's rebirth. Originally open only to members of Congress and the Supreme Court, the library has evolved from a congressional library to a de facto national library, but retains reference and research service for the Congress as its primary mission.

## CONGRESSIONAL SUPPORT AGENCIES

Four agencies support Congress's legislative pursuits: the Congressional Budget Office (discussed in Chapter 10), the Congressional Research Service, General Accounting Office, and Office of Technology Assessment. The congressional support agencies provide background information and analysis to support congressional decision making, and produce many of their reports in-house. Because support-agency publications are created expressly for Congress, there "is no automatic presumption of public access to this material." Support-agency publications reach only a small segment of the public "who know enough to use their congressional office contacts" and, to a lesser extent, to use the depository library program.[14]

The General Accounting Office (GAO) is Congress's auditor, assisting in oversight of federal programs and agencies through audits, investigations, and evaluations. GAO's concise "blue cover" reports (GA 1.13: ) summarize GAO findings, and are free from GAO or available in depository libraries. They can be traced using the monthly *Reports and Testimony* (GA 1.16/3: ) and the *Annual Index: Reports Issued in FY [year]* (GA 1.16/3-2: ), both free from GAO.

The Office of Technology Assessment (OTA) is Congress's "think tank," helping Congress plan for the consequences of technology through objective analyses of technological issues. Summaries of most OTA reports, the *OTA Publications List* (Y 3.T 22/2:9/P 96/yr/no), and *OTA Annual Report* are free from the Office of Technology Assessment. Full OTA reports are usually sold through GPO or NTIS.

## Congressional Research Service: "The Information Arm of Congress"

> Go over to the Library of Congress. It has the most beautiful interior in the world. Also, the greatest and richest treasury of knowledge. Work those people to death. They like it. They will do research for you over the phone, and deliver books to you, marked right where you want them.
> —Advice to new members of Congress from Rep. Maury Maverick of Texas, 1949

The Congressional Research Service (CRS) serves Congress exclusively and "in many ways is the present day form of what the entire Library of Congress was when it began."[15] Without partisan bias, CRS staff research and analyze information for Congress, providing confidential services ranging from in-depth policy analyses, legal research, legislative histories, and speech writing to basic question-answering and provision of free materials requested by legislators for their constituents. Much CRS work remains unpublished and confidential, the property of the legislator who requested it.

Public access to CRS publications is the exception rather than the rule because most were produced solely for Congress and are off limits to the public. In fact, congressional offices are warned not to distribute lists of CRS products to their constituents. The quarterly *Guide to CRS Products* and its monthly *Update* are printed in-house and stamped "For Congressional Office Use Only." Other CRS products printed in-house with restricted availability are *CRS Reports for Congress* (in-depth studies of legislative issues), *Issue Briefs* (concise briefings on issues in the news), and *Info Packs* (packets of background information). University Publications of America publishes the full text of *Issue Briefs* on microfilm, and indexes to them: *Major Studies and Issue Briefs of the Congressional Research Service: 1916-1989 Cumulative Index*, continued by *Major Studies and Issue Briefs of the Congressional Research Service*.

Although CRS cannot respond directly to citizen requests, some CRS products are accessible through "back door sources." A legislator can sponsor a constituent request, forwarding materials from CRS to the requester. *CRS Review* (LC 14.19: ), one of a handful of CRS titles sold through GPO, highlights major congressional issues and announces some CRS products. The January issue previews the agenda for the upcoming congressional term.

CRS reports sometimes appear as committee prints or reports, House or Senate documents, or speeches printed in the *Congressional Record*. These may be identified using *Monthly Catalog*, *CIS/Index*, or the *Congressional Record Index*. Congressional committee documents are also available to libraries through DocEx, a source of publications not sent to depositories and not for sale. University Publications of America sells CRS reports on microfiche as a subscription service.

## THE SERIAL SET (Y 1.1/2: )

> It would be difficult, if not impossible, to do historical documents research without having the Serial Set available. —Jean L. Sears and Marilyn K. Moody, *Using Government Publications*

The Serial Set, America's longest-running series, is a serially numbered collection of congressional publications dating back to 1789. It includes House and Senate Reports and Documents. These are initially issued individually in the course of each Congress, and later compiled for posterity into the permanently bound and numbered Serial Set. The terms "reports" and "documents" are not generic, but refer to congressional materials officially designated in either category. Both types serve as important historical records. The Serial Set includes not only congressional publications, but also noncongressional materials ordered printed by Congress and earmarked as House or Senate Documents.

The House and Senate Reports in the Serial Set are the familiar congressional committee reports on proposed legislation, probably the most important publication group in the Serial Set. Traditionally confidential, Senate Executive Reports have been part of the Serial Set since the 97th Congress (1980). House and Senate Documents are a diverse assortment of publications printed by order of Congress. These noncongressional materials include executive-agency documents such as presidential messages to Congress, annual or special reports to Congress, special studies and background information, and annual reports of some nongovernment veterans and patriotic groups (for example, the Boy and Girl Scouts of America, the Daughters of the American Revolution, and the American Legion). Senate Treaty Documents have been included, as Senate Documents, in the Serial Set since the 96th Congress (1978-79). Like the Reports, Documents are sequentially numbered within each Congress:

H. Doc. 98-1
S. Doc. 99-578

The Serial Set offers a fascinating patchwork of primary American history documentation: diaries of the Lewis and Clark expeditions, background on the assassinations of Presidents Lincoln and Kennedy, accounts of the sinking of the *Titanic*, reports from the McCarthy-era House Committee on Un-American Activities, details of World War II rationing, and records of the inquiry against President Richard M. Nixon. It has been said of the Serial Set that "there has rarely been a published series of its depth and breath of coverage, and none in this country as long-lived."[16] The Serial Set offers 180 years of the following publication types:

- Congressional journals, administrative reports, directories, manuals, and other internal publications
- Congressional reports on public and private legislation
- Reports of congressional investigations
- Annual reports from federal executive agencies
- Executive agency survey, research, and statistical publications
- Annual and special reports from nongovernmental agencies[17]

The Serial Set's consecutive serial numbering—it began in 1817 during the 15th Congress—results in a roughly chronological arrangement of documents for each congressional session. Earlier congressional publications for the first fourteen Congresses and some later Congresses are included in the American State Papers, which have been numbered 01-038, and have also been reprinted as the *National State Papers of the United States, 1789-1817* (M. Glazier, publisher). Copies of Serial Set documents may be purchased from GPO, CIS, and Readex Microprint Corporation, or consulted in depository libraries.

### CIS U.S. Serial Set Index

Covering the American State Papers and the Serial Set from 1789 to 1969, the Congressional Information Service's *Serial Set Index* allows searching by subject, names of people and organizations, Report and Document numbers, and serial volume numbers. The set indexes House and Senate Reports and Documents (plus the House and Senate Journals through 1952). Omitted are hearings, debates, and committee prints. Since 1970, Serial Set coverage has been provided by *CIS/Index*, although serial numbers are omitted (CIS is considering adding them to the *CIS/Index* multiyear cumulations). Serial numbers for titles identified in *CIS/Index* may be identified using the *United States Congressional Serial Set Catalog: Numerical Lists and Schedule of Volumes*, discussed below. The Congressional Information Service's CD-ROM *Congressional Masterfile 1* streamlines historical searching between 1789 and 1969 by merging CIS indexes

to the *Serial Set*, published and unpublished committee hearings, committee prints, and Senate Executive Documents & Reports. Purchasers may select all or some indexes for inclusion on their CD-ROM.

| SERIAL SET | |
|---|---|
| **Inclusions** | **Omissions** |
| Senate Reports, House Reports, Senate Documents, House Documents (including the House and Senate Journals through 1952) | Hearings, debates, committee prints |

### Serial Set Catalog (GP 3.34: )

Through the 96th Congress (1980), the *Numerical Lists and Schedule of Volumes of the Documents and Reports of Congress* referred from Document and Report numbers to the Serial Set volume where the text of the Report or Document could be found (numerical lists), and from serial numbers to the contents of each Serial Set volume (schedule of volumes). It was searchable by report, document, and serial numbers only, not by subjects or names.

Next, for a short time, this finding aid was issued as a supplement to the *Monthly Catalog*, undergoing a name change to *Monthly Catalog United States Congressional Serial Set Supplement* (GP 3.7/2: ). Issued following each Congress, this source had author, title, subject, series/report number, bill number, GPO stock number, and title keyword indexes. Since the 98th Congress (1983-84) it has been called the *United States Congressional Serial Set Catalog: Numerical Lists and Schedule of Volumes* (GP 3.34: ). The *Serial Set Catalog* includes a numerical list of congressional Reports and Documents, a schedule of serial set volume contents, and *Monthly Catalog* report/document entries enhanced with serial set numbers added in bold type (the original *Monthly Catalog* listing of same report/document lacks serial numbers). It is indexed by author, title, subject, and series/report and bill numbers.

## LEGISLATIVE PROCEDURE

The Constitution allows each chamber to determine its own rules. These are published in manuals that describe precedents and practices as well as the organization and operation of Congress. Mastering the bevy of congressional rules has been compared to learning a foreign language. House rules are adopted anew every two years, while the Senate's standing rules are rarely changed. The House parliamentary procedures were originally prepared by Thomas Jefferson and are popularly known as the *House Manual* (Y 1.1/7: ). This source contains the texts of the Constitution and *Jefferson's Manual*, plus rules with notes and annotations showing their history and interpretation. The House also has its own *Ethics Manual* (Y 4.St 2/3:Et 3/1981).

The *Senate Manual* (Y 1.1/3: ) contains rules affecting the Senate, plus the Articles of the Confederation and the Constitution, a list of presidents pro tempore since the first Senate, presidential election electoral votes since 1789, and lists of senators and Supreme Court justices since 1789.

## ADDRESSES

C-Span Cable Public Affairs Network, 400 N. Capitol St., N.W., Suite 650, Washington, DC 20001; (202) 737-3220, FAX (202) 737-3323

Capitol Switchboard: Any committee or subcommittee office can be reached by calling (202) 224-3121

The Congressional Sales Office, North Capitol and G. Streets, N.W., Washington, DC 20402 is open for walk-in business between 8:00 A.M. and 4:00 P.M.

General Accounting Office, Box 6015, Gaithersburg, MD 20877; (202) 275-6241

GPO: To buy congressional publications provide title, committee, date, and payment; (202) 275-3030.

National Standards Association, Inc., 1200 Quince Orchard Blvd., Gaithersburg, MD 20878; (800) 638-8094, (301) 590-2300

Office of Legislative Information, House Annex Number 2, Room 696, Washington, DC 20515; (202) 225-1772

## FREEBIES

The following subject bibliographies are available free from U.S. Government Printing Office, Superintendent of Documents, Washington, DC 20402:

197.    United States Code
228.    Congressional Directory

### *CIS/Index*

From Congressional Information Service, 4520 East-West Highway, Bethesda, MD 20814-3389; (301) 654-1550.

*CIS/Index User Handbook* (30 pages) and "CIS/Index Search Guide" (1 page)

### Congress

Single free copies of all congressional publications except committee prints and hearings are often available from the issuing committee, or from the House or Senate Document Rooms:

Senate Document Room, B-04 Hart Senate Office Bldg., Washington, DC 20510; (202) 224-7860. Request limit is 12 items daily. Group by document type (laws, bills, reports, documents) in numerical order.

House Document Room, B-18, Annex #2, Washington, DC 20515; (202) 225-3456. Request limit is 6 items daily; include a self-addressed gummed label, no envelope or postage.

### Library of Congress

From Library of Congress, Central Services Division, Printing and Processing Section, Washington, DC 20540 (LC 1.12/2:P 96/yr):

*Library of Congress Publications in Print*

### OTA

From Office of Technology Assessment, U.S. Congress, Washington, DC 20510-8025; (202) 224-8996:

*OTA Annual Report*

*OTA Publications List* (Y 3.T 22/2:9/P 96/yr/no)

Summaries of most OTA reports

## REFERENCES

1. Congressional Research Service, *Congress and Mass Communication: An Institutional Perspective*, Prepared for Joint Committee on Congressional Operations. 93rd Congress, 2nd Session (Committee Print) (GPO, 1974), p. v. (Y 4.C76/7:C 73)

2. Eric Redman, *The Dance of Legislation* (New York: Simon & Schuster, 1973), p. 16.

3. Beth Postema and Terry L. Weech, "The Use of Government Publications: A Twelve-Year Perspective," *Government Publications Review* 18 (May/June 1991):223.

4. The House *Calendars* are printed daily for members of the House of Representatives, but only the Monday issue is available on subscription from GPO.

5. House calendars: the Union Calendar, for legislation dealing with revenues, money, or property; the House Calendar, for legislation not involving money; the Consent Calendar, for noncontroversial measures on either the Union or House calendars; the Private Calendar, for private bills; and the Discharge Calendar, for motions to discharge committees.

6. Jerrold Zwirn, *Congressional Publications: A Research Guide to Legislation, Budgets, and Treaties* (Littleton, CO: Libraries Unlimited, Inc., 1983), p. 83.

7. Bernard A. Block, "The Congressional Record," *Serials Review* 6 (January/March 1980): 27.

8. James A. Miller, *Running in Place: Inside the Senate* (New York: Simon & Schuster, 1986), p. 101.

9. Robert D. Stevens, "But Is the Record Complete? A Case of Censorship of the *Congressional Record*," *Government Publications Review* 9 (January-February 1982): 75-80.

10. "Status of Bound Congressional Record As of March 29, 1991," *Administrative Notes* 12 (April 15, 1991):15-16. (GP 3.16/3-2:12/09)

11. *Task Force on the Congressional Record, Prepared for the Committee on House Administration of the U.S. House of Representatives, August 1990.* (Committee Print) GPO, 1990. p. 2 (Y 4.H 81/3:C 76/3)

12. Morris L. Cohen and Robert C. Berring, *How to Find the Law*, 8th ed. (St. Paul, MN: West Publishing Co., 1983), p. 315.

13. *United States Law: Finding Statutory Material* (CRS Report for Congress, 90-110 A). Washington, DC: CRS, 1990. p. CRS-3.

14. Office of Technology Assessment, *Public Access to Congressional Support Agency Information in the Technological Age: Case Studies*, by Stephen E. Frantzich. NTIS, 1989. PB89-225221 *CIS/Index* microfiche no. 89-J952-25, p. v.

15. Library of Congress, *Guide to the Library of Congress* (LC, 1982), p. 37. (LC 1.6/4:L 61/2)

16. Congressional Information Service, *User Handbook: CIS U.S. Serial Set Index* (Washington, DC: CIS, Inc., 1980), pp. 2, 10.

17. Congression Information Service, p. 10.

## FURTHER READING

Byrd, Robert C. "Reporters of Debates and the *Congressional Record*," in *The Senate 1789-1989: Addresses on the History of the United States Senate.* Vol. 2 (Bicentennial Edition, Senate Doc. 100-20) GPO, 1991. (Y 1.1/3:100-20/v. 2)

A detailed history of the *Congressional Record* , with rationale for editing of members' remarks.

Congressional Quarterly. *Congress A to Z: CQ's Ready Reference Encyclopedia.* Washington, DC: Congressional Quarterly, Inc., 1988.

This companion to *CQ's Guide to Congress* is a dictionary of congressional lingo.

————. *Congressional Quarterly's Guide to Congress.* 4th ed. Washington, DC: Congressional Quarterly, Inc., 1991.

An overview of the history, development, and operations of Congress.

————. *How Congress Works.* 2nd ed. Washington, DC: Congressional Quarterly, Inc., 1991.

A detailed guide to the operations of Congress.

Dole, Robert J. *Historical Almanac of the United States Senate: A Series of "Bicentennial Minutes" Presented to the Senate during the One Hundredth Congress.* (Senate Document 100-35) GPO, 1989. (Y 1.1/3:100-35)

Vignettes of Senate history since 1787, ranging from scandalous to inspirational.

Elliot, Jeffrey M. and Ali R. Sheikh. *The Presidential–Congressional Political Dictionary.* Denver, CO: ABC-Clio Information Services, 1984.

A source of concise, clear definitions and explanations of key congressional concepts and terms.

Hutson, James H. *To Make All Laws: The Congress of the United States, 1789-1989.* Washington, DC: Library of Congress, 1989. (LC 1.2:C76/11)

This catalog accompanying the bicentennial exhibit of the same name provides a history of Congress and its pursuits.

Johnson, Nancy P. *Sources of Compiled Legislative Histories: A Bibliography of Government Documents, Periodical Articles, and Books, 1st Congress - 99th Congress* (AALL Publ. Series No. 14) Littleton, CO: F. B. Rothman, 1988- . (loose-leaf for updating)

A guide to locating previously compiled legislative histories in print and online, with listings by subjects and by public law number, plus a bibliography of documents, finding aids, and compiling techniques.

Library of Congress. *For Congress and the Nation: A Chronological History of the Library of Congress* by John Y. Cole. GPO, 1977. (LC 1.2:C 76/6)

A history of the Library of Congress and review of its current role in the legislative branch.

Maier, Elaine C. *How to Prepare a Legal Citation.* Woodbury, NY: Barron's Educational Series, Inc., 1986.

A guide to proper citing according to the *Uniform System of Citation,* including sections on citing laws and legislative histories.

McCallum, S. V. "Legal Research for Non-Law Librarians." *Government Publications Review* 6 (1979): 263-73.

A detailed overview of legal publications from Congress and the courts.

Murphy, Cynthia E. "A Comparison of Manual and Online Searching of Government Document Indexes." *Government Information Quarterly* 2 (May 1985):169-81.

Print and online versions of *CIS/Index* are compared for search costs, recall, precision, overlap, and effort.

"Private Bills and Private Laws: A Guide to the Legislative Process," in Joe Morehead, *Essays on Public Documents and Government Policies.* New York: The Haworth Press, 1986.

A description of private legislation and related information sources.

Senate. Republican Policy Committee. *Glossary of Senate Terms: A Guide for TV.* GPO, 1986. (Y 1.3:S.prt. 99-157)

Although only nineteen pages long, this is a useful guide to common congressional parlance.

Simpson, Andrew L. *The Library of Congress.* (Know Your Government). New York: Chelsea House Publishers, 1989.

Although this looks like a kid's book, it is packed with information about LC's history and current status.

Springer, Michelle M. "The *Congressional Record:* 'Substantially a Verbatim Report?'" *Government Publications Review* 13 (May-June 1986): 371-78.

A history of the editing of the *Congressional Record.*

Willet, Edward F. *How Our Laws Are Made.* (Bicentennial ed., 1789-1989) (House Doc. 101-139) GPO, 1990. (Y 1.1/7:101-139)

The standard citizen's guide to the legislative process, often available free from members of Congress.

The following titles are excellent introductions to legal research and materials:

Coco, Al. *Finding the Law: A Workbook on Legal Research for Laypersons.* Prepared for the Bureau of Land Management, Denver Service Center. GPO, 1982. (I 53.2:L 41)

Cohen, Morris L., Robert C. Berring, and Kent C. Olson. *How to Find the Law.* 9th ed. St. Paul, MN: West Publishing Co., 1989.

Jacobstein, J. Myron, and Roy M. Mersky. *Fundamentals of Legal Research.* 5th ed. Westbury, NY: The Foundation Press, Inc., 1990. (Abridged version is *Legal Research Illustrated*)

McCallum, S. V. "Legal Research for Non-Law Librarians." *Government Publications Review* 6 (1979): 263-73.

## EXERCISES

1. Smokey Bear, the forest fire prevention symbol, was created by the Forest Service in the 1950s. Government-produced, and thus in the public domain, Smokey was ineligible for trademark protection so Congress outlawed unauthorized use of Smokey's name or image. Identify this 1952 law and any background materials in its legislative history.

2. In the late 1980s, the Office of Management and Budget initiated a controversial push to privatize the National Technical Information Service. A self-sustaining agency, NTIS had paid its own way since its inception. Witnesses in congressional hearings warned that privatization would be costly and risky, characterizing the proposal as "a triumph of ideology over common sense." Identify one hearing on the topic.

3. In 1912, a Senate special subcommittee investigated the sinking of the *Titanic*, which had killed many prominent Americans. Although no legislation was pending, the investigation was authorized by a Senate resolution, broadening the precedent for Senate investigations beyond immediate law-making. Identify the committee's report. Helpful tip: 1912 was the 62nd Congress.

4. Have there been recent attempts to improve the accuracy of the *Congressional Record*?

5. As part of its Library Awareness Program, the FBI asked librarians to alert them to Soviets seeking "sensitive but unclassified" information in libraries. After a flurry of unfavorable media attention, congressional hearings explored possible conflicts between FBI counterintelligence visits to libraries and individual privacy rights. Identify the hearing, which took place in the late 1980s.

6. In 1925, Congress appropriated $10,000 to dispose of old patent models. A fire had already destroyed one-third of the model collection, leaving 150,000 survivors, each no larger than 12 square inches. Some were transferred to the Smithsonian Institution or returned to their inventors, while thousands were auctioned off. Identify any congressional document pertaining to the disposal of the models. *Helpful tip*: 1925 was the 68th congress.

7. The Federal Information Resources Management Act of 1989 (S. 1742) was introduced to reauthorize the Paperwork Reduction Act. What was its status at the close of the 101st Congress?

8. Locate the legal basis that enables senators and representatives to send free *Congressional Record* subscriptions to constituents.

# CHAPTER 9
# Regulations

*Regulations are the engines of federal law.*
—Steven L. Katz, Attorney

## WHAT

Administrative regulations and adjudications, along with statutes and judicial opinions, are our nation's three primary sources of law. Regulations, sometimes called quasi-legislation or bureaucratic law, are authorized by law or by presidential executive order to be written by executive agencies. Like laws, they are binding upon those to whom they apply.

## HOW

Congress delegates to executive agencies and independent administrative agencies the power to issue regulations and adjudicate disputes. These agencies are sometimes called "the fourth branch" of government because they exhibit characteristics of all three branches of government.

## WHY

Although it may be easy to imagine federal bureaucrats maniacally pounding out regulations in windowless rooms, regulations are not created by whim but by law. They result from power granted to the president by the Constitution or power delegated by Congress.

## REGULATIONS AND AMERICAN LIFE

According to a 1982 Gallup poll commissioned by the League of Women Voters, Americans are a little fuzzy on the details of the regulatory process.[1] The poll results, which a League official characterized as "appalling," showed many Americans to be unclear about what regulations are, where they come from, and why they are promulgated. Half could not name a single regulation affecting their lives, and even more were unable to differentiate between regulations and laws. Only one in five Americans interviewed knew that executive agencies write regulations. Four out of five admitted they didn't know where regulations originated, or guessed incorrectly that they emanated from Congress or the courts.

Government regulations receive a lot of negative press. Read an article about regulations in a popular magazine and you'll probably find complaints about "bureaucratic red tape," "strangulation by regulation," and other depictions of regulatory villainy. Most people don't realize the extent to which regulations affect their daily lives. The care tags on your clothes, nutritional labeling on food packages, overhead storage on airplanes, the purity of the air, and the composition of many prepared foods—all are government-regulated. An understanding of the purpose and use of regulations leads to several conclusions: They have daily impact on our lives; they are not written to torture us (although that is sometimes a result); and citizens have a say in regulation writing.

---

**Nature's Buffet: Defects Allowable in Food[2]**

CHOCOLATE: up to 60 microscopic insect fragments per 100 grams or 90 insect fragments in one sample; or one rodent hair per 100 grams

CANNED CITRUS JUICE: fewer than 5 fly eggs or one maggot per 250 ml

BAY LEAVES: up to 5 percent moldy or insect-infested pieces or 1 mg mammalian excreta per pound

FROZEN BROCCOLI: fewer than 60 aphids, thrips, and/or mites per 100 grams

FISH: less than one-quarter of their surface with a definite odor of decomposition in less than 5 percent of the sample

---

Rules and regulations (the terms are synonymous) are a means of implementing laws enacted by Congress.

If every law spelled out the particulars of administering it, the statute books would overflow their shelves and Congress would be stalled in a quagmire of details (evidenced by the fact that the *Code of Federal Regulations* takes about three times the shelf space as the *U.S. Code*). Instead, lawmakers write laws as broad policy statements, with the expectation that specifics will be determined later by the executive agencies administering the laws day-to-day.

Laws often specify which agencies are required to write rules to carry out legislation. Look for language like:

The Department of _____ shall. . .
The Commissioner shall prescribe regulations which. . .

In this way Congress "delegates" authority to the executive administrative agencies to implement legislation by writing rules itemizing procedures and details. For this reason, regulations are sometimes described as "delegated legislation." Seen in this light, regulations are an extension of legislation in a logical evolution from general to specific.

The question of who controls the regulatory agencies is a long-standing constitutional debate. Is it the president, who heads the executive branch, or Congress, empowered to oversee the executive branch?[3] Since the 1980s, the Office of Management and Budget has carried out presidential oversight of rulemaking by approving regulations before their publication in the *Federal Register*. OMB's Office of Information and Regulatory Affairs (OIRA) is the hub of this activity, overseeing the government's regulatory, paperwork, and information-management activities. OMB's annual *Regulatory Program of the United States Government* (PrEx 2.30: ) overviews and describes agency regulatory programs. The "Unified Agenda of Federal Regulations," published in the *Federal Register* each April and October, projects regulatory activity in specific regulatory agencies.

## The *Federal Register* (AE 2.106: )

*While the* Federal Register *stands as the official organ of the government, it is a publication with limited circulation read by few ordinary citizens.*
—Congressional Office of
Technology Assessment

It all started with a merry mix-up. In July and August 1933, President Franklin D. Roosevelt issued a complicated series of six executive orders on petroleum quotas. The real problem began when a seventh executive order revoked the first, but chaotic recordkeeping cloaked the mistake. When the president's first petroleum executive order (which no longer existed) prompted a refining company to sue the government, the case

traveled all the way to the Supreme Court. There, Chief Justice Charles Evans Hughes realized the suit was predicated on a defunct executive order and issued a scathing denunciation of the plaintiffs, defendants, and lower courts for ignorance of the law, and the president and the secretary of the interior for failing to publicize their regulations.

In response, Congress passed the Federal Register Act, mandating a daily publication to document presidential proclamations and executive orders and agency regulations. The genesis of the *Federal Register* (FR) was Congress's stipulation that government regulations have no legal force until made public by publication. For the first time, Americans had a practical way to learn about regulations affecting them. Supplemental legislation called for codifying the rules in the *Code of Federal Regulations*. The primary function of the resultant *Federal Register/ Code of Federal Regulations* system is to inform the public about rules set by federal agencies.

Although "it graces few of America's coffee tables," the *Federal Register* is a major vehicle for regulating and governing the United States.[4] Several categories of documents must be announced in the *Federal Register* before they can be legally binding: presidential proclamations and executive orders, rules and regulations, proposed rules, notices, and Sunshine Act meetings.

### Proposed Rules

The rationale goes like this: Since regulations affect all of us, the public should have a say in regulation writing. After all, regulations are quasi-legislation, and citizen representation in the legislative process is an American tradition. Public participation broadens regulators' perspectives, ensures protection of citizen concerns, and balances the self-interested input of regulated industries. To achieve this, the law requires that agencies consider public input when writing regulations. This input occurs at the "proposed" rulemaking stage, when agencies must announce regulations being drafted and allow public comment on them. The vehicle for soliciting public input is the *Federal Register*.

In actuality, almost half of all regulations go on the books with no public comments at all.[5] The sheer volume of regulations and the vocabulary of "regulatory gobble-dygook" and legalese are hurdles to citizen understanding of both proposed and final rules. As a congressional report explained, "People cannot be expected to understand that which is incomprehensible."[6] Not only are regulations unclear to the general public, they can be unintelligible even to the people who wrote them. At a "plain-English" workshop, bureaucrats told to simplify their regulations often could not decipher what they had originally written.

The "Proposed Rules" section of the *Federal Register*
announces early or final drafts of rules with names,
addresses, and telephone numbers of contact people. A
deadline for written comments is announced, usually at
least two months hence. There are even rules governing
public comments: The *Federal Register* itemizes agency
guidelines for submitting comments. These should be
followed because, "the agencies' directions are a part of
a plan for analyzing a large volume of comments. If the
agency has to search for the point you are making, there
is the potential for missing or misinterpreting it."[7]

What happens to the public comments an agency
receives? The agency does more than blindly tally comments for various points of view: It must address all
issues raised in the comments. Public input does have
impact. The 1981 "catsup-as-a-vegetable" regulation is a
memorable example. The Department of Agriculture
made headlines by suggesting that catsup qualify as a
required vegetable component of school lunches. The
public furor that ensued convinced the USDA to recall
their proposed rules, and catsup reverted to its former
status as a condiment.

## Final Rules

*Regulation is the substitution of error for chance.*
    —Fred J. Emery,
    former director of the
    Office of the Federal Register

Proposed rules often evolve into final rules, ready
to take effect. The "Supplementary Information" section
of the final rule's preamble describes public comments
received during proposed rulemaking and the agency's
response to them. The rule's effective date, often different from its publication date, is also noted in the preamble. Since final rules published in the *Federal Register*
have the force of law, the effective date is when all
affected parties will be required to comply. At that point,
it will be too late for changes.

The *United States Code Congressional and Administrative News* reprints significant regulations from the *Federal
Register*, and *United States Law Week* digests administra-
tive-agency rulings.

Like the Government Printing Office, the Office of
the Federal Register has no control over the contents of
the material it prints. The OFR does require that each
agency begin its text with a preamble written in plain
English, concisely describing the regulation (see Figure
9.1). The "Action" section of the preamble identifies
whether a regulation is a final or proposed rule.

### *Federal Register* Citation

Regulations published in the *Federal Register* are
cited by volume and page, with the date sometimes
added in parentheses.

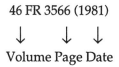

46 FR 3566 (1981)

Volume  Page  Date

### *Federal Register* Finding Aids

Commercial vendors such as Congressional Quarterly (Washington Alert database), DIALOG, LEGI-
SLATE, LEXIS, and WESTLAW include the full text of
the *Federal Register*. The *U.S. Code Service* (USCS) includes
the texts of pertinent sections of the CFR. Other vendors
sell the *Federal Register* in various formats; for example,
the Congressional Information Service (microfiche) and
Counterpoint Publishing (CD-ROM).

The cumulative, monthly *Federal Register Index* (AE
2.106:vol./no./ind.) is included with each *Federal Register* subscription and also published separately. It is helpful for tracking regulations, but not overwhelmingly so,
because of its broad indexing. The index is actually a
consolidation of *Federal Register* tables of contents, supplemented with general subject headings. The result is an
index of issuing agencies and very general topics. Terms
used in the *Federal Register* and CFR indexes are based on
the "Federal Register Thesaurus of Indexing Terms," free
from the Office of the Federal Register, and last published
in the *Federal Register* on September 18, 1990 (55 FR 38444).
The *Federal Register Index* also lists Privacy Act publications, a table of pages and dates referring from page
numbers to *Federal Register* issues, and a quarterly Guide
to Freedom of Information Indexes.

| LIFE CYCLE OF A REGULATION | |
|---|---|
| **Stage** | **Published in** |
| Proposed rule | *Federal Register* |
| Final rule | *Federal Register* |
| Codified final rules | *Code of Federal Regulations* |

The *CIS Federal Register Index* (FRI) is a comprehensive weekly index to daily *Federal Register* issues, which

**FIGURE 9.1: Preamble Requirements.**

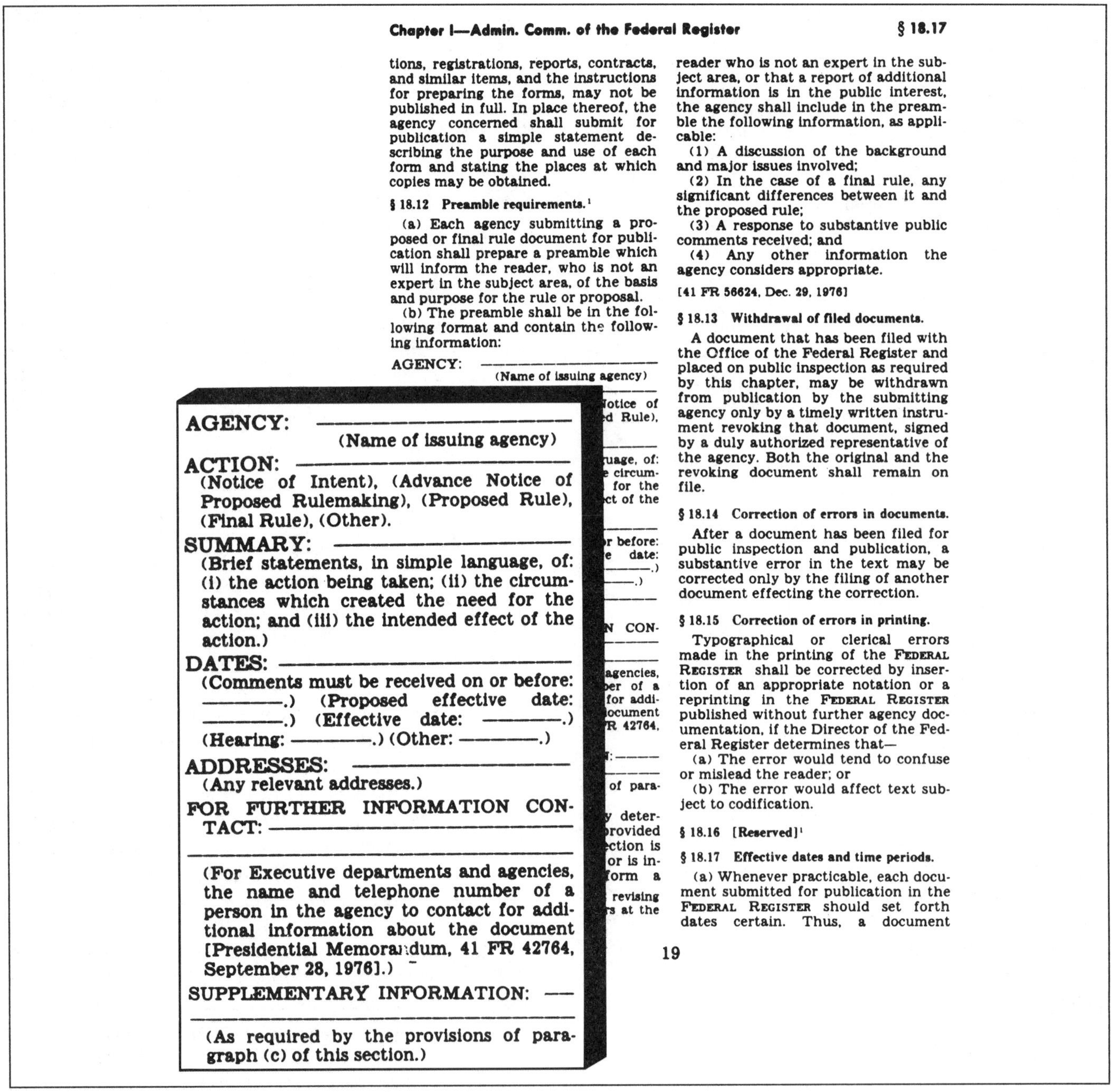

**Chapter I—Admin. Comm. of the Federal Register** **§ 18.17**

tions, registrations, reports, contracts, and similar items, and the instructions for preparing the forms, may not be published in full. In place thereof, the agency concerned shall submit for publication a simple statement describing the purpose and use of each form and stating the places at which copies may be obtained.

**§ 18.12 Preamble requirements.**[1]

(a) Each agency submitting a proposed or final rule document for publication shall prepare a preamble which will inform the reader, who is not an expert in the subject area, of the basis and purpose for the rule or proposal.

(b) The preamble shall be in the following format and contain the following information:

AGENCY: ————————
(Name of issuing agency)

**AGENCY:** ————————
(Name of issuing agency)

**ACTION:** ————————
(Notice of Intent), (Advance Notice of Proposed Rulemaking), (Proposed Rule), (Final Rule), (Other).

**SUMMARY:** ————————
(Brief statements, in simple language, of: (i) the action being taken; (ii) the circumstances which created the need for the action; and (iii) the intended effect of the action.)

**DATES:** ————————
(Comments must be received on or before: ————.) (Proposed effective date: ————.) (Effective date: ————.) (Hearing: ————.) (Other: ————.)

**ADDRESSES:** ————————
(Any relevant addresses.)

**FOR FURTHER INFORMATION CONTACT:** ————————

(For Executive departments and agencies, the name and telephone number of a person in the agency to contact for additional information about the document [Presidential Memorandum, 41 FR 42764, September 28, 1976].)

**SUPPLEMENTARY INFORMATION:** ——

(As required by the provisions of paragraph (c) of this section.)

reader who is not an expert in the subject area, or that a report of additional information is in the public interest, the agency shall include in the preamble the following information, as applicable:

(1) A discussion of the background and major issues involved;

(2) In the case of a final rule, any significant differences between it and the proposed rule;

(3) A response to substantive public comments received; and

(4) Any other information the agency considers appropriate.

[41 FR 56624, Dec. 29, 1976]

**§ 18.13 Withdrawal of filed documents.**

A document that has been filed with the Office of the Federal Register and placed on public inspection as required by this chapter, may be withdrawn from publication by the submitting agency only by a timely written instrument revoking that document, signed by a duly authorized representative of the agency. Both the original and the revoking document shall remain on file.

**§ 18.14 Correction of errors in documents.**

After a document has been filed for public inspection and publication, a substantive error in the text may be corrected only by the filing of another document effecting the correction.

**§ 18.15 Correction of errors in printing.**

Typographical or clerical errors made in the printing of the FEDERAL REGISTER shall be corrected by insertion of an appropriate notation or a reprinting in the FEDERAL REGISTER published without further agency documentation, if the Director of the Federal Register determines that—

(a) The error would tend to confuse or mislead the reader; or

(b) The error would affect text subject to codification.

**§ 18.16 [Reserved]**[1]

**§ 18.17 Effective dates and time periods.**

(a) Whenever practicable, each document submitted for publication in the FEDERAL REGISTER should set forth dates certain. Thus, a document

19

*Federal Register* regulations (1 CFR 18.12) require agencies to include a preamble in plain English to explain proposed and final rules. Source: *The Federal Register: What It Is and How to Use It*, 1978 ed.

CIS calls a "master guide to the *Federal Register*." FRI may be searched by subjects and names, CFR section numbers, agency docket numbers, and by effective dates and comment deadline dates to identify the subject of the rule and action taken, issuing agency, *Federal Register* issue and page, and type of rulemaking involved (proposed rule, final rule, etc.). A "Calendar of Effective Dates and Comment Deadlines" announces effective dates, along with deadlines for comments, hearings, and replies.

LEGI-SLATE not only provides the full text of the *Federal Register* online, but also indexes the contents of FR. The database is searchable by publication date, issuing agency, docket number, deadline dates, CFR parts affected, FR page, enabling law, and keywords.

The *Federal Index*, from National Standards Association, is a monthly index to the *Federal Register* as well as to the *Congressional Record* and the *Weekly Compilation of Presidential Documents*. NSA's *Federal Register Abstracts* also indexes and abstracts the daily *Federal Register*. Both NSA indexes are searchable online through DIALOG. NSA also sells microfiche copies of each day's *Federal Register* and operates a document retrieval service for GPO-printed regulatory documents.

Counterpoint Publishing's Compact Disc Federal Register (the *Federal Register* on CD-ROM) allows one-step searching of all FR issues from the last six months. The full text on CD-ROM can be searched by agency names, words and phrases, and FR citations.

## The *Code of Federal Regulations* (AE 2.106/3: )

Publication in the *Federal Register* is only the first stop on a regulation's journey (see Figure 9.2). The year's accumulation of new rules, amendments and deletions to old rules, presidential publications, and other materials in the daily *Federal Register* totaled more than 52,500 pages in 1990 alone. The final rules and presidential materials are incorporated yearly into the *Code of Federal Regulations* (CFR). Here the general and permanent rules originally published in the *Federal Register* are systematically arranged under fifty subject titles (about half of which cover the same subjects as the *U.S. Code*).

The fifty CFR titles are broken down into chapters (one for each rule-issuing agency), parts (general topics of regulation), and sections (the rules themselves), each with its own table of contents. The smallest component within the CFR is the "section," where the actual text of a regulation appears. The section is the basic unit of the CFR, with section numbers incorporating part and chapter numbers. CFR citations pinpoint the title (broadest division) and section (smallest division), referring the searcher to the beginning of the text of a regulation.

### *CFR* Citation

The *Code of Federal Regulations* is cited by title and section numbers, with the date sometimes added in parentheses.

40 CFR 211.10 (1978)

Title   Section   Date of Edition

### *CFR* Revisions

The fifty CFR titles are revised annually, at staggered intervals throughout the year. This means that the revision date on the cover of a CFR title must be carefully noted—depending on the revision schedule, some titles will be more up-to-date than others.

*United States Code Annotated* includes references to the CFR, with some USCA titles providing full text of regulations, and is searchable in print or on WESTLAW. Commercial vendors such as LEGI-SLATE, LEXIS, and WESTLAW include the full text of the *Code of Federal Regulations*.

### *CFR* Finding Aids

The approximately 175 volumes of the CFR span fifteen feet of shelves and harbor around 60,000 pages of fine print. Several aids expedite searching this mass of information. The *CFR Index and Finding Aids* (AE 2.106/3-2: ) is a separate volume of the CFR, included as part of the CFR subscription or purchased separately. Like the *Federal Register*, it indexes by agency names and broad subject headings, referring to CFR titles and parts (but not sections) where the regulation appears. Tables of laws and presidential documents cited as authority for regulations are included, along with tables by presidential document numbers. Using the finding-aids volume, one can use an authority table to translate a Public Law number into a CFR chapter and refer from laws that require publication in the *Federal Register* to *Statutes at Large* and *U.S. Code* citations. It also includes: (1) a list of agency-prepared indexes appearing in individual CFR volumes; (2) acts requiring publication in the *Federal Register*; (3) a list of CFR titles, chapters, subchapters, and parts; and (4) a list of agencies appearing in the CFR (also found in every CFR volume). Indexing terms are based on the "Federal Register Thesaurus of Indexing Terms."

The Congressional Information Service publishes an *Index to the Code of Federal Regulations*, which allows searching by subject, geographic entities and names, and CFR citations. Users are referred to both a CFR citation and to the CIS microfiche edition of the CFR.

*List of CFR Sections Affected* (AE 2.106/2: ). The *List of CFR Sections Affected* (LSA) serves as a bridge between newly published rules in the *Federal Register* and the CFR. As its title indicates, LSA lists CFR sections affected by rules and proposed rules published in the *Federal Register*. LSA can be used to answer the question: What new rules or proposed rules have been issued for this CFR title and section since its last revision?

LSA may be searched by CFR title, chapter, part, and section to identify *Federal Register* issues in which amendatory actions and proposed rules have been published since the last revision. It cannot be searched by subject—the searcher must know the CFR title and section to use LSA. Also included is a table of statutory authorities for regulations published in the FR, updating the authority table in the *CFR Index*.

The monthly LSA is cumulative and comes as part of the *Federal Register* subscription or can be bought separately. (Because of the staggered CFR revision schedule, four permanent issues of LSA must be saved during the year to ensure comprehensiveness until the next CFR revision.) To identify CFR provisions in force between 1964 and 1983, use *Code of Federal Regulations: List of CFR Sections Affected, 1964-1972* (GS 4.108:List/964-72/vol.), and *Code of Federal Regulations: List of CFR Sections Affected, 1973-1985* (AE 2.106/2-2: ).

**FIGURE 9.2: STAT/USC Compared with FR/CFR.**

## Parallel Codification of Legislation and Regulation

LEGISLATION
is published first as

is compiled annually in the

is codified in the

Slip Law
(Public Law 94–142)

U.S. Statutes at Large
(89 Stat. 773)

U.S. Code *
(20 U.S.C. 1401 et seq.)

## Legislation Is Implemented by Federal Agencies as Rules and Regulations

REGULATIONS
appear as
agency documents

which are published
daily in the

and codified annually in the

FR Doc. 77–36597

Federal Register
(42 FR 65082)

Code of Federal Regulations
(45 CFR 121a)

* Published by West Publishing Company under the direction of the Office of the Law Revision Counsel of the House of Representatives.

Source: *The Federal Register: What It Is and How to Use It,* 1978 ed.

## REGULATION DETECTIVE WORK: SEARCHING THE LATEST VERSION OF A RULE

People often become aware of a rule through a newspaper or magazine article, which may describe agency actions without clearly identifying them as regulations. Usually the *Federal Register* and the *Code of Federal Regulations* are not mentioned as sources for locating the text of the rule, and no publication date is given. This presents several challenges to someone wishing to learn more: first, recognizing that the action described is an executive agency regulation, and second, locating the text of the regulation.

To find the most up-to-date version of a regulation requires a search of the CFR, updated by searching the *Federal Register* and LSA. An excellent exercise that walks the reader through a complete search using government publications in the *Federal Register* system is described in *The Federal Register: What It Is and How to Use It* (AE 2.108:F 31). Commercial publications may also be used to identify relevant citations in the *Federal Register* and CFR.

| TRACKING REGULATIONS | |
|---|---|
| **If you know** | **Search these sources** |
| CFR citation | LSA; *CIS Federal Register Index; Federal Register* ("CFR Parts Affected in This Issue," and "CFR Parts Affected during [current month]"); *CFR Index and Finding Aids* or "Finding Aids" section in CFR volumes; LEXIS; WESTLAW |
| Subjects and names | *CIS Federal Register Index; Federal Index; Federal Register Index; NSA Federal Register Abstracts;* CIS *Index to the CFR; CFR Index and Finding Aids;* LEXIS; WESTLAW |

## ADJUDICATIONS

Administrative agency adjudications decide cases involving regulations. Like court opinions, agency opinions are issued first in slip form and advance pamphlets, and later cumulated into permanent, bound volumes of administrative reporters. Like laws and court opinions, they are issued either officially or unofficially (commercially published). Some may be searched online using LEXIS or WESTLAW. Official administrative publications are listed in *A Uniform System of Citation* and in Sears and Moody's *Using Government Publications;* both official and unofficial reporters have been described by Maclay.[8]

Shepard's *United States Administrative Decisions* cites decisions of many federal departments, along with those of courts (regulatory actions are subject to judicial review), boards, and commissions. The primary citator to administrative agency decisions and rulings is Shepard's *Code of Federal Regulations Citations*, a compilation of citations to the CFR from the Supreme Court, the *Statutes at Large*, various federal court reporters, and decisions of agencies, courts, boards, and commissions. It can be used to identify citations to judicial interpretation of CFR sections, presidential proclamations, executive orders, and reorganization plans.

## ADDRESSES

Congressional Information Service, 4520 East-West Highway, Bethesda, MD 20814-3389; (301) 654-1550.

National Standards Association, Inc., 1200 Quince Orchard Blvd., Gaithersburg, MD 20878; (800) 638-8094, (301) 590-2300

Office of the Federal Register, National Archives and Records Administration, Washington, DC 20408; (202) 523-5227

OMB Watch is a private, nonprofit organization that monitors the executive branch and the Office of Management and Budget: 1731 Connecticut Ave., N.W., Washington, DC 20009-1146; (202) 234-8494.

## FREEBIES

The following subject bibliography is free from U.S. Government Printing Office, Superintendent of Documents, Washington, DC 20402:

247. General Services Administration Publications

Free workshops on using the *Federal Register* and *Code of Federal Regulations* are offered in Washington, DC, and selected other cities. Look for announcements in the *Federal Register* or call the Office of the Federal Register at (202) 523-5227.

Short guides to using the *CIS Federal Register Index* are free from Congressional Information Service, Inc. (see "Addresses" above).

## REFERENCES

1. League of Women Voters, *Survey of Public Awareness of and Interest in Federal Regulations* (Washington, DC: The League, 1982).

2. Food and Drug Administration, *The Food Defect Action Levels: Current Levels for Natural or Unavoidable Defects in Food for Human Use That Present No Health Hazard,* (FDA, 1989). Updates are announced in the *Federal Register*. It should be noted that the preface to this pamphlet emphasizes that these levels are harmless, natural, and unavoidable.

3. *Federal Regulatory Directory.* 6th ed. (Congressional Quarterly, Inc., 1990), p. xv.

4. *Federal Regulatory Directory,* p. 18.

5. Senate, *Study on Federal Regulation. Vol. III Public Participation in Regulatory Agency Proceedings* (Senate Doc. 95-71) (GPO, 1977), p.viii. (Y 4.G 74/6:R 26/5/v.3)

6. Senate, p. 159.

7. Office of the Federal Register, *The Federal Register: What It Is and How to Use It* (GPO, 1985), p. 106, gives hints for writing effective comments. (AE 2.108:F 31)

8. Veronica Maclay, "Selected Sources of United States Agency Decisions," *Government Publications Review* 16 (May/June 1989):271-301.

## FURTHER READING

Congressional Quarterly. *Federal Regulatory Directory.* 6th ed. Washington, DC: Congressional Quarterly, Inc., 1990.

> Profiles of regulatory agencies and a directory of information contacts, plus a discussion of the regulatory process and using the FR and CFR.

————. *Regulation: Process and Politics.* Washington, DC: Congressional Quarterly, Inc., 1982.

> A thorough overview of the role of regulations in government and American life, with sketches of regulatory agencies.

Senate. *Reauthorization of OMB's Office of Information and Regulatory Affairs, Hearing before the Senate Committee on Governmental Affairs, February 21 and 22, 1990, 101-2.* (S. Hrg. 101- 588) GPO, 1990. (Y 4.G 74/9:S. Hrg. 101-588)

> The impact of OMB regulatory review.

Waldman, Steven. "Watching the Watchdogs." *Newsweek* 113 (February 20, 1989):34.

> Pros and cons of OMB's involvement in rulemaking.

## EXERCISES

1. In 1991, newspapers across the nation reported that the Food and Drug Administration had identified America's favorite fruits, vegetables, and fish. Bananas, potatoes, and shrimp topped the lists, compiled in response to the Nutrition Labeling and Education Act of 1990. Identify the FDA's "top-20" fruits, vegetables, and fish lists.

2. Find any of the following regulations in the FR or CFR, noting their proper citations.

   a. A regulation describing whether an inventor must submit a working model to secure a patent.

   b. OMB proposal for revision of Circular A-130, "Management of Federal Information Resources" (announced in FR)

   c. The presidential libraries display gifts sent by well-wishers from all over the world. Their museum collections are bolstered by the fact that government employees must relinquish gifts worth more than $200 to the National Archives. Locate the regulation that dictates this.

   d. A regulation that prescribes the contents of mayonnaise.

   e. A regulation that prescribes the contents of cottage cheese.

   f. A regulation that prescribes the size limitations for carry-on baggage on airplanes.

   g. A regulation related to child safety seats in cars.

# CHAPTER 10
# Executive Branch Information Sources

*The buck stops here.*
—Harry S. Truman

## WHAT

The president is the nation's chief executive and the administrative head of the executive branch of government, which includes the thirteen executive departments plus numerous temporary and permanent agencies.

## WHO

The president must be a citizen born in the U.S., no younger than thirty-five, who has lived in the United States for at least fourteen years.

## WHY

Article III, United States Constitution: "The executive power shall be vested in a President of the United States of America."

The constitutional powers expressly granted to the president include the role of commander in chief of the army and navy, the granting of reprieves and pardons, making treaties (with Senate concurrence), nominating Supreme Court justices, and vetoing acts of Congress. The Constitution directs the president to periodically inform Congress on the state of the Union and to recommend legislation.

## WHEN

The president's term commences at noon on January 20, every fourth year.

## HOW

Thirteen executive departments and their agencies administer the laws enacted by Congress. The executive branch also includes independent agencies such as the Veterans' Administration; independent regulatory commissions such as the Federal Trade Commission; government corporations like the Tennessee Valley Authority; and federally aided corporations including Gallaudet College and Howard University. Many documents of legal effect and significance are issued by the president, executive agencies, and independent administrative agencies.

## WHERE

Many presidential documents are published, while others are housed in the Library of Congress and presidential libraries, and some remain inaccessible to the public.

## PUBLICATIONS OF THE PRESIDENCY

*The papers of the presidents are among the most valuable sources of material for history. They ought to be preserved and they ought to be used.*
—Harry S. Truman

Hirshon has distinguished between four categories of presidential papers: public/published, executively controlled, official, and personal.[1] Of the four types, the public/published papers are the most accessible. These include materials issued by the White House, such as legally binding proclamations and executive orders, plus presidential messages, speeches, and statements. These materials are funneled into established sources of documentation, making them straightforward to trace. The bulk of this chapter will focus on this type of material.

Unlike the published papers, much presidential documentation is initially closed to the public, including personal, executively controlled, and official papers. A president's personal papers are those not created in the course of official duties, such as personal diaries and journals, family mementos, or love letters. Executively controlled documents are "privileged" from disclosure to Congress or the courts (and the public) because they incorporate national secrets, classified or legal information, or policy-making records. President Richard M. Nixon cited executive privilege when he withheld the White House audiotapes subpoenaed by the Senate Watergate Committee in 1973, claiming the tapes contained frank and private Oval Office conversations extraneous to the committee's investigation. (The Supreme Court later ordered the tapes released to the Watergate special prosecutor.)

Another restricted category of presidential documents are National Security Directives, issued by the president through the National Security Council. During the 1980s, National Security Directives authorized the U.S. invasion of Grenada and the order to restrict access to "sensitive but unclassified" information in computer databases (see Chapter 2 for a discussion of NSDD 145). Characterized as the president's "secret laws," National Security Directives are not required to be published or released to Congress or the public. Of the estimated 1,042 NSDs issued since 1961, only about 247 have been declassified.

Official presidential papers are working documents generated in the course of daily presidential activities. Goehlert and Martin, however, distinguish between unpublished working papers and final presidential decisions and actions, which are published. "Unlike the Congress and the Supreme Court, the decision-making process in the White House is closed to the public."[2] White House policy-making deliberations are documented internally in memos, drafts, notes, diaries, or tape recordings, which remain unpublished. In fact, until 1978, all official presidential records were considered the president's private property. Now the law mandates that they pass into the custody of the Archivist of the United States at the conclusion of the president's term. As a result, official papers are unpublished, but not inaccessible. After the president leaves office, most are archived in the presidential libraries, where they are available to scholars.

Raymond Geselbracht has identified four eras in the history of presidential papers, beginning with a chaotic epoch ushered in by George Washington.[3] When Washington left office, he took his official letters, notes, drafts, and working papers home to Mount Vernon, primarily because there was nowhere to archive them. Washington's action established a precedent for personal, not public, ownership of presidential papers—a privilege exercised freely by every exiting president until Richard Nixon.

As a result, the destiny of official presidential papers was haphazard. Geselbracht notes that "the papers of many of the nineteenth-century presidents were seriously damaged, and almost every collection suffered from neglect."[4] Some presidential papers simply vanished, while others were burned (intentionally and inadvertently), loaned to biographers and lost, distributed as souvenirs, cut up for autographs, or destroyed in the Civil War. A few were even sold back to the government.

| The Library of Congress Presidential Papers Collection* | |
| --- | --- |
| Chester A. Arthur | Abraham Lincoln |
| Grover Cleveland | James Madison |
| Calvin Coolidge | William McKinley |
| James A. Garfield | James Monroe |
| Ulysses S. Grant | James K. Polk |
| Benjamin Harrison | Theodore Roosevelt |
| William H. Harrison | William Howard Taft |
| Andrew Jackson | Zachary Taylor |
| Thomas Jefferson | George Washington |
| Andrew Johnson | Woodrow Wilson |

*Since Franklin D. Roosevelt, the presidents' papers have been in the custody of presidential libraries administered by the National Archives and Records Administration.

This tradition of neglect was reversed at the turn of the century, when the Library of Congress began collecting presidential papers. In what marked the beginning of the second era of preservation, LC's Manuscript Division was established as a repository, giving presidents the first real alternative to carting off their papers when their terms ended. But because LC lacked legal authority to demand presidential papers, its preservation efforts were dependent upon voluntary donations.

Today the Library of Congress's Presidential Papers Collection houses the papers of most of the presidents from Washington to Coolidge. The collection is located in the Library's Manuscript Division and includes letters, financial records, speeches, notes, and writings—all for sale to the public on microfilm. Published indexes in the *President's Papers Index Series* (LC 4.7: ) serve as guides to each president's collection, providing descriptions of contents and an index to the microfilm. An index accompanies each purchase of a microfilmed presidential collection or may be bought separately. A list of more than one hundred U.S. and foreign libraries owning complete or partial sets of Presidential Papers microfilm is available from the Manuscript Division, while indexes to the series may be consulted in many depository libraries. *A Guide to Manuscripts in the Presidential Libraries*, by Burton, Rhoads, and Smock (Research Materials Corp.) provides descriptions of manuscript collections, microfilm resources, and oral histories in seven presidential libraries.

*Franklin D. Roosevelt is the nation's answer to the historian's prayer.*

—Robert D. W. Connor,
the first archivist of
the United States

Franklin D. Roosevelt ushered in the third era of preservation by erecting the first presidential library in

1939. Roosevelt donated land, solicited private donations for construction, and then consigned the Roosevelt Library to the government to maintain. Harry S. Truman followed suit, donating his papers to his own library in Independence, Missouri. Later the 1955 Presidential Libraries Act formalized government maintenance of the presidential libraries with tax dollars. Like the Library of Congress's presidential papers program, presidential libraries were a compromise "between the competing private and public property claims to presidential papers."[5] The Presidential Libraries Act embraced the traditional view that presidents own their papers, and depositing them in a presidential library remained voluntary.

The fourth era began after Richard Nixon resigned, rekindling questions about ownership of presidential papers. Exercising a two-century-old precedent, ex-President Nixon claimed his presidential papers and tapes as personal property. But, in the wake of Watergate, the nation was in a cantankerous mood. To mollify objections, Nixon temporarily deposited his papers at the National Archives, restricting access and asserting his right to reclaim them and even to destroy the tapes. Congress seized the Nixon materials by passing a law giving the government control over them, with a second law designating presidential papers in general as national, not private, property.

As a result of the Presidential Records Act of 1978, official records of any president after 1981 belong to the nation, not the president. The Presidential Libraries Act is still on the books, but to ease the taxpayers' maintenance burden, recent legislation has mandated that new libraries established after Ronald Reagan have endowment funds.

---

**Presidents on the Presidency**

*The job is interesting, but the possibilities for trouble are unlimited.*
—John F. Kennedy

*They're all my helicopters, son.*
—President Lyndon B. Johnson
to an air force corporal who pointed out the presidential helicopter by saying, "This is your helicopter, sir."

*I can get up at nine and be rested, or I can get up at six and be president.*          —Jimmy Carter

*Is the country still here?*          --Calvin Coolidge
after a nap

---

## Public Statements

Official daily White House press releases announce administrative and presidential activities, providing the text of major addresses and remarks, proclamations,

executive orders, communications to executive departments, messages to Congress, letters to foreign heads of states, fact sheets, nominations and appointments, and presidential statements. Most of these are published in the various sources discussed below.

### Presidential Proclamations and Executive Orders

Soon after he took office, George Washington issued the first executive order, asking his Cabinet for "a clear account" of the infant government of 1789 (the first proclamation was also issued in 1789—declaring Thanksgiving Day). Executive orders were not numbered or issued uniformly until 1907, and until the birth of the *Federal Register* in 1936, the only systematic organization and numbering of executive orders was done by the State Department. It was the State Department that collected them from agencies throughout the Capitol in 1907 and began numbering them, designating an 1862 order from President Lincoln as number one. (President Washington's 1789 order is the earliest unnumbered executive order.) The mandate for announcement in the *Federal Register* signaled a new era—never before had presidential proclamations and executive orders been publicly available immediately after issuance.

Since 1936, presidential executive orders and proclamations have been published in the *Federal Register*, where they must appear to be legally binding. Later they are codified in Title 3 of the *Code of Federal Regulations*. Although proclamations and executive orders are numbered consecutively, they are cited by the *Federal Register* volume and page where they were issued. For example, Presidential Proclamation 4693 would be cited according to the FR volume and page where it was published: 44 FR 56669. Confidential or classified executive orders are issued but not published. They are numbered as executive orders, however, and are released to Congress.

Presidential proclamations and executive orders are legal documents, issued under statutory authority or according to presidential powers granted by the Constitution. Proclamations are issued by virtue of the president's office, by law, or in response to congressional joint resolutions. Executive orders are authorized by the president's statutory or constitutional powers. When issued with legal authority, both executive orders and proclamations have the same effect as laws.

Legally, there is no difference between a proclamation and an executive order, and the best way to differentiate between them is simply to accept the designation they have been assigned. In actual use, most proclamations address the general public, while executive orders are working documents often used to command government agencies or officials. There are two types of proclamations: ceremonial, which announce special observances, holidays, or events, such as Mother's Day and National Rice Month, and the more substantive, non-ceremonial proclamations, dealing with trade, imports and exports, and tariffs.

Commercial databases such as LEXIS and WESTLAW include the full text of the *Federal Register* and *Code of Federal Regulations*, including presidential proclamations and executive orders. Monthly when Congress is in session, the *U.S. Code Congressional and Administrative News* provides the full text of new presidential proclamations, executive orders, and executive branch reorganization plans. Proclamations and executive orders are indexed by number, referring to the subject and date of each and the location of the text in *U.S. Code Congressional and Administrative News*.

The *Statutes at Large* includes the text of proclamations but not executive orders. Some proclamations and executive orders issued under specific statutory authority are published with statutes in the *United States Code*. The *United States Code* has tables listing executive orders that implement laws, as well as tables of proclamations.

The *CIS Federal Register Index*, along with the NSA *Federal Index* and *Federal Register Abstracts*, indexes presidential documents in the *Federal Register*. Each is searchable online through DIALOG. *CIS Index to Presidential Executive Orders and Proclamations 1789-1983* indexes numbered and unnumbered executive orders and proclamations, with a companion microfiche full text collection. The index is searchable by subjects, names, organizations, geographic areas, and dates of issue, with cross-references to interrelated executive orders.

The *Codification of Presidential Proclamations and Executive Orders, April 13, 1945-January 20, 1989* (AE 2.113:945-89) gives the text of many proclamations and executive orders issued from the Truman to Reagan administrations, arranged in fifty subject chapters, with amendments incorporated. The cumulative codification allows referral from statutes, title, and the *U.S. Code* to presidential document number, and includes a table listing each proclamation and executive order issued between 1945 and 1989. This source is updated every four years.

SHEPARD'S *Code of Federal Regulations Citations* compiles citations to proclamations, executive orders, and presidential reorganization plans from the Supreme Court, the *Statutes at Large*, various federal court reporters, and other sources.

### Retrospective Searching

Between 1925 and 1936, when systematic publication commenced in the *Federal Register*, proclamations and executive orders were issued individually under SuDocs classification Pr ___.7: and Pr ___.5: (an individual number for each president followed the Pr prefix) and may be found in some depository library collections. The *Statutes at Large* has included proclamations since 1791, but there is no similar collection of executive orders.

| SEARCHING PROCLAMATIONS AND EXECUTIVE ORDERS | | |
|---|---|---|
| **Title** | **Access Points** | **Time Coverage** |
| **Indexes:** | | |
| *Weekly Compilation of Presidential Documents* | In index under "Proclamations" | Weekly since 1965 |
| *Federal Register Index* AE 2.106: | Under "Executive Orders," "Proclamations" | Monthly for current year |
| *CIS Federal Register Index* | In index by CFR section numbers (Proc. or E.O. numbers); under subject headings "Presidential Documents" and "Executive Orders" | Weekly since 1984 |
| *CIS Index to Presidential Orders and Proclamations, 1789-1983* | Subjects, names organizations, issue dates | 1789-1983 |
| *Code of Federal Regulations, Title 3—The President, 1936-1975 Consolidated Tables* GS4. 108/2:936-75/tab | Number, date, subject, *Federal Register* citation | 1936-75 |
| *Federal Index* | Subject | Monthly since 1976 |
| **Full Text:** | | |
| *Weekly Compilation of Presidential Documents* | "Proclamations" section | Weekly since 1965 |
| *U.S. Code Congressional and Administrative News* | Proc. or E.O. numbers | Since 1939 |
| *Federal Register* | "Presidential Documents" section | Daily since 1936 |
| Title 3 CFR | Proc. or E.O. numbers, statutes cited as authority | Yearly since 1936 |
| *Codification of Presidential Proclamations and Executive Orders* AE 2.113:945-yr | Subject; E.O. and Proc. numbers | Since 1945 |
| *Public Papers of the Presidents* | Date of issue | Yearly since 1957 |
| *CQ Almanac* | In order by date | Annually since 1948 |
| LEXIS | Full text | Since 1981 |
| WESTLAW | Full text | Since 1936 |

| SEARCHING FOR PRE-1936 PROCLAMATIONS AND EXECUTIVE ORDERS | | |
|---|---|---|
| **Title** | **Access Points** | **Time Coverage** |
| **Indexes:** | | |
| *CIS Presidential Orders and Proclamations, 1789-1983* | Subjects, names, organizations, issue dates | 1789-1983 |
| *Document Catalog* | "President of the U.S., Executive Orders"; subjects | 1893-1940 |
| *List and Index of Presidential Executive Orders* by Clifford L. Lord | Date of issue | 1789-1938 |
| *Presidential Executive Orders* by Clifford L. Lord | Number, subject | 1862-1938 |
| **Full Text:** | | |
| *Statutes at Large* | Proc. number (no E.O.s included) | Yearly since 1791 |
| *Proclamations and Executive Orders, Herbert Hoover (March 4, 1929-March 4, 1933)* | Proc. or E.O. numbers; subject | 1929-33 |
| *A Compilation of the Messages and Papers of the Presidents, 1789-1897,* by James D. Richardson | Date of issue | 1789-1897 |

## Presidential Messages

> *Presidential footprints almost inevitably lead to Capitol Hill, for there is little that a modern president does that does not somehow involve the Congress.*
> —G. Calvin Mackenzie,
> in *Studying the Presidency*

The president's oral and written communications to Congress and the public are called presidential messages. Messages to the public include speeches, radio addresses, press conferences, and press releases. Presidential messages to Congress may accompany bills introduced with the president's endorsement or treaties submitted for Senate consent, or may communicate the president's rationale for signing or vetoing an act. Many of these are ordered printed by Congress as House or Senate Documents and then included in the Serial Set, the *Congressional Record,* and the House and Senate *Journals*—making legislative search skills an asset for presi-

dential research. Messages may be traced through the indexes listed in the table below, as well as through the legislative histories summarized in slip laws and the *Statutes at Large,* which cite presidential statements published in the *Weekly Compilation of Presidential Documents.*

| **Presidential Messages** |
|---|
| PUBLIC MESSAGES |
| **Text:** |
|     *Weekly Compilation of Presidential Documents* |
|     *CQ Weekly Report* |
|     *CQ Almanac* |
|     Newspapers |
| **Indexes:** |
|     Cumulative index in each *Weekly Compilation of Presidential Documents* |
|     *Monthly Catalog* |
|     PAIS |
|     Newspaper indexes |
| MESSAGES TO CONGRESS |
| **Text:** |
|     Serial Set |
|     *Congressional Record* |
|     House and Senate Journals |
|     *CQ Weekly Report* |
|     *Congressional Quarterly Almanac* |
|     *U.S. Code Congressional and Administrative News* |
| **Indexes:** |
|     *CIS/Index* |
|     *CIS Serial Set Index* |
|     *Federal Index* |
|     House and Senate Journals |
|     *Monthly Catalog* |
|     PAIS |
|     Slip laws |
|     *Statutes at Large* |
|     *Congressional Record Index* |
|     Cumulative indexes in each *Weekly Compilation of Presidential Documents* |

### *Weekly Compilation of Presidential Documents* (AE 2.109:)

Each week the White House releases presidential materials, including transcripts of news conferences, messages to Congress, and public speeches and statements. The text of presidential materials released during the preceding week is provided in the *Weekly Compilation of Presidential Documents.* The *Weekly Compilation* also includes a monthly dateline, lists of laws approved by the president, nominations submitted to the Senate, and a checklist of White House releases. At the start of each month, the *Congressional Record Daily Digest* offers statistics on executive nominations.

Unlike the *Congressional Record*, the *Weekly Compilation of Presidential Documents* reprints speeches, remarks, and press conferences as delivered. A tape recording of the president's actual words is compared with prereleased transcripts to verify accuracy. When no tape is available, the *Weekly Compilation* notes that the published text is based on a press release rather than actual delivered remarks.

Each weekly issue of the *Weekly Compilation* has a cumulative index for the year, with separate indexes appearing quarterly, semiannually, and annually. A commercially published index covering the *Weekly Compilation of Presidential Documents* is the *Federal Index*, which also indexes the *Congressional Record* and *Federal Register*. The index is searchable through DIALOG.

### Public Papers of the Presidents of the United States (AE 2.114:)

> *Once you get into the great stream of history you can't get out.*                    —Richard M. Nixon

Before 1957, there was no systematic official compilation of the presidential messages and speeches. Except for presidential executive orders and proclamations published in the *Federal Register*, publicly issued presidential materials had not been accumulated and published by the government for more than fifty years. The first compilation of presidential messages and papers for Presidents Washington through McKinley had been authorized by Congress and compiled by James D. Richardson as *A Compilation of the Messages and Papers of the Presidents, 1789-1897*. Since then, the government had done nothing to organize and systematically record presidential materials released to the public.

This documentary gap was bridged in 1957 with the initiation of *Public Papers of the Presidents*, with the full text of presidential papers and speeches released from the White House by Herbert Hoover and every other president since Harry S. Truman. This is an official series containing the text of each president's speeches, news conferences, messages, statements, communications to Congress, executive orders, proclamations, nominations, and appointments. For example, the last item in the Nixon volumes is a letter to Secretary of State Henry Kissinger, dated August 9, 1974:

Dear Mr. Secretary:

I hereby resign the Office of President of the United States.
                                        Sincerely,
                                        Richard Nixon

The John F. Kennedy volumes end with JFK's last speech, delivered on November 22, 1963, in Fort Worth before his flight to Dallas. Preceding the text of speeches Kennedy had prepared to deliver that same afternoon is a footnote explaining that the president was shot and killed while driving in an open motorcade toward downtown Dallas.

Since 1977 *Public Papers* has incorporated all the material originally published in the *Weekly Compilation of Presidential Documents*. Because the set contained only selected material from the *Weekly Compilation* between 1965 and 1976, many libraries have saved older issues of the *Weekly Compilation*, but discard current issues after the annual *Public Papers* is received.

*Public Papers* volumes include subject and name indexes, with appendixes of supplementary material such as the president's public schedule, White House announcements, and a list of public and private laws. Individual volumes of *Public Papers* include indexes, but for a cumulated index to all the volumes, consult *The Cumulated Indexes to the Public Papers of the Presidents of the United States*, published by Kraus International Publications.

| SOURCES OF PUBLISHED PRESIDENTIAL PAPERS | |
|---|---|
| **Text:** | |
| *Compilation of the Messages and Papers of the Presidents, 1789-1897* | 1789-1897 |
| *Public Papers of the Presidents* | Since 1929-33; 1945-present |
| *Weekly Compilation of Presidential Papers* | Since 1965 |
| Serial Set | Messages to Congress since 1789 |
| Congressional Record | Messages to Congress |
| *U.S. Code Congressional and Administrative News* | Messages to Congress since 1939 |
| *CQ Weekly Report* and *CQ Almanac* | Weekly and annual coverage of speeches, press conferences, veto messages, and other communications |
| House and Senate Journals | Annual coverage of messages to Congress |
| **Indexes:** | |
| *CIS Serial Set Index* | Communications to Congress, 1789-1969 |
| *CIS/Index* | Communications to Congress, since 1970 |
| *Federal Index* | Various communications |
| *Monthly Catalog* | Various communications |
| PAIS | Various communications |
| *Congressional Record Index* | Communications to Congress |
| House and Senate Journals | Communications to Congress |

# THE FEDERAL BUDGET

*A billion here, a billion there—pretty soon it adds up to real money.* —Senator Everett Dirksen, Illinois

Although many people associate the federal budget with the thick, paperbound book displayed on the television news each January, "the budget" is not a single document. It is a series of executive and legislative publications issued throughout the federal fiscal year, October 1–September 30. Initiated by the executive branch, the budget is finalized by Congress—not with a single law, but piecemeal during the congressional budget process. The Congressional Budget and Impoundment Control Act of 1974 established a congressional budget process for reviewing the president's proposals according to overall guidelines. The budget act also created House and Senate budget committees which report and enforce budget resolutions, and the Congressional Budget Office, which provides budget analyses and information, but makes no recommendations.

The federal budget odyssey begins with a proposed budget, forwarded to Congress from the president (this is the document that makes headlines each January). Since 1991, the *Budget of the United States Government* has incorporated information previously issued in four supplements: the former *Appendix, Historical Tables, Special Analyses,* and *Budget in Brief.* The *Economic Report of the President* (numbered individually, Pr_.9: ) is the president's report to Congress on the nation's economic health, including the Annual Report of the Council of Economic Advisors, which reviews the economy and proposed spending. Congress holds annual hearings to review the *Economic Report of the President* (Y 4.Ec 7:Ec 7/2/yr.) and issues a *Joint Economic Report* (Y 1.1/8: ), the Joint Economic Committee's critique of the president's *Economic Report.*

---

**Beware Budget Blunders**

Remember that the president's *Budget of the United States Government* is a *proposal*. This means that totals for the current and upcoming fiscal year are projected, not actual, amounts. Figures for the past year (budget year minus 2) are factual, but data for the current (budget year minus 1) and next fiscal year are estimates that may be modified during budget execution and the congressional budget process.

---

Congress may approve, disapprove, or change the president's budget proposals, sending them through the same legislative machinery as any bill. Congress reacts to the president's budget proposals with an overall budget plan establishing spending ceilings and broad priorities, produced by the House and Senate budget committees with the assistance of the Congressional Budget Office. If the Senate and House adopt different budget plans, a conference committee resolves their differences. Finally, a budget plan designed solely to guide Congress in its budget deliberations is agreed upon by both houses in the form of a concurrent resolution.

With the budget resolution as a guide, Congress enacts authorization bills to create federal programs and appropriations bills to fund them. During the congressional budget process, legislation is introduced, committee reports and prints are issued, and hearings are held. Tracing documents generated during the congressional budget process requires a legislative search, using the resources discussed in Chapter 8, along with *American Statistics Index* to identify statistical budget documents, the status tables in the House *Calendars,* and the *Congressional Record*'s Daily Digest. Congressional Budget Office "scorekeeping" reports track action on revenue and spending bills. The CBO *List of Publications* cites analyses of alternative fiscal, budgetary, and program policies. Copies of most CBO publications are free to the public and can be traced using *Monthly Catalog* or *CIS/Index.*

# PRESIDENTIAL LIBRARIES

*We have papers from my forty years in public service in one place for friend and foe to judge, to approve or disapprove....This library will show the facts, not just the joy and triumphs, but the sorrow and failures, too.* —Lyndon Johnson, dedicating the Johnson Library, 1971

Modeled after FDR's library and administered according to Congress's ground rules, the presidential libraries and museums are built with private donations and then turned over to the government to administer. Except for the The Richard M. Nixon Library and Birthplace in Yorba Linda, California, they are maintained by the National Archives and Records Administration. The Nixon Library and Birthplace is privately operated, housing only Nixon's personal diaries and pre-presidential papers, along with some objects loaned by the National Archives. Nixon's official presidential papers and White House tapes remain national property, warehoused by the National Archives and Records Administration in Alexandria, Virginia.

Presidential libraries preserve "the real stuff of history"—not only papers and personal mementos of the president, but also of his associates, friends, and relatives. Their collections include manuscripts, artifacts, photographs, films, recordings, microfilm, and gifts from foreign heads of state. "Perhaps the most confusing thing about [presidential libraries] is their name—for they are neither collections of books about Presidents nor collections of Presidents' books."[6] Presidential "libraries" are actually archives and museums "dedicated to educating the public about a former President, his administration, and the office of the President in the American system of government."[7] Their collections include John F. Kennedy's rocking chair, the draft of Franklin Roosevelt's Pearl Harbor speech, Harry Truman's "The Buck Stops Here" sign, and Jimmy Carter's cardigan sweater. Visual and audio materials are important components of many of the collections. There are the Nixon audiotapes, which would take 4,000 hours to play and are supplemented by a 27,000-page finding aid. The John F. Kennedy Library, another example, houses thousands of photographs and films documenting almost every day of Kennedy's term.

Each presidential library has its own personality. At the Truman Library in Independence, Missouri, for example, visitors can see the actual 1941 Chrysler coupe driven by Vice President Truman and a fireplace mantle from the White House. The Roosevelt Library boasts museum exhibits that include locks of Roosevelt's baby hair, his christening gown and cradle, his first pony saddle, and the cane he used after his bout with polio. Eleanor Roosevelt's life is also reflected, in letters, personal papers, and photographs. The Kennedy Library has the papers of Ernest Hemingway, donated by Mary Hemingway, the author's widow.

Although presidential libraries have their critics (some deride them as "paper pyramids"), their contributions go beyond the archival preservation of papers and artifacts. These libraries touch not only scholars but also thousands of ordinary Americans who file through their doors to tour their museums and attend conferences, exhibitions, and special programs.

Although presidents may restrict access to materials in their libraries, restrictions can be appealed to the National Archives, and the bulk of material is quickly opened to the public (see Figure 10.1). The Iran-Contra documents in the Reagan Library will be sealed until at least 2002, to protect national security, foreign policy, and confidentiality. The "Accessions and Openings" section of *Prologue* (AE 1.111: ) lists new additions to presidential library collections, as well as opened or declassified records. *A Guide to Manuscripts in the Presidential Libraries*, published by Research Materials Corporation, describes collections in the libraries of Hoover, Roosevelt, Truman, Eisenhower, Johnson, Kennedy, and Ford, with an index that allows searching by names, subjects, government agencies, and countries. Frank L. Schick's *Records of the Presidency: Presidential Papers and Libraries from Washington to Reagan* (Oryx Press) describes legislation and agencies related to presidential records, bibliographic guides, plus the histories and contents of sets of presidential papers. Fritz Veit's *Presidential Libraries and Collections* (Greenwood Press) provides a review of presidential library collections and services, and their history and administration.

**FIGURE 10.1: The LBJ Library.**

Four floors of archives are visible from the museum area of the Lyndon Baines Johnson Library behind glass walls rising above the second floor of the Great Hall. Behind the glass are four stories of red document boxes, each bearing a gold presidential seal. Courtesy LBJ Library.

## FOREIGN RELATIONS

U.S. foreign relations are conducted by the executive branch and rooted in the constitutional powers of the president. The Department of State advises the president on foreign relations and negotiates treaties and agreements with other nations.

### Foreign Relations Publications

#### *US Department of State Dispatch* (S 1.3/5: )

In 1989, the *Department of State Bulletin* (S 1.3: ) was replaced by *Dispatch*, the official weekly documentary record of the State Department. *Dispatch* chronicles foreign policy, reprints speeches and congressional testimony of the president and secretary of state, and provides fact sheets, foreign policy analyses, maps, and profiles of countries in the news. *Dispatch* is indexed in the *Reader's Guide*, in the Congressional Information Service's *American Foreign Policy Index* and is available in full text on LEXIS and on the USDA's electronic bulletin board, CIDS. Rather than running its own bulletin board, the Department of State "piggybacks" on CIDS, selling access to subscribers through the Martin Marietta Corporation. Materials in CIDS include transcripts of press briefings, speeches, and congressional testimony; travel advisories; foreign policy summaries; and the full text of *Background Notes* and *Country Profiles*. Government subscribers to CIDS, including depository libraries, pay according to their use of the system.

### *Foreign Relations of the United States* (S 1.1:)

Another source of diplomatic background information is the Department of State's *Foreign Relations of the United States* (FRUS), the documentary record of U.S. diplomacy and foreign policy for more than a century. The policy of publishing the records of American diplomacy began in 1861, when Secretary of State Seward decided to publish his important diplomatic dispatches. Today, *Foreign Relations of the United States* is the oldest, most comprehensive publication of its kind in the world. The annual volumes form the official record of U.S. diplomacy, including background documents like diplomatic communications, memoranda, diplomatic notes and telegrams, and other documents tracing the formulation of foreign-policy decisions.

Special FRUS volumes are sometimes published for topics such as the Paris Peace Conference of 1919 and the summit meetings of World War II. Declassification procedures require at least a twenty-five-year interim before publication. Volumes for Vietnam 1958-1960, for example, were released in 1986, opening previously classified documents on U.S. Vietnam policy for public view. Recent concerns about the integrity and completeness of FRUS were addressed in 1991 in the Foreign Relations Authorization Act, which mandated that FRUS be compiled according to principles of historical objectivity and accuracy. The series was mandated by Congress to be free of alterations, unnoted deletions, or omissions aimed at concealing policy weaknesses.

### *American Foreign Policy: Current Documents* (S 1.71/2:)

*American Foreign Policy: Current Documents* (S 1.71/ 2: and microfiche supplement, S 1.71/2-2: ) is a related series, published under several titles since 1950.[8] Unlike *Foreign Relations of the United States*, which publishes declassified documents only after a quarter-century time lag, *American Foreign Policy: Current Documents* compiles publicly released contemporary materials. Included are foreign policy messages, addresses, statements, interviews, press briefings and conferences, plus congressional testimony by the president and representatives of the executive branch. Much of the contents was previously published in other official publications; other inclusions were never before published. The Congressional Information Service's *American Foreign Policy Index* and accompanying microfiche collection provide access to

key policy documents from the executive branch, Congress, and independent federal agencies

## TREATIES

Treaties are written agreements between nations, governed by international law. The U.S. Constitution identifies treaties as part of the supreme law of the land and grants the president power to make them, with the consent of Congress. The president may negotiate a treaty without Senate consent, but cannot ratify it without approval by two-thirds of the Senate. After ratification, treaties are proclaimed by the president and assume the same legal authority and force as statutes.

---

**Stages in the Treaty Process**

1. Negotiation by the president
2. Signature by the president
3. Transmittal to Senate
4. Ratification (after congressional approval)
5. Publication
6. Proclamation
7. Execution

---

## The Treaty Process

The treaty process begins when the president forwards a treaty to the Senate, where it is considered by the Foreign Relations Committee. The treaty, usually supplemented by a presidential endorsement, is designated a Senate Treaty Document (Y 1.1/4: ) and numbered sequentially during each Congress: Treaty Document 101-8, for example.

The Senate approves about ninety percent of the treaties submitted by the president. Only twenty have ever been killed by lack of a two-thirds vote (the Treaty of Versailles, for example, was rejected twice, keeping the United States out of the League of Nations). Senate inaction is a more common tactic, sometimes inducing the president to withdraw the treaty. Unlike other legislation, treaties do not die at the conclusion of a Congress—they remain vital until either acted upon by the Senate or withdrawn by the president. Treaties have been known to stagnate for years, even decades, awaiting Senate action.

Although Senate Treaty Documents can technically be kept confidential, the injunction of secrecy is usually lifted, allowing them to be printed without confidential classification. Senate Treaty Documents have been in the Serial Set since the 97th Congress (1980-81) and are available on microfiche from the Congressional Information Service. They are searchable in the *Monthly Catalog*, *CIS/Index*, *Congressional Masterfile 2*, and other legislative indexes (see Chapter 8). Before 1980, Senate Treaty Documents were called Senate Executive Documents and sequentially lettered: Exec. Doc. A, 99-1; Exec. Doc. B, 99-1. Since Senate Executive Documents and Reports were uncataloged and unindexed before *CIS/Index* began in 1970, the Congressional Information Service sells a complete indexed microfiche collection covering 1817-1969, *CIS U.S. Senate Executive Documents and Reports (not included in the Serial Set)*. Retrospective Senate executive reports and documents are also searchable through CIS's *Congressional Masterfile 1* , on CD-ROM.

In the Senate Foreign Relations Committee, the treaty proposal is translated into a bill and treated as any legislative measure: It may die, remain unaltered, or be amended. In the process, it may generate public or executive hearings. Executive hearings (also called executive sessions) are the opposite of public hearings—they are closed to the public and rarely printed. When treaty hearings are public, transcripts are usually printed and distributed by the committee. Treaty recommendations are reported from committee in Senate Executive Reports, which are numbered as other committee reports (Senate Report 99-326, for example). Traditionally confidential, Senate Executive Reports have been part of the Serial Set since the 97th Congress (1980).

The *Journal of the Executive Proceedings of the Senate* (Y 1.3/4: ), called the Executive Journal, is the official record of Senate actions on nominations and treaties. The Executive Journal compiles presidential nomination and treaty messages and proceedings of Senate executive sessions. The Senate Executive Calendar (Y 1.3/2: , not depository), an agenda of treaties and nominations reported from committee, lists treaties in calendar number order, noting subject, committee action, and executive report number.

Most treaties receive Senate approval and then are ratified and made public by presidential proclamation. The treaty's final ratification is up to the president, not the Senate, with the formal treaty promulgation issued under the president's name. The president is not legally obligated to accept any Senate treaty action, remaining free to withdraw the treaty from Senate consideration at any time, or to decline to ratify it even after Senate consent has been granted.

## Treaty Searches

Legislative action → TIAS → UST

Cohen and Berring identify three stages of treaty research: (1) locating the text, (2) determining whether the treaty is in force and the scope of its coverage, and (3) interpreting the text.[9] The first stage, locating the treaty text, is complicated by the fact that treaties can be elusive before ratification and entry into force. Treaty actions are announced in State Department press releases, *Dispatch*, and CIDS, the Agriculture Department's electronic bulletin board. About six months after its effective date, the treaty is numbered sequentially and issued in pamphlet (slip) form as part of the *Treaties and Other International*

*Acts Series* (TIAS) (S 9.10:1501-nos.). The contents of TIAS are indexed in *Monthly Catalog, Treaties in Force,* and Hein's *Current Treaty Index*. Treaties originally published in TIAS are then bound and cumulated in UST, *United States Treaties and Other International Agreements* (S 9.12: ). UST is a chronological arrangement of treaties, with country and subject indexes. (Subject headings are drawn from treaty titles, rather than a controlled vocabulary.) UST citations resemble those in the *U.S. Code* or *Code of Federal Regulations*: 26 UST 1793 is UST volume 26, page 1793.

Treaty texts before UST's starting date are available in the *Statutes at Large* (until 1950), and *Treaties and Other International Agreements of the United States of America, 1776-1949* (S 9.12/2: ). This title, (edited by Charles Bevans and often cited as "Bevans"), is considered "the definitive edition of U.S. treaties and international agreements for this time period."[10]

An ongoing series compiled by Kavass and Sprudzs and published by W. S. Hein includes *United States Treaty Index: 1776-1990 Consolidation*, indexing treaties since 1776 by number and chronologically under countries or subjects, and its update, *United States Current Treaty Index*. *United States Current Treaty Index* is a cumulative index of recent treaties too new to be published in TIAS. It indexes agreements and treaties numerically, chronologically, geographically, and by subject, giving TIAS number, title or description, and signature date. *United States Current Treaty Index* is also available on CD-ROM (Hein). *United States International Treaties Today, Unpublished and Unnumbered Treaties Index,* also from Hein, indexes treaties not published in TIAS. Peter Rohn's *World Treaty Index* covers twentieth-century (1900-1980) treaties registered in the League of Nations Treaty Series, the United Nations Treaty Series (UNTS), and national sources.

To determine whether a treaty is still in effect, check the annual TIF, *Treaties in Force* (S 9.14: ), which lists all treaties and other international agreements still in force on January 1 of each year. Kavass and Sprudzs' annual *A Guide to the United States Treaties in Force* is meant to be used with TIF, supplementing it by providing additional access points for searching. *United States Current Treaty Index* on CD-ROM (Hein) includes the full text of TIF.

Interpreting a treaty is aided by examining documents in its legislative history. Treaty Documents and Senate Executive Reports may be traced through the *Monthly Catalog, CIS/Index, Congressional Index, Congressional Record Index,* and the *Federal Index*. Copies of treaties are available from the Senate Executive Clerk. Although few can take advantage of it, most of the records of the Senate Committee on Foreign Relations are open to the public in the Capitol. Praised as the "most accessible [records] of any committee in Congress," they are available from 1816 through the early 1980s.[11]

| TREATY SEARCHES | |
|---|---|
| **Title** | **Scope** |
| **Indexes:** | |
| *Congressional Index* | Status table summarizes pending treaties awaiting Sentate consent and notes congressional action |
| *CIS/Index* | Cites Senate treaty documents and legislative history |
| *Current Treaty Index* | Slip treaties too recent to be in TIAS |
| *Treaties in Force* (TIF) (S 9.14: ) | Citations to the text of active treaties |
| *A Guide to the United States Treaties in Force* | Citations to active treaties |
| *United States Treaty Index: 1776-1990 Consolidation* | Citations to treaties since 1776 |
| *United States Congressional Serial Set Catalog: Numerical Lists and Schedule of Volumes* GP 3.34: | The series/report index is searchable by treaty document numbers |
| *United States International Treaties Today, Unpublished and Unnumbered Treaties Index* | Unnumbered treaties not published in TIAS |
| *CIS Index to U.S. Executive Documents & Reports* | Senate Executive Documents and Reports issued 1817-1969 |
| *Congressional Masterfile 1* | Senate Executive Documents and Reports issued 1817-1969 |
| **Text:** | |
| *Statutes at Large* | Treaties before 1950 |
| *Treaties and Other International Agreements of the United States of America 1776-1949* | Treaties before 1950 |
| *U.S. Treaties and Other International Agreements* (UST) (S 9.12: ) | The official, chronological series cumulating full text of slip treaties since 1950 |

## Executive Agreements and Legislation

Most international agreements bypass the treaty process by taking the form of executive agreements or legislation. Executive agreements are understandings between the president and foreign governments, and are more common than either treaties or legislative actions. In 1989, the United States had 5,117 executive agreements on the books, compared to 890 treaties. In fact, the treaty has been called "an all-but-discarded procedure."[12] Unlike treaties, executive agreements are not mentioned in the Constitution. Less binding and formal than treaties, executive agreements require no Senate consent, simplifying their handling. While treaties are considered laws

and may supersede earlier laws or treaties, executive agreements must operate within the boundaries of existing law and cannot alter it. The 1981 release of fifty-two American hostages from Iran was negotiated by President Carter as an executive agreement, as was much of the United States' involvement in the Vietnam War, and the Lend-Lease Agreement of World War II. Sometimes executive agreements are used to execute treaties.

The Senate may use joint resolutions for treaty action, with passage in both houses substituting for a two-thirds Senate approval. Texas and Hawaii were annexed to the United States this way. Congress occasionally tries to induce the president to negotiate a treaty by passing joint or concurrent resolutions.

## THE EXECUTIVE OFFICE

The basic structure of today's presidency emerged in 1939 with the creation of the Executive Office of the President. The idea was to provide executive assistants to help the president work with agencies and departments. The burgeoning staff of the Executive Office resulted in a "dramatic expansion in the size of the Presidency."[13] The influential Office of Management and Budget is a subunit of the Executive Office of the President, as is the White House staff, the Council of Economic Advisors, and many smaller bodies.

The *Federal Staff Directory* includes information about the Executive Office of the President. Executive Office publications can be identified using the quarterly *Publications of the Executive Office of the President* (NTIS), the *Monthly Catalog*, *CIS/Index*, PRF, PAIS, and *American Statistics Index*, which despite its appellation, is "the best source of comprehensive information" for executive branch publications.[14]

## EXECUTIVE BRANCH PUBLICATIONS

It is estimated that half of executive agency documents are missed by the depository library system. Frederic J. O'Hara's *Guide to Publications of the Executive Branch* describes executive publications useful in school, public, and college libraries. *CIS Index to U.S. Executive Branch Documents, 1789-1909*, covers departmental documents of the executive departments, including most executive branch titles in the *Checklist of United States Public Documents, 1789-1909* (the "1909 Checklist") except those in the Serial Set (departmental annual reports and materials submitted to Congress). CIS sells a companion microfiche collection.

The working documents of the White House are somewhat inaccessible. Goehlert and Martin emphasize that other than "the published papers of the executive branch, there is no published record of the White House staffers, such as policy and political advisors, the legislative liaison, press secretaries, and special counsels and consultants."[15]

## REORGANIZATION PLANS

A president uses reorganization plans to change executive-branch structure by combining, abolishing, or transferring agencies. Reorganization plans are transmitted to Congress as executive orders, published in the *Congressional Record* and *Federal Register*, printed as House or Senate Documents for inclusion in the Serial Set, and printed in the House and Senate Journals. Reorganization plans automatically become law unless disapproved by Congress before a specified deadline, and are cumulated in Title 3 of the *Code of Federal Regulations*, in Title 5 of the *U.S. Code*, as well as in the *Statutes at Large*. DeToro recommends the *U.S. Code* as the best source for reviewing enacted reorganization plans, where they are published "following the specific reorganization acts by which they are authorized, together with associated presidential messages and executive orders."[16]

## ADDRESSES

CIDS: Martin Marietta Corp., 4795 Meadow Wood Lane, Chantilly, VA 22021; (703) 802-5700.
> Questions about content should be addressed to Office of Public Communication, Bureau of Public Affairs, State Dept., Room 6805, Washington, DC 20520-6810.

Congressional Budget Office—copies of most CBO publications are free to the public: Office of Intergovernmental Relations, Congressional Budget Office, House Office Bldg. Annex # 2, Second and D Streets, S.W., Washington, DC 20515; (202) 226-2809.

## FREEBIES

The following subject bibliographies are available from U.S. Government Printing Office, Superintendent of Documents, Washington, DC 20402:

106.   Presidents of the United States
204.   Budget of the United States Government and Economic Report of the President
210.   Foreign Relations of the United States
282.   Congressional Budget Office Publications

From Executive Office of the President Publications, 726 Jackson Place, N.W., Room 2200, Washington, DC 20503; (202) 395-7332:

> List of OMB circulars

> "Publications of the Executive Office of the President, January 20, 1981-December 31, 1986"

From Library of Congress, Manuscript Division, Washington, DC 20540; (202) 287-5383:

> *Library of Congress Publications in Print*

> "Reference Aids to Manuscript Collections in the Library of Congress"

From Public Affairs Office, National Archives and Records Administration, Washington, DC 20408; (202) 523-3099:

> *News from the Archives* (AE1.117:) free quarterly newsletter with information about happenings at the presidential libraries, accessions, openings, and declassifications, and National Archives publications and grants

## REFERENCES

1. Arnold Hirshon, "The Scope, Accessibility and History of Presidential Papers," *Government Publications Review* 1 (1974): 363-90.

2. Robert U. Goehlert and Fenton S. Martin, *The Presidency: A Research Guide* (Denver, CO: ABC-Clio Information Services, 1985), p. xix.

3. Raymond Geselbracht, "The Four Eras in the History of Presidential Papers," *Prologue* 15 (Spring 1983): 37-42. (AE 1.111: 15/1)

4. Geselbracht, p. 37; a detailed summary of the fate of papers of individual presidents is given in Arnold Hirshon, "The Scope, Accessibility and History of Presidential Papers," in *Government Publications: Key Papers*, ed. by Bernard M. Fry and Peter Hernon (New York: Pergamon Press, 1981), pp. 156-73.

5. Geselbracht, p. 39.

6. Donald B. Schewe, "Establishing a Presidential Library: The Jimmy Carter Experience," *Prologue* 21 (Summer 1989) p. 125. (AE1.111: 21/2)

7. Schewe, p. 125.

8. *American Foreign Policy: Current Documents* continues the State Department series begun in 1950 with *A Decade of American Foreign Policy: Basic Documents, 1941-49*, and the subsequent 1957 publication of *American Foreign Policy, 1950-1955: Basic Documents*. Between 1956 and 1967, annual volumes entitled *American Foreign Policy: Current Documents* were issued. No further volumes were published until *American Foreign Policy: Basic Documents, 1977-1980* (1983), followed by annual volumes of *American Foreign Policy: Current Documents*.

9. Morris L. Cohen and Robert C. Berring, *How to Find the Law*, 8th ed. (St. Paul, MN: West Publishing Co., 1983), p. 184.

10. Jennifer DeToro, "A Guide to Information Sources," in *Studying the Presidency*, ed. by George C. Edwards and Stephen J. Wayne (Knoxville, TN: University of Tennessee Press, 1983), p. 140.

11. "Senate Foreign Relations Committee Opens Bulk of Archival Records," *Prologue* 18 (Summer 1986): 139. (AE 1.111: 18/2)

12. Loch K. Johnson, *The Making of International Agreements: Congress Confronts the Executive* (New York: New York University Press, 1984), p. 6.

13. National Study Commission on Records and Documents of Federal Officials. *Final Report of the National Commission on Records and Documents of Federal Officials* (GPO, 1977), p. 13. (Y 3.R 24/2:1/977)

14. DeToro, p. 142.

15. Goehlert and Martin, p. xx.

16. DeToro, p. 139.

# FURTHER READING

Bennett, Donna and Philip Yannarella. "Locating Presidential Proclamations and Executive Orders—A Guide to Sources." *Legal Reference Services Quarterly* 5 (Summer/Fall 1985): 177-85.

A thorough review of sources of recent and retrospective presidential proclamations and executive orders.

Burke, Frank G. "Taking the Presidency to the People." *Prologue* 18 (Summer 1986): 72-73. (AE 1.111:18/2)

A concise chronicle of the history of presidential libraries, recent legislation pertaining to them, and access to their collections.

Congressional Quarterly, Inc. *CQ Guide to Current American Government, Spring 1991.* Washington, DC: Congressional Quarterly, Inc., 1991.

Clearly written overviews of the three branches of government include a discussion of the presidency.

Edwards, George C. and Stephen J. Wayne, eds. *Studying the Presidency.* Knoxville, TN: University of Tennessee Press, 1983.

Articles include practical tips for performing research in presidential libraries, studying executive-legislative relations, and information resources for presidential research.

Elliot, Jeffrey M. and Ali R. Sheikh. *The Presidential-Congressional Political Dictionary.* Denver, CO: ABC-Clio Information Services, 1984.

A source of clear, concise definitions and explanations of key concepts and terms related to the presidency and executive branch, including the Executive Office of the President.

Goehlert, Robert and Hugh Reynolds. *The Executive Branch of the U.S. Government: A Bibliography.* (Bibliographies and Indexes in Law and Political Science, no. 11) New York: Greenwood Press, 1989.

A listing of nongovernmental literature about the history, development, organization, procedures, rulings, and policy of federal executive departments.

Haldeman, H.R. "The Nixon White House Tapes: The Decision to Record the Presidential Conversations." *Prologue* 20 (Summer 1988):79-87. (AE 1.111:20/1)

An insiders' account of the Nixon Oval Office recording system.

Herman, Edward. *The Federal Budget: A Guide to Process and Principal Publications.* Ann Arbor, MI: The Pierian Press, 1991.

An in-depth review of the federal budget, related information sources, and tips for locating and interpreting information in the budget.

Hoag, Gary. "The Search for Orders: CIS Presidential Executive Orders and Proclamations, 1789-1983." *Microform Review* 18 (Fall 1989): 222-34.

Dating back to George Washington's presidency, proclamations and executive orders have frequently been elusive to trace.

Horn, Miriam and Mike Tharp. "All the Truth That's Fit to Tint." *U.S. News and World Report* 111 (November 11, 1991): 36, 38.

"Presidential museums are hardly objective."

House of Representatives. Committee on Government Operations. *Presidential Records Act of 1978: Hearings Before a Subcommittee of the Committee on Government Operations, 95th Congress, 2nd Session on H.R. 10998 and Related Bills to Amend the Freedom of Information Act to Insure Public Access to the Official Papers of the President, and for Other Purposes, February 23, 28; March 2 and 7, 1978.* GPO, 1978. (Y 4.G74/7:P 92/5)

Background information on the disposition of presidential and executive-branch papers before the passage of the Presidential Records Act of 1978.

———. *Presidential Directives and Records Accountability Act, Hearing before the House Committee on Government Operations, August 3, 1988.* 101-2. GPO, 1989. (Y 4.G 74/7:P 92/9)

Testimony reveals the controversial nature of presidential directives.

Keller, W. Eric. "To Mr. President—Simple Gifts Of, By and From the People." *Smithsonian* 21 (December 1990):82-88.

A look at handmade gifts to the presidents, "an orgy of Americana."

Library of Congress. *Special Collections in the Library of Congress: A Selective Guide.* comp. by Annette Melville. Library of Congress, 1980. (LC 1.6/4:C 68)

Describes the Presidential Papers Collection, which includes papers of twenty-three presidents, and guides to accessing materials in the collection.

McCoy, Donald R. "The Beginnings of the Franklin D. Roosevelt Library." *Prologue* 7 (Spring 1975): 137-50. (AE 1.111:7/3)

A history of the nation's first presidential library.

Miller, Gordon W. "Researching Treaty Information: An Annotated Guide to Key Reference Sources." *RQ* 25 (Winter 1985): 204-12.

A selected, annotated bibliography of current and retrospective U.S. and international treaty information sources.

OMB. *The Budget System and Concepts of the United States Government.* GPO, 1992. (PrEx 2.2:B 85/5/992)

A clear, concise introduction to the federal budget.

Pell, Eve. "The Backbone of Hidden Government." *The Nation* 248 (June 19, 1989): 833, 848.

A discussion of National Security Directives, "perhaps the most powerful and hidden tool of the Oval Office."

Peterson, Trudy Huskamp. "Documents in Time: The Archives of the United States and the National Archives and Records Service." *Government Publications Review* 8A (1981): 285-94.

Describes the Presidential Records Act of 1978 and the Presidential Libraries Act which preceded it, along with a discussion of access to materials in presidential libraries.

Plischke, Elmer. *U.S. Foreign Relations: A Guide to Information Sources* (American Government and History Information Guide Series, vol. 6). Detroit, MI: Gale Research Co., 1980.

This annotated bibliographic guide to official and unofficial foreign relations documents is also a guide to publications of the executive and legislative branches of government.

Price, Miles O. and Harry Bitner. *Effective Legal Research.* Boston: Little, Brown, and Co., 1953.

The first edition of this title provided a listing of retrospective sources of proclamations and executive orders (pp. 143-48).

*Prologue* 21 (Summer 1989) (AE 1.111:18/2)
> Entire issue is devoted to presidential libraries.

Senate. Committee on the Budget. *The Congressional Budget Process: How It Works* (Committee Print, S. Prt. 99-74) GPO, 1985. (Y 4.B 85/2:S. prt. 99-74)
> A concise overview of the congressional budget process.

Wolff, Cynthia J. "Necessary Monuments: The Making of the Presidential Library System." *Government Publications Review* 16 (January/February 1989):47-62.

A history of the archival and political foundations of the presidential libraries.

Zwirn, Jerrold. *Congressional Publications and Proceedings: Research on Legislation, Budgets, and Treaties.* 2nd ed. Littleton, CO: Libraries Unlimited, Inc., 1988.
> A thorough overview of Congress's budget and treaty processes and related information sources.

## EXERCISES

1.  The United States is party to the Patent Cooperation Treaty (PCT), providing reciprocal patent protection and filing rights for member countries. Locate the text of this treaty and citations to its legislative history.

2.  Following World War II, Allied reconnaissance teams shipped tons of captured Nazi documents to the United States. To handle the flood of German documents, President Truman issued Executive Order 9568, establishing the Office of the Publication Board. Locate the text of Truman's executive order.

3.  The recent portrayal of young Americans as "geographically illiterate" has triggered annual presidential proclamations declaring Geography Awareness Week. Locate any recent Geography Awareness Week proclamation.

4.  In 1982, President Reagan issued an executive order described popularly as "when in doubt, classify." The executive order instructed government officials to err on the side of classification whenever they were unsure whether information warranted secrecy. Identify this executive order.

# CHAPTER 11
# Judicial Information Sources

*There is no liberty if the power of judging be not separated from the legislative and executive powers.*
—C. S. Montesquieu

## WHAT

The United States has two judicial systems: state and federal. At the pinnacle of each are supreme courts, below which are appellate courts and trial courts (called U.S. district courts at the federal level). In addition, there are special courts established to consider particular issues. The federal judiciary is headed by the nine-member Supreme Court, plus courts of appeals, district courts, and various special courts, all created by Congress.

## WHY

The United States courts were established by Congress under authority of the Constitution; state and local courts function under the authority of individual state governments.

## WHO

Federal judgeships are presidential appointments, requiring Senate approval for confirmation. The federal judiciary has been called "an anomaly" in our democratic society, with nonelected judges holding office not for a specific time, but contingent upon "good behaviour."[1]

## HOW

Court rulings may be published ("reported") in both official (government-published) and unofficial (commercially published) reporters. Official court reporters are government documents, and many are available to depository libraries—allowing depository libraries to maintain basic legal collections. Unofficial reporters reprint and enhance the official version by adding explanatory material and finding aids. Three leading commercial legal publishers are West Publishing Company (the primary publisher of federal court opinions), Lawyers Cooperative Publishing Company, and Shepard's/McGraw-Hill, Inc.

*Most Americans are certified at birth, licensed at marriage, and registered at death. In each instance, they are touched by the law. In fact, it is hard to find a facet of American life that is not affected or regulated by legal procedure.*
—Robert M. Warner,
archivist of the United States

Alexander Hamilton observed that "laws are a dead letter without courts to expound and define their true meaning and operation." Judicial opinions (case law), along with statutes and administrative regulations and adjudications, are our nation's three primary sources of law. Court decisions interpret both statutory and administrative law, and are important for determining whether a law or presidential action is constitutional (see Figure 11.1).

The doctrine of *stare decisis* dictates that judicial decisions be based upon legal precedent. As Lavin points out, the "critical point to remember about legal research is that the past can never be ignored."[2] The uses of court reporters go beyond legal precedent, however. Fascinating historical information is tucked into federal court records, revealing Wyatt Earp's prosecution as a horse thief; bankruptcy papers of the H. J. Heinz Company which claimed "pickles and relish" as assets; a "custody" battle between two companies claiming patent and trademark ownership of Raggedy Ann, the rag doll.[3] Many, but not all, court rulings are published. Opinions that break new ground or go beyond previous decisions are ordered to be published. A general rule of thumb is that the higher the court, the more likely its decisions have been published. However, even at the federal level, publication is not comprehensive—not even the Supreme Court publishes all its decisions. All federal courts do file case documentation with the clerk of the court, including the initiating complaint, orders, answers, mo-

**FIGURE 11.1: Legislative/Judicial/Executive Relationships.**

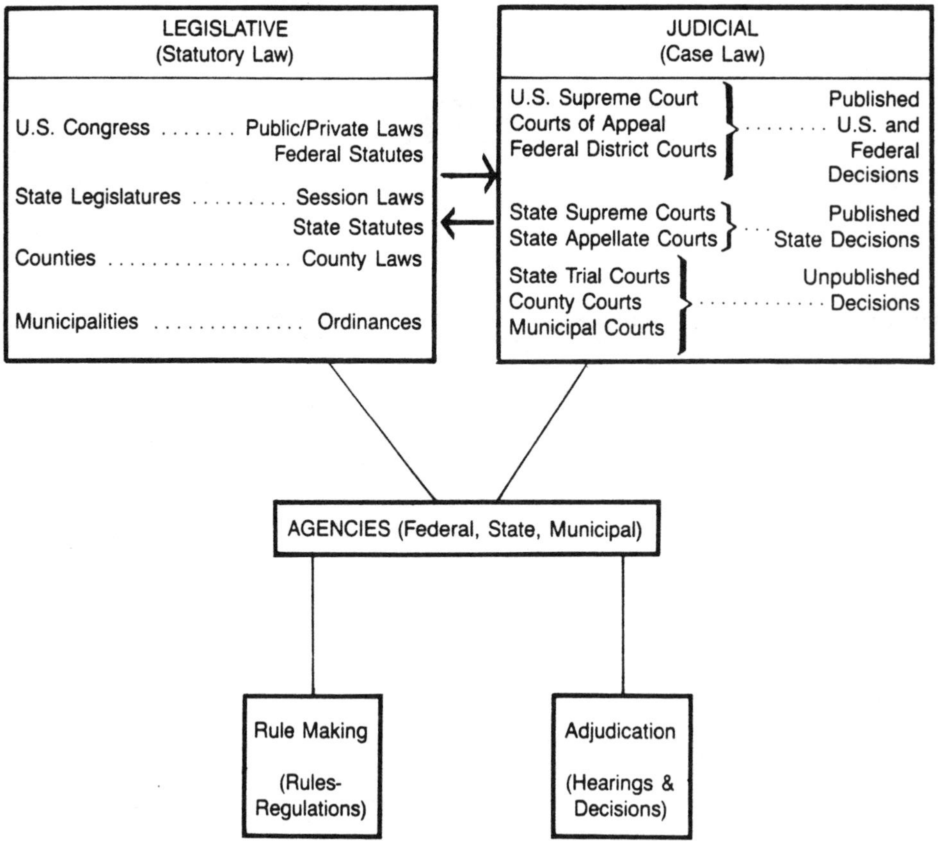

Source: *Finding the Law: A Workbook on Legal Research for Laypersons,* 1982

tions, and subpoenas. While not always published, this documentation is publicly available through on-site examination or requests for photocopies (fees are charged). Each court establishes its own procedures for access. Many unpublished decisions are also available through online legal databases.[4]

The United States court system is like a pyramid, with the Supreme Court at the apex and the U.S. courts of appeals and U.S. district courts on the two levels below (see Figure 11.2). This pyramidal structure allows the courts of appeals to correct errors made in trial courts, and ensures uniformity through Supreme Court review.

For a court to render a valid judgment it must have the authority, or jurisdiction, to decide the case. The United States courts cannot decide all cases—only those qualifying as federal cases (thus the popular saying, "Don't make a federal case out of it," a warning not to overemphasize the importance of something). The Constitution and laws enacted by Congress prescribe what cases may be considered by the United States courts, leaving others to be tried in state courts.

| FEDERAL COURT REPORTERS: ABBREVIATIONS | |
|---|---|
| **Abbreviation** | **Reporter** |
| F., F.2d. | *Federal Reporter* |
| F.Supp. | *Federal Supplement* |
| L.Ed., L.Ed.2d. | *U.S. Supreme Court Reports,* Lawyers Edition |
| S. Ct. | *Supreme Court Reporter* |
| U.S. | *United States Reports* |

## THE UNITED STATES SUPREME COURT: THE COURT OF LAST RESORT

*Virtually every issue of significance in American society eventually arrives at the Supreme Court.*
—Bob Woodward and Scott Armstrong, in *The Brethren*

As the nation's highest court, the United States Supreme Court is the final forum for appeal in the American judicial system. Its decisions are final, creating legal precedents that guide future lower court and Supreme Court decisions. Many view the Supreme Court as the most powerful entity in federal government—not only can it declare presidential actions illegal, it can also strike down acts of Congress as unconstitutional, through the process of judicial review.

The Supreme Court can preempt other courts and hear cases first (called "original jurisdiction") when foreign diplomats or states are involved. Fewer than six original jurisdiction cases are filed each term, making them the rarest of Supreme Court cases. More numerous are the appellate jurisdiction cases, in which the Court hears appeals from lower courts. Between the first Monday in October and June, about 4,000 cases thread their way up through state and federal courts to the Supreme Court. Except for some cases that have to be considered, the Supreme Court can opt to review lower court decisions or let them stand. Most are dismissed with a brief decision that the subject is either improper or too insignificant to warrant review. Only about 200 cases rate oral arguments before the Court each term, with another 100 or so decided without oral argument.

Cases are decided by majority vote, with the opinions reported both officially and unofficially, and searchable online through services such as LEXIS and WESTLAW. The pilot Project Hermes Bulletin Board tested electronic dissemination of Supreme Court slip opinions, and will be evaluated in 1992–93. Although often used interchangeably, legal opinions and decisions can be differentiated: The decision tells whether the court upheld or reversed a lower court decision; the opinion explains why, giving the legal reasoning for the judgment. Although the majority rules in deciding cases, any justice may write a separate opinion to accompany the majority opinion. These may be concurring opinions (in agreement with the majority but for different reasons) or dissenting opinions (disagreeing with the majority).

*The people can change Congress but only God can change the Supreme Court.* —George W. Norris

The nine justices of the U.S. Supreme Court are appointed for life by the president of the United States, with the advice and consent of the Senate. In 200 years the Senate has rejected roughly one out of every five

## FIGURE 11.2: Federal and State Judicial Systems.

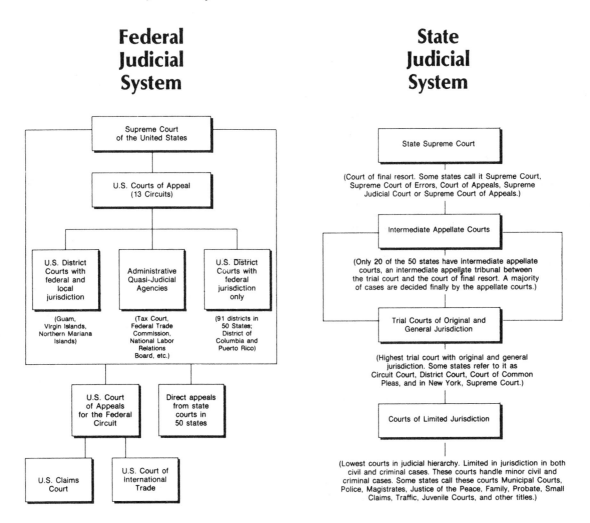

Reprinted with the permission of Congressional Quarterly, Inc. from *CQ Guide to Current American Government*, Spring 1988.

Supreme Court nominees and has argued passionately about others. The decision is far-reaching—once confirmed, Supreme Court justices may be removed only by impeachment (something that has never happened in the nation's history).

---

**Biographical Information about Justices**

*The American Bench* (Forster-Long, Inc.)
*Federal Judiciary Almanac* (Wiley; searchable on LEXIS)
*Judicial Staff Directory* (Staff Directories, Ltd.)

---

## Supreme Court Reporters

Within a few weeks, Supreme Court opinions are published individually as numbered slip opinions (Ju 6.8/b: ). These are accumulated throughout the term in official advance sheets, called Preliminary Prints (Ju 6.8/a: ), supplemented with headnotes or syllabi (summaries of significant legal issues in the case), names of counsel, indexes, and tables of cases. The final, bound, official record of Supreme Court opinions appears as *United States Reports* (Ju 6.8: ). All are for sale from GPO and available to depository libraries. The Congressional Information Service sells microfiche subscriptions to *United States Reports*. The pilot Project Hermes Bulletin Board (PHBB) offered full text Supreme Court opinions within hours of their release. The daily *Journal—Supreme Court of the United States* (Ju 6.5: ) summarizes the Court proceedings.

Supreme Court opinions are also published unofficially, first as paperbound "advance sheets" containing several decisions, which are later replaced by bound volumes. Like their official counterparts, unofficial reporters include the text of opinions, but are augmented with annotations and supplemental information, and are available faster than the official reporters. Because of their speedy publication and editorial additions, "most lawyers and researchers prefer using them to the *United States Reports*."[5]

*United States Supreme Court Reports* (Lawyers' Edition) has two series and may be searched online. The first series (cited as L.Ed.) covers opinions from volumes 1 to 349 of *United States Reports*; the second series (L.Ed.2d.) began with volume 350. (Multiple series are commonly used in court reporters to prevent unwieldy numbering.) The annually supplemented *Desk-Book to the United States Supreme Court Reports, Lawyers Edition*, contains tables of cases in L.Ed.2d., a table of Supreme Court justices since 1789, and an index to L.Ed.2d. annotations.

*Supreme Court Reporter* (West Edition), part of the West Publishing Company's National Reporter System, is also searchable online. *Supreme Court Reporter* begins with volume 106 of the official set (1882) and omits cases reported in volumes 1-105.

Two weekly loose-leaf services are especially useful for tracing actions during the current Supreme Court term. Commerce Clearing House's weekly *U.S. Supreme Court Bulletin* reproduces the full text of the Court's opinions, with information on docketed cases and the Court's disposition of them. Its loose-leaf format allows fast reporting, an advantage shared by the weekly legal reporting service, *United States Law Week*, Supreme Court edition, available online through LEXIS and BNA. *U.S. Law Week* (USLW) includes full texts of Supreme Court decisions along with status reports on developing cases—from docketing through denial or formal review. (For tracing the disposition of a recent Supreme Court case using USLW, novices may find Maier's how-to discussion helpful.[6]) The Supreme Court section of *U.S. Law Week* includes information on court proceedings, summary digests, tables of cases, and a Supreme Court index and is searchable online through LEXIS. A companion resource, Supreme Court Today, is an electronic news service from BNA Online (available from LEXIS and WESTLAW) listing all U.S. Supreme Court decisions and case summaries reported by *U.S. Law Week*.

Legal digests are subject indexes to court decisions. *United States Supreme Court Digest* (West) and *United States Supreme Court Reports/Digest: General Index to Decisions, Annotations, and Digest* (Lawyers Co-operative) are complete indexes to Supreme Court decisions. The *Federal Practice Digest* covers the entire federal court system.

Supreme Court records and briefs are reprinted by several commercial publishers, including the Congressional Information Service, which sells microfiche transcripts of Supreme Court oral arguments for all argued cases since the 1969/70 term, and also Supreme Court records and briefs on microfiche, including petitions, jurisdictional statements, appendixes, and memos. Audiotapes of oral arguments heard by the Court are kept in the National Archives.

### Legal Citations

The most respected guide to legal citing is the Harvard Law Review Association's *A Uniform System of Citation*, popularly known as the "Bluebook" because of its blue cover. The "preferred" citation for Supreme Court decisions is to *United States Reports*, the official reporter. Here is an example:

---

*Roe v. Wade*, 410 U.S. 113 (1973)

The case name, derived from the last names of the parties involved. The first name cited is the plaintiff; the second is the defendant. The "v." is an abbreviation for "versus."

Citation to volume 410, page 113 of *United States Reports*, where the text begins. The case was decided in 1973.

---

To locate the text of a decision for which you have a citation, consult the volume and page of the reporter abbreviated in the cite. Cases are sometimes referred to only by the names of plaintiff and defendant. The "Pentagon Papers" case, for example, is *New York Times Company* v. *United States*. One way to locate the decision when you have a reference to the parties involved is to consult the alphabetical tables of cases in legal digests. These will refer to cites for the case. The *United States Supreme Court Reports/Digest, United States Code Annotated*, and *Shepard's Acts and Cases by Popular Names, Federal and State* allow cross-referencing from a popular case name (the "Pentagon Papers" case, for example) to case citations.

Parallel citations cite the same material in unofficial reporters, using the same format and substituting the unofficial reporter abbreviation for the *U.S. Reports* abbreviation. The Bluebook recommends West's *Supreme Court Reporter* as the "preferred unofficial" citation, used when the official publication is unavailable. The two unofficial reporters have their own numbering systems, but also give the *United States Reports* citation (sometimes called "star-pagination"). The unofficial reporters also have cross-reference tables referring from official to unofficial citations.

## LOWER COURTS

Below the Supreme Court stand the United States courts of appeals, the intermediate appellate courts that review district court decisions. They render judgments that either affirm or reverse those of the lower district courts, and their decisions are final unless reviewed by the Supreme Court. The federal appeals courts are busy: Over the last thirty years, the number of appeals has grown sixteen times faster than the population. Since only about one percent of appealed cases rate Supreme Court review, the federal courts of appeals are the end of the judicial road for most Americans. As one federal appeals court judge explained: "Yes, the Supreme Court is above us, but in practice we are nearly always the final court of review."

The United States is divided into twelve judicial circuits, each of which has a court of appeals serving several states. There is also a United States Court of Appeals for the Federal Circuit, with national jurisdiction. This court was created by merging the former U.S. Court of Claims with the U.S. Court of Customs and Patent Appeals. The resultant Court of Appeals for the Federal Circuit hears appeals from all district courts in patent and "Little Tucker Act" cases (claims against the United States) plus all appeals from the U.S. Claims Court, the U.S. Court of International Trade, the Boards of Contract Appeals, the Patent and Trademark Office, and the Merit Systems Protection Board and the International Trade Commission.

At the lowest rung of the federal court hierarchy are the United States district courts, the trial courts of the federal government, where cases are initially decided. Each state has at least one district court, with larger states having as many as four (see Figure 11.3).

**FIGURE 11.3: U.S. Court System.**

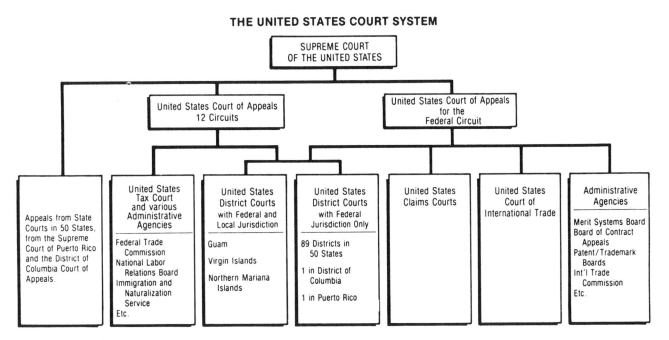

**THE UNITED STATES COURT SYSTEM**

Source: *The United States Courts: Their Jurisdiction and Work*, 1989

## Lower Court Reporters and Citators

Although no official reporter exists for the U.S. courts of appeals or U.S. district courts, some are unofficially reported by West Publishing Company. West's National Reporter System's *Federal Reporter 2d*, documenting opinions from U.S. courts of appeals and some district courts, is available in print and online through WESTLAW. West's *Federal Supplement*, reporting opinions of the U.S. district courts, is also available in print or online. Both sets are issued first as advance sheets and later in bound volumes. Jacobstein and Mersky emphasize that the *Federal Supplement* contains only a small percentage of district court decisions and that others are published in special-subject loose-leaf services.[7] The weekly *West Federal Case News* summarizes Supreme Court and other federal decisions, plus selected cases from state courts. The *National Reporter Blue Book* refers from official citations to unofficial National Reporter citations.

Case citators document changes in the legal effect of court cases, identifying any subsequent legal action that may have reversed or overruled an earlier decision. This updating is sometimes referred to as "Shepardizing" a case, since Shepard's Citations is a popular citator. Citators are useful for determining the disposition of an appealed case, identifying interim opinions for the same case, locating parallel citations, tracing subsequent opinions, verifying the current status of an opinion, and obtaining subsequent cases, law review articles, or annotations citing the case. Novices to citators will find Maier's step-by-step guide to using Shepard's Citations a helpful introduction.[8]

## SPECIAL COURTS

There are also special national courts that handle specific types of cases. The United States Court of International Trade (formerly the United States Customs Court) deals with cases involving international trade and customs duties. The United States Claims Court, known as "the keeper of the nation's conscience," is where citizens, corporations, and some aliens bring suits against the federal government for money damages. The United States Tax Court is a special court in the legislative branch which settles disputes between taxpayers and the Internal Revenue Service. The government publishes decisions of many special courts.

## THE CONSTITUTION

*The Declaration of 1776 gave us our independence, but the Constitution of 1787 gave us our government.*
—Frank G. Burke, acting archivist of the United States

| FEDERAL COURT DECISIONS | |
|---|---|
| **Supreme Court** | **Official Reporters** |
| | Slip opinions (Ju 6.8/b: ) |
| | Preliminary prints (Ju 6.8/a: ) |
| | *United States Reports* (Ju 6.8/a: ), cited as U.S. |
| | **Unofficial Reporters** |
| | *Supreme Court Reporter* (S. Ct. or Sup. Ct.) |
| | *United States Supreme Court Reports* (L.Ed., L.Ed.2d.) |
| | *Loose-leaf Services* |
| | *United States Law Week* (U.S.L.W.) (USLW) |
| | *U.S. Supreme Court Bulletin* |
| **U.S. Courts of Appeals** | *Federal Reporter* (F., F.2d) |
| **U.S. District Courts** | *Federal Supplement* (F. Supp.) |
| **Online Access** | BNA ONLINE |
| | LEXIS |
| | WESTLAW |
| **Citators** | *Shepard's United States Citations*: decisions of the U.S. Supreme Court and statutes enacted by Congress |
| | *Shepard's Federal Citations*: federal courts of appeals and districts courts (both available on LEXIS and WESTLAW) |
| **Digests** | *American Digest System* Federal and state decisions |
| | *Federal Practice Digest* (West) Federal court system |
| | *United States Supreme Court Digest* (West) |
| | *United States Supreme Court Reports/Digest* (Lawyers Cooperative) |

Although not as familiar as Independence Day, September 17, 1787, is a milestone in our national history. On that day more than two centuries ago, thirty-nine delegates from twelve states signed a document that began, "We the people of the United States"—the United States Constitution, the oldest written constitution on earth. Only fifteen other nations have constitutions written before World War II, and fully two-thirds of the world's constitutions were adopted after 1970.

The United States Constitution is the cornerstone of American democracy. America claimed freedom on July 4, 1776, with the Declaration of Independence, but eleven years later the Constitution secured that freedom. That same year, Alexander Hamilton, James Madison, and John Jay issued the first of the *Federalist Papers* under a pseudonym. The *Federalist Papers* argued for the states' ratification of the proposed Constitution and are today considered among the clearest constitutional explanations ever written.

## Annotated Constitution

Annotated constitutional texts provide judicial decisions that have interpreted or applied the Constitution, along with scholarly analysis. Examples are West's *United States Code Annotated: Constitution of the United States Annotated* and the Lawyers Co-operative Publishing Company's *United States Code Service: Constitution Volume.* The government-published *Constitution of the United States of America, as Amended: Analytical Index, Unratified Amendments* (X 95-2: doc. 256) provides the text of the Constitution, amendments and their ratification dates, background on proposed but unratified amendments, and a detailed analytical index. The Senate's *Constitution of the United States, Analysis and Interpretation*, often referred to as the "Annotated Constitution" or "Constitution Annotated" (Y 1.1/3:99-16 and 1990 supplement Y 1.1/3:101-36), supplements the Constitution with annotations to historic Supreme Court cases, along with laws declared unconstitutional. It also lists federal, state, and local laws determined to be unconstitutional and Supreme Court decisions overruling previous decisions. The format is an article-by-article, amendment-by-amendment treatment of the Constitution, with commentaries based on historical and legal considerations. The "Constitution Annotated" is prepared by the Congressional Research Service and revised each decade, with cumulative supplements issued every two years. Cohen and Berring point to its infrequent supplementation as the major weakness of this source.[9]

## Annotated Codes

Annotated codes are supplemented with citations and case notes for court and administrative agency decisions, with cross-references to the *Code of Federal Regulations*, and historical notes on the development of the law. Two unofficial annotated editions of federal statutes are the *United States Code Service, Lawyers Edition* (USCS) and *United States Code Annotated* (USCA).

## STATE COURTS

The fifty states have independent judiciaries, called state courts, with which citizens most often have contact (see Figure 11.2). Located in towns and cities across the nation, the state courts are empowered to decide almost any type of case, subject only to limitations of state law. Many states publish slip opinions and advance sheets, often unofficially. The National Reporter System is one example, publishing state appellate court opinions according to a geographic breakdown of regional and state reporters.

## FREEBIES

The following subject bibliography is available free from U.S. Government Printing Office, Superintendent of Documents, Washington, DC 20402:

25. United States Reports

From the Office of the Clerk of the Court, U.S. Supreme Court Bldg., 1 First St., N.E., Washington, DC 20543; (202) 479-3011:

Supreme Court Slip Opinions: (A few free copies of Supreme Court opinions are available immediately after their announcement)

## REFERENCES

1. Daniel Meador, *Consumers of Justice: How the Public Views the Federal Judicial Process* (Washington, DC: Federal Judicial Center, [1975]), p. 5.

2. Michael R. Lavin, *Business Information: How to Find It, How to Use It* (Phoenix, AZ: Oryx Press, 1987), p. 229.

3. Robert M. Warner, "The Law and American Society," *Prologue* 16 (Winter 1984):212-13. (AE 1.111: )

4. Mark J. Newman, "Shortcuts for Better Research: Online Searches," *The National Law Journal* 14 (February 17, 1992):31, 32, 36.

5. J. Myron Jacobstein and Roy M. Mersky, *Fundamentals of Legal Research*, 3rd ed. (Mineola, NY: The Foundation Press, Inc., 1985), p. 34.

6. Elaine C. Maier, *How to Prepare a Legal Citation* (Woodbury, NY: Barron's Educational Series, Inc., 1986), pp. 38-40.

7. Jacobstein and Mersky, p. 36.

8. Maier, pp. 35-38.

9. Morris L. Cohen and Robert C. Berring, *How to Find the Law*, 8th ed. (St. Paul, MN: West Publishing Co., 1983), p. 144.

## FURTHER READING

Baum, Lawrence. *The Supreme Court.* 3rd ed. Washington, DC: CQ Press, 1989.
> A thorough introduction to the Court and how it functions.

"Celebrating the Constitution." *Prologue* 17 (Fall 1985). (AE 1.111:17/3)
> This special issue is devoted to a review of the Constitution's history and its role in American life.

Coco, Al. *Finding the Law: A Workbook on Legal Research for Laypersons.* Prepared for Bureau of Land Management, Denver Service Center. GPO, 1982. (I 53.2:L 41) Reprinted, W. S. Hein, 1986.

A clearly written introduction to legal literature from the courts and Congress.

Cohen, Morris L. and Robert C. Berring. *How to Find the Law.* 9th ed. St. Paul, MN: West Publishing Co., 1989.

A standard legal textbook that thoroughly reviews legal literature from all levels of government.

Congress. Senate. Committee on the Judiciary. Subcommittee on the Constitution. *Amendments to the Constitution: A Brief Legislative History* (Committee print, S. 99-87) 99th Congress, 1st session. GPO, 1985. (Y 4.J 89/2:S. prt. 99-87)

A historical review of every congressional amendment to the Constitution.

Congressional Quarterly. *Congressional Quarterly's Guide to the U.S. Supreme Court.* 2nd ed. Washington, DC: Congressional Quarterly, Inc., 1990.

A key reference covering the history, procedures, and landmark decisions of the Supreme Court, with biographies of justices.

Department of Justice. *Bibliography of Original Meaning of the United States Constitution.* GPO, 1988. (J 1.20/2:C 76/2)

A list of materials discussing the meanings of Constitutional provisions as understood by the framers of the Constitution, including Supreme Court cases.

Elliott, Stephen P. *A Reference Guide to the United States Supreme Court.* New York: Facts on File Publications, 1986.

A scholarly history of the Court with summaries of landmark cases and biographies of justices.

Geel, T. R. van. *Understanding Supreme Court Opinions.* New York: Longman, 1991.

A guide to reading and interpreting Supreme Court opinions.

Harrell, Mary Ann. *Equal Justice under Law: The Supreme Court in American Life.* 4th ed. Washington, DC: The Supreme Court Historical Society, 1982.

A simple introduction to the Supreme Court and its impact on American life.

Jacobstein, J. Myron and Roy M. Mersky. *Fundamentals of Legal Research.* 5th ed. Westbury, NY: Foundation Press, Inc., 1990.

A detailed review of federal, state, local, and international legal literature.

Maier, Elaine C. *How to Prepare a Legal Citation.* Woodbury, NY: Barron's Educational Series, Inc., 1986.

To be used as a companion to *Uniform System of Citation,* this is a guide to proper citing, checking legal citations for accuracy, verifying missing or incomplete citations, and updating citations using *Shepard's* and *U.S. Law Week,* with programmed exercises for self-instruction.

National Park Service. *The Framing of the Federal Constitution* (Handbook 103). National Park Service, 1986. (I 29.9/5:103)

A vivid, illustrated account of the drafting of the Constitution and the people and places that share its history.

*A Uniform System of Citation.* 15th ed. Cambridge, MA: Harvard Law Review Association, 1991.

The key reference for legal citation format, also called the "Bluebook."

## EXERCISES

1. Ex-President Richard M. Nixon sued the government after Congress seized his presidential papers and tapes in 1974, charging that the confiscation was unconstitutional. In 1977, the Supreme Court upheld a lower court decision denying Nixon's right to control his papers, overthrowing the 200-year precedent of presidential ownership and setting the stage for the Presidential Records Act of 1978. Identify this Supreme Court decision.

2. After the 1980 census, the Census Bureau was beset by lawsuits alleging a population undercount. The most publicized suit, filed by the city of Detroit, was *Young* v. *Klutznick.* Identify the full cite.

3. An article discussing the judicial opinion that "There simply is no first amendment right to receive a verbatim transcript of the proceedings of Congress" cites the following court case: *Gregg* v. *Barrett,* 771 F.2d 539 (D.C. Cir 1985). What court and source are being cited?

4. Which of the following are citations to Supreme Court decisions?
798 F.2d.731
102 S. Ct. 87
454 U.S. 812
468 F.Supp. 927
77 L.Ed.2nd 317

# CHAPTER 12
# Statistics

*Statistics: the heart of democracy.*
—Simeon Strunsky

## WHAT

Statistics are both an American tradition and a national resource. One of the federal government's major functions is collecting and analyzing data to satisfy legal requirements and emerging national needs. The United States, cranking out more statistics than any other entity in the world, has long been looked to as a source of reliable, consistent, and comparable data about national demographic, social, and economic trends. It is a task so complex that only the federal government has the facilities and funds to accomplish it.

## WHERE

Federal statistical activity is decentralized, with more than 100 agencies authorized to collect and disseminate statistics. Three agencies supply the most used data in the nation: the Bureaus of the Census, of Economic Analysis, and of Labor Statistics. These three multipurpose collection agencies join five other statistical agencies as the eight major statistical organs of the federal government, accounting for more than one-third of the nation's annual $2 billion statistical tab. The remainder of federal statistical activity is scattered among other agencies whose statistical work supports their administrative, regulatory, or operating functions. Federal statistical activity is coordinated by the Office of Management and Budget (OMB).

## WHY

Agencies collect statistics to support their missions and to satisfy legislative mandates requiring data collection. Between one-half and three-quarters of the federal budget is allocated based on statistics and statistical formulas.

## HOW

Federal statistics are collected by federal agencies and received from state and local governments and private sources. Although federal and state statistical programs generally operate independently, some federal-state data collection is coordinated: The national vital statistics records, for example, are compiled nationally based on state and local reporting.

The 1980s brought concern about coordination of federal statistical activity, with cost-cutting and staff reductions. Amid general consensus that data collection could be more efficient and less duplicative, there was concern that cutbacks not cause deterioration in the quality, quantity, and utility of federal statistics.[1]

## WHEN

Federal data collection was launched with the constitutionally mandated decennial census, and has been a national enterprise since the earliest days of our republic.

## STATISTICAL STANDARDS

Because standard definitions and classifications increase the comparability and usefulness of government statistical programs, several standards are applied across numerous agencies. Geographic units such as Metropolitan Areas have been defined by the Census Bureau and are used throughout government and in private and nonprofit organizations (a metropolitan area is a city and suburbs with a population of at least 100,000). The *Standard Industrial Classification Manual* (PrEx 2.6/2:In 27/yr) classifies industries by their activities and lists standard industrial classification (SIC) codes. Initially designed for government to ensure compatibility of economic statistics, the SIC is now widely used by business, trade, and professional organizations. The *Standard Occupational Classification Manual* (C 1.8/3:Oc 1/yr) provides a coding system and nomenclature for classifying occupations, allowing cross-referencing and aggregating of occupational data collected for various social and economic programs. Its companion volume, *Dictionary of Occupational Titles* (L 37.302:Oc 1), describes occupations arranged alphabetically and by industry.

---

**Major Federal Statistical Agencies**

Bureau of the Census: the nation's chief collector of economic and demographic data, and the central federal statistical agency

Bureau of Economic Analysis (Commerce Department): develops the national economic accounts, preparing the national income and product accounts and analyses of business conditions

Bureau of Justice Statistics: crime and criminal-justice data

The Bureau of Labor Statistics: the government's chief source of information on labor-related aspects of the economy, including employment and unemployment, prices, living standards, wages and benefits, industrial relations, and productivity

Energy Information Administration: energy data and analysis to support energy decisions of government, industry, and the public

The National Agriculture Statistics Service: national and state agricultural statistics, estimates, and forecasts

National Center for Education Statistics: statistics about preschool through postsecondary education

National Center for Health Statistics: health, population, health care, family changes, vital statistics

---

# CENSUSES

A census is an official count of a nation's population (or anything else), usually conducted at regular intervals. Counting people is one of government's oldest activities. There is evidence of Babylonian censuses as early as 3800 B.C., and in ancient China, food-conscious bureaucrats counted mouths instead of noses. Nine hundred years ago a census resulted in the famous Domesday Book, when William the Conqueror counted the English under his rule.

Computerization has both streamlined modern censuses and unnerved respondents, making anti-census campaigns a sign of the times. In West Germany a census was finally taken in 1987, after a 17-year stalemate. West Germans had balked at the length and complexity of the questionnaire and feared leaks to government databanks. Opponents pressured for a census boycott under the slogan, "Only sheep let themselves be counted." Fear of "big brother" also struck in Holland, where a national census has been stalled on the drawing board since 1981. Since Holland's last census in 1971, the government has resorted to monitoring population growth through municipal residence records. In the United States, initial response to the 1990 census was sluggish, reflecting the public's changing attitudes, reluctance to tackle complicated questionnaires, and fear

of "big brother." A "reformed" U.S. census is being considered for 2000.

## The Decennial Census

Soon after the thirteen colonies broke away from England, a national head count was taken—not only to establish the House of Representatives, but also to divvy up the Revolutionary War debt among taxpayers. With a constitutional mandate to reapportion House of Representatives seats based on district boundaries that shift with population changes, the United States became the first nation to incorporate regular censuses into its Constitution.

Since 1790, the entire population has been counted each decade. The decennial census of population and housing has become the cornerstone of the nation's statistical system. The three primary uses of census data are redistricting within states and reapportionment of the House of Representatives, allocation of federal funds, and economic decision making in the public and private sectors.

The decennial census counts heads and gathers housing facts, providing a snapshot of social, demographic, and economic characteristics, with data on age, sex, race, marital status, and income, plus many others. The census describes the nation as a whole and its components like regions, states, and metropolitan areas. Unlike other data-collection programs, the decennial census also provides statistics for small parcels like counties, congressional districts, cities, towns, and even neighborhood blocks. By including historical time series, each decennial census also allows comparison with previous censuses.

### Selecting Census Questions

When attendees at a census conference were urged to describe their census data needs, one user asked how many Americans owned horses. The expectation that the census would gather horse-ownership data highlights an important concept: Although it may seem that every possible question is asked in the census, determining census questions is actually painstakingly selective. Public input is solicited to select new questions and delete obsolete ones. Question changes over the last twenty decades mirror the nation's shifting interests and data needs. Americans are no longer asked, for example, whether they own television sets: Virtually every home now boasts at least one. Questions on appliance ownership, kitchen sinks, electric lights, and refrigerators were abandoned for similar reasons. Exploring "modern" trends, the 1990 census added questions on "blended families," asking about stepchildren, foster children, and grandchildren and added solar heating to the list of home heating fuels. Some questions of limited use are never asked—horse ownership, for example. Others are reworded to reflect changing attitudes: The "head of household" concept, meaning the husband in a husband/wife household, was replaced in 1980 with the more neutral "person in column one."

As Ann Scott notes in *Census USA*, "choosing and wording of questions may well be the most fascinating part of census planning."[2] The impossibility of including every question useful to someone, somewhere, means careful choices must be made. "Over the years the Bureau has turned down appeals for statistics on dogs, cats, and parakeets, smoking, auto accidents, union membership, child spacing, boat ownership, and hundreds of other subjects of vital interest to some group or other."[3]

---

**Question Suggestions Rejected by the Census Bureau[4]**

Ask everyone's height and weight so you can determine the national obesity rate
How many people suffer from hay fever?
Do you take vitamins daily?
How many cigarettes do you smoke?
Have you ever had a paranormal or psychic experience?
Do you dream in color?

---

The first census in 1790 asked only five questions, allowing publication of results in a modest fifty-six-page volume. By 1790 legislation had already expanded the census beyond the simple head count stipulated in the Constitution, adding questions to tally free white men and women, free blacks, and slaves, plus recording the ages of free white men as either under or over sixteen (see Figure 12.1). James Madison, who had been instrumental in expanding the scope of census questions, wanted occupational information gathered as well, but Congress balked. The 1790 census enumerated 3,929,214 Americans, but left Indians uncounted and recorded every five slaves as only three people. By the time the tenth census rolled around in 1880, questions had been added about the ages of white women, health, literacy, and employment. By 1890, the scope of the census leapt from five subjects to 235. To review questions from the first twenty population and housing censuses, consult *200 Years of U.S. Census Taking: Population and Housing Questions, 1790-1990* (C 3.2:T 93).

## "There Ought to be a Machine"

By 1890, census staff were overwhelmed by mountains of data spilling onto their desks. Hunched over bookkeeping and accounting ledgers, they tallied by hand on ruled sheets, stroke by stroke, like this: ⊥ℍ⊤. It was Dr. John Shaw Billings, head of Vital Statistics at the Bureau of the Census, who dreamed of mechanically counting the census and staged a contest to encourage inventors. The winner was young Herman Hollerith, a census office engineer whose tabulation machine would

**FIGURE 12.1: The First Census.**

| DISTICTS | Free white Males of 16 years and upwards, including heads of families. | Free white Males under sixteen years. | Free white Females, including heads of families. | All other free persons. | Slaves. | Total. |
|---|---|---|---|---|---|---|
| Vermont | 22435 | 22328 | 40505 | 255 | 16 | 85539 |
| N. Hampshire | 36086 | 34851 | 70160 | 630 | 158 | 141885 |
| Maine | 24384 | 24748 | 46870 | 538 | NONE | 96540 |
| Massachusetts | 95453 | 87289 | 190582 | 5463 | NONE | 378787 |
| Rhode Island | 16019 | 15799 | 32652 | 3407 | 948 | 68825 |
| Connecticut | 60523 | 54403 | 117448 | 2808 | 2764 | 237946 |
| New York | 83700 | 78122 | 152320 | 4654 | 21324 | 340120 |
| New Jersey | 45251 | 41416 | 83287 | 2762 | 11423 | 184139 |
| Pennsylvania | 110788 | 106948 | 206363 | 6537 | 3737 | 434373 |
| Delaware | 11783 | 12143 | 22384 | 3899 | 8887 | 59094 |
| Maryland | 55915 | 51339 | 101395 | 8043 | 103036 | 319728 |
| Virginia | 110936 | 116135 | 215046 | 12866 | 292627 | 747610 |
| Kentucky | 15154 | 17057 | 28922 | 114 | 12430 | 73677 |
| N. Carolina | 69988 | 77506 | 140710 | 4975 | 100572 | 393751 |
| S. Carolina | 35576 | 37722 | 66880 | 1801 | 107094 | 249073 |
| Georgia | 13103 | 14044 | 25739 | 398 | 29264 | 82548 |
|  | 807094 | 791850 | 1541263 | 59150 | 694280 | 3893635 |

| Total number of Inhabitants of the United States exclusive of S. Western and N. Territory. | Free white Males of 21 years and upwards. | Free Males under 21 years of age. | Free white Females. | All other Persons. | Slaves. | Total |
|---|---|---|---|---|---|---|
| S.W. territory N. Ditto | 6271 | 10277 | 15365 | 361 | 3417 | 35691 |

This page from the printed report of the 1790 census shows the five categories of information gathered in the first census.

rescue the Bureau from the manual drudgery that had dogged the previous nine decades.

The Bureau leased fifty-six of Hollerith's machines, hoisted them outside the building to the third floor, and connected them by wires to primitive batteries in the basement. Census clerks, "nice-looking girls in cool white dresses," worked at long rows of counting machines that resembled pianos (see Figure 12.2). It was muggy July, 1890, and while electric fans hummed, bells on the "statistical pianos" rang with every touch of the keys. For the first time in history, electricity was being used to count population.[5]

---

**Profile: Herman Hollerith (1860–1929)**

By the late 1880s census counting had barely evolved from the ancient Babylonian tallies chipped onto clay tablets. The 1880 census was scarcely finished before the 1890 census rolled around. Census counting methods, using pencil strokes on paper, inspired one observer to marvel that census clerks didn't go blind or crazy.

A contest was staged to find a "census machine" for computing the 1890 census. Herman Hollerith's entry, an electric, punched-card system, was pitted against color-coded paper and cards that were hand counted and sorted by his two rival contestants. Hollerith's machine finished in seventy-two hours, beating his first and second runners-up by thirty-nine and seventy-two hours.

A contemporary newspaper reporter predicted that since Hollerith's patents would only be useful to governments, Hollerith would "not likely get very rich." Nevertheless, Hollerith's Tabulating Machine Company netted $1,210,500 when he sold it in 1911 to the company that later became IBM.

**FIGURE 12.2: The Census Machine.**

Herman Hollerith's census tabulating machine saved the Census Bureau $5 million in two years, and created new jobs for women after men were found to be inferior at using Hollerith's machines, 1904.

## Confidentiality

The Census Bureau is unique among federal agencies, enjoying specific legal protection of information gathered from respondents, households, or firms, to ensure the data's use solely for statistical analysis. The classic challenge to Census Bureau confidentiality arose during World War II, when the War Department requested names and addresses to expedite the internment of Japanese Americans. The Census Bureau refused, turning over only aggregate statistics describing the ethnic composition of neighborhoods. Similar refusals were issued when immigration authorities wanted addresses of people sought for deportation, and when the Labor Department requested names and addresses for a survey of all working women in Rochester, New York.

Only after enjoying a seventy-two-year cloak of secrecy are census records opened to scholars and researchers (72 years was the average American's life span as estimated in 1952). The decennial census schedules are the National Archives' most heavily used record group, containing a wealth of information about westward expansion, local history, immigration, and genealogy, plus proof of citizenship. The National Archives sells microfilmed census schedules from 1790 to 1920, and allows on-site searches of the files. Unfortunately, most of the 1890 census records were destroyed by fire.

Four catalogs identify microfilm copies of the schedules: *Federal Population Censuses, 1790-1890* (GS 4.2:P 81/2/790-890), *1900 Federal Population Census* (GS 4.2:P 81/2/900), *The 1910 Federal Population Census* (GS 4.2:P 81/2/910), and *The 1920 Federal Population Census*, published by the National Archives Trust Fund Board (the 1920 records, unlocked on March 2, 1992, take up 3,400 miles of microfilm). The inexpensive catalogs are for sale from the Publications Branch (NEPS), National Archives, Washington, DC 20408; the 1920 catalog is sold by the National Archives Trust Fund, Box 10073, Atlanta, GA 30384. Census schedules may be purchased in microfilm or paper, consulted at the National Archives in Washington, DC, or at any of NARA's twelve regional archives, through the National Archives Microfilm Rental Program, and at many libraries and genealogical societies. "Special List 24," a list of institutions owning copies of National Archives microfilmed census records, is free from the National Archives and Records Administration.

## The 1990 Decennial Census

*The founding fathers never said counting the population was going to be easy.*
—Michael R. Darby,
Department of Commerce

The 200th anniversary of the decennial census was greeted halfheartedly by the 249,632,692 Americans it enumerated. Although nine out of ten realized the census was imminent, only about two-thirds had returned their questionnaires a month later. Low response was attributed to "mailbox glut" from junk mail and surveys, the questionnaire's complexity, rising illiteracy, and changing attitudes. A *New York Times* poll of nonrespondents found half were too busy or forgot to answer census questions. Others called the census irrelevant or "none of the government's business." Despite assurances of confidentiality, nonrespondents and respondents alike worried that the Bureau would leak information to other agencies such as the IRS or Immigration and Naturalization Service.[6]

# User Aids

## *Census Catalog and Guide* (C 3.163/3: )

This annual publication is a mainstay for any user of census statistics. The Census Bureau calls it "the only one-stop guide to every Census Bureau data product and service," recommending it as "the book to buy before you buy any of our others." The *Catalog and Guide* helps users sort through thousands of data products and formats (print, microfiche, CD-ROM, diskettes, etc.) and understand Census Bureau programs and services. Product summaries describe contents, scope, and geographic coverage; format; and how to order. The *Catalog and Guide* includes telephone numbers of bureau specialists, plus lists of regional offices, State Data Centers, and other service centers.

To identify Bureau of the Census publications from the first through 1972 censuses, consult *Bureau of the Census Catalog of Publications, 1790-1972* (C 56.222/2-2:790-972). Annual guides were issued throughout the balance of the 1970s. Information from 1980 to 1988 is cumulated in the *Census Catalog and Guide: 1989*, which should be kept as a permanent reference. All previous guides are available from Census Customer Services.

## *Factfinder for the Nation* (C 3.252: )

No user of census statistics should overlook the handy *Factfinder for the Nation* series. These concise and extremely useful pamphlets explain sources of data for specific topics, summarize Census Bureau data gathering, and cite key references. Number 5 in the series, "Reference Sources," is an annotated bibliography of Bureau reference publications. The entire set costs about $5; single copies are free from the Bureau's Census History department; (301) 763-7936, and many are reprinted in the *Catalog and Guide*.

### *Factfinder for the Nation* Titles

| | |
|---|---|
| No. 1 | Statistics on Race and Ethnicity |
| No. 2 | Availability of Census Records about Individuals |
| No. 3 | Agriculture Statistics |
| No. 4 | History and Organization |
| No. 5 | Reference Sources |
| No. 6 | Housing Statistics |
| No. 7 | Population Statistics |
| No. 8 | Census Geography Concepts and Products |
| No. 8a | 1990 Census Geography |
| No. 9 | Construction Statistics |
| No. 10 | Retail Trade Statistics |
| No. 11 | Wholesale Trade Statistics |
| No. 12 | Statistics on Service Industries |
| No. 13 | Transportation Statistics |
| No. 14 | Foreign Trade Statistics |
| No. 15 | Statistics on Manufactures |
| No. 16 | Statistics on Mineral Industries |
| No. 17 | Statistics on Governments |
| No. 18 | Census Bureau Programs and Products |
| No. 19 | Enterprise Statistics |
| No. 20 | Energy and Conservation Statistics |
| No. 21 | International Programs |
| No. 22 | Data for Small Communities |

## *Census and You* (C 3.238: )

This monthly newsletter announces new Census Bureau products, census and survey plans, and federal statistical program developments, and summarizes newsworthy statistics. Although these contents may sound dry, the newsletter is interesting and well written—a pleasant way to keep up with the numbers. For a free sample copy, contact the Data User Services Division. The December issue includes an index for the previous year. Substantial excerpts are available online through CENDATA, the Census Bureau's online system. A companion source, *Monthly Product Announcement*, alerts readers to new products and is incorporated into CENDATA.

### Personal Assistance

The Census Bureau operates numerous outlets with staff ready to help the public find and use statistics, including Regional Offices, State Data Centers, and a National Clearinghouse. A directory is included in the *Census Catalog and Guide* or will be sent free from the Data User Services Division.

### CENDATA: "The Census Bureau Online"

This online system provides current statistics, news releases, and ordering information. Most statistics are for the nation as a whole; many are for states, and a few cover counties, metropolitan areas, and cities. The *Census Catalog and Guide* summarizes CENDATA contents. CENDATA is available through DIALOG and CompuServe.

## DATA FORMATS

Census Bureau statistics are available in numerous formats, including printed reports, magnetic tape, floppy disks, online, microfiche, maps, and CD-ROM. Every printed report has a corresponding computer tape containing additional statistical and geographic detail. A stack of the 1980 printed reports would reach the top of a fifteen-story building, yet would contain only ten percent of the data collected. Thus the printed reports in depository libraries represent only the tip of the statistical iceberg, containing only about one-tenth of the total 1980 and 1990 census data: The bulk is computer-accessible only. Computerized data are available sooner than printed reports and allow data manipulation and customized printouts. The Census Bureau will download data from magnetic tapes to floppy disks. The 1990 census abandoned the preliminary, advance, and provisional release sequence in which earlier reports were superseded by later ones, and 1990 data releases have been speedier than those for 1980.

## DEPOSITORY LIBRARIES

Federal depository libraries are the primary hubs for accessing census publications, archiving more than one-quarter of the total reports printed for the 1980 census. Until the 1990 census, depository census collections were largely in paper and microform. While there is still an abundance of printed reports, electronic formats are on the rise. Depositories have CD-ROMs of 1990 census data, containing series formerly released only on computer tape. Many depository libraries rely on their State Data Centers for access to supplemental census computer tapes, while academic libraries may also refer to Inter-University Consortium for Political and Social Research (ICPSR).

### Census Depository Libraries

To augment collections of Census Bureau publications in federal depository libraries, the Census Bureau sends copies of its printed reports to census depository libraries (listed in the *Census Catalog and Guide.*) The Bureau of the Census library in Suitland, Maryland, and the Department of Commerce Reference Room in Washington, DC, have the most extensive collections in the country.

## WHAT DOES THE CENSUS BUREAU DO FOR THE REST OF THE DECADE?

People who imagine census staff napping or watching soap operas during the remainder of the decade underestimate the Bureau's work load. In fact, the Bureau never rests, planning the next decennial census years ahead, plus performing intercensal surveys and other censuses. Intercensal surveys are those completed between regular censuses, producing annual, quarterly, and monthly data updates. They are sample surveys—not 100 percent censuses—primarily covering large areas.

Planning for the next decennial census begins mid-decade, and citizen input has long been a tradition. In 1888, Alexander Graham Bell submitted forty-two suggested questions about deafness for the 1890 census. For recent censuses, public meetings across the U.S. have allowed citizens and special-interest groups to suggest census questions and clarify their special needs. Field tests and "dress rehearsals" allow pretesting methods and technology to reveal problems that need solving before Census Day.

## Other Censuses

A census can count anything, from people and homes in the Census of Population and Housing to businesses, farms, even governments themselves (see Figure 12.3).

### Economic Censuses

Every five years the Census Bureau performs a monumental juggling act, simultaneously conducting six economic censuses and related economic programs, plus the censuses of agriculture and governments. The Economic Censuses (formerly called the Census of Business before a scope expansion) collect data on many topics and trades. Census Bureau economic products generally provide data such as number of establishments, employees, and payrolls for specific industries. The 1987 Economic Censuses are available on CD-ROM (C 3.277:Ec 7/987/CD/vol.), and overviews are available in introductory slide sets sold by Census Customer Services. User guides are included as part of each economic census publication set.

| Programs Covered in the Economic Censuses |
|---|
| *Censuses* |
| Construction |
| Manufacturing |
| Mineral industries |
| Retail trade |
| Service industries |
| Wholesale trade |
| *Related Programs* |
| Census of outlying areas |
| Census of Transportation |
| Enterprise statistics |
| Survey of minority-owned businesses |
| Survey of women-owned businesses |

User Aids: *Guide to the 1987 Economic Censuses and Related Statistics* (C 3.253:Ec 87-R-2) describes the scope, coverage, classifications, data items, and products for the economic census and related surveys. Single copies are free from Customer Services. *The 1987 Economic Censuses* (videotape) overviews the scope and coverage of the economic surveys, and is available for about $10 from Data User Services Division, Customer Services.

**Manufactures.** Twice each decade since 1809, the census of manufactures has generated data about manufacturing for industries, small geographic areas, products shipped, and materials consumed. Conducted as part of the economic censuses, the census of manufactures generates data on employment, payroll, supplementary labor costs, assets, capital expenditures, rents, depreciation, inventories, materials costs, fuels consumed, value of shipments, and value added by manufacture.

User Aids: *Factfinder for the Nation*, no. 15, "Statistics on Manufactures."

**Mineral Industries.** Also a component of the economic censuses, the census of mineral industries shows data for industries, geographic areas, and subjects. It provides statistics on number of establishments, employment, payroll, hours worked, materials costs, value added, capital expenditures, materials consumed, and products shipped.

User Aids: *Factfinder for the Nation*, no. 16, "Statistics on Mineral Industries."

### Census of Transportation

The Census of Transportation has been taken every five years since 1963. It includes the truck inventory and use survey and transportation industry statistics. Three other economic censuses also generate transportation statistics: the surveys of minority- and women-owned businesses, and the business enterprise statistics program.

User Aids: *Factfinder for the Nation*, no. 13, "Transportation Statistics."

### Census of Agriculture

This census generates complete, consistent agricultural data for the nation, the fifty states, and every county. Data are gathered on farming, ranching, land use, sales of agricultural products, poultry, livestock, crops, and energy costs. The 1987 Agriculture Census is available on CD-ROM in depository libraries (C 3.77:Ag 8/987/CD/vol.).

User Aids: *Guide to the 1987 Census of Agriculture and Related Statistics* (C 3.6/2:Ag 8/2/987, free from Census Customer Services), and *Factfinder for the Nation*, No. 3, "Agriculture Statistics."

### Census of Governments

The census of governments focuses on state and local governments, gathering data on taxable property, number of employees, payrolls, revenues, expenditures, debts, and assets.

User Aids: *Government Statistics Data Finder* (C 3.163/6:G74) and *Factfinder for the Nation*, no. 17, "Statistics on Governments."

## STATISTICAL COMPENDIA

Dear Gentlemen:

I saw your census lady today. Why do you have to spend so much money to take the Census?

You could get all the figures from the World Almanac for free.

Yours truly,
Mrs. Ethel _____, Ohio
(a letter to the Census Bureau)

Census Bureau statistics are probably the most quoted, and least credited, in the nation. Census Bureau data are used not only in almanacs, but also in encyclopedias, newspaper articles, and by researchers, and federal, state, and local government agencies. The fact is that most government statistics originate from the Census Bureau (by some estimates, 98 percent), even though other agencies sometimes release them.

When a statistical question arises, searching original census data may be inefficient. Many questions can be answered more quickly and easily using statistical compendia, which digest data from numerous sources. Statistical compendia serve two purposes: data summary and referral to additional sources. When choosing a

**FIGURE 12.3: Census Retrospective Coverage.**

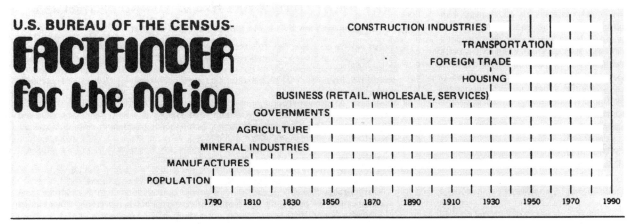

Each census has been gathered for a different span of time. Source: *Factfinder for the Nation*, 1992

compendium, consider the special strengths of each, weighing the importance of subject versus geographic detail. Currency and time coverage should also be considered.

| COMPENDIA STRENGTHS | |
|---|---|
| *Statistical Abstract* | Detail |
| *Historical Statistics* | Time series |
| *County and City Data Book; State and Metropolitan Area Data Book* | Data for smaller geographic areas |
| *USA Statistics in Brief* | Handy, quick reference; online through CENDATA |
| *U.S. Statistics at a Glance* | Monthly updating; online through CENDATA |

## The *Statistical Abstract of the United States* (C 3.134: )

*It's the best book the government publishes.*
—Robert J. Samuelson, *Newsweek*

A government document that inspires testimonials? If you thought only blockbuster movies and best-selling novels could generate quotable praise, it's time to take another look at the *Statistical Abstract of the United States*. Since 1878, the *Statistical Abstract* (note that it's "Abstract," not "Abstracts") has been the single most authoritative source of facts about our nation's people, institutions, and economy. Daniel Boorstin, former Librarian of Congress, characterized it as "the standard national inventory which leaves no part of our lives untouched." It is so brimming with social, political, and economic facts that a Census Bureau advertising flier dares to challenge: "Pick a question! The *Statistical Abstract* has just about all the answers!"

It's a rare library that doesn't own the *Statistical Abstract*. In 1991 it ranked nineteenth among the most-owned serials in the OCLC database.[7] It is available in paper, microfiche, and magnetic tape and is excerpted in CENDATA.

Not only does the *Abstract* offer statistics, it also directs readers to more detailed data through chapter introductions, table source notes, and appendices. The original sources cited include more information than can be summarized in the *Abstract*'s tables and graphs, making the *Statistical Abstract* a reference to federal and private sources of data as well as a fact source (see Figure 12.4). Appendixes list key statistical sources for the United States, state, and foreign governments. Appendix I includes "Guide to Sources of Statistics," a handy subject index of titles of Census Bureau publications on specific topics.

---

| Statistical Documents in Every Depository Library* |
|---|
| *Budget of the United States Government* |
| *Census Bureau Catalog and Guide* |
| Census of Housing [state] |
| Census of Population [state] |
| *Congressional District Data Book* |
| *County-City Data Book* |
| *Historical Statistics of the United States* |
| *Statistical Abstract of the United States* |

\* Titles recommended for every depository library collection by the Depository Library Council.

## Historical Statistics of the United States, Colonial Times to 1970 (C 3.134/2:H 62/970/pt.1,2)

*Historical Statistics of the United States* is a statistical synopsis of social, economic, political, and geographic development from 1610 to 1970. Data after 1970 are given in the *Statistical Abstract*, which includes an historical appendix linking the historical series to specific *Abstract* tables. *Historical Statistics'* coverage includes population, vital statistics, health, labor, prices, income, welfare, climate, agriculture, forestry, fisheries, minerals, construction, housing, manufactures, transportation, communications, energy, commerce, banking, and government. A summary, *Historical Statistics at a Glance*, is included in CENDATA.

## County and City Data Book (C 3.134/2: )

This *Statistical Abstract* supplement gives social and economic data for states, counties, cities, and census regions and divisions. It is published irregularly and, like many Census Bureau publications, is available in numerous formats including microfiche, floppy disk, and computer tape. Excerpts from *County and City Data Book* are included in CENDATA and are available on CD-ROM.

## State and Metropolitan Area Data Book (C 3.134/5: )

*State and Metropolitan Area Data Book* supplements the *Statistical Abstract* by providing data on states, metropolitan areas, counties, and cities. It is published irregularly, and is available in print, on floppy disk, and on computer tape. Excerpts are included in CENDATA.

## USA Statistics in Brief (C 3.134/2-2: )

For data-on-the-go, this pocket-sized *Statistical Abstract* supplement offers quick, easy-to-use tables. It may be purchased separately or plucked from a new copy of the *Statistical Abstract*, where it is included as an insert. It is also incorporated into CENDATA.

## U.S. Statistics at a Glance

This monthly and annual summary of demographic and economic indicators for the last fifteen years is included in issues of *Census and You* and online through CENDATA.

## A Sampling of Statistical Compendia

While the *Statistical Abstract* and its supplements offer general data, other statistical compendia focus on particular topics.

- Agriculture:
  *Agricultural Statistics*. Annual. A 1.47:
- Business and Labor:
  *Business Statistics, 1961-1988*. C 59.11/3:989
  *Economic Indicators*. Monthly. Y 4.Ec7:Ec7/date
  *Handbook of Labor Statistics*. Irregular. L 2.3/5:
- Communications:
  *Statistics of Communications Common Carriers*. Annual. CC 1.35:
- Criminal Justice:
  *Sourcebook of Criminal Justice Statistics*. Annual. J 29.9/6:
  *Uniform Crime Reports*. Annual. J 1.14/7:
- Earth Sciences:
  *Minerals Yearbook*. Annual. I 28.37:
  *United States Earthquakes*. Annual. I 19.65/2:
- Education:
  *Condition of Education*. Annual. ED 1.109:
  *Digest of Education Statistics*. Annual. ED 1.326:

- Energy:
  *International Energy Annual*. Annual. E 3.11/20:
  *Annual Energy Review*. Annual. E 3.1/2:
- Health:
  *Health, United States*. Annual. HE 20.6223:
  *Mental Health, United States*. Biennial. HE 20.8137:
  *Vital Statistics of the United States*. Annual. HE 20.6210:
- Housing/Urbanology:
  *HUD Statistical Yearbook*. Annual. HH 1.38:
- Libraries:
  *Library Statistics of Colleges and Universities. Institutional Data*. Annual. ED 1.122:
  *Statistics of Public Libraries*. Quadrennial. ED 1.122/2:
- Population:
  *World Population Profile*. Biennial. C 3.205/3:WP-yr.
- Public Lands:
  *Public Land Statistics*. Annual. I 53.1/2:
- Transportation:
  *FAA Statistical Handbook of Aviation*. Annual. TD 4.20:
  *Highway Statistics*. Annual. TD 2.23:
  *National Transportation Statistics*. Annual. TD 10.9:
  *Transport Statistics in the United States*. Annual. IC 1.25:
- Weather:
  *Monthly Climatic Data for the World*. Monthly. C 55.211:

**FIGURE 12.4:** *Statistical Abstract* **Referral to Other Sources.**

Excerpts from the Referral Information Provided in Selected Statistical Abstract Tables

NO. 95. BIRTHS TO UNMARRIED WOMEN, BY RACE AND AGE OF MOTHER: 1950 TO 1978

[Prior to 1960, excludes Alaska and Hawaii. Beginning 1970, excludes births to nonresidents of U.S. Includes estimates for States in which marital status tata were not reported. No estimates included for misstatements on birth records or failures to register births. See also Appendix III and *Historical Statistics, Colonial Times to 1970*, series B 28–35]

| RACE AND AGE | 1950 | 1955 | 1960 | 1965 | 1970 | 1973 | 1974 | 1975 | 1976 | 1977 | 1978 |
|---|---|---|---|---|---|---|---|---|---|---|---|
| Total live births (1,000) | 141.6 | 183.3 | 224.3 | 291.2 | 398.7 | 407.3 | 418.1 | 447.9 | 468.1 | 515.7 | 543.9 |
| Percent of all births[1] | 4.0 | 4.5 | 5.3 | 7.7 | 10.7 | 13.0 | 13.2 | 14.2 | 14.8 | 15.5 | 16.3 |
| White (1,000) | 53.5 | 64.2 | 82.5 | 123.7 | 175.1 | 163.0 | 168.5 | 186.4 | 197.1 | 220.1 | 233.6 |
| Black and other (1,000) | 88.1 | 119.2 | 141.8 | 167.5 | 223.6 | 244.3 | 249.6 | 261.6 | 271.0 | 295.5 | 310.2 |
| Percent of total | 62.2 | 65.0 | 63.2 | 57.5 | 56.1 | 60.0 | 59.7 | 58.4 | 57.9 | 57.3 | 57.0 |
| Percent White of all White | 1.7 | | 2.3 | | | 6.4 | | | 7.7 | | |

[1] For total births, see table 85. [2] Rate per 1,000 unmarried (never-married, widowed, and divorced) women aged 15–44 years enumerated as of April 1 for 1950, 1960, and 1970, and estimated as of July 1 for all other years.

Source: U.S. National Center for Health Statistics, *Vital Statistics of the United States*, annual, and unpublished data.

NO. 101. LEGAL ABORTIONS—ESTIMATED NUMBER, RATE, AND RATIO BY RACE: 1972 TO 1978

[Refers to women 15–44 years old at time of abortion. Minus sign (−) denotes decrease]

| ITEM | 1972 | | 1975 | | 1976 | | 1977 | | 1978 | |
|---|---|---|---|---|---|---|---|---|---|---|
| | White | Black[1] | White | Black[1] | White | Black[1] | White | Black[1] | White | Black[1] |
| Total women, 15–44 yr old (1,000) | 38,381 | 6,014 | 40,485 | 6,633 | 41,254 | 6,855 | 42,022 | 7,071 | 42,741 | 7,288 |
| Number of abortions (1,000) | 455.3 | 131.5 | 701.2 | 333.0 | 784.9 | 394.4 | 891.2 | 429.1 | 969.4 | 440.2 |
| Annual percentage change | (x) | | 15.5 | 36.3 | | 18.4 | 13.5 | | 8.8 | |

X Not applicable. [1] Includes other races.

Source: Alan Guttmacher Institute, New York, N.Y. unpublished data. Includes data from U.S. Bureau of the Census, U.S. National Center for Health Statistics, and U.S. Center for Disease Control, Atlanta, Ga.

In some cases general references are provided (arrow B); other references cite specific publications as the source of data (arrow A), or refer to additional data sources (arrow C). Source: Bureau of the Census. *Census '80: Projects for Students*, 1981.

## Nothing Is as Simple as It Looks: Interpreting Tables

*Ordinary reading ability is no more effective in reading a table than an ordinary can opener in opening a can of sardines, and if you go at it with a hammer and chisel you are likely to mutilate the contents.*
— W. A. Wallis and H. V. Roberts,
*Statistics, A New Approach*

Statistical compendia appear quick and easy to use, but their detailed data compressed into concise tables demand sophisticated interpretation. Whether using statistical compendia or the original reports upon which they are based, hasty or careless reading can result in misinterpretations or selection of incorrect answers. Before attempting to extract data from statistical tables, review the introduction or preface, which summarizes data sources and important concepts, and read the notations and footnotes for individual tables (see Figure 12.6). The extra time invested can make the difference between correct data interpretation and misinterpretation.

## Pitfalls Aplenty: Interpreting Census Reports

*An eighth of everyone in this country lives in California.*
— Newspaper caption

When consulting census reports rather than summaries in compendia, preliminary preparation can save time and prevent misinterpretation. First, determine whether the information sought was gathered in the census at all and its availability for the geographic area

**FIGURE 12.5: Census Report Numbering.**

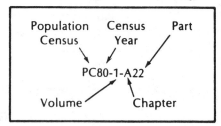

Source: *1980 Census User Guide*, 1980

desired. Next, verify whether the question was in the population or housing component of the census questionnaire, and whether it was a complete count or a sample question. Answers to questions like these will determine which census reports hold the desired data. Answers can be found in the *1980 Census User's Guide,* or in individual reports themselves (a user guide for the 1990 census will eventually be released). Lavin concisely summarizes census-report coverage in his chapter on the decennial census.[8] *200 Years of U.S. Census Taking: Population and Housing Questions, 1790-1990* (C 3.2:T 93) lists all questions asked since the first census.

Since census reports are issued in state volumes and in national summary volumes, users should determine whether they want detailed state or more general national data and should be aware that tables are numbered differently in the two types of publications. (Table-hopping among state volumes is simplified by the fact that subject tables have the same numbers for all states.) Once inside any census report volume, users should remember that general summary tables precede more detailed breakdowns.

**FIGURE 12.6: Parts of a Census Statistical Table.**

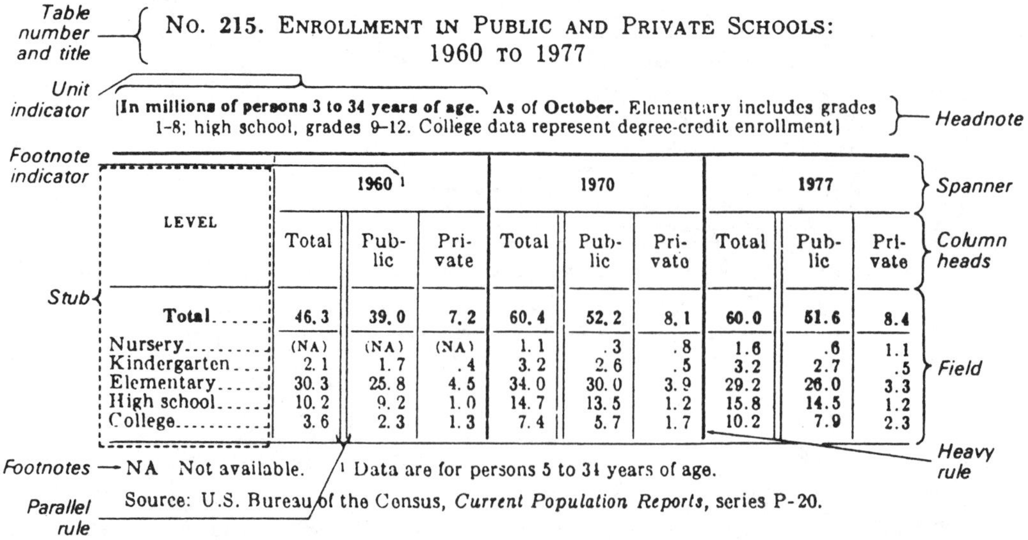

No. 215. ENROLLMENT IN PUBLIC AND PRIVATE SCHOOLS: 1960 TO 1977

[In millions of persons 3 to 34 years of age. As of October. Elementary includes grades 1–8; high school, grades 9–12. College data represent degree-credit enrollment]

| LEVEL | 1960 [1] | | | 1970 | | | 1977 | | |
|---|---|---|---|---|---|---|---|---|---|
| | Total | Public | Private | Total | Public | Private | Total | Public | Private |
| Total | 46.3 | 39.0 | 7.2 | 60.4 | 52.2 | 8.1 | 60.0 | 51.6 | 8.4 |
| Nursery | (NA) | (NA) | (NA) | 1.1 | .3 | .8 | 1.6 | .6 | 1.1 |
| Kindergarten | 2.1 | 1.7 | .4 | 3.2 | 2.6 | .5 | 3.2 | 2.7 | .5 |
| Elementary | 30.3 | 25.8 | 4.5 | 34.0 | 30.0 | 3.9 | 29.2 | 26.0 | 3.3 |
| High school | 10.2 | 9.2 | 1.0 | 14.7 | 13.5 | 1.2 | 15.8 | 14.5 | 1.2 |
| College | 3.6 | 2.3 | 1.3 | 7.4 | 5.7 | 1.7 | 10.2 | 7.9 | 2.3 |

NA Not available. [1] Data are for persons 5 to 34 years of age.

Source: U.S. Bureau of the Census, *Current Population Reports*, series P-20.

*(Labels: Table number and title; Unit indicator; Footnote indicator; Stub; Headnote; Spanner; Column heads; Field; Heavy rule; Footnotes; Parallel rule)*

Source: Bureau of the Census. *Census '80: Projects for Students*, 1981

| CENSUS BUREAU COMPENDIA[9] | | | |
|---|---|---|---|
| Title | Time Coverage | Geography | Subject Detail |
| *Statistical Abstract* | Recent | U.S., regions, divisions, states, MAs, selected cities, foreign countries | Most |
| *Historical Statistics* | 1610-1970 | U.S., states, selected cities | |
| *State and Metropolitan Area Data Book* | Since 1970 | Regions, divisions, states, MAs, counties, central cities | |
| *County and City Data Book* | Since 1980 | Regions, divisions, states, counties, larger cities | Least |

## Definitions

Census language is precise. Terms have specific meanings that do not always duplicate their popular usage, and definitions should not be guessed or assumed. What, for instance, is the census term for an unmarried person? (It depends: Has the person never married, or is he or she widowed, divorced, or separated?) How do census reports describe cohabitating unmarried couples? (After a brief fling with POSSLQ, Persons of the Opposite Sex Sharing Living Quarters, the Bureau settled on "unmarried partners.") Even seemingly obvious definitions should be verified: "Person" seems self-explanatory, but in 1790 American Indians were left uncounted because they paid no taxes, and five slaves were tallied as only three persons. Proper use of terminology is essential for interpreting statistical tables. To verify current Census Bureau definitions, check the "Glossary" in *1980 Census User's Guide* (C 3.223:80-R-1B) or appendixes in each published report.

## Census vs. Samples

Census users should recognize differences between "complete-count" and sample data. A complete-count is a true census or head-count, in which everyone is counted. Complete-counts are also called "100 percent," indicating the target response rate (despite a slow start, the 1990 census concluded with a 97 percent response). Samples, on the other hand, are estimates derived from a statistical sampling of the population.

The 1990 short and long census questionnaires are examples of a census and a sample, respectively. The short form was sent to every household (a complete-count), while the thirty-five additional long-form questions were appended to one out of every six questionnaires (a sample). The Census Bureau estimated the fourteen short-form questions would take about four-teen minutes to answer, with the long form clocking in at about forty-three minutes.

Sometimes both complete-count and sample data are available, often giving different totals for the same component. For the 1980 census, the *Census User's Guide* "Glossary" notes whether items were sample or complete-count (see Figure 12.7). Nineteen Ninety Census Summary Tape Files (STFs) include 100-percent population and housing data, and are available in depository libraries on CD-ROM (C 3.282: ). Summary data are the kind found in printed tabulations; microdata are "raw" records of individual responses, requiring computer manipulation to be meaningful. Public Law 94-171 data are population counts required for redistricting the fifty state legislatures. P.L 94-171 CD-ROMs are available in depository libraries (C 3.281: ), and include population data for states, counties, voting districts, minor civil divisions, places, American Indian/Alaska Native areas, census tracts, block groups, and blocks.

## Census Geography

Census Bureau geographic units are either governmental (states, counties, cities) or statistical (metropolitan areas, urbanized areas, census tracts, block groups, blocks). The larger the geographic area, the greater the number and detail of statistics published. Especially for small areas, more data are available on computer tape than in print.

The 1990 census witnessed a juncture in census mapping with the creation of TIGER, a coast-to-coast computerized map database. Using TIGER, some 90,000 maps were created for the 1990 census, ten times the number for the 1980 census. Some were issued on paper, while others are available on microfiche, CD-ROM, magnetic tape and through census regional offices and State Data Centers. TIGER files for specific counties are for sale, and described in the free booklet, *TIGER: The Coast-to-Coast Digital Map Data Base.* TIGER is also repackaged and sold commercially by data vendors.

---

**Hierarchy of Census Geography for Data Products**

United States
  Region
    Division
      State
        County
          Minor civil division/census county division
            Place
              Census tract/block numbering area
                Block group
                  Block

Source: *1990 Census of Population and Housing: Tabulation and Publication Program,* 1989, p. 11

**FIGURE 12.7: 1990 Census Content.**

### 100-PERCENT COMPONENT

| POPULATION | HOUSING |
|---|---|
| Household relationship | Number of units in structure |
| Sex | Number of rooms in unit |
| Race | Tenure—owned or rented |
| Age | Value of home or monthly rent |
| Marital status | Congregate housing meals (included in rent) |
| Hispanic origin | Vacancy characteristics |

### SAMPLE COMPONENT

| POPULATION | HOUSING |
|---|---|
| *Social characteristics:* | Year moved into residence |
| Education—enrollment and attainment | Number of bedrooms |
| Place of birth, citizenship, and year of entry to U.S. | Plumbing and kitchen facilities |
| Ancestry | Telephone in unit |
| Language spoken at home | Vehicles available |
| Migration (residence in 1985) | Heating fuel |
| Disability | Source of water and method of sewage disposal |
| Fertility | Year structure built |
| Veteran status | Farm residence |
| *Economic characteristics:* | Shelter costs, including utilities |
| Labor force | |
| Occupation, industry, and class of worker | |
| Place of work and journey to work | |
| Work experience in 1989 | |
| Income in 1989 | |
| Year last worked | |

Note: Questions in the 100-percent component were asked of all persons and housing units. Those covered by the sample component were asked of a sample of the population and housing units. Source: *Census Catalog and Guide 1991*, p. 164.

## MACHINE-READABLE DATA

The days when printed reports provided comprehensive access to government statistics are past. Statistics, so well suited to computer storage and manipulation, are at the forefront of the government computer revolution, rendering increasing amounts of government data available only electronically. The Census Bureau, as an example, cuts costs by publishing only a fraction of the data stored in its computers. In the next century, census reform could involve a paperless census, with enumerators counting people using handheld microcomputers or telephones.

The electronic revolution offers advantages and disadvantages. On one hand, users now enjoy the option of accessing raw data, tailoring computer manipulation to their specific needs, and accessing data quickly through electronic bulletin boards and news services. On the other hand, fees are sometimes charged for accessing data formerly available free in printed depository publications. Depository libraries do not receive free copies of computerized files, even those produced at government expense. Limiting the number of Census Bureau printed reports meant that depository libraries received less information from the 1980 census than from the 1970 census. This trend is expected to continue.

Descriptions of Census Bureau machine-readable data are provided in the *Census Catalog and Guide* and the 1980 *Census User's Guide*, part C, "Index to Summary Tape Files."

## NTIS

The National Technical Information Service (NTIS) serves as a central source for many government statistical data files, many of which are described in *Directory of U.S. Government Datafiles for Mainframes and Microcomputers*, which describes federal numeric and textual data sold by NTIS. NTIS operates the Federal Computer Products Center, which sells government software and datafiles to the public. Government software and datafiles can be identified by searching the NTIS Bibliographic Database, and through free NTIS catalogs, including "Energy Datafiles" (PR-712) and "NCHS Datafiles" (PR-716). NTIS issues a free Federal Computer Products Center newsletter, *CenterLine* (PR-838). The monthly *NTIS Alert* on Computers, Control & Information Theory describes new software and datafiles added to the Federal Computer Products Center collection, with abstracts of research related to computers and information technology. NTIS offers free brochures describing files available on tape and diskette, while the more comprehensive NTIS Bibliographic Database and GRA & I cite government-produced software packages and statistical data files.

NTIS offers online access to the Commerce Department's Economic Bulletin Board (EBB), which provides federal economic data from the Bureau of Economic Analysis, Bureau of Labor Statistics, and Bureau of the Census. The twenty-four-hour bulletin board provides updated statistics on U.S. industry, foreign trade, money, and most principal indicators. Additional information is available from the Commerce Department's Office of Business Analysis and Economic Affairs; (202) 377-1986.

Many agencies' machine-readable data collections fall outside the NTIS net and are unavailable from NTIS. These must be traced through commercially published guides or through agency guides listed in the *Monthly Catalog, American Statistics Index,* and the agency's own newsletters and announcements. Agencies will often send requesters free copies of pamphlets or catalogs describing their print and electronic publications.

## INTERNATIONAL DATA

The Census Bureau's Center for International Research (CIR), which the bureau calls its window on the world, gathers and publishes demographic and economic data on world nations. CIR is a research group funded by government and private organizations. One of its best-known publications is Series WP, the biennial *World Population Profile* (C 3.205/3:WP-yr.), containing demographic profiles of 208 countries and territories with populations of at least 5,000. Substantial excerpts are available through CENDATA. CIR sells the International Data Base Machine Readable File: 1990, with demographic and economic data since 1950 and some projections to 2050. IDB includes figures for population, age, sex, urban/rural residence, vital statistics, migration rate, and literacy, with projections.

The Center for International Research also publishes Series ISP-DP, *Country Demographic Profiles* (C 3.205/3:DP-nos.) with detailed data on selected countries of Africa, Latin America, and Asia. Country profiles include population totals and projections since 1950, age and sex distributions, vital statistics, migration, education, and labor force.

The *Statistical Abstract* includes some international data, and a "Guide to Foreign Statistical Abstracts," in the appendixes. It also includes a section devoted to comparative international statistics.

The National Trade Data Bank (NTDB), the Commerce Department database and CD-ROM, includes information about foreign country demographics incorporated in the CIA's *World Factbook*. NTDB is available in depository libraries (C 1.88: ), or can be purchased on subscription from NTIS.

### Index to International Statistics

*Index to International Statistics* (IIS), from Congressional Information Service, indexes and abstracts data published since 1983 by major international intergovernmental organizations (IGOs). Covered are IGOs such as the United Nations, the European Community, and the Organization for Economic Cooperation and Development; the Organization of American States; commodity organizations; development banks; and other regional and special purpose organizations. *Index to International Statistics* may be searched in print, online, or on CD-ROM (*Statistical Masterfile*).

## AGRICULTURE

The National Agriculture Statistics Service (NASS) prepares estimates and reports on production, supply, price, and other items related to the U.S. agricultural economy. The service collects data about farms and farmers, crops, production, livestock, prices, wages, and uses of agricultural products. Another USDA statistical agency is the Economic Research Service (ERS), responsible for analyzing the outlook for domestic and foreign farm products.

The USDA's electronic bulletin board, CIDS, contains timely agricultural data. CIDS is available on subscription through Martin Marietta Corporation, but is not free through depository libraries. Subscribers to CIDS, including depository libraries, pay according to use.

## BUREAU OF ECONOMIC ANALYSIS

The Commerce Department's Bureau of Economic Analysis (BEA) prepares basic economic indicators and analyzes business trends. The BEA constructs the national income and product accounts, "which are based on several hundred statistical series and are among the most comprehensive measures of economic activity."[10] The BEA also calculates the international balance of payments and foreign expenditures. Timely BEA data are available through the Commerce Department's Economic Bulletin Board.

## CRIMINAL JUSTICE

The National Institute of Justice (NIJ) is the primary criminal justice research arm of the Department of Justice. NIJ is rare among federal agencies in requiring the deposit of data sets for funded research. Public-use data tapes of Bureau of Justice Statistics and criminal justice data sets are available from the National Archive of Criminal Justice Data (formerly CJAIN), Box 1248, Ann Arbor, MI 48106; (800) 999-0960.

NIJ operates an international information clearinghouse, the National Criminal Justice Reference Service (NCJRS). NCJRS's computer database of criminal-justice literature is available through DIALOG, on CD-ROM, or through NCJRS. Users of NCJRS resources may wish to consult the *National Criminal Justice Thesaurus* (J 28.2:T 34/986), used to index the NCJRS document database. NCJRS also operates a public reading room; provides information, referral, and distribution services; and oversees clearinghouses on AIDS, juvenile justice, crime victims, and statistics.

The NCJRS statistical clearinghouse is the Justice Statistics Clearinghouse, operated by the Bureau of Justice Statistics. The Bureau of Justice Statistics (BJS) gathers statistics on crime, courts, and corrections. BJS's largest statistical series is the National Crime Survey, which measures victimization by rape, robbery, assault, larceny, burglary, and auto theft. The annual *Sourcebook of Criminal Justice Statistics* (J 29.2: ) is a one-volume compendium of data from more than one hundred sources. BJS's Justice Statistics Clearinghouse responds to statistical and information requests, suggests additional sources of criminal justice statistics, and performs custom searches of the NCJRS database: (800) 732-3277.

The NCJRS Electronic Bulletin Board posts BJS press releases, statistics, news, publication announcements, and conference calendars. For information call (800) 732-3277.

## EDUCATION

The federal government began gathering educational statistics in 1867, when the Department of Education was established. Calling itself "America's education fact-finder," the Office of Educational Research and Improvement (OERI) is the Department of Education's primary research organ. OERI sponsors research and library programs, reports on the condition of education, disseminates information, and collects statistics. The National Center for Education Statistics (NCES) is a subunit of OERI.

The National Center for Education Statistics collects statistics about U.S. and foreign education and disseminates data in print and electronic form. The center's data collection programs cover public and private elementary and secondary education, higher education, and vocational and adult education.[11] Data are available on disk, tape, and print, and special tabulations may be requested for a fee. Answers to questions about education statistics, research, publications, and data tapes may be obtained by calling the OERI Information Office at (800) 424-1616 or accessing the OERI Electronic Bulletin Board at (800) 222-4922 or (202) 219-2011 in the Washington, DC, area. Additional information is available by calling (202) 219-1547. *American Statistics Index* offers comprehensive coverage of NCES statistical publications.

## ENERGY

The Energy Information Administration (EIA) is the Department of Energy's statistical and analytical arm, responsible for data about energy reserves, production, demand, consumption, distribution, and technology. EIA also serves as a clearinghouse for energy information. EIA's electronic bulletin board, EPUB, provides timely access to data in EIA statistical reports. Instructions are in *Electronic Publishing System (EPUB) Quick Start Users Guide* (E 3.8:El 2), free from EIA's subunit, the National Energy Information Center (NEIC). The annual *EIA Publications Directory* (E 3.27: ), free from EIA, abstracts Energy Information Administration publications, with information on EIA data files and modeling programs. EIA sells computer data files and modeling programs through NTIS. EIA's annual report to Congress (E 3.1: ) includes information on surveys, data collection, and publications, and is free from EIA. *Energy and Conservation Statistics*, number 20 in the *Factfinder for the Nation* series, is a guide to energy data collected in the censuses and surveys of agriculture, foreign trade, the economy, and government. *American Statistics Index* offers comprehensive coverage of Energy Information Administration statistical publications.

## HEALTH

The National Center for Health Statistics (NCHS) collects and disseminates statistics about public health. NCHS's programs of vital and health statistics provide data on health and nutrition, illness and disability, health resources, health expenditures, and official vital statistics.

Vital statistics report life events, including births and deaths, health and disease, abortions, fertility, life expectancy, marriages, and divorces. *Vital Statistics of the United States* (HE 20.6210: ) has been called a "basic building block of demographic analysis."[12] It is published annually in three volumes, covering natality, mortality, and marriage and divorce. The *Vital and Health Statistics Series* (HE 20.6209: ) includes dozens of titles, covering numerous health topics (see Subject Bibliography SB-121 for a list of series titles for sale from GPO).

The Congressional Information Service's *Index to Health Information: A Guide to Statistical and Congressional Publications on Public Health* (IHI) consolidates health-related citations and abstracts from *American Statistics Index, Statistical Reference Index, Index to International Statistics*, and *CIS/Index. American Statistics Index* offers comprehensive coverage of NCHS statistical publications.

## LABOR

The Bureau of Labor Statistics (BLS) is the nation's chief fact-finder for labor economics. BLS gathers data on topics such as the labor force, employment, hours and earnings, productivity, and foreign labor. BLS produces key economic indicators including the Consumer Price Index, the Producer Price Index, and Employment Situation. Many BLS economic indicators (prices, wages, employment) are available immediately through the BLS Electronic News Release Service, a subscription service provided through Boeing Computer Services. The BLS 24-hour hotline offers recorded messages regarding recent news releases about the Consumer Price Index, Producer Price Index, the Employment Situation, and the Employment Cost Index; (202) 523-1221. *American Statistics Index* offers comprehensive coverage of BLS statistical publications.

The Commerce Department's Economic Bulletin Board includes timely statistics and economic news from the Bureau of Labor Statistics. The Economic Bulletin Board is "a one-stop source for current economic information," containing timely statistics and economic news not just from Commerce, but also from NTIS, the International Trade Commission, Bureau of Economic Analysis, Bureau of Labor Statistics, Federal Reserve Board,

and Treasury Department. Access in depository libraries was tested as an electronic pilot project, and is now being evaluated. Subscribe through NTIS; (703) 487-4630. For information, call the Commerce Department's Office of Business Analysis; (202) 482-1986; Economics and Statistics Administration, Room 4885, HCH Bldg., Washington, D.C. 20230.

The National Trade Data Bank (NTDB) is a Commerce Department database and CD-ROM (distributed by GPO) containing international trade and economic information. Conceived as a "warehouse of trade data," NTDB includes full text of government publications (the *U.S. Industrial Outlook*, for example), tables, and time series from fifteen federal statistical agencies. The monthly NTDB discs can be used in depository libraries (C 1.88: ) or purchased on subscription from NTIS. For more information, contact the NTDB Help Line at (202) 377-1986 or the Department of Commerce's Business Statistics and Information Systems Division. The U.S. Department of Commerce will soon release a second database, the National Economic, Social, and Environmental Data Bank (NESE-DB). Available on CD-ROM (C1.88/2:), the NESE-DB contains full text of numerous government publications focusing on the nation's economic growth, education, health, crime, and the environment. Additional information is available from the Department of Commerce's Economics and Statistics Administration.

## FINDING AIDS

There is no single index to all federal statistics. Individual agencies often publish guides to their own data, identifiable by searching the *Monthly Catalog* or *American Statistics Index*. Evinger's *Federal Statistical Source: Where to Find Agency Experts & Personnel*, is a guide to identifying experts to answer questions and direct users to unpublished sources. Several Census Bureau aids deserve special mention. The *Catalog and Guide* and the *Factfinder for the Nation* series (especially no. 5, "Reference Sources") cover so many subjects that any serious statistics hunter can benefit by reviewing them before initiating a search. Each was discussed in detail earlier in this chapter. Two highly respected indexes to government and nongovernment statistics, published commercially by the Congressional Information Service, are discussed below.

### American Statistics Index

*American Statistics Index* (ASI) is a master guide to federal government statistics. The ASI editorial staff scan for statistics in every type of federal publication except highly scientific or technical ones, perusing depository, nondepository, and non-GPO publications; maps; CD-ROMs; and microfiche. Included are any federal publications that are wholly or partially statistical, with social, economic, demographic, or natural-resources data, plus selected scientific and technical data. Coverage is comprehensive for the Census Bureau and Bureau of Labor Statistics, the National Center for Health Statistics, the National Center for Education Statistics, Energy Information Administration, and the Crop Reporting Board; and selective for other agencies.

ASI covers tables of data, and also maps, charts, listings, and text that help locate statistics or clarify agency statistical activities. This provides access to discussions of methodology, classification guides, directories, and bibliographies that include significant references to statistical materials. Statistical publications are indexed and abstracted within about six to nine weeks after publication, cited with full bibliographic information, including SuDocs numbers, depository status, prices, and ordering information. Every document cited is sold by CIS on microfiche, and many may also be used in depository libraries or purchased from the government.

ASI provides coverage retrospective to the 1960s. Selected congressional publications appear in both ASI and *CIS/Index*, which indexes publications of Congress. ASI may be searched by subjects, names, titles, or report numbers, and by geographic, economic, or demographic categories (a helpful time-saver). The ASI accession numbers that identify entries are useful only within ASI, and should not be given as part of general bibliographic citations except to provide access to ASI microfiche. ASI is accessible online, on CD-ROM (*Statistical Masterfile*), or by using the print index. The Congressional Information Service's *Guide to 1980 U.S. Decennial Census Publications: Detailed Abstracts and Indexes Derived from the American Statistics Index* cumulates ASI abstracts for 1980 census reports issued through 1986.

### Statistical Reference Index

*Statistical Reference Index* (SRI) is a companion to ASI, focusing on U.S. statistics from nonfederal private and public organizations. It indexes and abstracts business, financial, and social statistical data from U.S. associations and institutes, businesses, commercial publishers, independent research centers, state governments, and universities. The publications indexed provide national, state, local, and foreign data. SRI indexes, abstracts, and sells microfiche copies of most of the documents listed, and can be searched by subjects, names, categories, issuing sources, and titles. Coverage began in late 1979. *Statistical Reference Index* may be searched in print, online, or on CD-ROM (*Statistical Masterfile*).

## ADDRESSES

### Census

Bureau of the Census, Data User Division, Customer Services, Washington, DC 20233; (301) 763-4100: the "Census Information Number"

Census map products: (301) 763-4100, FAX (301) 763-4794

Center for International Research, Bureau of the Census, Room 614, Scuderi Bldg., Washington, DC 20233; (301) 763-4811

---

**Statistical Search Aids**

*Statistical Abstract* section, "Guide to Sources of Statistics"
*Census Catalog and Guide*
*1980 Census User's Guide* (a 1990 update is forthcoming)
*Guide to 1980 U.S. Census Publications* (CIS)
Individual census reports: Table Finding Guide, Data Index sections
*American Statistics Index*
*Statistical Reference Index*
*Index to International Statistics*
*Factfinder for the Nation*, no. 5, "Reference Sources," and *Factfinders* on specific topics
Evinger, *Directory of Federal Statistical Data Bases*
Ondrasik, *Data Map: Index of Published Tables of Statistical Data*
Sears and Moody, *Using Government Publications. Vol. 2: Finding Statistics and Using Special Techniques*

---

### Energy, Health, and Justice

National Center for Health Statistics, 3700 East-West Hwy., Hyattsville, MD 20782; (301) 435-8500

National Energy Information Center, Energy Information Administration, Forrestal Bldg., Room 1F-048, Washington, DC 20585; (202) 586-8800

Justice Statistics Clearinghouse, Box 6000, Rockville, MD 20850; (800) 732-3277, (301) 251-5500 in Maryland and the Washington, DC, area.

### Labor

BLS Electronic News Release Service is sold through Boeing Computer Services, 7980-90 Boeing Court, Vienna, VA 22180-9990; (703) 821-6306

## FREEBIES

The following subject bibliographies are free from U.S. Government Printing Office, Superintendent of Documents, Washington, DC 20402:

   83. Educational Statistics
118. Annual Reports
121. Vital and Health Statistics
146. Census of Manufactures
149. Census of Transportation
152. Census of Business
156. Census of Governments
157. Census of Construction
162. Agricultural Research, Statistics, and Economic Reports
181. Census of Population
273. Statistical Publications
277. Census of Agriculture

## Agriculture

From Economic Research Service, 1301 New York Ave., N.W., Washington, DC 20005-4788; (800) 999-6779; in Washington, DC, 786-1512:

*ERS Database Catalog*
*ERS Electronic Products*
*Publications and Data Products*

## Census

From Customer Services, Data User Services Division, Bureau of the Census, Washington, DC 20233; (301) 763-4100, FAX (301) 763-4794:

*Census, CD-ROM, and You!*

*Monthly Product Announcement*

*Census '90 Basics* (C 3.2:B 29), nontechnical background information about census preparation, data collection, subject coverage, data limitations, census geography, publication formats, and sources of assistance.

*Hidden Treasures! Census Bureau Data and Where to Find It!*, a guide to identifying local sources of census information.

*TIGER: The Coast-to-Coast Digital Map Data Base*

## Congressional Information Service

From Congressional Information Service, 4520 East-West Highway, Bethesda, MD 20814; (800) 638-8380, (301) 654-1150:

Search guides for *American Statistics Index, Statistical Reference Index,* and *Index to International Statistics*

## Crime

From BJS, Department of Justice, Washington, DC 20531:

"Telephone Contacts" (J 29.11/4: )

"How to Gain Access to BJS Data"

From National Institute of Justice/NCJRS User Services, Box 6000, Rockville, MD 20850; (800) 851-3420 or (301) 251-5500 for Washington, DC, Maryland, and Alaska:

*Data Resources of the National Institute of Justice* (J 28.2:D 26/2), a catalog of data sets from NIJ-sponsored research.

*National Institute of Justice Catalog*, a bimonthly publications list.

*National Institute of Justice Journal*, articles about NIJ research and programs.

*NIJ Publications Catalog: 1983-89, Your Guide to NIJ Research Findings* lists NIJ free or inexpensive publications and videotapes.

*User Guide to NCJRS Products and Services*

*NCJRS Computer Based Products and Services: Your Direct Route to Criminal Justice Information*

## Department of Commerce

From Economics and Statistics Administration, Room 4885, HCH Bldg., Washington, DC 20230; (202) 482-1986, FAX (202) 482-2164:

Information about National Trade Data Bank and the National Economic, Social, and Environmental Data Bank.

## Economic Indicators

From Department of Commerce, Bureau of Economic Analysis, Washington, DC 20230; (202) 523-0777:

*A User's Guide to BEA Information: Publications, Computer Tapes, Diskettes, and Other Information Services*

## Education

From OERI, Information Services, 555 New Jersey Ave., N.W., Washington, DC 20208-5570; (800) 424-1616, in Washington, DC, 219-1513:

*OERI Bulletin*, a newsletter (ED 1.303/2: )

*OERI Publications Catalog*

## Energy

From National Energy Information Center, EI-231, Energy Information Administration, Forrestal Bldg., Room 1F-048, Washington, DC 20585; (202) 586-8800:

*EIA New Releases*, bimonthly (E 3.27/4: )

*EIA Publications Directory*, annual

*Energy Information Directory*

"Energy Datafiles" (PR-712 from NTIS, 5285 Port Royal Road, Springfield, VA 22161; (703) 487-4650)

## Health

From National Center for Health Statistics, Scientific and Technical Information Branch, Division of Data Services, 6525 Belcrest Rd., Hyattsville, MD 20782; (301) 435-8500:

*Catalog of Electronic Data Products*

*Catalog of Publications 1980-88*

*Data Tape Update* (updates *Catalog of Public Use Data Tapes* )

*NCHS Catalog of Publications 1980-88*

*National Center for Health Statistics Datafiles* (PR-716 from NTIS, 5285 Port Royal Road, Springfield, VA 22161; (703) 487- 4650)

From ODPHP National Health Information Center, Box 1133, Washington, DC 20013-1133; (800) 336-4797; in Washington, DC, and Maryland (301) 565-4167:

"Health Statistics," a list of reference sources and guides to statistics, agencies, and organizations that publish data, and publicly available data files.

## Labor

From the Bureau of Labor Statistics, U.S. Department of Labor, 441 G St., N.W., Washington, DC 20212 or from BLS Regional Offices in Boston, New York, Philadelphia, Atlanta, Chicago, Dallas, Kansas City, and San Francisco:

"BLS Data Diskettes"

*BLS Update* is a quarterly newsletter announcing new BLS publications and services.

*BLS Data Files on Tape* is a list of major data series on magnetic tape (Office of Publications).

*Major Programs of the Bureau of Labor Statistics* (BLS Report 793) (L 2.125: )

*Where to Find BLS Statistics on Women* (Report 762), a guide to identifying data about working women.

BLS 24-hour Current Data Hotline (202) 523-1221 tells how to obtain BLS information and provides summaries of data and news releases.

## NTIS

From NTIS, 5285 Port Royal Rd., Springfield, VA 22161; (703) 487-4650):

"CD-ROMs & Optical Discs Available from NTIS" (PR-888)

## REFERENCES

1. Katherine K. Wallman, *Losing Count: The Federal Statistical System* (Washington, DC: Population Reference Bureau, 1988).

2. Ann Herbert Scott, *Census U.S.A.: Fact Finding for the American People, 1790-1970* (New York: Seabury Press, 1968), p. 121.

3. Scott, p. 121.

4. Bureau of the Census, *Census '80: Continuing the Factfinder Tradition* (GPO, 1980), p. 276.

5. Geoffrey D. Austrian, *Herman Hollerith: Forgotten Giant of Information Processing* (New York: Columbia University Press, 1982), pp. 58-73.

6. "Mixed Reception Likely to Greet Census Takers Today, Poll Finds," *New York Times* (April 29, 1990): A1, B13; House. Committee on Post Office and Civil Service. *Preliminary Indications from the 1990 Census: Hearing before the Subcommittee on Census and Population, Committee on Post Office and Civil Service, House of Representatives, 101-2, August 8, 1990.* (Serial no. 101-71) GPO, 1990. (Y 4.P 84/10:101-71); Michael Schrage, "Census Is Regarded as Just More Junk Mail," *Los Angeles Times* 109 (May 17, 1990):D15

7. *OCLC Newsletter* (March/April 1991):28.

8. Michael R. Lavin, *Business Information: How to Find It, How to Use It*, 2nd ed. (Phoenix, AZ: Oryx Press, 1992), pp. 303-11.

9. Bureau of the Census, *Census '80: Projects for Students* (GPO, 1981), p. 16. (C 3.2:C 33/36)

10. Commission on Federal Paperwork, *Statistics: A Report of the Commission on Federal Paperwork* (GPO, 1977), p. 23. (Y 3.P 19:2 St 2)

11. Senate, *Quality of U.S. Education Information, Hearings before the Subcommittee on Government Information and Regulation of the Committee on Governmental Affairs, 100-1: Overview of National Goals, October 23, 1989; Availability and Quality of National Education Databases, November 1, 1989.* (Y 4.G74/9: S. hrg. 101- 411)

12. Michael R. Lavin, *Business Information: How to Find It, How to Use It* (Phoenix, AZ: Oryx Press, 1987), p. 171.

## FURTHER READING

Anderson, Margo J. *The American Census: A Social History.* New Haven, CT: Yale University Press, 1988.

A history of the decennial census and its impact on the nation.

Bureau of the Census. *Reflections of America: Commemorating the Statistical Abstract Centennial.* GPO, 1980. (C 3.2:Am 3/5)

A collection of articles by admirers of the *Statistical Abstract of the United States.*

Congress. Office of Technology Assessment. *Statistical Needs for a Changing U.S. Economy: Background Paper.* (OTA-BP-E-58) GPO, 1989. (Y 3.T 22/2:2St 2/2)

An overview of how the national statistical system impacts upon understanding key economic issues.

Evinger, William R. *Federal Statistical Data Bases: A Comprehensive Catalog of Current Machine-Readable and Online Files.* Phoenix, AZ: Oryx Press, 1988.

Emphasis is on magnetic tape files; lists companion print sources and reports; updates 1981 *Directory of Federal Statistical Data Files,* formerly published by the Department of Commerce.

————. *Federal Statistical Source: Where to Find Agency Experts & Personnel.* Phoenix, AZ: Oryx Press, 1991.

Subject and agency index to executive agency statistical programs, giving names, addresses, telephone numbers of key personnel, and a guide to principal sources of information about these activities.

Farrington, Polly-Alida. *Subject Index to the 1980 Census of Population and Housing.* Clifton Park, NY: Specialized Information Products, 1985.

A detailed index to subject coverage of the 1980 census, with an explanation of the organization of census data.

Fishbein, Meyer H., ed. *The National Archives and Statistical Research.* Athens, OH: Ohio University Press, 1974.

A guide to statistical materials in the National Archives.

House. Committee on Post Office and Civil Service. *Preliminary Indications from the 1990 Census: Hearing before the Subcommittee on Census and Population, Committee on Post Office and Civil Service, House of Representatives, 101-2, August 8, 1990.* (Serial no. 101-71) GPO, 1990. (Y 4.P 84/10:101-71)

A look at census accuracy and the undercount.

Lavin, Michael R. *Business Information: How to Find It, How to Use It.* 2nd ed. Phoenix, AZ: Oryx Press, 1992.

Practical advice for finding and using statistics from the censuses, an introduction to statistical reasoning, plus overviews of economic and industry statistics.

Ondrasik, Allison. *Data Map: Index of Published Tables of Statistical Data.* Phoenix, AZ: Oryx Press, 1990.

A computer-generated index to contents of thousands of statistical tables, including those in U.S. government and

United Nations publications and those of other public and private organizations.

McClure, Charles R. and Peter Hernon. *Use of Census Bureau Data in GPO Depository Libraries: Future Issues and Trends. Final Report for United States Bureau of the Census 21st Century Decennial Census Planning Staff.* Manlius, NY: Information Management Consultant Services, 1990. (C 3.2:D 26/9)

An examination of issues and trends in public access to census data through depository libraries.

Morehead, Joe. "The Uses and Misuses of Information Found in Government Publications," in *Essays on Public Documents and Government Policies.* New York: The Haworth Press, 1986.

A discussion of the need for intelligent interpretation of government statistics, with cautions about specific data weaknesses.

Schulze, Suzanne. *Population Information in Nineteenth Century Census Volumes.* Phoenix, AZ: Oryx Press, 1983.

————. *Population Information in Twentieth Century Census Volumes, 1900-1940.* Phoenix, AZ: Oryx Press, 1985.

————. *Population Information in Twentieth Century Census Volumes, 1950-1980.* Phoenix, AZ: Oryx Press, 1988.

A subject index to data in decennial census volumes; especially useful for census volumes before 1940, which were published without guides.

Sears, Jean L. and Marilyn K. Moody. *Using Government Publications. Vol. 2: Finding Statistics and Using Special Techniques.* Phoenix, AZ: Oryx Press, 1986.

A how-to manual for finding government statistics on dozens of topics; 2nd edition is forthcoming.

Stanfield, Rochelle L. "Statistics Gap." *National Journal* (April 13, 1991): 844-49.

A review of recent government statistical woes.

# EXERCISES

1. What is the population of the United States?
2. Using statistical reference tools, identify the answer or a probable answer source for the questions below. Cite the answer source and the reference you consulted to identify it.
   a. How scientifically literate are Americans?
   b. A magazine article mentions a 1991 Harris poll that found four out of five Americans to be concerned about threats to their personal privacy. Identify the survey.
   c. What percent of U.S. patents are granted to non-Americans?
   d. How can I get Charles McClure and Peter Hernon's report on depository library use of census data?
   e. What is the relationship between these two NTIS titles: *Directory of Computerized Data Files* and *Directory of U.S. Government Datafiles for Mainframes and Microcomputers?*

# CHAPTER 13
# Nonprint and Primary Resources

## WHAT

The United States is the nation's biggest producer of audiovisual materials. In addition to the growing legions of government-produced videotapes, there are films (a waning medium), audiotapes, posters, charts, maps, picture sets, photographs, and databases, many of which are available to the public.

## WHERE

Government AV production is decentralized, without a central hub similar to GPO. Practically every government agency has created audiovisuals at one time or another, frequently by contracting out their productions. Except for maps, however, most fall through cracks in the depository library system because agencies fail to send copies to GPO for depository distribution.

## HOW

Central clearinghouses like the National Audiovisual Center and Earth Science Information Centers help link the public with the wealth of government AV resources. New technologies allow "electronic libraries" of photograph and film collections to be disseminated nationwide in programs like the Library of Congress's American Memory Project.

## AUDIOVISUAL MATERIALS

*If we put on "Uncle Sam's Saturday Night at the Movies," in one year we [would have] enough material to run for twenty-two years with no summer reruns.*
—Lester A. Fettig,
Office of Management and Budget

The federal government has been called "Hollywood on the Potomac" because it creates so many audiovisual productions—almost $48,000,000 worth in 1990, more than three-quarters of which were videotapes.

National Audiovisual Center figures, which are acknowledged to be incomplete (the Department of Defense, for example, does not report its media expenditures), calculate a federal audiovisual tab of $85,979,000 for 1990, including production, duplication, purchases, and library services.[1]

Federal audiovisual management has some acknowledged problems: duplication, poor use of facilities, and sketchy information on the volume and cost of productions. The federal AV scene has been characterized as wasteful and inefficient—in a state of "overall confusion."[2] And, although federal audiovisual productions are unique historical records, their preservation has been neglected.[3] Many federal films have been lost; posters have been depreciated and poorly maintained. One agency that cranked out six to twelve posters yearly for thirty years has kept not a single copy.

## Audiovisual Searches

It is important to realize that not only is there no governmentwide master list of AV materials, but also that many of the indexes relied upon for tracing printed documents are weak when it comes to AV. The *Monthly Catalog* lists printed guides to AV productions, such as the free National Audiovisual Center (NAC) subject brochures, but does not offer comprehensive coverage of AV resources themselves. After a hopeful flurry of activity in the early 1980s, a program of cooperative cataloging among the GPO, NAC, and Library of Congress evaporated, leaving few AV citations in the *Monthly Catalog*. Currently, *Monthly Catalog* coverage emphasizes GPO/depository-distribution AV items like the posters listed in Subject Bibliography 57. To locate nondepository audiovisuals, several sources must be consulted. The NAC *Media Resource Catalog* and database offer the broadest (although not comprehensive) coverage of federal AV output. To identify medical audiovisuals, use the National Library of Medicine AV catalogs.

## National Audiovisual Center (NAC)

The National Audiovisual Center is the government's primary audiovisual distributor, with a collection among the largest and most diverse in the country. The center serves as a central information and distribution source for federally produced audiovisuals, including newer electronic media such as CD-ROM and videodisc. NAC disseminates federal AV productions to the public through purchase or rental, and also supplies copies of supplementary materials like study guides and teacher's manuals.

NAC catalogs and computer files are the primary bibliographies for nonmedical audiovisuals. The *Media Resource Catalog* (AE 1.110/4: ) is a free, annotated bibliography of new and popular NAC videos, films, filmstrips, multimedia kits, and slide sets, but reflects only a partial listing of NAC titles. The total collection is recorded in the NAC Master Data File, which can be searched by NAC Customer Service staff in response to telephone or written inquiries. Supplementing the NAC's general catalog are the *Quarterly Update*, a free newsletter listing new NAC materials and services (AE 1.109: ), and free special subject brochures. Subject brochures are announced in the *Media Resource Catalog*, or can be identified through the *Monthly Catalog*.

## National Library of Medicine

NLM's online catalog, AVLINE, and *National Library of Medicine Audiovisuals Catalog* document NLM's audiovisual collection. The collection focuses on a wide range of biomedical subjects "from Anatomy to Zoonoses," on film, videocassette, videodisc, slides, filmstrips, x-rays, and computer software. AVLINE includes all audiovisuals cataloged by NLM since 1975, with some abstracts and evaluative information for pre-1982 citations. Availability (at the time of cataloging) is also noted. AVLINE may be searched online on MEDLARS.

Several printed catalogs are culled from AVLINE. The quarterly *National Library of Medicine Audiovisuals Catalog* (HE 20.3609/4: ) lists audiovisuals cataloged by NLM and includes distributor information. An annual cumulation substitutes for the fourth quarterly issue. The microfiche *Health Sciences Audiovisuals Catalog* (HE 20.3614/5: ) includes all AV titles cataloged between 1975 and 1988. This title ceased in 1988, and the last issue, cumulative for 1975-88, should be saved. Access is now through AVLINE and the *National Library of Medicine Audiovisuals Catalog*. For help identifying or locating NLM audiovisuals, contact Reference Section, NLM, 8600 Rockville Pike, Bethesda, MD 20894; (800) 272-4787. Most NLM audiovisuals are available through interlibrary loan by contacting NLM's Collection Access Section; (800) 272-4787, FAX (301) 496-2809.

## Agency Catalogs

Supplementing the NAC and NLM guides are numerous catalogs describing audiovisuals available from specific agencies. Some agency catalogs are listed in Subject Bibliographies 57 and 73, available free from the Government Printing Office. Others must be identified using the *Monthly Catalog*, which lists bibliographies of audiovisuals, but often not the audiovisuals themselves.

Some agencies will provide free loans of their AV productions, even those in the NAC collection. Agency loans are best arranged directly through the agency or one of its field offices. Agencies may also arrange for commercial film distributors to lend some of their films without charge. Although the National Audiovisual Center does not lend materials, it can refer requesters to federal-agency lending libraries and commercial loan sources.

### National Union Catalog

The *National Union Catalog: Audiovisual Materials* (LC 30.8/4: ) is a quarterly microfiche listing of films, videos, filmstrips, transparency sets, and slide sets released in the United States or Canada and cataloged by the Library of Congress. It continues *Audiovisual Materials: Films and Other Materials for Projection* and *Library of Congress Catalog: Motion Pictures and Filmstrips*, which provided coverage between 1953 and 1982. The NUC register/index may be searched by name, title, subject, and series.

### Library of Congress

*Special Collections in the Library of Congress* (LC 1.6/4:C 68) offers overviews of the library's prized collections, including drawings, films, maps, prints, photographs, sound recordings, videotapes, and other nonprint formats. Brief descriptions focus on the history, content, scope, subject strengths, and organization of each special collection.

## Photographs and Prints

*We introduced Americans to America.*
—Roy E. Stryker, director of the Farm
Security Administration, 1935-43

From the late 1800s to the early 1930s, government staff photographers flourished, particularly during Franklin Roosevelt's administration, when photographs portraying the ravages of the Depression galvanized social change. The 1930s saw government photographs featured in books, pamphlets, magazines, newspapers, and even entered as evidence in congressional hearings.[4] A quarter of a million photos were taken by the Farm Security Administration alone, in a massive documentary project now archived at the Library of Congress.

These same photographs inspired John Steinbeck to write *The Grapes of Wrath* after spending several days studying "those tragic, beautiful faces."[5]

**Figure 13.1: Migrant Mother.**

In the 1930s, Farm Security Administration photographers like Walker Evans, Gordon Parks, and Dorothea Lange produced some of the best known images of the twentieth century. "Migrant Mother," snapped by Lange in 1936, is the Library of Congress's most requested photo.

Often overlooked as historical documents, photographs form a hauntingly detailed record of times past. As primary sources, photographs often provide information unavailable through the written word. Studying Civil War images, for example, can provide information about uniforms, equipment, battlefields, and camps. The Park Service's accurate restoration of Ford's Theater might have been impossible without stereographic photos taken immediately after Lincoln's assassination.

The Library of Congress's Prints and Photographs Division is a cache of prints, negatives, transparencies, and stereographs, with images produced from almost every photographic technology, old and new. The collection was nurtured by the copyright law of 1865, which required that a copy of each copyrighted "book, pamphlet, map, chart, musical composition, print, engraving, or photograph" be deposited in the Library of Congress. Copies may be purchased through the Library's Photoduplication Service, but requests must be identified by a negative number.

Although the Prints and Photographs reading room opens its photograph collections to visitors, "public awareness of the library's photographs has been indirect and random."[6] The collection's frequent visitors include historians, picture researchers, photography students, authors seeking book illustrations, and individuals trying to identify their family photos.

Technology has catapulted some of the LC collections beyond the Capitol through the Library of Congress American Memory project, a six-year pilot launched in 1991. The American Memory electronic library of Library of Congress photographs and other materials will be distributed to test sites on optical and compact discs, and eventually online. The American Memory Project will allow electronic libraries of some of the Library of Congress's most treasured collections to be scattered across the nation.

Although much of the Prints and Photographs collection remains uncataloged, a few guides exist. A general introduction to the collection is the fascinating *A Century of Photographs, 1846-1946* (LC 1.2:P 56/5/846-946), a visual history of documentary photography beginning with daguerreotypes. *Graphic Sampler* (LC 25.2:G 76) focuses on drawings and prints created between the fifteenth century and the 1960s. Other guides include exhibition catalogs, identifiable through the free Library of Congress *Publications in Print* (LC 1.12:P 96/yr) or *Monthly Catalog*.

The National Archives is such a rich source of pictorial history it has been dubbed a "photographic time machine." Visitors to Washington may pursue picture research in the Archives' Still Pictures Branch Research Room (researcher appointments should be arranged at least two days ahead). The Still Pictures Branch also has some 13,000 federal posters, copies of which can be purchased as slides. The National Archives and Records Administration's Audiovisual Archives Division has images documenting America's history since colonial times, with emphasis on the nineteenth and first half of the twentieth centuries. The *Guide to the Holdings of the Still Picture Branch of the National Archives and Records Administration* (AE 1.108:St 5) provides an overview of the collection.

The Forest Service Photograph Collection, the world's largest forestry photo collection (begun in 1898), is also disseminated through laser disc. Forest Service photographs can be perused on-site at NAL or at selected Forest Service Units and Land-Grant libraries by browsing the Forest Service Photo Laser Disc, a word-searchable database of images and image information from the Forest Service Photo Browsing Collection at NAL. It includes photos, slides, posters, illustrations, and maps. An accompanying database may be searched for additional information. Some Forest Service photos circulate, while others can be ordered as prints of negatives from the National Archives.

The Capitol's concentration of government agencies and national-organization headquarters makes it a rich source of pictorial resources. The Library of Congress and National Archives collections are only two of dozens in the Capitol. *Pictorial Resources in the Washington, D.C., Area* (LC 1.32/2:P 58) is a guide to the availability and content of government, international, and private organization collections, many of which respond to telephone or mail queries.

| AV FINDING AIDS | |
|---|---|
| **Scope** | **Title** |
| General | NAC's *Media Resource Catalog,* updated by *Quarterly Update,* NAC Master Data File |
| Medicine | AVLINE: *NLM Audiovisuals Catalog* |
| Depository titles | *Monthly Catalog* |
| Special subjects | Agency catalogs, NAC subject brochures |
| Pictorial materials | Guides to special collections, such as those in the Library of Congress and National Archives |
| Bibliographic verification | *Monthly Catalog; NUC: Audiovisual Materials; NUC: Cartographic Materials;* special subject databases and indexes: OCLC |

## MAPS

*Maps are part of the understanding of all humankind.*
—Peter Steinhart, contributing editor
to *Audubon* magazine

For more than two hundred years, surveying, compiling, and publishing maps have been recognized as official obligations of government. Since our nation's infancy, the government has recognized map and chart making as vital to national development and defense. As early as 1777, General George Washington appointed a staff geographer and surveyor to make sketches and maps for the Continental Army. Later, major geographic features of the nation's new territories were delineated through public land surveys; the West was explored by government-sponsored expeditions like that of Lewis and Clark; and the nation's waterways were charted and surveyed to safeguard commercial and naval vessels. In 1807 Congress created the government's first scientific office, the Survey of the Coast (now embedded within the National Oceanic and Atmospheric Administration) to chart America's coastal waters. And in 1879 the army surrendered its role as the nation's chief mapper to a fledgling agency called the Geological Survey. But mapping had flourished on the continent long before white men took an interest in it: In 1869, when a U.S. coast survey geographer asked Chilkat Indians to describe the Sitka, Alaska, landscape, they spent three days drawing him a detailed, accurate map.

By some estimates, about 80 percent of all maps are officially published by national, state, county, or municipal governments. As a result, the most comprehensive map collections are found in official government agencies and in the world's national libraries. Numerous federal agencies collect and prepare cartographic data, creating maps not only for specific cartographic programs but as working tools and for communicating information.

## Cartographic Literacy

*I'm at the corner of Walk and Don't Walk.*
—Unknown

Are you cartographically literate? The United States recently placed sixth among eight nations in a National Geographic Society assessment of geographic knowledge. Americans came in dead last when eighteen to twenty-four-year-olds were compared across the globe. In other studies, one-third of college undergraduates studying geography couldn't find France or Japan on a map, and more than half were fuzzy on the whereabouts of Chicago. More than 14 percent of Americans interviewed couldn't locate the United States on a world map.[7]

Cobb and Seavey stress the need for librarians to be knowledgeable about maps in order to help users interpret them: "Almost never does one have to teach the patron how to *read* a book. This is not the case with maps. Often the patron will need assistance in actually interpreting the data presented by the cartographic format."[8]

### A Cartographic Primer

Cartography is the science of mapmaking. GIS, or geographic information systems, create computerized maps.

Charts are maps that aid navigation in water, air, or space. Mapping and charting are not limited to the earth, but can also illustrate planets, satellites, and the heavens.

Atlases are collections of maps or charts, while national atlases focus on an entire country and are often government publications. The *National Atlas of the United States* (I 19.2:N 21a), published by the U.S. Geological Survey in 1970, was a monumental work and the first U.S. national atlas ever produced. It included hundreds of maps depicting general, physical, historical, economic, sociocultural, and administrative aspects of the nation, along with sections on mapping, charting, and the world. Although the volume is now out of print, selected *National Atlas* maps are still sold by USGS, which will send a price list on request.

Topographic maps show the shape and elevation of terrain using contour lines (called "terrain relief"). With practice, a map reader can visualize hills and valleys from the contour lines that convey the shape of the land on a topographic map. Symbols are the graphic language of maps, their shapes, sizes, locations, and color all having special meaning. On USGS topographic maps a symbol's color indicates the feature represented: Water is blue, human-made features like roads are black, wooded areas are green, while brown contour lines represent the earth. Planimetric maps do not show terrain relief.

Base maps are used to organize and display information, which is "overlaid" on the base map. The USGS prepares base maps for the nation.

Thematic maps depict data through color and shading. The location and intensity of earthquakes, for example, could be depicted using defined colors on a map (see Figure 13.2).

The map margin, the border around the map's outer edges, provides bibliographic information. Marginal information corresponds to a book's table of contents and introduction, noting how the map was made, by whom, and when. Like books, maps can be bibliographically described by title, publisher, and date, along with characteristics unique to maps, like scale and contour.

Scale is the relationship between map distance and real distance, usually expressed as a ratio. A scale of 1:63,360, for example, means that one inch on the map represents 63,360 inches (one mile). The larger the second number in the ratio, the smaller the map scale and the less detail shown.

Quadrangles are the most common publication format for modern maps. The most common scale for topographic maps is 1:24,000, called 7.5 ("seven-and-a-half") quadrangle maps because they cover 7.5 minutes of latitude and longitude. These are fairly large-scale maps, showing details of natural and human-made features like buildings, campgrounds, ski lifts, water mills, bridges, fences, roads, and even drive-in theaters. Smaller-scale maps (1:250,000 and smaller) show large areas and predominant features like boundaries, state parks, airports, major roads, and railroads. The USGS's National Mapping Program produces 7.5 quadrangle maps for each of the fifty states.

Index maps are guides to maps of specific areas, using a base map with an overlaid grid that breaks the area into named segments.

Gazetteers are geographic dictionaries, alphabetical lists of places with descriptions. *The National Gazetteer of the United States* (I 19.16:1200) is issued in separate volumes for states, territories, and other special listings, all published as USGS Professional Paper 1200 and collectively called *The National Gazetteer of the United States of America. The National Gazetteer of the United States of America-United States Concise 1990* volume (I 19.16:1200-

US) covers the entire nation and its territories, describing significant features and places. A cooperative endeavor of the USGS and the U.S. Board on Geographic Names, the gazetteer provides a national standard for names of places, features, and areas. The gazetteer is derived from the USGS's National Geographic Names Database, which can be used to produce special listings of geographic names in bound reports, magnetic tape, or microfiche.

| A SAMPLING OF GOVERNMENT MAPPERS | |
| --- | --- |
| Census Bureau | Demographic maps, MSA maps, congressional district maps |
| CIA | Country and world maps |
| Corps of Engineers | River navigation charts, topographic maps, geodetic surveys |
| Defense Mapping Agency | Hydrologic maps, nautical and aeronautical charts |
| State Department | Atlases, maps, charts, and tables showing basic aspects of U.S. foreign relations |
| Geological Survey | Moon and planetary maps, polar maps, U.S. maps |
| Federal Highway Administration | Transportation and county highway maps |
| Library of Congress | Maps, charts, atlases, historical and military reproductions |
| NASA | Aerial and space photos |
| National Oceanic and Atmospheric Administration | Nautical and aeronautical charts, bathymetric maps, historical maps, climate maps, Civil War map reproductions, storm evacuation maps |
| Forest Service | Aerial photos, national forest maps, recreation maps |

## The Nation's Primary Mapmakers

The three major agency distributors of maps to depository libraries are the U.S. Geological Survey, Defense Mapping Agency, and National Ocean Service. Most maps arrive in depositories folded, cataloged with SuDocs numbers assigned, and are listed in the *Monthly Catalog*. The *Federal Depository Library Manual* includes a section on "Maps in Depository Libraries," with suggestions for handling and processing depository maps, plus "Maps, Charts, and Atlases Available for Selection by Depository Libraries," which lists GPO item numbers, issuing agencies, and Sudocs number stems.

**FIGURE 13.2: Thematic Maps.**

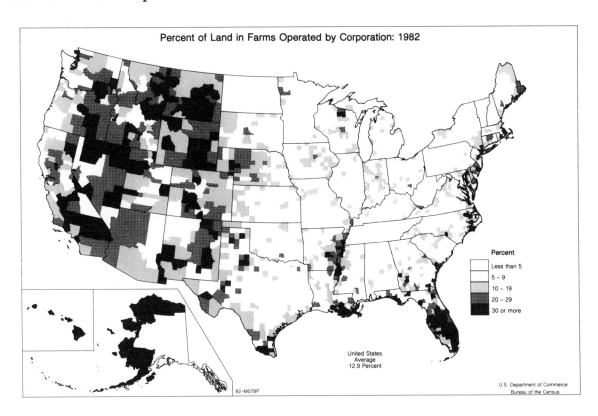

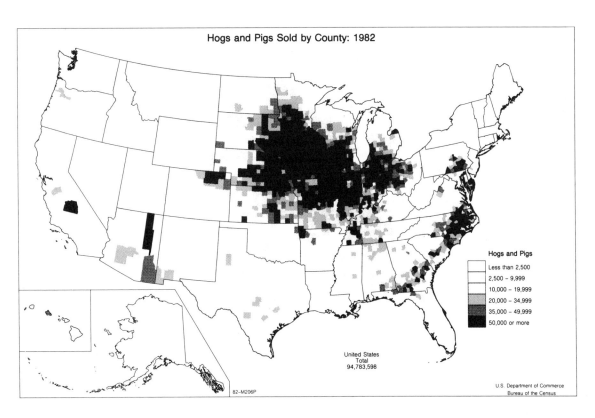

Source: Bureau of the Census

## U.S. Geological Survey

The U.S. Geological Survey (USGS) is a national information source for geology, hydrology, cartography, geography, remote sensing, energy, land use, and mineral and water resources. The USGS disseminates this information in many formats, including books, maps, photographs, CD-ROMs, and computer files. In 1984 USGS terminated its separate depository program and merged with GPO's depository system. Now every major USGS map series is available to depositories, and USGS is considering including their CD-ROMs in the Depository Library Program. USGS maps are usually photo-revised every five to ten years. New maps are announced in the free monthly *New Publications of the Geological Survey* (I 19.14/4:) and the annual *Publications of the Geological Survey* (I 19.14:). The free annual pamphlet "Price and Availability List of U.S. Geological Survey Publications" lists USGS books and thematic maps for sale.

The USGS Library System is one of the world's largest earth-science libraries, with a main library in Reston, Virginia, and branches in Denver, Colorado; Flagstaff, Arizona; and Menlo Park, California. The Denver branch includes a field records depository for the original materials produced during USGS geologic field investigations and a photographic library dating back to the late 1800s.

## Defense Mapping Agency

Much government mapping in the United States and virtually every other modern nation relates to military operations. The Defense Mapping Agency is the Pentagon's mapmaker, sometimes called "the military's AAA." The Defense Mapping Agency offers little domestic mapping, focusing instead on preparing maps and charts of all corners of the world to support the nation's defense and security. For national security reasons, only about one percent of DMA maps and charts are available to the public: by purchase through the USGS distribution branch, or through the Federal Depository Library Program (DMA aeronautical, hydrographic, and topographic maps). DMA sales items are listed in its public sales catalogs for topographic maps and publications (D 5.351/3:) and for aeronautical charts and publications (D 5.351/3-2:). DMA also publishes map indexes.

## National Ocean Service

An agency within the National Oceanic and Atmospheric Administration (NOAA, pronounced "Noah"), the National Ocean Service is responsible for domestic charting, both nautical (U.S. waters and navigable waterways) and aeronautical. Since its own map depository program ended in 1988, the National Ocean Service has sent nautical and aeronautical charts to federal depository libraries. Depository copies are stamped "not to be used for navigation" since they may be out of date by the time they reach depository shelves (NOS maps and charts are usually revised every 28-56 days). Catalogs of nautical and aeronautical charts for sale by NOAA are free from NOAA's distribution branch (C 55.418: and C 55.418/2: ). Charts are also sold by NOAA chart agents.

## Census Bureau

Censuses and surveys depend upon accurate mapping. Census Bureau programs generate geographic information in maps, publications, and computer files. The Bureau keeps maps for all counties, incorporated villages, towns, cities, county subdivisions, census tracts, enumeration districts, and city blocks. The Census Bureau publishes outline maps showing names and boundaries of geographic areas, and statistical (thematic) maps, which illustrate data using color and shading.

Some 90,000 maps were computer-generated for the 1990 census using TIGER, "the Coast-to-Coast Digital Map Database." TIGER is the first computerized database to map the entire nation: 3.6 million square miles. To create TIGER, the USGS scanned or manually digitized its 1:100,000-scale maps of the United States and gave the Census Bureau the computer tapes, which were merged into a seamless map database. Selected TIGER files are available to the public on magnetic tape and CD-ROM. Census maps have been issued on paper, microfiche, CD-ROM, and computer tape. The regional census centers sell maps for their regions, and state data centers have copies of all their state's maps.

Number 8 in the Census Bureau's *Factfinder for the Nation* series, "Census Geography—Concepts and Products," is an excellent introduction to census cartographic data, and is free from Data User Services Division and reprinted in the *Census Catalog and Guide*.

# Foreign Country Maps

*When we take no joy in maps, we take no joy in distant places.*                  —Peter Steinhart,
contributing editor to *Audubon* magazine

The CIA, Defense Mapping Agency, State Department, and USGS publish world and foreign maps and charts. Many of these are available to depository libraries in the series shown in the table below. Other foreign maps and producing agencies may be identified using *Monthly Catalog*. Earlier CIA maps were released through Doc Ex, and since 1980, through NTIS or GPO.

| FOREIGN AND WORLD MAPS | |
|---|---|
| CIA | PrEx 3.10/4: |
| DMA | D 5.355: |
| State Department | S 1.33/2: |
| USGS | I 19.81: |
| | I 19.102: |
| | I 19.108: |

The government's primary publisher of foreign gazetteers is the Board of Geographic Names, within the Defense Mapping Agency. Each gazetteer (D 5.319: ) covers a specific country or geographic region and lists official place names approved by the federal government. The DMA's free public sales catalogs include lists of titles. The Congressional Information Service's Foreign Gazetteers of the U.S. Board on Geographic Names is a microfiche file of Defense Mapping Agency gazetteers since 1950.

## Map Collections

*Maps, like faces, are the signatures of history.*
—Will and Ariel Durant,
*The Story of Civilization*

### Library of Congress

When the Library of Congress was established in 1800, its holdings included three maps and four atlases. Today the Library's Geography and Map Division boasts the world's largest and most comprehensive cartographic collection, containing not only maps but also atlases, reference materials, globes, three-dimensional plastic relief models, and other formats. The Library's Geography and Map Division provides cartographic and geographic information to Congress, the nation, and the world. It has been estimated that the Library of Congress acquires copies of three-quarters of the world's unrestricted maps and charts. Because surveying and mapping are official functions of the federal government, many maps and atlases in the collection are deposited by official sources, such as the U.S. Geological Survey and the National Oceanic and Atmospheric Administration. Private and commercial cartographic works arrive via the Library of Congress's Copyright Office, while foreign maps are received by exchange or purchase.

The library's collections include familiar formats along with rarities: treasure maps taken from Spanish galleons by Sir Francis Drake; Micronesian charts fashioned from sticks, pebbles, and coconuts; Chinese maps painted on fans; neckerchief maps worn by British aviators in WW II; maps carved on gunpowder horns from the French and Indian War; Pierre L'Enfant's original 1791 sketch of Washington, DC, with Thomas Jefferson's handwritten marginal notes.

The collections are for on-site reference use only, with maps and atlases unavailable for public loan, sale, or free distribution. (Loans are available to members of Congress and federal agencies, and through occasional interlibrary loans to research libraries.) Many map and atlas reproductions can be purchased through the Library of Congress's Photoduplication Service, however. The library's collections are reflected in several card and book catalogs, including the *Bibliography of Cartography* (G.K. Hall), which shows photo-offset copies of cards

from the library's major reference tool, the Bibliography of Cartography Card File. The "B of C" is an author and subject index to books and journal articles about maps, mapmaking, interpretation, use, preservation, history, and map librarianship. The *National Union Catalog: Cartographic Materials* on microfiche includes the complete Library of Congress map database, including entries for newly cataloged maps. *Special Collections in the Library of Congress* is a selective guide to some of the library's prized research material held in special collections. Maps are included, with brief descriptions of the history, content, scope, subject strengths, and organization of the library's map collections.

### The National Archives

The National Archives oversees the nation's largest aerial photograph collection and second-largest map collection. Although published in 1971, *Guide to Cartographic Records in the National Archives* (GS 4.6/2:C 24) continues to be the key to the National Archives cartographic collection.

## Accessing Maps

To identify map collections, consult the American Library Association's *Guide to U.S. Map Resources*, a comprehensive directory of the nation's map libraries and cartographic resources in public, private, state, and federal agencies. Federal depository libraries serve as map depositories by receiving maps from the Geological Survey, Defense Mapping Agency, and National Ocean Service in a cooperative program administered by the Government Printing Office. In addition, there are U.S. Geological Survey Map Reference Libraries housing selected USGS maps for public use. Their addresses are available from Earth Science Information Centers and from USGS Public Inquiries Offices, and are listed on the *Index to Topographic Maps* for each state.

USGS maps may be purchased from Earth Science Information Centers, known as "map stores," by mail from the USGS Denver Distribution Center, or from authorized local dealers. The *Index to Topographic and Other Map Coverage [state]* (I 19.41/6-3: ) includes a directory of map sales locations and addresses of map libraries in the state. *Catalog of Topographic and Other Published Maps [state]* (I 19.41/6-2: ) provides current ordering information. Maps from agencies other than USGS must be purchased from their issuing agencies or GPO.

### Earth Science Information Centers

A network of Earth Science Information Centers (ESICs, pronounced "ee-sicks") are the central source for USGS cartographic information. ESICs respond to questions by mail, telephone, or on-site at more than 75 locations (get addresses by calling 800-USA-MAPS or requesting an address list from USGS). The Earth Science Information Centers provide information about earth science, the earth's surface and interior, and even the space surrounding Earth. ESICs help requesters locate maps, charts, aerial and satellite photos and imagery, digital map data, earth science databases, and even non-government map data using their Cartographic Catalog, a bibliography of government and private cartographic products. The range of ESIC sales items is vast: Aerial photos of your neighborhood, views of the earth taken from space, computer data, color slides, and out-of-print map reproductions are only a few examples. One of the most popular photographs for sale is a color panoramic view of New York City showing the Statue of Liberty, the New Jersey coast, Queens, and Manhattan.

### Finding the Right Map

Unlike books, many maps are uncataloged. Rather than using the library catalog as a finding tool, the map seeker uses techniques specially designed for maps. One of the most common finding aids is the map index. USGS map indexes divide the fifty states, Puerto Rico, Guam, American Samoa, and the Virgin Islands into named grids representing mapped quadrangles. Grids are named after a prominent place or natural landmark within their boundaries. After identifying a grid name, the corresponding map can be retrieved from alphabetically arranged map cabinets. To identify state maps, use the *Index to Topographic and Other Map Coverage [state]* (I 19.41/6-3: ). A companion booklet, *Catalog of Topographic and Other Published Maps [state]* (I 19.41/6-2: ), is a catalog for ordering, with map prices and availability. Map indexes and catalogs are free from USGS.

Cobb and Seavey point out that atlases can serve as indexes to library map collections by helping identify the location to be searched on an index map: "'I know it's somewhere east of Magnetogorsk' can be pinned down very quickly using the gazetteer [place name index] that virtually all atlases have, or simply by scanning the small scale maps in the atlas itself."[9] Cobb and Seavey liken this approach to finding "the forest before looking for a specific tree."

Bibliographic information for maps appears in the *Monthly Catalog*, in OCLC, the NTIS database and GRA & I, and in *National Union Catalog: Cartographic Materials*. The *Monthly Catalog* concentrates on maps sent to depository libraries, with sparse coverage of nondepository maps. Separate maps are rarely included in the NTIS collection, which emphasizes maps that are integral components of reports. When a map is available from NTIS, the keyword "Maps" is listed as a descriptor in the database, with "Mapping" used for reports describing how maps are made. OCLC allows qualification of name or title searches by format: /**map** to retrieve maps, and /**med** to retrieve audiovisual materials. The *NUC Carto-graphic Materials* is a quarterly microfiche publication that reproduces catalog records of cartographic materials from the Library of Congress and contributing libraries, including the entire retrospective LC MARC database since 1969. It may be searched through any of five cumulative indexes: name, title, subject, series, and geographic classification code. The *Catalog of Copyright Entries*, published by the Copyright Office, lists maps, atlases, and other cartographic works registered for copyright in part 6, *Maps. The Map Catalog: Every Kind of Map and Chart on Earth and Even Some Above It*, from Random House, is a guide to maps and map products for the earth, sky, and water. The catalog provides an introduction to dozens of map types, with advice on where to get them.

## Digital Maps

Federal geographic information systems (GIS), or computerized maps, are the wave of the future in cartography. Not since Mercator produced maps depicting a round Earth has mapping been so revolutionized. Longitude-latitude coordinates, which provide a number code for every place on Earth, are easily computerized. Digital maps have simplified map storage and expanded versatility, allowing customized maps to be created on demand.

Agency GIS applications are widespread, currently focusing on natural resource management and environmental assessment. Two of the major federal digital map producers are USGS and the Census Bureau, creator of TIGER, the 1990 census geographic database. Digital data and customized maps from both agencies are for sale to the public. USGS Earth Science Information Centers provide free information packages describing digital cartographic data. The Federal Geographic Data Committee, which oversees computerized federal mapping, envisions a National Geographic Data System which will pool spatial databases developed by government agencies.

## ELECTRONIC INFORMATION

*Modern computerized information systems are forcing a reevaluation of the role of government agencies in the dissemination of information.*
> —Glenn English, chairman of the
> House Subcommittee on Government
> Information, Justice and Agriculture

For two centuries our government documented its activities on paper. Although paper still dominates, the U.S. government maintains the world's largest inventory of computer equipment, and acquires personal computers so quickly it can't keep track of their numbers (there are more than one million, however). Increasingly, the federal government uses computers for collection, maintenance, and dissemination of public information. The prevalence of electronic agency records created with word processing and database management programs, spreadsheets, imaging, computer modeling, and E-mail is changing the way information is collected, stored, and disseminated. It has been predicted that by the year 2000, three-quarters of government transactions will be electronic. [10]

A federal inventory taken in 1991 identified more than 1,789 major program-related electronic databases worthy of transfer to the National Archives.[11] Among the government records suited to computer processing are statistical, administrative, textual, graphic, and index/ cross-reference files. While many federal electronic records have paper counterparts, others exist only electronically, creating continuing challenges for archival storage. Electronic records are those stored in a form that only a computer can process. This format encompasses many electronic media, including magnetic tape, CD-ROMs, and floppy disks. Technological obsolescence is the primary threat to the electronic historical record, rendering future computer hardware and software incapable of reading records created with contemporary technology. It has already hobbled access to the original data tapes from the 1960 census—they can only be run on two machines, one in the Smithsonian Institution, the other in Japan. A similar fate has incapacitated Department of Defense audiotapes made on Vietnam battlefields: The machinery to replay them is no longer available. Even if obsolete hardware remains available, there may be no one able to run it and no surviving instruction manuals.

## Expert Systems

Expert systems are computer software packages that help perform a task, solve problems, or make logical decisions. The federal government is the foremost user of expert systems, responsible for about three-quarters of the market. Military, intelligence, and space agencies have been especially active in expert systems research and development.

## The National Archives

Although the law forbids destroying federal records without authorization from the Archivist of the United States, in reality key federal records have already been lost, electronically altered, or erased. The National Archives and Records Administration (NARA) oversees federal electronic record-keeping. In 1990, the House Committee on Government Operations released *Taking a Byte Out of History: The Archival Preservation of Federal Computer Records* (Y 1.1/8:101-978), which galvanized concern about preservation of electronic archival records. NARA has spent the last two decades working to sensitize federal agencies to the importance of preserving the nation's machine-readable memory, collecting more than 8,000 data files for its collections.

NARA's Center for Electronic Records is responsible for maintaining electronic government records, storing computer files from Congress, the courts, and the Executive Office of the President; presidential commissions; and government agencies and their contractors. The basic finding aids for machine-readable records in the National Archives collection are the *Catalog of Machine-Readable Records in the National Archives of the United States* (GS 4.17/3:R 24), published in 1977, and the more current and periodic "Center for Electronic Records Title List (A Partial and Preliminary List of the Datasets in the Custody of the National Archives)." The free "Title List" is compiled using the Center for Electronic Records' database. Copies of most of NARA's data sets may be purchased from the Center. Evinger's *Federal Statistical Data Bases: A Comprehensive Catalog of Current Machine-Readable and Online Files* includes NARA data sets.

## Databases

*Even with the help of the most lovable librarian, if you rely on information in a paper-based library, using paper-based methods, you can waste time, money, and sanity.*
—Elizabeth Ferrarini, in *Informania*

The federal government maintains thousands of electronic databases, including demographic, bibliographic, personnel, financial, and statistical files, primarily in the sciences and social sciences. Electronic formats are becoming the preferred mode for many categories of information, with some government data available solely in electronic form. There are government databases on a mind-boggling range of topics: from bird-banding and boating accidents to Sudden Infant Death Syndrome and working women.

Although there is no governmentwide list, numerous commercially published database directories list government databases. Sources such as *The Directory of Online Databases* and Martha Williams' *Computer-Readable Databases: A Directory and Data Sourcebook* may be identified in local library catalogs by searching the subject headings "On-line bibliographic searching—Directories," "Information storage and retrieval systems—Directories," "Data Bases—Directories," or "Machine-readable bibliographic data—Directories." Individual agencies may issue database directories, free information brochures, or create online guides to their databases in the form of computer "menus." Lesko's *The Federal Data Base Finder: A Directory of Free and Fee-Based Data Bases and Files Available from the Federal Government* is useful for identifying government databases. While there are no plans to compile a comprehensive list of federal CD-ROMs, they are included in commercial directories such as *CD-ROMs in Print* and *The Directory of Portable*

*Databases.* The Office of Management and Budget has released Government Information Dissemination Products and Services, a data file listing government periodicals and publicly available machine-readable data files, software, online database services, and electronic bulletin boards. Many government employees are members of SIGCAT, Special Interest Group on CD-ROM Applications & Technology, which operates an electronic bulletin board out of the USGS; (703) 648-4168. SIGCAT has compiled a list of government CD-ROMs, *SIGCAT CD-ROM Compendium* (GP3.2:Sp 3/2).

### Electronic Access

Many agencies release their databases to the public through commercial vendors (which charge for online searching). Database vendors have been characterized as database "supermarkets," offering their subscribers a variety of databases that can be searched using similar search strategies.[12] Such services may be subscribed to by individuals searching on personal computers, accessed through public and academic libraries, or through the services of a private information broker. To identify information brokers, check the telephone directory yellow pages or sources such as the *Directory of Online Databases* or call the reference desk at your local library. Many libraries subscribe to government databases on CD-ROM, allowing the public to search at no cost. Depository copies of electronic media often have SuDocs numbers ending with "/CD" (CD-ROMs), "/floppy" (floppy disk), or "/doc." (accompanying paper documentation).

Some agencies operate regional offices or search centers which search their databases for the public. Unfortunately, many government databases are not publicly available, labeled "internal use only," or accessible only to government agencies and their grantees and contractors. Government information entrepreneur Matthew Lesko emphasizes that public access is still possible, even to restricted databases. He suggests requesting information anyway, since government personnel often "will query their databases for you and send you a printout, often free of charge."[13]

There has been increasing pressure to make government databases available free to the public through the Depository Library System. Congressman Glenn English, chair of the House committee concerned with electronic information dissemination, has cautioned that without access to government databases, "the whole depository library program will be undermined."[14] During the 102nd Congress, several bills were introduced that underscored growing concern about charging taxpayers twice for electronic data: first when government creates it, and again to access it through private vendors reselling "value added" electronic government information. Congressman Charlie Rose, chair of the Joint Committee on Printing, introduced H.R. 2772, to establish GPO as a hub for public access to federal databases. The bill, popularly known as "GPO WINDO," would allow taxpayers to easily access public electronic information without paying high vendor charges: at a reasonable fee for individual subscribers, and free to depository libraries. If GPO WINDO or similar bills fail to be enacted during the 102nd Congress, they will probably be reintroduced in succeeding Congresses.

### National Technical Information Service

Although there is no central information point for all government databases, NTIS serves as the prime vendor for government-produced machine-readable files and software, both bibliographic and nonbibliographic. Government databases can be purchased or leased directly from NTIS (on magnetic tape, floppy disk, video disc, CD-ROM), searched online through commercial vendors, or purchased on commercially produced CD-ROMs.

| DATABASES AVAILABLE FROM NTIS | |
|---|---|
| **Title** | **Coverage** |
| AGRICOLA* | World literature of agriculture |
| AGRIS* | Elusive world agricultural literature |
| Energy Science and Technology Database* | World energy literature; companion print index is *Energy Research Abstracts* |
| FEDeral Research in Progress (FEDRIP)* | Federally funded research projects |
| USGS Library Database and Geoindex | USGS materials; references to maps of the U.S. and its territories |
| National Institute for Occupational Safety and Health Technical Information Center (NIOSHTIC)* | Literature of occupational safety and health |
| NTIS Bibliographic Database* | U.S. and foreign technical reports; government patents; translations; government machine-readable databases. Companion resource: GRA & I |
| Selected Water Resources Abstracts (SWRA)* | Water-related topics in the life, physical, and social sciences; water conservation, control, use, and management |

*Discussed more fully in Chapter 6.

The sale and lease of electronic products is NTIS's fastest growing pursuit, accounting for about one-quarter of its yearly revenues. NTIS offers nonbibliographic databases in business and science, with statistical, numeric, and full-text data files from numerous federal agencies. These include health and vital statistics from the National Center for Health Statistics, nutrition and food intake data from the Department of Agriculture, and regulatory licensee data from the Federal Communications Commission. Additional federal data files are announced in NTIS's *Directory of U.S. Government Datafiles for Mainframes and Microcomputers* (C 51.11/2-2: ) which describes federal numeric and textual data available for sale. NTIS's *Directory of U.S. Government Software for Mainframes and Microcomputers* (C 51.11/2-2: ) describes programs developed by federal agencies and sold by NTIS. NTIS operates the Federal Computer Products Center, which sells government software and datafiles to the public and issues the free Federal Computer Products Center newsletter, *CenterLine* (PR-838).

Government software and data files can be identified by searching the NTIS Bibliographic Database, and through free NTIS sales catalogs, listed in NTIS's products catalog. The monthly *NTIS Alert* on "Computers, Control & Information Theory" describes new software and data files added to the Federal Computer Products Center collection, with abstracts of research related to computers and information technology.

### Government Bulletin Boards

Electronic bulletin boards allow online access to government information using a computer, modem, communications software, and telephone. Some agencies, such as Agriculture and Commerce, pump massive amounts of data into bulletin boards, frequently "time sensitive" or perishable data that will be quickly superseded. In the next decade, it is expected that most federal agencies will operate electronic bulletin boards to distribute everything from statistics to technical reports. Although there is great demand for one, there is currently no comprehensive list of federal EBBs.[15]

## PRIMARY SOURCES

### The National Archives

*The National Archives and the Manuscript Division of the Library of Congress are our major archival collections, both of them places so seductive that, notwithstanding nutritional handicaps, historians have been known to enter and never emerge, or at least never publish because they cannot bear to bring their research to an end.* —Barbara Tuchman, Historian

---

**The National Charters**

The three most famous documents in American history are here: the Declaration of Independence, the parchment copy of the Constitution, and the Bill of Rights. The actual documents may be viewed in the National Archives Building Exhibition Hall, in an atmosphere described as "distinctly High Church—buffed marble, shuffling feet, the occasional cough or whisper."[16] There, in the unobtrusive shadow of an armed guard, the Charters of Freedom are displayed in hermetically sealed, helium-filled, bulletproof cases with special filters to repel harmful light. At closing time the Great Charters are lowered into a fifty-five-ton vault constructed of reinforced concrete and steel.

---

Imagine a place where you can see Edison's original light bulb patent, read journals of polar explorers and the passenger list for the *Lusitania*'s last voyage, examine Japanese surrender documents from World War II and a wanted poster for Butch Cassidy and the Sundance Kid, view Mathew Brady Civil War photographs and Eva Braun's photo albums, and hear Tokyo Rose's radio propaganda, the Nixon tapes, news broadcasts, and the Nuremberg trials. You could experience all of this and more in the National Archives of the United States, the nation's memory.

The National Archives records two centuries of U.S. history in documents, photographs, maps, films, recordings, and computer files. These records span the three branches of government and date back to the First Continental Congress.

---

**Profile: R.D.W. Connor, First Archivist of the United States (1878-1950)**

Robert Connor, archivist, college professor, and author, began his crusade for preservation of historical records in North Carolina in the 1920s. He urged his home state to salvage records not already lost forever by rescuing them from "dark corners and dusty archives, in pigeon holes, vaults, desks, attics, and cellars."[17] His crusade led to the establishment of North Carolina's State Historical Commission, and as its first secretary he urged the public to donate records for posterity. In 1934 Connor was tapped by President Franklin D. Roosevelt to be the nation's first archivist. One contemporary newspaper ran his photograph under the headline "He's U.S. Archivist," with the added explanatory note: "No, dear children, an archivist is not a radical. He is one who preserves historical documents."

Connor's work began with a philosophical battle over the archives' role. Fighting for the preservation of ordinary office files alongside the nation's key historical documents, he battled opponents who debunked bureaucratic records as dusty trash. Connor convinced Congress that it was absurd to erect a spacious $12 million building solely to house the Declaration of Independence, the Constitution, and a few hundred treaties. Today, the "ordinary" records championed by Connor offer an irreplaceable link with the nation's past.

The massive National Archives building in Washington, DC, is part of a geographically scattered network that includes regional archives branches, Federal Records Centers, and presidential libraries (discussed in chapter 10), all administered by the National Archives and Records Administration.

Before the creation of our National Archives in 1934, the nation's records were haphazardly stored and generally inaccessible, not only to citizens but also to government. The documents of our history were scattered throughout the Capitol in basements, attics, stables, and odd cubbyholes (see Figure 13.3). Most agencies were nonchalant about the moldering papers in their custody, and many national records were already lost or damaged by the time the National Archives opened its doors. Historians acknowledge that 1934 was "astonishingly late" to pull the nation's archives under one roof, compared with other Western countries whose archives date from the mid-nineteenth century.[18] When the archives cornerstone was laid in 1933, Herbert Hoover called the building the "temple of our history." Although the motto inscribed on the archives building was "The Written Word Endures," the archives began to gather not only government written records, but also films, sound recordings, photographs, maps, drawings, punch cards, and nongovernment material that illuminated U.S. history, including the everyday memorabilia of the nonfamous.

### The Collections

*What is Past is Prologue.*
  —Words from Shakespeare's
  *The Tempest,* carved on
  the National Archives building

If you've ever cleaned an attic, you can imagine the National Archives' task of culling the accumulated official papers of the nation—growing by billions of pieces each year. Federal records cannot be destroyed without authorization from the Archivist of the United States, who oversees the preservation of those judged to have enduring value—about two to three percent each year. But that tiny fraction has added up to billions of pages of text, millions of photographs, thousands of movie reels and sound recordings, maps, charts, and aerial photos. Just to listen to all the sound recordings in the archives would take 30,000 hours.

The National Archives also has the most inclusive permanent collection of federal government publications, about 2.4 million of them. The bulk of the collection was added in 1972, with the acquisition of the Superintendent of Documents collection, which has titles dating back to 1789. The archives sells copies of these documents. An introduction to the archives' government document collection is given in the free General Information Leaflet No. 28, "Looking for an Out-of-Print U.S.

Government Publication?" (AE 1.113:28). The *Cumulative Title Index to United States Public Documents, 1789-1975,* compiled by Daniel Lester (U.S. Historical Documents Institute), is a listing of titles from the GPO collection now housed in the National Archives.

### Access

> *An archives is not a library. While a library houses books. . . an archives houses the raw materials from which books are written.*
>   —Herman Viola, Museum of Natural
>   History, Smithsonian Institution

Archival collections are not subject-classified or accessed through familiar library tools like card catalogs. Instead, they are organized according to their source of origin in "record groups," containing records of a single agency. The National Archives publishes guides, special lists, indexes, and other finding aids for researchers seeking specific records within the vast National Archives holdings. The free pamphlet "Publications from

### FIGURE 13.3: Before the National Archives.

When records were amassed for transfer to the new National Archives building in the 1930s, they were recovered from attics, abandoned theaters, warehouses, and the White House garage. More than half were damaged from neglect, fire, dirt, insects, or the elements. The photo above shows War Department records before their transfer to the archives.

the National Archives" lists guides and indexes to specific collections, catalogs of microfilmed records, and special archival publications useful to scholars, archivists, historians, and researchers. An overview of National Archives collections is provided in *Guide to the National Archives of the United States* (AE 1.108:N 21), a 1987 reprint of the 1974 edition (with new prefatory material and an appendix of record groups added between 1970 and 1977). A new edition is forthcoming. *Prologue* (AE 1.111: ), the National Archives' award-winning quarterly journal, offers fascinating articles and current announcements. *Microfilm Resources for Research: A Comprehensive Catalog* (AE 1.102:M 58/2) is a comprehensive list of microfilmed federal records, containing a wealth of information for researchers. Photocopies of NARA documents and microfilm rolls may be purchased on-site or by mail, and many large research libraries also own copies.

The National Archives research rooms are open to the public. Researchers should write or call the Reference Services Branch (NNRS) before visiting. "National Archives Primary Reference Contact List," published in *News from the Archives* or free from NARA, lists archivists responsible for records on particular topics. Researchers can request "Information about the National Archives for Prospective Researchers," General Information Leaflet Number 30, and register for the regularly offered four-day course "Going to the Source: An Introduction to Research in Archives," by contacting the Chief, Education Branch, National Archives, Washington, DC 20408; (202) 523-3298.

The Records Declassification Division of the National Archives systematically reviews security-classified documents after they reach thirty years of age. Records dealing with cryptology and intelligence activities are reviewed after fifty years. Priority for review is given to records of research interest, and to those of which a significant portion could be declassified.

### Regional Branches

> *Time and accident are committing daily havoc on the originals deposited in our public offices. . . .The lost cannot be recovered; but let us save what remains... by such a multiplication of copies, as shall place them beyond the reach of accident.*
> —Thomas Jefferson, 1823

Twelve regional archives branches house basic archival collections, records of regional and local interest, plus copies of many NARA microfilm publications. Many branches offer basic collections of records, including those of U.S. district courts since the mid-1940s, the U.S. courts of appeals, the Bureau of Indian Affairs, the Bureau of Customs, and the Office of the Chief of Engineers. A list of regional archives is given in the *U.S. Government Manual*, and in the free booklet, "Regional Branches of the National Archives" (General Information Leaflet Number 22), from NARA. The holdings of regional archives are described in branch publications and in *The Archives: A Guide to the National Archives Field Branches*, from Ancestry, Inc.

### The Library of Congress

In 1991, the Library of Congress launched a six-year pilot test of the American Memory project. American Memory is an electronic library reproducing some of the Library's collections of photographs, graphics, sound recordings, music, films, manuscripts, pamphlets, and books. American Memory optical and compact discs will be distributed nationwide, allowing primary historical material to be "freed from the page or shelf. . . and made accessible to the American nation." Eventually the American Memory CD-ROMs and laser videodiscs will be supplemented by online access. The electronic collections will be accompanied by interactive, electronic "exhibitions," to introduce the collections, as well as user guides, interpretive materials, and bibliographies. Initial American Memory collections will focus on American history and culture, with two or three new collections added yearly.

## ADDRESSES

### Agriculture

Special Photo Collections Office, NAL, 14th Floor, 10301 Baltimore Blvd., Beltsville, MD 20705; (301) 344-3876

### American Memory Project

American Memory, Special Projects, Library of Congress, Washington, DC 20540; (202) 707-6233

### Census

Bureau of the Census, Census Geography Division, Geographic Reference and Assistance Staff, Washington, DC 20233; (301) 763-5720

### National Archives

Center for Electronic Records (NNX), National Archives and Records Administration, Washington, DC 20408; (202) 501-5579, TIF@NIHCU.BITNET

Still Pictures Branch Research Room, National Archives Building, Room 18N, 7th Street and Pennsylvania Avenue, Washington, DC 20408; (202) 523-3236. (Researcher appointments should be arranged at least two days ahead.)

### National Audiovisual Center

National Audiovisual Center, Customer Services Section PY, 8700 Edgeworth Dr., Capitol Heights, MD 20743-3701; (800) 788-NAVC, (301) 763-1891, FAX (301) 763-6025

## NTIS

Federal Computer Products Center, NTIS, 5285 Port Royal Rd., Springfield, VA 22161; (703) 487-4807

## U.S. Geological Survey

National Geographic Names Database, descriptions of services and costs, are available from Chief, Branch of Geographic Names, USGS, 523 National Center, Reston, VA 22092; (703) 648-4544, FAX (703) 648-5585.

Public Affairs Office, USGS, 119 National Center, Reston, VA 22092; (703) 648-4460

# FREEBIES

The following subject bibliographies are available free from the U.S. Government Printing Office, Superintendent of Documents, Washington, DC 20402:

51. Computers and Data Processing
57. Posters, Charts, Picture Sets and Decals
73. Motion Pictures, Films, and Audiovisual Information
102. Maps and Atlases (United States and Foreign)
183. Surveying and Mapping

## CIA

From Office of Public and Agency Information, Washington, DC 20505; (703) 351-2053:

*CIA Maps and Publications Released to the Public*

### Defense Mapping Agency

From DMA Office of Distribution Services, 8613 Lee Highway, Fairfax, VA 22031-2139; (703) 285-9368:

"Public Sale Catalog"

### National Archives

National Archives "General Information Leaflets" (AE 1.113: ) are free from Publications Services (NEPS), National Archives and Records Administration, Washington, DC 20408:

"Cartographic and Architectural Branch," General Information Leaflet Number 26

"Information about the National Archives for Prospective Researchers," General Information Leaflet Number 30

"Motion Pictures & Sound and Video Recordings in the National Archives," General Information Leaflet Number 23

"Regional Branches of the National Archives," General Information Leaflet No. 22

"Select List of Publications of the National Archives and Records Administration," General Information Leaflet No. 3

"Using Records in the National Archives for Genealogical Research," General Information Leaflet No. 5

From NARA Public Affairs Office:

"Calendar of Events" (AE 1.117: )

"Gifts from the National Archives" from National Archives Trust Fund Board, Washington, DC 20408

"National Archives Primary Reference Contact List" from Textual Reference Division (NNR), NARA, Washington, DC 20408

*News from the Archives*, a quarterly newsletter announcing news, accessions, openings, declassifications, publications, and grants

## NOAA

From NOAA Distribution Branch, N/CG33, National Ocean Service, Riverdale, MD 20737; (301) 436-6990:

*Catalog of Aeronautical Charts and Related Products*

## NTIS

From NTIS, 5285 Port Royal Rd., Springfield, VA 22161; (703) 487-4807:

"CD-ROMs & Optical Discs Available from NTIS" (PR-888)

## U.S. Geological Survey

From Books and Open File Reports Section, USGS, Box 25425, Federal Center, Denver, CO 80225:

USGS Circular 900, *Guide to Obtaining USGS Information* (I 19.4/2:900) describes sources of USGS products and how to get them.

From USGS Map Sales, Box 25286, Denver, CO 80225; (303) 236-7477:

Map indexes and catalogs.

From USGS New Publications, 582 National Center, Reston, VA 22092:

*New Publications of the Geological Survey* (I 19.14/4: )

*Publications of the Geological Survey* (I 19.14: )

"Price and Availability List of U.S. Geological Survey Publications" lists USGS books and thematic maps for sale.

From any Earth Science Information Center, or by calling (800) USA-MAPS:

*Catalog of Cartographic Data*

*Catalog of Maps*

*National Atlas Maps*

# REFERENCES

1. National Audiovisual Center, *Federal Audiovisual Activity: Fiscal Year 1990* (NAC, 1991), p. 6.

2. *Federal Audiovisual Materials Policy and Programs: Hearings Before a Subcommittee of the Committee on Government Operations, House of Representatives, 95th Congress, 2nd Session, September 21 and October 26, 1978* (GPO, 1979), p. 107. (Y 4.G 74/ 7:Au 2/5)

3. National Archives and Records Administration, *The Management of Audiovisual Records in Federal Agencies: A General Report* (NARA, 1991).

4. Karin Becker Ohrn, *Dorothea Lange and the Documentary Tradition* (Baton Rouge: Louisiana State University Press, 1980).

5. John Newlin, "Bargain of the Century: A Treasure Trove of Photos for Just $12 and Up; Give Gifts by Walker Evans, Dorothea Lange, etc." *Roll Call* (December 16, 1991), NEXIS Current Library.

6. Library of Congress, *A Century of Photographs, 1846-1946, Selected from the Collections of the Library of Congress* (LC, 1980), p. vii. (LC 1.2:P 56/5/846-946)

7. Connie Leslie, "Lost on the Planet Earth," *Newsweek* (August 8, 1988): 31; Dennis Kelly, "Getting Kids Acquainted with the Globe," *USA Today* (November 30, 1990): 10D.

8. David A. Cobb and Charles A. Seavey, *An Introduction to Maps in Libraries: Maps as Information Tools* (Chicago: Association of College and Research Libraries, [1982]), p. 19.

9. Cobb and Seavey, pp. 25-26.

10. House Committee on Government Operations, *Taking a Byte Out of History: The Archival Preservation of Federal Computer Records.* H. Rpt. 101-978 (GPO, 1990), p. 2. (Y 1.1/8:101-978).

11. *The Archives of the Future: Archival Strategies for the Treatment of Electronic Databases: A Study of Major Automated Databases Maintained by Agencies of the U.S. Government* (Washington, DC: National Academy of Public Administration, 1991), p. 15.

12. Matthew Lesko, *The Computer Data and Database Source Book* (New York: Avon Books, 1984), p. 2.

13. Lesko, p. 369.

14. House of Representatives, Committee on Government Operations, *Electronic Collection and Dissemination of Information by Federal Agencies, Hearings before a Subcommittee of the Committee on Government Operations, 99th Congress, 1st Session, April 29, June 26, and October 18, 1985* (GPO, 1986), p. 476. (Y 4.G 74/7:El 2/5)

15. Florence Olsen, "Bulletin Boards Give Users the Line on Federal Information," *Administrative Notes* 12 (June 30, 1991) 20-23 (a partial list of government bulletin boards starts on p. 21; reprinted from *Government Computer News*).

16. Alfred Meyer, "Daily Rise and Fall of the Nation's Revered Documents," *Smithsonian* 17 (October 1986): 134-43.

17. Hugh T. Lefler, "Robert Digges Wimberly Connor," in *Keepers of the Past*, ed. by Clifford L. Lord (Chapel Hill, NC: University of North Carolina Press, 1965), p. 111.

18. Senate, Committee on Governmental Affairs, *National Archives and Records Administration Act of 1983: Hearings Before the Committee on Governmental Affairs, United States Senate 98th Congress First Session on S. 905 Entitled the "National Archives and Records Administration Act of 1983" July 29, 1983* (S. Hrg. 98-488) (GPO, 1984), p. 37. (Y4.G7419: S. HRG. 98-488)

## FURTHER READING

Army. *Map Reading.* (Army Field Manual FM 21-26) GPO, 1969 (reprinted 1983). (D 101.20:21-26/4/rep.)
> Between these army-drab covers is a wealth of information about interpreting and using maps and aerial photos.

"Avoiding Federal Amnesia: The Role of Electronic Records." *Prologue* 18 (Summer 1986): 138. (AE 1.111:18/2)
> Summarizes the need for electronic records management to avoid federal amnesia.

Butler, Stuart L. and Graeme McCluggage. "Taking Measure of America: Records in the Cartographic and Architectural Branch." *Prologue* 23 (Spring 1991):41-57. (AE 1.111: )
> An introduction to the National Archives' Cartographic and Architectural Branch collection of maps, charts, and aerial photos, with a list of "Finding Aids Relating to Cartographic and Architectural Models."

Kirby, Diana Gonzalez. "Managing Government-Sponsored Posters in the Academic Library." *Government Information Quarterly* 6 (August 1989): 283-94.
> A guide to organizing and maintaining poster collections, which includes a list of SuDocs number stems for posters from numerous agencies.

Londos, Eutychia G. *AV Health: Current Publications of the United States Government.* Metuchen, NJ: Scarecrow Press, 1982.
> An annotated bibliography of catalogs, indexes, and guides to federal health-related AV, including catalogs of films on special topics.

McCoy, Donald R. *The National Archives: America's Ministry of Documents, 1934-1968.* Chapel Hill, NC: University of North Carolina Press, 1978.
> A comprehensive history of the National Archives and presidential library system, with a lengthy bibliography.

Miles, Wyndham D. *A History of the National Library of Medicine: The Nation's Treasury of Medical Knowledge.* (NIH Publication No. 82-1904) (GPO, 1982). (HE 20.3602:H 62)
> This NLM historical chronicle includes a chapter on the National Medical Audiovisual Center, pp. 433-41.

National Archives and Records Service. *Inside the National Archives* (slide/audiotape program). Distributed by the National Audiovisual Center. 1977. 10 min., color.
> An introduction to the services and collections of the archives, using selected items from the rich collections to trace the nation's history.

National Library of Medicine. *Guide to Locating Patient Education Audiovisual Materials.* NLM, 1989.
> A finding guide for NLM audiovisuals created for patient information.

Sears, Jean L. and Marilyn K. Moody. *Using Government Publications. Vol. 2: Finding Statistics and Using Special Techniques.* Phoenix, AZ: Oryx Press, 1986, pp. 157-61.
> A chapter on "National Archives" describes a search strategy for accessing National Archives records and lists microfilm catalogs and special subject guides.

Steinhart, Peter. "Names on a Map." *Audubon* 88 (May 1986): 8-11.
> A review of the wonders of maps.

Viola, Herman J. *The National Archives of the United States.* New York: Harry N. Abrams, Inc., 1984.
> This dazzling volume of color photographs and vivid narrative recounts the history of the National Archives and gives the reader a taste of its collections.

## Exercises

1.  After the Presidential Commission on the Space Shuttle Challenger Accident (Rogers Commission) concluded its investigation, its records were transferred to the National Archives for permanent preservation. Included are reports, photographs, correspondence, memoranda, electronic datasets, transcripts, affidavits, videotapes, and sound recordings. How can researchers find out exactly which Rogers Commission records are available in the National Archives?

2.  How can I peruse the same Farm Security Administration photos that inspired John Steinbeck to write *The Grapes of Wrath*?

3.  What videos has the government produced about libraries?

4.  What is the National Archives' most-requested photo?

# CHAPTER 14
## Overcoming Barriers to Access: Using Documents Reference Sources

*A couple of months in the laboratory can frequently save a couple of hours in the library.*
—Frank Westheimer, Harvard chemist

It's no news to librarians that many people consider libraries to be castles of torture. Finding and using library materials is often viewed as confusing and frustrating, an experience to avoid. If general library materials pose problems for users, government documents can be even more threatening and obscure. The prospect of grappling with government publications makes many potential users balk. And for people lacking government literacy, the mental agony and frustration can be real. There are many barriers to using government information in libraries, barriers that can create similar frustrations for both users and uninitiated librarians. In fact, if Greek mythology were rewritten today, one of Hercules' twelve labors might be to bibliographically verify and obtain a copy of a specific government document.

## BARRIERS FOR USERS

Picture yourself at home, reading the evening newspaper, when you spot an article about burglarproofing your home. The article makes a hazy reference to a Justice Department booklet on the same topic, called *How to Protect Yourself from Crime*.

## Problem 1:
### Popular media rarely give complete citations to government publications.

You want to obtain this document and learn more about burglarproofing. How would you go about it? Your first strategy might be to visit the closest depository library.

Since grade school you have probably been drilled about the splendors of the library catalog: a natural place to look up your document title, right?

## Problem 2:
### Even when documents are listed in a depository library's catalog, you may encounter problems.

Filing rules and the complexity of organizational hierarchies thwart many a catalog user. (Online catalogs help by allowing keyword searching.) This particular burglarproofing booklet, for example, was issued by the Office of Community Anti-Crime Programs of the Law Enforcement Assistance Administration of the U.S. Department of Justice. Other problems result from popular versus "official" titles of documents. The Warren Report is a good example. It may be filed under its official title, *Report of the President's Commission on the Assassination of President John F. Kennedy*, with no cross-reference from its better-known, popular title.

## Problem 3:
### Government publications are not comprehensively listed in many library catalogs.

Although online catalogs have sucked government publications into the mainstream in many libraries, some libraries still omit government documents from their catalogs. Others catalog some, but not all. Many libraries don't catalog depository documents because they can rely on specialized bibliographies and indexes like the *Monthly Catalog*, complete with titles and SuDocs numbers, instead.

Ideally, librarians who understand documents cataloging gaps will intercede for hapless users, yet some librarians do not realize the limitations of their own library catalogs. Hernon and McClure found that library staff rebounded from fruitless author or title card catalog searches by incorrectly assuming their library did not own the requested document.[1] The fact that this misconception occurred even in libraries that rarely cataloged documents underscores the need for library staff to acquaint themselves with the idiosyncrasies of their own library's documents policies.

## Problem 4:
### Documents may be housed in a separate collection, integrated with the regular collection, or a combination of both.

In a library with a separate documents department, documents are often assigned Superintendent of Documents classification numbers rather than the Dewey or Library of Congress numbers used for the regular collection. In these cases, the catalog may omit documents, with specialized bibliographies and indexes relied upon for access. In an integrated collection, documents are intershelved with other materials, under the same classification system. Documents in integrated collections are assigned Dewey or Library of Congress classification numbers, while government periodicals might be in the periodical room, government pamphlets in the vertical file, and so on. In this scenario, the library catalog is usually the primary key to the documents collection. A partially integrated collection offers a little of both: some documents in a separate department (possibly listed in the library catalog), others integrated with the regular collection (listed in the library catalog). All of this affects search strategy for finding a document. The only absolute rule of thumb is that individual libraries vary.

## Problem 5:
### Documents lack visibility.

The fact that you know *How to Protect Yourself from Crime* exists is a miracle in the first place. Documents are usually ignored in book reviews, disregarded by book clubs, absent from many library "new books" displays, and overlooked by the popular media. And, when documents *are* mentioned in magazines or newspapers, how to acquire them is often left undisclosed. For example, how often have you read phrases like this: "A report released by the Defense Department...," "An Agriculture Department booklet . . . ," "An EPA study...," or "A Census Bureau factsheet . . . "?

References to government issuing agencies are clues that help people with government literacy recognize "an EPA study," for instance, as a government publication. But think of the average Joe—unaware that he's seeking a government publication, he may make a vain attempt to locate the title using traditional library skills. Overcome with frustration, he may give up before he can be intercepted by a knowledgeable librarian. While it is impractical to expect even librarians to recognize the government origin of all document citations without bibliographic verification, verification itself may be impossible using some library catalogs. By acknowledging any catalog limitations, users and librarians can turn to specialized documents reference sources or OCLC before declaring a title nonexistent or unavailable. If documents bibliographic aids are not housed in the reference department, reference librarians can refer patrons to another department or library.

## Problem 6:
### Buying or borrowing copies of documents can be difficult.

Obtaining a copy of a trade book may mean visiting a bookstore, ordering from the publisher, or borrowing from a library. Acquiring copies of documents is similar, but different. Don't bother taking your documents shopping list to a mainstream bookstore. Instead, you must refer to a specialized outlet such as a GPO bookstore, or order by mail from GPO, NTIS, or the issuing agency. Since there is no central source for buying all documents, you may have to deal with several suppliers. Then there's the problem of availability—some documents are not sold to the public in the first place, while others may be out of print. Your local depository library may own the title you seek (but since most don't receive and keep all documents, there's no guarantee). And, the title's absence from the shelves doesn't mean it has been checked out—it may be in microfiche rather than paper, tucked away in a microfiche cabinet.

## Problem 7:
### Documents come in unusual formats.

Documents often don't even physically resemble books. They range from flimsy single-sheet fliers to cumbersome boxes, from table-sized maps to microfiche that nestle in your hand. And some government-information formats can't be held at all—electronic databases and bulletin boards, archives, information clearinghouses, and government experts are easily overlooked as information resources. This mix of formats may scatter government information throughout library collections, necessitates user familiarity with numerous bibliographic tools, and occasionally bedevils users by supplanting their beloved hard copy with alternative formats.

## USER STUDIES

Because of access barriers, it is no surprise that documents collections are notoriously underused, due partly to underestimating the scope of government resources, coupled with confusion about how to access them. User studies indicate that most academic faculty use library documents collections only about once yearly, feeling they have "no need" for government publications. Browsing, one of two favorite ways faculty discover documents, is haphazard at best (see Chapter 3). Tracking documents cited in footnotes and bibliographies, another favorite, often requires SuDocs number verification before a title can be retrieved and may lead to dead ends if traditional library skills are relied upon.[2]

A New England telephone survey revealed some interesting documents use patterns among "average citizens." A walloping 83 percent used government publications at work, but many had obtained them directly from agencies, bought them from GPO, or requested them from members of Congress.[3] Fully three-quarters of the forty-six people questioned were unaware of depository libraries. Respondents were hesitant to use libraries to obtain documents because they expected the experience to be time-consuming and troublesome. Not only was it easier to request documents directly from issuing agencies or from members of Congress, they were also motivated by the desire to have personal copies to keep. Apparently the time and money spent avoiding libraries when accessing documents was deemed a worthwhile investment.

## THE LIBRARY LINKAGE

Library users need librarians' help to overcome barriers to documents access. Because finding government information is difficult for the general public, librarians' documents proficiency is crucial. Knowledge of documents reference strategies and resources empowers information professionals to play key roles in linking government publications with people who need them. This linkage is the job not only of documents staff, but also of reference librarians. In fact, high-caliber reference work demands basic government information skills.

The fact that reference and documents departments are frequently physically separate fosters the illusion that there are "reference" questions and "documents" questions. This is often an equivocal dichotomy for library users, who bring their questions to either desk. Since more than three-fourths of depository collections are staffed by one or fewer full-time professionals (backed up by paraprofessionals, clerks, and student workers), there may be many occasions when the only professional librarian available to help a documents seeker is at the reference desk.[4]

In their unobtrusive 1983 study of documents reference service, McClure and Hernon found depository library staff unable to answer 63 percent of their documents test questions, and reported even more pessimistically on the performance of reference librarians.[5] Reference staff fared better in Hernon and McClure's second unobtrusive test, with a 59 percent correct answer rate for documents questions.[6] In both studies, inaccurate answers resulted from lack of the most rudimentary documents skills: having superficial knowledge of documents reference sources, being unable to match questions to answer sources or even to recognize questions as documents-related, offering incorrect answers, incorrectly claiming the library didn't own the answer source, or admitting "I don't know," without offering alternatives or referral. In fact, when faced with a question they couldn't answer, reference staff rarely referred patrons to another answer source, not even to their own library's depository collection. Fortunately, weaknesses such as these need not be chronic if updating documents skills becomes a priority.

## REFERENCE SOURCES

A mountain may be climbed "because it's there," but bibliographic aids don't always command the same respect or recognition. Take social scientists, for example: Although heavy documents users, they ignore documents indexes, relying instead upon random citations in professional journals and browsing shelves to keep abreast of government titles.[7] These habits are shared by numerous documents users.[8] Admittedly, using documents bibliographic aids is complicated by their numbers and diversity, with no single source offering comprehensive coverage. However, knowledge of the sources described in chapters 3 through 13, coupled with an awareness of reference sources for federal, state, local, and foreign documents, will be an asset to any documents seeker. Titles discussed below that pertain to more than one government jurisdiction or require clarification of scope are keyed with the following code:

Fed = Federal, S = State, L = Local, F = Foreign

The list is selective rather than comprehensive, with many titles referring to additional sources.

## Background Reading

### Historical Sources

Boyd, Anne M. *United States Government Publications*. 3rd ed. revised by Rae E. Ripps. New York: H. W. Wilson, 1949, reprinted 1952. 627 p. (Fed)
   This classic is a valuable source of historical information about government printing, publishing, and distribution.

Schmeckebier, Laurence F. and Roy B. Eastin. *Government Publications and Their Use*. Washington, DC: Brookings Institution, 1969. 502 p. (Fed)
   A key resource for tracing the history of documents indexes, bibliographies, and catalogs.

### Current Texts

Herman, Edward. *Locating United States Government Information: A Guide to Sources*. Buffalo, NY: Hein & Co., 1983. 250 p. (Fed)
   A practical guide to government publications, with workbook exercises.

Morehead, Joe and Mary Fetzer. *Introduction to United States Government Information Sources*. 4th ed. Littleton, CO: Libraries Unlimited, Inc., 1992. 450 p. (Fed)
   An overview of federal government publishing with descriptions of key information resources.

Nakata, Yuri. *From Press to People: Collecting and Using Government Publications*. Chicago: American Library Association, 1979. 212 p. (Fed)
   A readable introduction to federal publishing and documents reference sources, designed as a handbook for beginning librarians.

## Guides to Reference Materials

*Government Reference Books.* Littleton, CO: Libraries Unlimited, Inc., 1970- . Biennial. (Fed)

A comprehensive, annotated subject guide to all types of government-published reference books issued during the previous two years.

Robinson, Judith Schiek. *Subject Guide to U.S. Government Reference Sources.* Littleton, CO: Libraries Unlimited, Inc., 1985. 333 p. (Fed)

A selective, annotated bibliography of key government information sources for general reference and the social sciences, sciences, and humanities.

Schwarzkopf, LeRoy C. *Government Reference Serials.* Englewood, CO: Libraries Unlimited, 1988. (Fed)

Companion to *Government Reference Books*, with the same subject arrangement.

## Professional Update Sources

*Documents to the People.* Chicago: American Library Association, 1972- . Bimonthly. (Fed, S, L, F)

Known as *Dttp*, this information-packed newsletter from the ALA Government Documents Roundtable has a no-frills format and a reasonable price.

Government Documents Roundtable (GODORT) is ALA's unit that focuses on government documents at all government levels, including consideration of federal information policy, access to government information, and the impact of new technologies. *A History of the Government Documents Round Table of the American Library Association 1972-1992* by Lois Mills (published by the Congressional Information Service) chronicles the history of GODORT and *Documents to the People.*

*Government Information Quarterly: An International Journal of Resources, Services, Policies, and Practices.* Greenwich, CT: JAI Press, 1984- . Quarterly. (Fed, S, L, F)

Articles and columns cover aspects of government information dissemination, current developments, and information resources.

*Government Publications Review: An International Journal of Issues and Information Resources.* New York: Pergamon Press, 1982- . Bimonthly. (Fed, S, L, F)

Articles and columns cover government information programs, policies, and information resources at all levels of government—U.S., foreign, and international.

*Microform Review.* Westport, CT: Microform Review Inc., 1972- . Quarterly. (Fed, S, L, F)

Focuses on trends and issues related to microforms, with the fall issue devoted to government publications in microform.

The "Discussion of Government Document Issues" electronic bulletin board is Govdoc-L: GOVDOC-L@PSUVM.BITNET. Moderator is Diane K. Kovacs, Instructor and Reference Librarian for the Humanities, Kent State University Library, Kent, OH 44240; (216) 677-4355 after 5:00p.m. Bitnet: DKOVACS@kentvm or LIBRK329@kentvms; Internet: DKOVACS@library.kent.edu or LIBRK329@ksuvxa.kent.edu

The ALA Washington Office Newsline provides updates on the Federal Information Scene: ALA-WO@UICVM. Questions or comments should be addressed to Fred King, American Library Association, 110 Maryland Ave. N.E., Washington, DC 20002; (202) 547-4440.
Bitnet: NU_ALAWASHB@CUA;
Internet: NU_ALAWASH@CUA.EDU

## Recurring Columns

*Booklist:* Appearing three times yearly are annotated bibliographies of titles for sale from GPO or free from issuing agencies.

*Government Publications Review:* Each year's final issue is devoted to notable documents for the year; other columns cover theses in documents, news from Washington, technical reports, and recent literature on government information.

*Inform: The Magazine of Information and Image Management:* Offers a column on federal records management and dissemination.

*Library Journal:* Contains annual "Notable Documents" list compiled by GODORT's Notable Documents Panel; lists federal, state, local, and international titles

*Microform Review:* Includes a column reviewing federal depository documents issued in microfiche.

*Serials Review:* A regular column reviews materials for documents collections.

Regular columns discussing documents-related issues are found in *Collection Building, Serials Librarian*, and *Wilson Library Bulletin.* Issues of *ALA Washington Newsletter* and *Information Hotline* frequently discuss government publications, access, and information policy.

## Special Topics

American Library Association. Government Documents Round Table. *The Complete Guide to Citing Government Documents: A Manual for Writers and Librarians*, by Diane L. Garner and Diane H. Smith. Bethesda, MD: Congressional Information Service, 1984. 142 p. (Fed, S, L, F)

A style manual for citing federal, state, local, regional, and international documents.

Bernier, Bernard A. and Karen Wood, comps. *Popular Names of U.S. Government Reports: A Catalog.* 4th ed. Library of Congress, 1984. 272 p. (LC 6.2:G 74/984) (Fed)

The key to identifying official titles and issuing agencies when only the short, popular name of a government report is known.

Ekhaml, Leticia T. and Alice J. Wittig. *U.S. Government Publications for the School Library Media Center.* 2nd ed. Englewood, CO: Libraries Unlimited, 1991.

An annotated guide to documents for elementary and secondary school libraries.

Evinger, William R., ed. *Guide to Federal Government Acronyms.* Phoenix, AZ: Oryx Press, 1989.

Acronyms, initialisms, and abbreviations for agencies, programs, products, services, surveys, position titles, laws and the legislative process, budgeting.

Voorhees, Donald J. *Government Publications for School Libraries: A Bibliographic Guide and Recommended Core Collection.* New York: New York Library Association (Government Documents Roundtable), 1988.

## Directories

American Library Association. Government Documents Round Table. *Directory of Government Documents Collections and Librarians,* ed. by Judy Horn. 6th ed. Bethesda, MD: Congressional Information Service, 1991. 690 p. (Fed, S, L, F)
    A directory listing of documents libraries by states and cities, with information about collections, depository status, subject specialties, and staff names; a directory of library school documents faculty; state document authorities; names to know; subject terms; and agency names and acronyms.

Evinger, William, ed. *Directory of Federal Libraries.* 2nd ed. Phoenix, AZ: Oryx Press, 1993. 384 p. (Fed, F)
    A worldwide listing of addresses, telephone numbers, contact people, special collections, database services, electronic mail networks, and more.

Larson, Donna Rae. *Guide to U.S. Government Directories, 1970-1980.* Phoenix, AZ: Oryx Press, 1981. 160 p. (Fed); *Guide to U.S. Government Directories, Vol. 2: 1980-1984.* Phoenix, AZ: Oryx Press, 1985. (Fed)
    Descriptions of government-issued directories include information about availability, coverage, arrangement, issuing agency, SuDocs number, and frequency. For directories prior to 1970, consult *Directories of Government Agencies* by Sally Wynkoop and David Parish, published by Libraries Unlimited, Inc.

Office of the Federal Register. *U.S. Government Manual.* GPO, 1935- . Annual. (AE 2.108: ) (Fed)
    Known as the "official handbook of the federal government," the USGM is really a directory of agencies and personnel in the three branches of government. Few libraries do not own it. The *Manual* summarizes agency responsibilities and gives addresses, telephone numbers, and names. It also gives information on quasi-official agencies, international organizations, boards, committees, and commissions. Appendixes cover abolished and transferred agencies, abbreviations and acronyms, and agencies appearing in the *Code of Federal Regulations.*

## Bibliographies

Andriot, Donna, ed. *Guide to U.S. Government Publications.* McLean, VA: Documents Index, Inc., 1973- . (Fed)
    A valuable aid for verifying documents citations, SuDocs numbers, or publication history. This is an annotated bibliography of key federal series, periodicals, and important reference materials issued within series, with a complete SuDocs number list since 1900.

Bailey, William G. *Guide to Popular U.S. Government Publications.* 2nd ed. Englewood, CO: Libraries Unlimited, 1990.
    Popular and best-selling titles primarily since the mid-1980s, arranged by subjects, with annotations.

*Bibliographic Guide to Government Publications—U.S.* Boston: G. K. Hall and Co., 1975- . Annual. (Fed, S, L); *Bibliographic Guide to Government Publications—Foreign.* Boston: G. K. Hall and Co., 1975- . Annual. (F)

These are comprehensive annual subject bibliographies of government publications cataloged by The Research Libraries of the New York Public Library and Library of Congress, regardless of language or format. These two titles update G. K. Hall's 1972 *Catalog of Government Publications.*

*Business Serials of the U.S. Government.* 2nd ed. Chicago: American Library Association, 1988.
    A subject guide for small and medium-sized public and academic libraries, with notes on special features, indexing sources, and SuDocs numbers.

*Government Publications Review: An International Journal of Issues and Information Resources.* New York: Pergamon Press, 1982- . Bimonthly. (Fed, S, L, F)
    A regular annotated bibliography, "Recent Literature on Government Information," was preceded by retrospective bibliographies of monographic and periodical literature in the field.

Library of Congress. *Government Publications: A Guide to Bibliographic Tools,* by Vladimir M. Palic. 4th ed. GPO, 1974. (LC 1.12/2:G 74) 441 p. (Fed, S, L, F)
    A bibliography of current and retrospective documents and indexes to documents of federal, state, local, and foreign governments, including a list of materials describing foreign government organization. A Pergamon Press reprint of this title includes Palic's *Government Organization Manuals: A Bibliography* (LC 1.6/4:G 74), which is also free to U.S. libraries and institutions from Library of Congress, Central Services Division, Printing and Processing Section, Washington, DC 20540.

O'Hara, Frederic J. *Informing the Nation: A Handbook of Government Information for Librarians.* New York: Greenwood Press, 1990.
    Reprints of key materials related to government documents, with introductory comments.

Richardson, John, Jr. *Government Information: Education and Research, 1928-1986.* (Bibliographies and Indexes in Library and Information Science, No. 2) New York: Greenwood Press, 1987. 186 p. (Fed, S, L, F)
    A detailed review of graduate research in government publications, with an analysis of trends. Supplemented by Richardson's column on "Theses in Documents" in *Government Publications Review* in issues numbered 2 and 5. The column cites and describes specialization papers, theses, and dissertations about publications of any level of government.

Schorr, Alan Edward. *Federal Documents Librarianship, 1879–1987.* Juneau, AK: The Denali Press, 1988. (Fed)
    A comprehensive bibliography of literature about U.S. government information, spanning 109 years.

Scull, Roberta A. *A Bibliography of United States Government Bibliographies, 1968-1973.* Ann Arbor, MI: Pierian Press, 1975. 353 p. (Fed); *A Bibliography of United States Government Bibliographies, 1974-1976.* Ann Arbor, MI: Pierian Press, 1979. 310 p. (Fed)
    An annotated bibliography of federal bibliographies on various topics, arranged by subjects.

Zink, Steven D. *United States Government Publications Catalogs.* 2nd ed. Washington, DC: Special Libraries Association, 1988. 292 p. (Fed)

An annotated bibliography of federal agencies' own publication lists, including AV lists and electronic information.

## State Documents

### State Depository Libraries

Like federal depositories, state depository libraries are legally designated to receive publications and make them publicly available. Although the libraries in the federal depository system are scattered across the nation, each operates under the same congressional statutes. State depositories, on the other hand, are legally mandated by individual state legislatures, making each an independent system. Some states have no depository laws. State depository systems vary in quality and comprehensiveness.

Dow, Susan L. *State Document Checklists: A Historical Bibliography.* Buffalo, NY: W. S. Hein & Co., 1990.
    Compiled primarily from *Monthly Checklist of State Publications* 1910-1988, this is a chronological bibliography of checklists for each state, with acquisitions information for current lists, and an overview of the history of bibliographic control of state documents.

Lane, Margaret T. *State Publications and Depository Libraries: A Reference Handbook.* Westport, CT: Greenwood Press, 1981. 573 p.
    An overview of state depository systems and state-by-state descriptions of depository programs, with a bibliography and discussion of the literature related to state depositories.

———, comp. *The Documents on [State] Documents Collection, 1973-1979 and 1980-1983.* Chicago: ALA, Government Documents Round Table, State and Local Documents Task Force, 1984 and 1985. (ERIC ED 247940 and ED 263923)
    A collection of materials for administering state documents depository programs, including sample contracts, forms, manuals, surveys, classification schemes, and promotional materials. Compiled from voluntary submissions sent by states to the GODORT State and Local Documents Task Force of the American Library Association, the retrospective collection is divided into two parts: 1973-79 and 1980-83. User guides are available for both sets (ERIC ED 247939 and ED 263922). Current materials are circulated through interlibrary loan.

### Checklists

Library of Congress. Exchange and Gift Division. *Monthly Checklist of State Publications.* GPO, 1910- . Monthly. (LC 30.9: )
    This annotated list of publications received by the Library of Congress from the fifty states is available free to state agencies sending their publications to LC. It lists voluntary submissions to LC only, but nevertheless remains the most comprehensive national list of state publications. Margaret T. Lane calls it "unparalleled in the state documents field."[9] The *Monthly Checklist* provides the sole bibliographic record of publications from the handful of states without their own state checklists. Citations include issuing agency, title, publication date, and number of pages, along with occasional LC card numbers, prices, and availability information.

Many state publications are available free upon request, but the request must move quickly. Most titles listed in the *Monthly Checklist* may be requested from their issuing agencies (agency addresses are usually omitted, so addresses must be garnered from state directories). An annual index is provided. Browsing is the primary access mode throughout the year, by skimming citations for agencies that might publish on a certain topic, or by reviewing all the entries for states of particular interest. Issues for June and December contain a periodicals list, while an annual index to monographs appears early each year.

Most states publish their own documents checklists, listing publications issued by state agencies. The checklists vary from mere agency/title listings to full bibliographic citations, with their ease of use ranging from frustrating to friendly. State checklists can be identified by looking for asterisked titles in the *Monthly Checklist of State Publications* and Parish's *State Government Reference Publications.* Libraries often subscribe to their own state's checklist along with the *Monthly Checklist of State Publications.*

### Bluebooks

Sometimes they are called bluebooks, sometimes redbooks, government manuals, or government handbooks. They describe state government workings and interactions with federal and local governments, and may be published officially or unofficially. They have been called "probably the best general reference available on state government organization."[10]

Hellebust, Lynn, ed. *State Blue Books, Legislative Manuals and Reference Publications: A Selective Bibliography.* Topeka, KS: Government Research Service, 1990. 142 p.
    An annotated bibliography of state bluebooks; legislative handbooks, manuals, and directories; general directories and statistical compilations.

### Legislative Manuals and Directories

Legislative manuals describe the organization of state legislatures, frequently giving names, committee memberships, rules, and procedures. State directories provide lists of agency personnel, most often covering the entire state but occasionally limited to individual agencies that publish their own.

*National Directory of State Agencies.* Bethesda, MD: National Standards Association, 1986- . Annual.
    A directory of agencies and personnel.

*State Bluebooks, Legislative Manuals and Reference Publications: A Selective Bibliography.*
    (See previous section.)

*State Legislative Sourcebook: A Resource Guide to Legislative Information in the Fifty States.* Topeka, KS: Government Research Services, 1986- . Annual.

A guide to sources of information about state legislatures, legislators, procedures, and activities.

## Legislation, Regulations, Courts

Each of the fifty states publishes session laws (after each legislative session) and annotated codes, either officially or unofficially (sometimes both). Many do not publish reports and hearings that lead to legislation. Cohen and Berring note that bibliographic control of state regulations is "at almost the same primitive level as in the federal government before 1935."[11] State regulations are not uniformly published and can be difficult to track down. While some states publish an equivalent to the *Federal Register* or *Code of Federal Regulations*, others require contacting agencies to identify regulations in force. State judicial decisions are documented in official, or frequently, unofficial reporters. The *National Reporter System* covers the nation according to regions (*Northeastern Reporter*, *Pacific Reporter*, etc.), printing state appellate court decisions. *Shepard's State Citations* cites appellate court references to state laws.

The Bluebook, *A Uniform System of Citation*, is a handy source for identifying state statutory compilations, session laws, administrative registers and compilations, and court hierarchies. (The guides to legislative searching listed in the "Further Reading" section of Chapter 8 also discuss state legislative materials).

Fisher, Mary L. *Guide to State Legislative Materials.* 3rd ed. (AALL Publications Series No. 15) Littleton, CO: Fred B. Rothman & Co., 1985. (1v., various pagings)

This title is a state-by-state compendium of sources of legislative and administrative information.

## Bibliographies

Parish, David W. *A Bibliography of State Bibliographies, 1970-82.* Littleton, CO: Libraries Unlimited, Inc. 1985. 267 p.

An annotated bibliography of bibliographies issued by state agencies, arranged by states and subjects.

March issues of *Documents to the People* include a "State and Local Documents Bibliography."

## Reference Sources

*The Book of the States.* Lexington, KY: The Council on State Governments, 1935- . Biennial.

This handbook describes "the state of the states," with information about state constitutions; executive, legislative, and judicial branches of government; elections, finances, management, activities, issues, and services; intergovernmental affairs; and statistics. Three supplemental directories are issued from the Council on State Governments: *State Elective Officials and the Legislatures; State Legislative Leadership, Committees and Staff; and State Administrative Officials Classified by Function.*

Jones, Geraldine U. and Norman D. Prentiss. *State Information Book.* Vienna, VA: INFAX Corporation, 1987. 863 p.

Facts, background information, statistics, and directory information for the fifty states.

Parish, David W. *State Government Reference Publications: An Annotated Bibliography.* 2nd ed. Littleton, CO: Libraries Unlimited, Inc., 1981. 355 p.

An annotated bibliography of official state bibliographies, bluebooks, legislative manuals, statistical sources, directories, audiovisual guides, maps, and other formats, plus an extensive bibliography on the literature of state publications and reference tools.

Public Affairs Information Service. *PAIS International.* New York: PAIS, 1991- . Monthly.

PAIS indexes all state legislative manuals and subject compilations of state laws received by The New York Public Library, a comprehensive collection of public affairs materials. State and local documents coverage is strongest for New York, New Jersey, and California, and New York City.

*Statistical Reference Index.* (CIS). Bethesda, MD: CIS, Inc., 1980- . Bimonthly with annual cumulation. (S, L)

Covers major state statistical publications and major reports issued by state data centers.

## Statistics

Bureau of the Census. *County and City Data Book.* GPO, 1949- . Irregular. (C 3.134/2:C 83/2/yr.) (S, L)

Social and economic statistics for counties, MAs, and large cities are augmented by information about standard federal administrative regions, census regions and divisions, and states.

———. *State and Metropolitan Area Data Book.* GPO, 1979- . Irregular. (C 3.134/5: ) (S, L)

A compendium of statistics for states, MAs, census divisions, and regions.

———. *Statistical Abstract of the United States.* GPO, 1878- . Annual. (C 3.134: ) (Fed, S, L, F)

This statistical compendium includes appendices with a guide to sources of state government statistics, state statistical abstracts, selected state rankings, and an index to state data.

Congressional Information Service. *American Statistics Index.* Bethesda, MD: CIS, Inc., 1973- . Monthly with annual cumulation. (F, S, L)

This is an index to federally generated statistics, with abstracts. Many of the statistical publications may be purchased from CIS on microfiche or accessed in depository library collections.

Congressional Information Service. *Statistical Reference Index.* Bethesda, MD: CIS, Inc., 1980- . Bimonthly with annual cumulation. (S, L)

This is an index to nonfederal statistical data, including publications of state agencies. This source abstracts and indexes social, governmental, economic, and demographic reports from the fifty states and the District of Columbia, as well as state statistical compendia, periodicals, and annual reports. Many of the statistical publications may be purchased from CIS on microfiche.

## Maps and Audiovisual Materials

State agencies producing audiovisual materials may issue their own AV catalogs, or statewide lists may be issued. The *Monthly Checklist of State Publications*, and David Parish's *State Government Reference Publications*, discussed earlier, are aids to identifying such lists.

In plain truth, access to state and local maps "is very much a question of luck."[12] Some states operate a central map information center, similar to the USGS Earth Science Information Centers, while others offer little help in tracking down maps. The Library of Congress has issued a list of "Sources of Official State Maps," which is available free from the Geography and Map Division, Washington, DC 20540.

Free USGS index maps show named map quadrangles for sale for each state. To identify USGS state maps, use the *Index to Topographic and Other Map Coverage [state]* (I 19.41/6-3: ). A companion booklet, *Catalog of Topographic and Other Published Maps [state]* (I 19.41/6-2: ), is a catalog for ordering, with map prices and availability. Both are free from USGS.

Cobb, David A. and Peter B. Ives. *State Atlases: An Annotated Bibliography.* (CPL Bibliography No. 108) Chicago: CPL Bibliographies, 1983. 21 p.
   An annotated guide to state atlases.

## Local Documents

*The County Yearbook.* Washington, DC: National Association of Counties, 1975- . Annual.
   A summary of trends, finances and employment, services and administration, with county profiles, a directory section, and a bibliography.

Hernon, Peter et al., eds. *Municipal Government Reference Sources: Publications and Collections.* (edited for the American Library Association Government Documents Round Table) New York: R. R. Bowker, 1978. 341 p.
   An annotated bibliography of municipal publications, libraries, and databases.

*Index to Current Urban Documents.* New York: Greenwood Press, 1972- . Quarterly. (L, F)
   ICUD is an index to documents issued by large cities, counties, states, regional planning agencies, civic organizations, universities, and research institutes. Most of the indexed titles are available in full text on microfiche through the *Urban Documents Microfiche Collection* sold by Congressional Information Service. Searchers should consult the companion resource, *Contemporary Subject Headings for Urban Affairs.*

*The Municipal Yearbook.* Washington, DC: International City Management Association, 1934- . Annual. (L, F)
   An annual summary of management and trends, intergovernmental relations, staffing and compensation, local government profiles, and directories of contacts in American local governments and chief appointed administrators of foreign countries, and a bibliography.

March issues of *Documents to the People* include a "State and Local Documents Bibliography."

## Maps

County and local maps produced by government agencies are often created for internal agency use rather than for public information. Bibliographic control of local or county maps is almost nonexistent, making acquisition troublesome.

## Foreign Countries/International

American Library Association. Government Documents Roundtable. *Guide to Official Publications of Foreign Countries.* Bethesda, MD: Congressional Information Service, 1990. 359 p.
   A selective bibliography annotated by specialists on each country, describing key publications from 157 nations and from International Governmental Organizations (IGOs).

Army. *Country Study Series.* GPO, irregular. (D 101.22:550-no.)
   This series replaced the *Area Handbooks.* Individual titles profile single countries, focusing on historical, cultural, political, and socioeconomic characteristics, with emphasis on the people. The Government Printing Office's Subject Bibliography SB-166 lists titles for sale.

Central Intelligence Agency. *World Factbook.* GPO, 1981- . Annual. (PrEx 3.15:)
   A source of maps and concise national profiles describing land, water, people, government, economy, communications, and defense, especially for small and Third World countries.

Department of Defense. American Forces Information Service. *Pocket Guides.* GPO, irregular. (D 2.14:PG-no.)
   These short booklets written for military personnel provide summary information for visitors to individual countries, including customs, money, sights, people, and language.

Department of State. *Background Notes on the Countries of the World.* GPO, 1980- . (S 1.123: )
   These short factual pamphlets describe land, people, history, government, politics, economy, and foreign relations for foreign countries, U.S. territories, and selected international organizations. The Government Printing Office's Subject Bibliography SB-93 lists titles available for sale; also available on the CIDS bulletin board.

Hajnal, Peter I. *Directory of United Nations Documentary and Archival Sources.* New York: Kraus International, 1991.
   An annotated bibliography of UN titles arranged by subject and type of resource.

———. ed. *International Information: Documents, Publications, and Information Systems of International Government Organizations.* Englewood, CO: Libraries Unlimited, 1988. 339 p.
   Bibliographic essays about acquiring and managing publications and computerized information from intergovernmental organizations, particularly the European Economic Community (EEC) and UN.

Public Affairs Information Service. *PAIS International.* New York: PAIS, 1991- . Monthly.
   An index to public affairs publications covering foreign government documents in English, French, German, Italian, Portuguese, and Spanish, including international organizations' statistical publications, directories, studies,

and reports related to public policy issues. This title absorbed the former *PAIS Foreign Language Index* and is searchable online and on CD-ROM. Users should refer to *PAIS Subject Headings* in planning their searches.

Turner, Carol A. *Directory of Foreign Document Collections.* New York: UNIPUB, 1985. 148 p.
  Descriptions of U.S. and Canadian libraries with foreign documents collections, with addresses and phone numbers.

## Statistics

Many countries publish national statistical compendia or yearbooks summarizing demographic, economic, and social statistics, similar to the *Statistical Abstract of the United States.* The Congressional Information Service (CIS) sells a "master collection of foreign statistics" on microfiche, called *Current National Statistical Compendiums.* Compendia from more than eighty countries are reproduced and may be purchased as a complete set or by continental groups (Europe, North and Central America, South America, Asia and Middle East, Oceania, and Africa).

In addition to foreign-issued statistics, many federal publications provide statistics about foreign nations. (Several of the statistical compendia listed in Chapter 12 include international data.) *American Statistics Index* (also described in Chapter 12), is an excellent source for identifying U.S. publications that include statistics about foreign countries. The *Statistical Reference Index*, Congressional Information Service's index to nonfederal statistics, includes data about foreign countries. SRI indexes and abstracts world economic and demographic trends; international finance, investment, and trade data; as well as social and economic data for foreign countries, frequently organized to allow comparison with U.S. data. Many of the publications listed are available on microfiche from CIS. A short "Guide to Statistical Reference Index" is free from Congressional Information Service, Inc., 4520 East-West Hwy., Suite 800, Bethesda, MD 20814. *Index to International Statistics*, also from Congressional Information Service, indexes statistics issued by international intergovernmental organizations (see Chapter 12). Finally, because Congress keeps tabs on international issues, *CIS/Index* is also a source of statistics on foreign nations.

Bureau of the Census. Center for International Research.
  This agency, discussed in Chapter 12, disseminates demographic information on foreign countries, publishing *World Population* reports and *Country Demographic Profiles*, and producing the Census Bureau International Data Base.

Central Intelligence Agency. *Handbook of Economic Statistics.* GPO, 1981- . Annual. (PrEx 3.10/7-5: )
  A source of statistics for all Communist countries and selected non-Communist countries, with maps, charts, and tables.

## Maps

A national atlas is a source of valuable reference information about a country. Cobb and Seavey emphasize the value of national atlases, recommending that even libraries without map collections collect national atlases.[13]

Several federal agency foreign map series are noted in Chapter 13. "Selected Sources for Maps Published by International Organizations" and "A List of National Bibliographies Containing References to Maps and Atlases" are free from Library of Congress, Geography and Map Division, Washington, DC 20540.

*World Mapping Today.* Boston: Butterworths, 1987.
  Maps and map catalogs from various countries.

## FREEBIES

The following subject bibliographies are free from U.S. Government Printing Office, Superintendent of Documents, Washington, DC 20402:

  93.  Background Notes
  102. Maps and Atlases (United States and Foreign)
  150. Libraries and Library Collections
  166. Foreign Area Studies

## REFERENCES

1. Peter Hernon and Charles McClure, "Unobtrusive Reference Testing: The 55 Percent Rule," *Library Journal* 111 (April 15, 1986): 40.

2. Beth Postema and Terry L. Weech, "The Use of Government Publications: A Twelve-Year Perspective," *Government Publications Review* 18 (May/June 1991): 223-38; Emily Jean Fraser and William H. Fisher, "Use of Federal Government Documents by Science and Engineering Faculty," *Government Publications Review* 14 (1), pp. 33-44; Steven D. Zink, "Clio's Blindspot: Historians' Underutilization of United States Government Publications in Historical Research," *Government Publications Review* 13 (January-February 1986): 67-78.

3. David C. R. Heisser, "Marketing U.S. Government Depository Libraries," *Government Publications Review* 13 (January-February 1986): 58.

4. Peter Hernon, Charles R. McClure, and Gary R. Purcell, *GPO's Depository Library Program: A Descriptive Analysis* (Norwood, NJ: Ablex Publishing Corp., 1985), p. 94.

5. Charles R. McClure and Peter Hernon, *Improving the Quality of Reference Service for Government Publications* (Chicago: American Library Association, 1983).

6. Peter Hernon and Charles McClure, "Unobtrusive Reference Testing," pp. 38-41.

7. Peter Hernon, *Use of Government Documents by Social Scientists* (Norwood, NJ: Ablex Publishing Corp., 1979), pp. 65-70.

8. Postema and Weech.

9. Margaret T. Lane, *State Publications and Depository Libraries: A Reference Handbook* (Westport, CT: Greenwood Press, 1981), p. 34.

10. *State Bluebooks and Reference Publications: A Selected Bibliography* (Lexington, KY: The Council on State Governments, 1983), p. iv.

11. Morris L. Cohen and Robert C. Berring, *How to Find the Law*, 8th ed. (St. Paul, MN: West Publishing Co., 1983), p. 371.

12. Charles A. Seavey, "Government Map Publications: An Overview," in *Communicating Public Access to Government Information, Proceedings of the 2nd Annual Library Government Documents and Information Conference*, ed. by Peter Hernon. (Westport, CT: Meckler Publishing, 1983), p. 88.

13. David A. Cobb and Charles A. Seavey, *An Introduction to Maps in Libraries: Maps as Information Tools* (Chicago: Association of College and Research Libraries, [1982]), p. 26.

## FURTHER READING

Batson, Donald W. "State Government Publications: Selection, Acquisition, and Reference Service." *RQ* 29 (Summer 1990): 554-59.

> Study of state documents collections in academic libraries with recommendations for further study.

Castonguay, Russell. *A Comparative Guide to Classification Schemes for Local Government Documents Collections.* Westport, CT: Greenwood Press, 1984.

> A summary of acquisition, classification, and cataloging practice for local documents, with an assessment of the advantages and disadvantages of various classification schemes and a bibliography.

Dalton, Lisa K. "Doc Soup: Dealing with Documents in Small Non-Depository Libraries." *North Carolina Libraries* 48 (Summer 1990): 91-94.

> Selecting, acquiring, and organizing federal and state documents in small public libraries and school media centers.

Elliot, Jeffrey M. and Sheikh R. Ali. *The State and Local Government Political Dictionary.* (Clio Dictionaries in Political Science No. 12) Santa Barbara, CA: ABC-Clio, 1985.

> A source of clear explanations of topics, political personalities, facts, institutions, and processes in state and local government.

Harley, Bruce L. and Knobloch, Patricia J. "Government Documents Reference Aid: An Expert System Development Project." *Government Publications Review* 18 (January/February 1991): 15-33.

> Expert systems help library users match documents sources to their information needs.

Hernon, Peter and Charles R. McClure. *Public Access to Government Information: Issues, Trends, and Strategies.* 2nd ed. Norwood, NJ: Ablex Publishing Corp., 1988.

> Areas discussed include local, state, and international documents.

Moody, Marilyn K. "State Depository Microform Publications." *Microform Review* 14 (Fall 1985): 232-36.

> A review of microform programs in state depositories, with a discussion of pros and cons.

————. "State Documents: Basic Selection Sources." *Collection Building* 7 (Spring 1985): 41-44.

> An annotated bibliography of state documents selection tools, with practical suggestions for their use.

Nakata, Yuri, Susan J. Smith, and William B. Ernst, Jr. comps. *Organizing a Local Government Documents Collection.* Chicago: American Library Association, 1979.

> A handbook for organizing local government documents in libraries.

Ratcliffe, John W. "International Statistics: Pitfalls and Problems." *Reference Services Review* 10 (Fall 1982): 93-95.

> Weaknesses and potential problems related to national statistics generated by foreign countries.

Schumaker, Earl and Jane Rishel, eds. *Illinois Libraries* 71 (November 1990).

> Entire issue covers access to federal, state, and municipal government information.

Sims, E. Norman. "The Council of State Governments, A National Information Provider." *Government Information Quarterly* 3 (1986): 407-17.

> An introduction to the Council of State Governments: a nonprofit information broker for the fifty states.

Smith, Karen. "POINTER vs. *Using Government Publications:* Where's the Advantage?' *The Reference Librarian* 23 (1989): 191–205.

Stwalley, Louise. "A Microcomputer Catalog for Municipal Documents." *Government Publications Review* 16 (January/February 1989): 63-72.

> A description of a computerized catalog with multiple access points for retrieval of municipal documents.

## EXERCISES

1. What was the official title of the Nixon-era Watergate report?
2. Where can I get statistics on the ethnic composition of counties in my state?
3. Where can I get data about foreign countries?

# CHAPTER 15
# Foreign and International Documents

## by Karen Smith

Foreign is a relative term; if you were living in Canada or France U.S. documents would be foreign to you. International, on the other hand, is a concept that transcends individual countries. The documents produced by foreign national governments and those issued by international governmental organizations fulfill, to an extent, the need for worldwide information and may be used interchangeably. However, since each country of the world has a unique governmental structure and a unique publishing program (as does each international organization), it is impossible to describe them all here. This chapter will offer representative examples to establish some general approaches to foreign and international documents.

## WHAT

International organizations whose members are countries, such as the United Nations, are known as international governmental organizations or IGOs. Some IGOs are organized on a regional basis—for instance, the Organization of American States (OAS) and the Council of Europe. Others are bonded together by common interests, such as the Organization of Petroleum Exporting Countries (OPEC). Both foreign countries and international governmental organizations produce official publications.

## WHY

No nation is self-sufficient. We must interact with, and thus have information from and about, other nations. For certain kinds of information, foreign and international documents may be the only, best, or least expensive source available.

## WHEN

Records of government activity have existed from earliest times. The clay tablets of Ashurbanipal survive in the British Museum today.

## WHERE

Although all types of libraries collect some foreign and international documents, the largest collections are to be found in academic and governmental libraries.

## WHO

Countless United States residents have ties to foreign countries through business, professional, or personal interest. Professors, students, business people, environmentalists, reporters, lawyers, government officials, and the intelligence community are among those interested in using foreign and international documents.

## HOW

Gaining access to foreign and international documents is a challenge for both librarians and users. Access depends on the ability to find out what has been produced, the cultivation of sources from which desired documents can be obtained, the appropriate organization of collections in libraries, and the availability of user friendly reference tools.

## A WEALTH OF INFORMATION

Foreign and international documents contain a wealth of information, not unlike U.S. government publications. They record the organizational structure of government or international bodies, information that can be useful when a person wants to know whom to write about a problem. Documents record the operations of the country or organization, information that is of interest to historians, reporters, and political scientists, among others. They describe and evaluate various social experiments and government programs, such as the value-added tax or child allowances, which may be considered for adoption here. Like other government documents, those issued by foreign governments and international organizations are a rich source of demo-

graphic and economic statistics. Scientific data and research findings are also financed and published by individual governments and by international organizations.
Finally, the authoritative texts of laws, treaties, conven-
tions, international agreements, and other legal materials
are issued as official documents.

Just as all types of people may need foreign and
international documents, from the high school student
involved in Model United Nations competition to the
scientist involved in Star Wars research, so do all types of
libraries collect foreign and international documents.

This chapter will discuss how the library learns
about, acquires, and organizes foreign and international
documents, and how these documents can be found and
retrieved in the library. Since describing the documents
of just one country or organization could occupy a
lifetime and fill a book, the discussion here will be quite
general.

## The Most Important Principle

The most important principle to be gleaned from
this chapter is *know your government*. The more you know
about how a country or IGO is organized and how it
carries out its work, the more successful you will be in
predicting where needed information will appear in the
recorded output of that organization and the more efficient you will be in selecting and pursuing appropriate
documents for use.

## BIBLIOGRAPHIC CONTROL

### Publisher's Catalogs

There are several ways to learn about foreign and
international documents. Theoretically, there is the
government's (or the organization's) own bibliographic
apparatus such as the publication lists put out by a
country's government printing office or by individual
government agencies—the equivalent of the *Monthly
Catalog*. In actuality, such lists may be slow coming out,
incomplete, or may not even exist. There may not even be
a centralized government printing office. One way to
verify the existence, name, and address of a country's
government printing office is to use the *Europa World Year
Book*.[1] A great deal of information is provided for each
country in a standardized format, including the structure
of the government and names and addresses of various
ministries or agencies. Such information will be useful if
you have to inquire about publication lists. The country's
government publishing house will be clearly identified at
the end of the list of publishers. The description of an
international organization in the *Europa World Year Book*
includes a listing of major publications but the sales agent
is not identified.

We don't always think of publishers' catalogs as
reference tools, but in the case of international organiza-

tions, sales catalogs are invaluable. They are readily
available by writing to the organization and are often the
best source of bibliographic information. The library,
however, may use them behind the scenes and not
catalog them.

---

**Searching the Library Catalog**

To find a publisher's catalog or sales list search:
[name of country]—**Government publications—Bibliography**
[name of IGO]—**Bibliography—Catalogs**
[name of IGO]—**Bibliography—Periodicals**
**International agencies—Bibliography**
**International agencies—Bibliography—Catalogs**
**Catalogs, Publishers'**—[geographic area or country]

---

## National Bibliographies

If there is a recognized national bibliography published for a country it may include official government
documents, often in a separate supplement or section.
Works such as Barbara L. Bell's *An Annotated Guide to
Current National Bibliographies*[2] and G. E. Gorman and J.
J. Mills' *Guide to Current National Bibliographies in the Third
World*[3] are useful for determining the existence, title, and
scope of national bibliographies. In their quest to be
comprehensive, however, national bibliographies are
also apt to be slow in appearing; they are thus often more
useful for historical research than for current information.

---

**Searching the Library Catalog**

To find a national bibliography, search:

[name of country]—**Imprints**

To find a guide to or list of national bibliographies,
search:

**Bibliography, National—Bibliography**

---

## General Catalogs and Indexes

A catalog that includes documents from many
countries is the *Bibliographic Guide to Government Publications—Foreign*[4], an annual publication produced from the
cataloging records of The Research Libraries of the New
York Public Library and the Library of Congress and
published by G. K. Hall. The "foreign" designation in the
title refers not just to foreign national documents but also
to publications of international and regional agencies;
foreign, state, and provincial governments; and major
foreign cities—all of which are represented in this bibliographic guide.

*International Bibliography*[5] is a compilation of information about the publications of many different international organizations. It comes out quarterly, has a detailed subject index, and includes a section that lists the
titles of articles in recent issues of IGO periodicals.

Certain other subject indexes include many foreign and international documents. *PAIS International in Print*[6], for one, is available on CD-ROM now.

---

**Searching the Library Catalog**

To find general catalogs and indexes search:
**Government publications—Bibliography— Catalogs—Periodicals**
**International agencies—Bibliography—Periodicals**

---

## Statistics

*Population Index*[7], published by Princeton University's Office of Population Research, lists census and demographic reports of the countries of the world. *Population Index* is available online as a database called POPLINE.[8]

For statistics published by international organizations, the *Index to International Statistics* (IIS)[9] published by Congressional Information Service is the prime tool. IGO documents are a rich source of comparative information about countries, and IIS provides an especially detailed approach by name of country. The index serves to provide access to the text as well as the numbers contained in these international documents. The documents indexed are available in a companion microfiche set[10] keyed to the abstract or entry number. IIS is one of the indexes included in the CD-ROM product *Statistical Masterfile*.[11]

## Science and Technology

In the scientific and technical area, don't overlook the National Technical Information Service (NTIS). NTIS has been handling foreign government publications since World War II, when its predecessor, the Publication Board, was established to disseminate to U.S. business and industry the technical data captured from foreign sources during the war. In FY 1990, NTIS acquired and made available 1,500 Japanese and 20,000 other foreign reports. Scan the "Corporate Author Index" of *Government Reports Announcements and Index* (C51.9/3:) to get a feel for the types of documents included. For instance, a recent issue had entries for the International Bank for Reconstruction and Development Living Standards Measurements Study as well as the Israel Atomic Energy Commission. Searching the electronic versions of the NTIS database[12] is the most efficient means of retrieving records for foreign and international documents.

## Education and Library Studies

The Educational Resources Information Center (ERIC) is a source of official publications dealing with education. It is particularly strong for UNESCO material and also includes reports of the International Federation of Library Associations (IFLA). The "Institution Index"

of *Resources in Education* (ED1.30:) summarizes the variety of foreign and international material to be found. The ERIC database[13] is also searchable online and through various CD-ROM products.

## Guides to the Literature

Aside from actual listings of publications, there are guides to the official literature of many countries and international organizations. Typically, these guides will explain how the government is organized; describe major series of publications; suggest useful bibliographic approaches; provide addresses; and list other books and articles for further reading.

---

**Searching the Library Catalog**

To find guides to the literature look for the subheading **—Government publications** after the name of the particular country or IGO:

[name of country]—**Government publications**
[world area]—**Government publications**
[name of organization]—**Government publications**

---

The *Guide to Official Publications of Foreign Countries*,[14] compiled by the International Documents Task Force of the American Library Association's Government Documents Roundtable, is the most comprehensive guide to the publications of foreign governments. For each of the 157 countries covered, standardized information is given concerning:

> Guides to Official Publications
> Bibliographies and Catalogs
> Sources of General Information on the Country
> Government Directories and Organization Manuals
> Statistical Yearbooks
> Laws and Regulations
> Legislative Proceedings
> Statements of Government Policy
> Economic Affairs
> Central Bank Publications
> Development Plans
> Budgets
> Census Results
> Health Titles
> Labor Titles
> Education Titles
> Court Reports

Emphasis is on titles published during the 1980s. Only the principal publications of the government are mentioned, but if the government has not produced a title in a particular category, a nonofficial publication has often been included. Entries for most titles include a brief description of contents plus English translations of any titles or agency names not in English. This guide is invaluable for both reference and acquisitions work.

The best overall guide to IGO material is *International Information: Documents, Publications, and Information Systems of International Governmental Organizations*[15] edited by Peter I. Hajnal. It covers the organizational setting, bibliographic control, collection development, arrangement of collections, reference work, citation forms, microforms, and computerized information systems.

Pergamon Press publishes a series called "Guides to Official Publications." Number 1 in that series is a combined report of Vladimir Palic's *Government Publications: A Guide to Bibliographic Tools* (LC 1.12/2:G74) and *Government Organization Manuals* (LC 1.6/4 G74), both originally published by the Library of Congress[16]. Palic describes the catalogs, bibliographies, and other sources for countries and international organizations. This book can be used as a starting point for finding out about foreign and international documents.

## Guides to Primary Sources

Guides to individual types of primary source material are also very useful. For statistics issued by national statistical offices there is the *Bibliography of Official Statistical Yearbooks and Bulletins*,[17] compiled by Gloria Westfall. Joan Harvey has produced guides to statistics for various areas of the world. Her *Statistics Africa*,[18] *Statistics America*,[19] *Statistics Asia and Australasia*,[20] and *Statistics Europe*[21] include nongovernmental as well as official publications.

---

**Searching the Library Catalog**

To find statistical compilations search:

[name of country]—**Statistics**
[topic]—**Statistics**

---

The *Checklist of Government Directories, Lists and Rosters*,[22] from Meckler Publishing, is an annotated guide to the types of publications that provide a working knowledge of the organization, administrative scope, and personnel of national governments.

---

**Searching the Library Catalog**

Organization manuals can be tricky to find in the subject catalog. Some Library of Congress headings to search are:

**Administrative agencies**—[name of country]
**Legislative bodies**—[name of country]
[name of country]—**Executive departments**
[name of country]—**Officials and employees**

---

Official gazettes are an important type of national publication. These "official journals" often combine information similar to that in separate United States publications such as the *Congressional Record*, *Statutes at Large*,

*Federal Register*, and the *Weekly Compilation of Presidential Documents*. The content will vary from country to country. Topics covered may include new legislation, regulations, orders and decisions, official announcements, texts of international agreements, court decisions, and legislative debates. The law library of the Library of Congress maintains an extensive collection of official gazettes and has issued *A Guide to Official Gazettes and Their Contents*[23] covering all the countries of the world.

---

**Searching the Library Catalog**

To find a guide that lists official gazettes search under:

**Gazettes—Bibliography**

To find official gazettes using the subject catalog search:

[name of country]—**Politics and government**

---

## The Library Catalog

A library's own catalog may be helpful, not only for determining call numbers when bibliographic information is known, but also for determining the extent of the library's holdings for particular countries or international bodies. Entries for official publications generally begin with the name of the country. It is fairly easy to browse through the cards filed under France, for example, in a card catalog; perhaps less easy to browse through the entries retrieved in an online catalog when you enter "France" as author or corporate author. Entries under government agency or international organization names can be lengthy and complicated. They present many opportunities for the searcher to make mistakes whether by looking in the wrong place alphabetically or by typing in misspellings.

---

**Searching the Library Catalog**
To find official publications in catalogs and indexes that use AACR cataloging rules look first under the name of the country or IGO.

---

Furthermore, when dealing with government documents one should always be alert to the possibility that the library's holdings are not reflected in the general catalog. Documents may be in a separate catalog or the library may rely entirely on printed catalogs and indexes for access plus a simple shelflist to verify holdings.

Finding out about the existence of foreign and international documents may take some digging: bibliographic control for official publications has not been mastered by the world's libraries. Whether this is because government publishing is too decentralized, too voluminous, varied, changeable, or too much like archival material is an unanswered question. The problems are well known; the solutions remain to be found.

# ACQUIRING FOREIGN AND INTERNATIONAL DOCUMENTS

## Collection Development Policies

A library's holdings of foreign and international documents will be governed by its collection development policy and the needs of its patrons. When a library decides to collect foreign documents, it might start with English-language materials such as those from Great Britain or Canada. Aside from a subject approach, there are two main ways to collect documents: by country or by type of material. Many libraries endeavor to collect a wide range of publications from a particular country. Others may collect certain types of material such as organization manuals and/or statistical abstracts from numerous countries.

## Microform Collections

Some microform publishers, such as Inter Documentation Company AG, Chadwyck-Healey, Readex, and Micromedia Limited, offer attractive packages of foreign and international material for sale to libraries. The subject volume of the *Guide to Microforms in Print*,[24] published by Microform Review, includes some sixty pages of foreign and international document listings under heading number **690: Official Documents**. Norman Ross Publishing[25] is the leading distributor of foreign microforms in the United States providing convenient centralized services. Sometimes, however, microforms are only available directly from a country's government or from an international organization's sales outlet.

## Interlibrary Loan

A library may decide not to collect foreign and international documents at all, but instead rely on interlibrary loan to satisfy the infrequent needs of its patrons. The Official Publications Section of the British Library Lending Division receives about 30,000 requests a year for documents. The Center for Research Libraries in Chicago houses foreign documents for its members. The collection of several hundred thousand volumes from more than 100 foreign governments is particularly strong for Western Europe, Latin America, and Southeast Asia. An attempt is being made to catalog these documents which are described in a general way in the Center's *Handbook*.[26] Libraries that are not Center members have limited borrowing privileges for a prepaid transaction fee. The *Directory of Government Document Collections and Librarians*,[27] published by Congressional Information Service, shows which libraries collect documents from particular international organizations or foreign countries. In 1985 Carol A. Turner's *Directory of Foreign Document Collections*[28] was published, providing even more comprehensive and detailed descriptions of library holdings for foreign documents at the national, state, provincial, and local levels.

## Verification

The first step in acquisitions is to identify the item bibliographically—sometimes a problem since bibliographic control for this material ranges from difficult to nonexistent. Use the sources described above or a cataloging utility such as OCLC or RLIN to verify bibliographic information before ordering. Foreign documents usually take from six months to a year to appear in OCLC with Library of Congress copy. Some never do appear. Since speed is important in acquiring government publications, you may be forced to order with incomplete information. For instance, it may be impossible to determine the price before ordering. Indeed, many government documents cost nothing. If you insist on a price quote before ordering you risk a fatal delay, since documents are generally printed only in small quantities. You might specify a maximum price, asking that the order be canceled if the cost is higher.

## Vendors

After you have pulled together pertinent bibliographic information—such as title, issuing body, date, and number of pages—the next step is determining where to send your order. Some of the tools described above, in particular *International Bibliography* for international documents and the *Guide to Official Publications of Foreign Countries* for foreign documents, include specific instructions and addresses for ordering the material. "A Selective Directory of Government Document Dealers, Jobbers, and Subscription Agents," compiled by Susan Dow, appeared in the *Serials Librarian* in 1988.[29] UNIPUB[30] is the major distributor of international organization publications in the United States.

Without a jobber, libraries must deal directly with the issuing government or organization. Organization manuals, directories, telephone books, lists of publishers in national bibliographies, and the OCLC name-address directory are sources for locating the proper addresses. Embassies are another—either the American embassy in the foreign country or the foreign embassy in this country. The internal address and correspondence files built up by librarians over the years can be a very important acquisitions resource.

Some foreign agencies prefer to receive requests written in their native language. Form letters can be translated into various languages. On college campuses there are generally native speakers from other countries who can be hired to translate. Some libraries maintain lists of local resource people by language. When it comes to coping with foreign languages you may find a book like ALA's *Language of the Foreign Book Trade*[31] handy to have nearby.

## Payment

Paying for the item can present further problems. Since exchange rates are unstable, the price at the ordering stage may differ from the final price. If pre-payment is required and your library is a public institution, you may have another problem. Librarians are often caught in the middle of a situation where one government requires the money before releasing the item and the other government requires the item before releasing the money. Sometimes deposit accounts can ameliorate this situation. One of the advantages of working with a vendor is that business dealings are generally smoother.

## Claiming

Once you have sent the order, experience will tell you when to expect receipt. If it doesn't come, send a follow-up request. If it still doesn't come, either follow up again, try another approach, or give up. Experience will indicate the point of diminishing returns. You may think you have set up a standing order for a foreign serial, but since government departments can be unreliable about maintaining mailing lists, to ensure receipt of an annual report or other serial publication you must write for it yearly around its issue date.

## Special Methods of Acquiring Documents

Under certain circumstances exchange agreements can be mutually advantageous for a pair of libraries in two different countries. Sometimes your own university publications can be used for barter. Or faculty members who work or travel in foreign countries can collect materials for the library. Or, best of all, the librarian gets to go on buying trips.

## Depository Arrangements

Depository libraries receive shipments of publications automatically thus obviating much of the workload associated with acquiring publications. Except for Canada, few foreign countries maintain U.S. depositories—whereas international organizations have depositories all over the world. On the other hand, international organizations frequently turn major publications over to private publishers, completely bypassing the depositories and making it difficult to keep track of what is available. Furthermore, some publications are produced through regional offices in the far corners of the world and are never even listed in the catalogs which emanate from headquarters, let alone distributed to depository libraries.

Sometimes the challenge for the foreign and international documents librarian is knowing what not to acquire; assessing how much the library can afford to process and store; setting up cooperative agreements with other libraries; knowing what can be borrowed; and knowing what will be used.

## ORGANIZING FOREIGN AND INTERNATIONAL DOCUMENTS

Once you acquire foreign and international documents you must decide how to handle them. Where will they be shelved? How will they be classified? What level of cataloging will be provided for them?

## Shelving

Libraries in the United States are about equally divided between those that keep documents in a separate collection and those that integrate them into the regular collection. Integrated collections keep subjects together but may scatter the publications of a particular nation or organization. A separate shelving sequence for documents makes it easier to keep all the publications of a body together, an arrangement often preferred by knowledgeable patrons, but may increase the level of complexity facing the casual user of a library. Pemberton argues that every library should have a documents and reports collection because these materials constitute a third form of literature distinct from monographs and serials in that the source from which they emanate is of particular interest to the user. In addition to official publications he would include the publications of political parties, pressure groups, and trade unions in the documents and reports collection.[32]

## Classification

Unlike U.S. federal documents, some foreign and international documents have document classification numbers printed right on them. This greatly facilitates processing and housing in a separate documents collection. The user who finds these numbers in printed indexes and catalogs can go directly to the shelves to retrieve the publication. Whether or not the documents come with numbers, the body may have developed an official classification scheme for its own documents that the library can adopt. Or the library may use an overall scheme into which it can fit all documents and reports. Several such systems are described in *The Bibliographic Control of Official Publications*[33] edited by John E. Pemberton. The important characteristic of a document classification system is that it groups together all the publications of a given country or a particular international organization.

Those who prefer a subject arrangement of documents have recourse to the Library of Congress, Dewey Decimal, or other classification system that the library uses. It should be noted that documents can be classified by subject using the library's established system and still be kept in a separate documents collection (just as reference books are classified but shelved separately). Likewise, a library could modify its classification to provide a common class for all the publications of a particular country or organization so that they would stand together in the stacks.

Generally speaking it is good practice to have a call number notation on every piece of library material so it can be retrieved from its proper place and be put back there. However, libraries have been known to shelve documents by agency name and title or by organization and then broad subject area. Sometimes color coding is used. Sometimes "filing" phrases are underlined on the cover of the document.

## Cataloging

Whether and/or how documents are classified (and shelved) is an entirely independent issue from whether and/or how documents are cataloged. Bibliographic descriptions of the documents owned may be included in the library's general catalog, maintained as a separate documents catalog, or exist only in a shelflist. AACR2 rules are not particularly hospitable to the documents cataloger, which is why GODORT produced a companion manual on documents cataloging.[34] Many libraries trying to catalog and integrate documents into their regular collections get bogged down with processing and develop large backlogs which, in essence, become separate documents collections. Every library has hidden files and special collections which are not yet reflected in the catalog. Until they are, it is incumbent upon both users and librarians to query each other about alternative or additional resources.

## USING FOREIGN AND INTERNATIONAL DOCUMENTS

How much are foreign and international documents actually used? One study in the field of international relations[35] found that citations to documents in journal articles were 19 percent of the total and over half of the document citations were to publications of foreign governments or international organizations. Documents in foreign languages made up just over 10 percent of all documents cited. Use does, of course, vary by discipline.

Studies have shown that scholars often have their own means of acquiring documents and may not rely heavily on libraries. However, the international documents specialist at the Library of Congress receives some 65 questions a month that require his extensive expertise to answer.[36] Often the answer or a clue to the answer comes from his personal filing cabinet. Sometimes a telephone call to another expert is required. Frequently queries are in response to publicity in the newspaper about documents that are too new to have been received or cataloged. Although none of these problems are unique to foreign and international documents they serve to emphasize the importance of the librarian being inti-

mately familiar with the collection. The questions the librarian gets may be typical in that they can be grouped into categories, such as requests for statistics, legislation, development plans, or international agreements. Handling them, however, is seldom routine. A request for the official election returns from Costa Rica may lead to a search for a statistical yearbook from the country, verification of the name of the agency responsible for elections (Tribunal Supremo de Elecciones), or frustration over the fact that indexing tools are not consistent in their use of terms, listing entries under both **Costa Rica—Elections** and **Elections—Costa Rica.** Some particular pitfalls of foreign and international document use, pitfalls that can be avoided by the alert and experienced librarian, are described below.

## PECULIARITIES OF FOREIGN AND INTERNATIONAL DOCUMENTS

### Language

Many international and some foreign documents are printed in more than one language, sometimes with parallel text in English and another language. If you do not spot the English text immediately you may become confused, waste time, or even abandon the book needlessly. Dealing with parallel titles in several languages is one of the factors that makes cataloging more time consuming for documents than for other material and makes finding such documents in the catalog more problematic and confusing.

However, there are more subtle problems than the simple inability to read foreign languages. The English language is used differently in different countries and by different international organizations. This leads to subject heading variations in catalogs and indexes. Use of the wrong terminology leads to poor retrieval results.

---

**Be Aware of Differences in Terminology!**

natural language uses **Multinational corporations**
United Nations uses **Transnational corporations**
Library of Congress uses **International business enterprises**

United States uses **Antitrust**
Canada uses **Competition**

Library of Congress uses **Hijacking of aircraft**
United Nations uses **Aerial interference**

United Nations uses **Human rights**
Library of Congress uses **Civil rights**

---

### Types of Publications

Official publications are a reflection of the process of governing. As governing bodies differ so do their documents. It is necessary to be open to learning about the importance of new types of publications when working with foreign and international documents. For instance, the United Nations carries on its work through the adoption of resolutions. Great Britain has its white papers (departmental policy statements) and green papers (preliminary versions of the white papers) and bluebooks (commission reports).

Particularly with regard to international organizations it is important to understand the distinction between publications and documents. Publications are materials produced for distribution to the public. They may be priced or unpriced, but generally there is some attempt made to publicize them. Documents, on the other hand, are records of organization activity produced primarily for the participants, not for wide public distribution. Examples include minutes, proceedings and draft reports. Such documents may be cited but impossible to obtain.

## Subject Matter

The documents of different nations reflect differing concerns: for instance, there are more religious topics where there is a state religion, as in Israel. Women are not allowed to drive automobiles in Saudi Arabia because the predominant religion forbids it. Countries with nationalized industries and crown corporations issue different kinds of statistics and reports. International organizations grapple with problems of global significance. It is necessary to be open minded about the type of subject matter that may be covered by foreign and international documents.

## Interpreting Citations

Librarians are wizards at deciphering bibliographic citations. However, not all librarians would be aware that the difference between Cmd.1 and Cmnd.1 is approximately 30 years. The British Command Papers series is a well-known and important part of that nation's parliamentary papers. Command Papers are numbered continuously, through several sessions of Parliament, from 1 to not more than 9999. The various series are distinguished by their prefix, as follows:

| Years: | Cite as: |
| --- | --- |
| 1833-1869 | 1 - 4222 |
| 1870-1899 | C1 - C9550 |
| 1900-1918 | Cd.1 - Cd.9239 |
| 1919-1956 | Cmd.1 - Cmd.9889 |
| 1956- | Cmnd.1 - |

The nuances of proper citation can be very important for the full identification of documents. A rule of thumb is to write down all the numbers, rather than overlook the one number that may prove most important for document retrieval in a particular library.

# ALTERNATIVE SOURCES OF INFORMATION

## United States Documents

Foreign national documents are not the sole source of foreign country information. Indeed, few libraries collect documents from more than a few countries. United States documents, however, contain much valuable information about other nations. The Departments of Commerce, Defense, and State are among the most prolific publishers in this regard. The Area Handbooks series, now called "Country Studies" (D101.22:550-no.), is especially valuable, as is *Overseas Business Reports* (C61.12:) and the *World Factbook* (PrEx3.15:). The State Department's annual report on human rights practices (Y4.F76/1-15:) is eagerly awaited each year. Even the *Statistical Abstract of the United States* (C3.134/2:C83/2/yr) has an appendix on world statistics.

## International Organization Publications

The publications of international organizations are a rich source of comparative information about countries. Member nations tend to be cooperative about releasing information to the IGOs, and the international organizations tend to be conscientious about publishing it in a consistent and comparable format. Much of this information is statistical in nature. However, the International Labor Office monitors legislation dealing with labor and social security issues in all countries and prints the laws in the annual *ILO Legislative Series*.[37] A similar undertaking by the World Health Organization results in the publication *International Digest of Health Legislation*.[38]

## Commercial Publications

Commercial publications, ranging from textbooks and travelogues to expensive business loose-leaf services, also help fill the need for international information. The bimonthly *International Legal Materials*,[39] from the American Society of International Law, reprints or translates significant documents from all over the world. It includes judicial and similar proceedings, treaties and agreements, legislation and regulations, reports and other documents.

Some information sources are hidden away in reference books that normally serve an entirely different purpose. For instance, one might easily overlook the foreign law digests in the last volume of the Martindale-Hubbell[40] directory of lawyers and law firms. These law digests provide understandable foreign legal information which is probably excelled only by the collections of the very best and largest law libraries.

Information about international governmental organizations may be located in *The Yearbook of International Organizations*,[41] which describes over 24,000 international organizations, only 5,000 of which are intergovernmental.

(International organizations whose members are not countries, such as the International Federation of Library Associations or IFLA, are known as nongovernmental organizations or NGOs.) Entries include organization names (in all applicable languages); addresses, telephone, and telex; name of principal executive officer; main activities; history, goals, and structure; personnel and finances; technical and regional commissions; consultative relationships; memberships by country; publications; and interorganizational links. This is the definitive source of information for international bodies.

## ELECTRONIC ACCESS

Electronic access to bibliographic information about foreign and international documents has changed from dream to reality in recent years. Ready access is now available through cataloging utilities, online databases, and CD-ROM products. For example, Chadwyck-Healey now markets a CD-ROM index to the British government documents, while the British Museum offers online access to the same material.[42] To determine whether such a database exists for a particular country or organization consult *Computer-Readable Databases: A Directory and Data Sourcebook.*[43]

## PROFESSIONAL UPDATE SOURCES

Good sources for keeping up-to-date on foreign and international documents include *Documents to the People,*[44] *Government Publications Review,*[45] and the newsletter of the IFLA Official Publications Section.[46] Recently, a new means of communication has gained popularity—discussion lists on BITNET. GOVDOC-L is a general documents forum, while INT-LAW[47] is specifically intended to be a quick electronic means of exchanging information on and talking about issues related to foreign and international legal publications, including documents of international organizations and foreign governments. Anything relating to acquisitions, reference work, databases, CD-ROM products, cataloging, and classification can be discussed.

## CANADIAN GOVERNMENT DOCUMENTS

### Canadian Documents in Libraries

Because Canada is our national neighbor and issues official publications in English (French, too, of course), many U.S. libraries collect Canadian documents. The Canadian government has established 150 depository libraries in the United States. Selective Canadian depositories are entitled to receive one free copy of any publication from the *Weekly Checklist of Canadian Government Publications.*[48] The Library of Congress, the only full Canadian depository in the U.S., automatically receives weekly shipments of all publications listed on the checklist.

## Acquisition of Canadian Government Publications

Because of its timeliness, the *Weekly Checklist* is a good acquisitions tool. Nondepository libraries outside Canada can subscribe to it for a fee. Orders should be addressed to the Canada Communication Group, Publishing Division, Ottawa, ON Canada K1A 0S9. Libraries not collecting in depth can get on the mailing list for "Book News," which announces important new publications on single sheet flyers with order forms attached.

## Borrowing Canadian Documents through Interlibrary Loan

The National Library of Canada (NLC), the library of last resort for international ILL requests, now accepts requests via the OCLC ILL Subsystem (symbol NLD). NLC has a unique collection of tools for identifying Canadian and foreign locations of publications and will provide a location service when requested. DOBIS,[49] an online union catalog supported by NLC, includes records generated by Canadian federal government libraries.

## Guide to the Literature of Canadian Documents

In *Canadian Official Publications,*[50] Olga B. Bishop describes the types of publications issued by the Parliament and the departments and agencies of the federal government as well as the types of information to be found in particular documents.

## Canada's Government Manual

The guide to Canada's federal government most closely equivalent to our *U.S. Government Manual* is entitled *Organization of the Government of Canada*[51] (Canadian Class No. BT1-2). It is published irregularly and since 1990 is co-published by the Canadian Chamber of Commerce. The *Guide to Federal Programs and Services*[52] (Canadian Class No. P38-4/1) emphasizes programs rather than structure but is probably the best source for addresses and telephone numbers.

## Canada's Official Gazette

Canada's official gazette is called the *Canada Gazette*[53] (Canadian Class No. SP-1, SP-2, and SP-11). Part I of the *Canada Gazette* contains notices, proclamations, and other material required to be published; Part II contains regulations; and Part III contains the public acts (i.e., laws) that have received Royal Assent.

## Canada's National Bibliography

The national bibliography of Canada is entitled *Canadiana*[54] (Canadian Class No. SN2-1). Official publications are intermixed. *Canadiana* is a valuable aid for Canadian Studies and is available in printed and microfiche formats and on magnetic tape.

## Bibliographic Sources for Canadian Publications

The most important bibliographic tool for document reference purposes is the *Government of Canada Publications*[55] catalog issued quarterly by the Canadian Government Publishing Centre (Canadian Class No. IC6-1). Each issue is bilingual, in English and French.

## Canadian Document Microforms

Micromedia Ltd. offers many Canadian documents for sale on microfiche and provides a comprehensive index, *Microlog*,[56] to both federal and provincial level material. They also sell a CD-ROM version.

## Canadian Statistics

Like the U.S. Bureau of the Census, Statistics Canada collects and publishes numerical data on social and economic activity. Publications available for purchase from the agency are described in the annual *Statistics Canada Catalogue*[57] (Canadian Class No. CS11-204). A retrospective volume, the *Historical Catalogue of Statistics Canada Publications, 1918-1980*[58] (Canadian Class No. CS11-512), provides a complete record of the cataloged publications of Statistics Canada and its predecessor, the Dominion Bureau of Statistics.

The actual statistics are found in *Historical Statistics of Canada*,[59] 2nd edition, 1983 (Canadian Class No. CS11-516). Most tables in this volume provide time series data for approximately fifty years. *Canada Handbook*[60] (Canadian Class No. CS11-403) is like a statistical abstract with pictures, a mini-encyclopedia about Canada. Other statistical data can be tracked down using the *Bibliography of Federal Data Sources Excluding Statistics Canada 1981*[61] (Canadian Class No. CS11-513).

Only 10 percent or less of the data available from Statistics Canada is in printed form. Online numeric databases such as CANSIM[62] are increasingly important.

*Canadian Statistics Index*,[63] published by Micromedia Ltd., indexes both government and nongovernment statistics. A companion microfiche collection is available.

## Classification of Canadian Publications

Canada has managed to do what GPO cannot; that is, print the catalog or classification number in the document itself. Preprinted numbers facilitate the processing of documents by the library. An explanation of the system is available in *Government of Canada Publications: Outline of Classification*,[64] 4th ed., 1984, (Canadian Class No. IC91-1984).

## UNITED NATIONS PUBLICATIONS AND DOCUMENTS

The United Nations, while not the oldest international governmental organization, is probably the best known and the largest, with 157 member nations. The UN proper has six principal organs: the General Assembly, the Security Council, the Economic and Social Council, the Trusteeship Council, the International Court of Justice, and the Secretariat. Seventeen other organizations, known as the "specialized agencies," are related to the United Nations by special agreements and work through the coordinating machinery of the Economic and Social Council. Although they report annually to the United Nations, organizations such as ILO, FAO, UNESCO, and WHO are separate, autonomous organizations with separate lists of member countries and separate publishing programs. Thus, a library that collects United Nations documents does not necessarily collect documents from these specialized agencies.

## Guide to the Literature of the United Nations

The basic library guide for the United Nations proper is Peter Hajnal's book *Guide to United Nations Organization, Documentation and Publishing*.[65] It contains excellent tips for students, researchers, and librarians.

The United Nations' own guide, *Everyone's United Nations*,[66] (United Nations Sales No. E.85.I.24) describes the structure and activities of the United Nations and the specialized agencies and is a handy place to find the Charter of the United Nations.

Two publications are of value to the inexperienced user or librarian: *United Nations Documentation: A Brief Guide*[67] (ST/LIB/34/Rev.1) and *Instructions for Depository Libraries Receiving United Nations Material*[68] (ST/LIB/13/Rev.3).

## Reference Tools for UN Research

The history of the United Nations is chronicled year by year in a series entitled *Yearbook of the United Nations*.[69] The *Yearbook*, which has extensive bibliographies and references to publications and documents, may often prove a more satisfactory bibliographic tool than the basic index, described below. However, there is a time lag of several years before the *Yearbook* comes out.

The acronym for the UN's index has varied over the years as UNDI, UNDEX, and now UNDOC but the subtitle remains the same: *United Nations Documents Index*.[70] The quarterly is a product of the computer-based integrated online United Nations Bibliographic Information System (UNBIS). Each issue has nine sections:

1. Checklist of documents and publications with full bibliographic description arranged by series symbol.
2. List of *Official Records*
3. List of sales publications arranged by sales number
4. List of documents republished in the *Official Records*
5. Language table
6. Subject index
7. Author index
8. Title index
9. List of new document series symbols

So many documents are listed in UNDOC that it is no longer feasible to produce hard-copy cumulations. The 1984 cumulative edition was the first distributed in microfiche, with five-year fiche cumulations planned for the future.

## Official Records of the United Nations

Most procedural information published by the United Nations is incorporated into the Official Records of the Economic and Social Council, the Security Council, the General Assembly, and the Trusteeship Council. The Index to Proceedings[71] of the organ provides very detailed access to procedural information. In fact, questions can be answered using the appropriate *Index to Proceedings* that cannot be answered using UNDOC.

## Magazine of the United Nations

References to recent publications and UN happenings can be found in the periodical *UN Chronicle*,[72] which changed from a monthly to a quarterly publication in 1986.

## Treaties Recorded by the United Nations

One of the important series published by the United Nations, although not in a timely manner, is the *Treaty Series*,[73] which includes authentic texts of multilateral treaties and international agreements.

## Statistics of the United Nations

The *Demographic Yearbook* and other publications of the UN Statistical Office are extremely important. Each issue of the *Demographic Yearbook*[74] (UN Document No. ST/ESA/STAT/ser.R) includes a lengthy article on a special topic as well as tables on population, mortality, natality, nuptiality, divorce, and migration.

## United Nation Concerns

The *Yearbook on Human Rights*[75] is a country-by-country report on civil and political rights, economic and social rights, and freedom of information. Also in demand are the publications of the UN's Centre on Transnational Corporations, as is anything to do with developing countries.

## United Nations Depository Libraries

The United Nations depository library system differs from most in that the libraries are expected to pay an annual fee. There are forty-two UN depository libraries in the United States. A complete list of depositories can be found in *Directory of the United Nations Information Systems, Vol.II: Information Sources in Countries.*[76]

## Acquisition of United Nations Publications

Sales publications can be ordered from United Nations Publications, Room DC2-0853, New York, NY 10017, which will send a catalog of publications in print upon request. A standing-order service provides automatic receipt of documents by subject category or by serial title. Vendors such as UNIPUB also handle UN publications.

Readex supplies microfiche of United Nation documents and now provides an electronic index on CD-ROM to access them.[77]

## Classification of UN Materials

Not all UN publications are assigned document numbers. There is a numbering system for official records, for documents, and for sales publications—categories which are not mutually exclusive. The fact that a title can have more than one "official" number assigned to it can cause confusion.

## EUROPEAN COMMUNITY PUBLICATIONS AND DOCUMENTS

The European Community (EC) is a regional international organization striving to become a national government by uniting the countries of Europe. By December 31, 1992, the European Community hopes to be a true "common market" where national borders are no more a barrier to trade and free movement than state borders are within the United States. As the goals of the original three communities, the European Coal and Steel Community (ECSC), the European Economic Community (EEC), and the European Atomic Energy Community (EAEC or Euratom) are finally being realized and extended, the three are increasingly referred to, in the singular, as the European Community. However, main entries in library catalogs tend to be under the original three community names or under the names of the common institutions. Lack of uniformity in the formation of these headings adds a degree of difficulty to the searching process.

---

**Searching the Library Catalog**

European Community material is found under headings such as:

Commission of the European Communities
European Community Information Service
European Economic Community
European Parliament
Statistical Office of the European Communities

Phrases in subject headings include:

European Communities
European Economic Community Countries

---

## European Community Depository Libraries

Although the United States is, of course, not a member, the EC thinks it important for Americans to be informed about and supportive of its goals and accomplishments. Therefore, the EC is committed to maintaining a presence in the U.S. through a depository library system. There are 51 European Community depositories in the United States, headed by the library of the Commission of the European Communities Delegation to the United States in Washington, DC.

## Magazines of the European Communities

The Washington delegation issues a monthly journal called *Europe*[78] which describes the current activities of the EC and highlights important new publications.

The Secretariat General of the Commission puts out the *Bulletin of the European Communities*,[79] a more formal publication which follows the activities and policies of the EC closely and has a section called "New Publications" each month. Supplements reprint official documents of the Commission such as communications to the Council, reports, and proposals.

## Language in the European Communities

When Great Britain joined the European Community in 1973, English became one of the official languages. Presently, everything the EC publishes must be issued in nine languages: French, English, German, Danish, Spanish, Italian, Portuguese, Dutch, and Greek. Many publications show parallel titles in all the languages on the title page. Since catalogers are instructed to use the first such title and since the English title is seldom the first one listed, the catalog records for these publications can be quite intimidating.

---

**Tip!** Don't automatically bypass foreign language titles, especially when searching for statistical information. Look for an English version of the title in the same record.

---

The standardized terminology of the EC is set out in *EUROVOC*,[80] an annex to the index of the *Official Journal*. This thesaurus appears in various forms. Each language version consists of an alphabetical section, a subject-oriented section, a permuted index, and a diagram (Terminogrammes) section—all monolingual—plus a multilingual index section.

## Acquisition of European Community Material

The official distributor for EC publications in the United States is UNIPUB. Their free catalog, *European Communities Official Publications*,[81] covers publications by and about the EC including monographs, yearbooks, periodicals and document subscriptions in both paper and microfiche.

EC's official printer, the Office for Official Publications (OOPEC), also has a free subject catalog of its popular publications entitled, *The EC as a Publisher*.[82]

## Official Gazette of the European Community

The texts of legislation and other official acts of the EC are published in the *Official Journal of the European Communities*.[83] It is divided into several parts:

**Legislation.** The "L" section includes regulations, directives, and other binding acts. Texts of a temporary duration are printed in normal typeface; those with permanence in bold. Regulations are numbered consecutively from the beginning of each year with the number first, followed by the year, i.e., 222/89. Other acts, such as directives, are also done consecutively for each year but the order is reversed, i.e., 89/222. A regulation is a law that is binding on all member states. A directive is binding as to the result to be achieved but the choice of method is left to the individual states. Businesses affected by a directive must take account of the national implementing legislation as well as the directive.

**Information and Notices.** The "C" section includes nonbinding decisions, resolutions, and other communications requiring publication. Proposals and amendments issued by the Commission are usually published here but without the explanatory memorandum that appears only in the original mimeographed series of *COM Documents*.[84] Opinions and minutes of proceedings of the European Parliament appear here approximately three months after the plenary session. Opinions of the Economic and Social Committee are grouped in particular issues. The operative text of each decision of the Court of Justice is published here. And this is where you can find the ECU (European Currency Unit) exchange rate on a daily basis.

**Supplement.** The "S" section includes notices of invitations to tender for development contracts financed by the European Development Fund, public works and supply contracts of the member states open to bidding by companies within the Community, and procurement contracts open for bids under the GATT procurement code.

**Annex.** The annex prints the debates of the European Parliament. Reports of the European Parliament are issued separately as part of a series called *Session Documents.*[85]

**Index.** The alphabetical index to the *Official Journal*, issued monthly and cumulated annually, covers only the "L" section plus the decisions of the Court of Justice from the "C" section. The debates of the European Parliament in the Annex have their own index. The methodological index provides a way to find an *Official Journal* citation when you already know the number of a regulation or directive.

---

WAYS THE OJ HAS BEEN CITED:

Official Journal 1979 No. L 50
OJL 13, 17.1.90 p34
OJ C 135/88
OJ 1985 L199
OJ Eur Comm. no.L209 (Aug. 2, 1988)

---

## Guides to the Literature of the EC

The most recent guide to the literature of the EC is Ian Thomson's *The Documentation of the European Communities*[86] published by Mansell in 1989. Thomson outlines the structure and function of the various component organizations of the EC, describes their publications and documents, and provides suggestions for obtaining further information. This book extends the historical information to be found in the earlier guide to the literature of the EC by John Jeffries: *A Guide to the Official Publications of the European Communities*,[87] 2nd ed. Mansell, 1981. The Jeffries guide contains the following:

1.  Introduction
2.  Publications of the European Communities
3.  Commission—General publications
4.  Commission—Nonstatistical publications
5.  Eurostat—Publications of the Statistical Office of the European Communities
6.  Council of Ministers
7.  European Parliament
8.  Court of Justice of the European Communities
9.  Other Bodies
10. Bibliographic aids
    Appendix I. Addresses to which orders for publications should be sent.
    Appendix II. European Documentation Centres and Depository Libraries.
    Appendix III. Further reading on the European Communities.
    Index

## Reference Tools for EC Research

There has been no one overall, cumulative, alphabetical index to EC documentation in paper since *EC Index*,[88] which covered the years 1984 to 1986, ceased publication. The EC's own *SCAD Bulletin*[89] comes out weekly, does not cumulate, and has a classified subject arrangement with a descriptor index in French. It covers official publications and documents of the EC plus articles dealing with the work of the community that appear in commercially published periodicals. There is a SCAD database[90] that can be searched online which solves the noncumulating problem.

*European Access*[91] is a current awareness service published by Chadwyck-Healey which covers both EC documentation and material about the EC appearing in a wide assortment of books, journals, and newspapers. Here again a classified arrangement is used and there is no cumulation. However, each bimonthly issue also includes bibliographical review articles on EC policies and activities and descriptions of EC databases and how to use them. This may be the most timely source of information for acquisitions purposes as well.

## Statistics of the European Communities

The EC's statistical abstract is *Basic Statistics of the Community*.[92] It provides general statistical comparisons of the EC with other countries. This title and the many others produced by Eurostat (the Statistical Office of the European Communities) are indexed in detail by *IIS* described above. Eurostat has three numeric databases available to the general public: Cronos—macroeconomic time series data; Regio—regional breakdowns; and Comext—trade statistics.[93]

## Classification of EC Publications

Although publications of the EC frequently have a "catalogue number" printed on them and although that number may be included in the cataloging description, it is not a number that lends itself to being used as a shelf number. The EC itself uses the Universal Decimal Classification which has not been adopted to any great extent in the United States. Consequently, libraries in the United States often classify EC documents by Library of Congress or Dewey and disperse them throughout the regular collection.

## FREEBIES

The following subject bibliographies are free from U.S. Government Printing Office, Superintendent of Documents, Washington, DC 20402:

93.   Background Notes
166.  Foreign Area Studies
278.  Canada

## REFERENCES

1. *Europa World Year Book.* 30th- 1989- (annual). (London: Europa Publications). Continues *Europa Year Book.*

2. Barbara L.Bell. *An Annotated Guide to Current National Bibliographies.* (Alexandria, VA: Chadwyck-Healey, 1986).

3. G. E. Gorman and J. J. Mills. *Guide to Current National Bibliographies in the Third World* (London: H. Zell, an imprint of K. G. Saur, 1983).

4. New York Public Library. Research Libraries. *Bibliographic Guide to Government Publications - Foreign.* 1975- (annual). (Boston: G. K. Hall).

5. *International Bibliography.* Vol.16- 1988- (quarterly). (White Plains, NY: Kraus International Publications).

6. *PAIS International in Print.* 1991- (monthly). (New York: Public Affairs Information Service, Inc.). *PAIS on CD-ROM.* 1972- (New York: Public Affairs Information Service). Also available from Silver-Platter Information, Inc.

7. *Population Index.* Vol.3- 1937- (quarterly). (Princeton, NJ: Office of Population Research, Princeton University).

8. *POPLINE.* 1970- Online availability through the National Library of Medicine's MEDLARS system; CD-ROM available from SilverPlatter Information, Inc.

9. *Index to International Statistics : IIS.* Vol.1- 1983- (monthly). (Washington, DC: Congressional Information Service).

10. *IIS Microfiche Library.* 1983- (Washington, DC: Congressional Information Service).

11. *Statistical Masterfile.* [CD-ROM] (Washington, DC: Congressional Information Service).

12. *NTIS Bibliographic Data Base.* Available online through BRS and DIALOG; CD-ROM versions available from DIALOG, SilverPlatter, and OCLC.

13. *ERIC.* Available online through BRS, OCLC EPIC, and DIALOG; CD-ROM versions available from DIALOG, OCLC, and SilverPlatter.

14. *Guide to Official Publications of Foreign Countries.* (Bethesda, MD: Congressional Information Service, 1990).

15. *International Information: Documents, Publications, and Information Systems of International Governmental Organizations,* edited by Peter I. Hajnal. (Englewood, CO: Libraries Unlimited, 1988).

16. Vladimir M. Palic. *Government Publications; A Guide to Bibliographic Tools, Incorporating Government Organization Manuals;* a Bibliography. (Oxford: Pergamon Press, 1977).

17. Gloria Westfall. *Bibliography of Official Statistical Yearbooks and Bulletins.* (Alexandria, VA: Chadwyck-Healey, 1986).

18. Joan M. Harvey. *Statistics Africa.* 2nd ed. (Beckenham, Kent: CBD Research, 1978).

19. _____. *Statistics America.* 2nd ed. (Beckenham, Kent: CBD Research, 1980).

20. _____. *Statistics Asia and Australasia.* 2nd ed. (Beckenham, Kent: CBD Research, 1983).

21. _____. *Statistics Europe.* 5th ed. (Beckenham, Kent: CBD Research, 1987).

22. *Checklist of Government Directories, Lists, and Rosters.* (Westport, CT: Meckler Pub., 1982).

23. John E. Roberts. *A Guide to Official Gazettes and Their Contents.* (Washington, DC: Library of Congress, 1985). (nondepository; Law Library of Congress general publications have SuDoc stem LC42.2:).

24. *Guide to Microforms in Print.* Subject. 1978- (annual). (Westport, CT: Microform Review Inc.).

25. For more information write to Norman Ross Publishing Inc., 330 West 58th Street, New York, NY 10019.

26. Center for Research Libraries. *Handbook.* 1969- (irregular) (Chicago, IL: The Center).

27. *Directory of Government Document Collections & Librarians.* 1974- (Bethesda, MD: Congressional Information Service).

28. Carol A. Turner. *Directory of Foreign Document Collections.* (New York: UNIPUB, 1985).

29. Susan Dow. "A Selective Directory of Government Document Dealers, Jobbers, and Subscription Agents." *Serials Librarian* 14 (1988): 157-86.

30. For further information write to UNIPUB, 4611-F Assembly Drive, Lanham, MD 20706-4391.

31. Jerrold Orne. *The Language of the Foreign Book Trade; Abbreviations, Terms, Phrases.* 2nd ed. (Chicago: American Library Association, 1962).

32. *The Bibliographic Control of Official Publications.* Edited by John E. Pemberton. (Oxford: Pergamon, 1982), pp.151-52.

33. Ibid.

34. *Cataloging Government Documents: A Manual of Interpretation for AACR2.* Edited by Bernadine A. Hoduski. (Chicago: American Library Association, 1984).

35. Margaret S. Brill. "Government Publications as Bibliographic References in the Periodical Literature of International Relations: A Citation Analysis." *Government Information Quarterly* 7 (1990): 427-39.

36. Robert W. Schaaf. "International Organizations Documentation: Serving Research Needs of the Legal Community." *Government Publications Review* 13 (January-February 1986): 123-33.

37. International Labor Office. *Legislative Series.* 1919- (annual). (Geneva: International Labor Office).

38. *International Digest of Health Legislation.* 1- 1948- (quarterly) (Geneva: World Health organization).

39. *International Legal Materials.* Vol.1- 1962- (bimonthly). (Washington, DC: American Society of International Law).

40. *Martindale-Hubbell Law Directory.* 1932- (annual). (Summit, NJ: Martindale-Hubbell, Inc.). CD-ROM available from Bowker Electronic Publishing.

41. *Yearbook of International Organizations.* 11th- 1966/67- (irregular). Edited by Union of International Associations. (Munich: K.G. Saur).

42. *United Kingdom Official Publications.* [CD-ROM] 1980- (Cambridge: Chadwyck-Healey Ltd.). Available online through BLAISE-LINE and DIALOG.

43. *Computer-readable Databases.* 1989- (Detroit: Gale Research Inc.).

44. *DttP. Documents to the People.* 1972- (quarterly) (Chicago: American Library Association).

45. *Government Publications Review.* 1982- (bimonthly) (New York: Pergamon Press).

46. International Federation of Library Associations and Institutions. Official Publications Section. *Newsletter - IFLA Official Publications Section.* No.1- 1978- (irregular). (London, The Section).

47. INT-LAW is moderated by Mila Rush (M-RUSH@UMINN1.BITNET, phone (612) 625-0793) and Lyonette Louis-Jacques (L-LOUI@UMINN1.BITNET, phone (612) 625-5086 or (612) 626-7702). Both are at the University of Minnesota Law Library.

48. *Weekly Checklist of Canadian Government Publications.* 1978- (Ottawa: Canada Communication Group, Publishing Division).

49. *DOBIS Canadian Online Library System.* Available through the National Library of Canada, Information Technology Services, 395 Wellington St., Ottawa, ON, Canada K1A 0N4.

50. Olga B. Bishop. *Canadian Official Publications.* (Oxford: Pergamon Press, 1981).

51. *Organization of the Government of Canada.* 1990- (irregular) (Ottawa: Information Canada : Canadian Chamber of Commerce).

52. *Guide to Federal Programs and Services.* 1987- (annual) (Ottawa: Department of Supply and Services).

53. Canada. *The Canada Gazette* Part I, v.104- Jan. 3, 1970- (weekly). Part II: Statutory Instruments, 1972- (biweekly). Part III: Statutes of Canada, v.1- Dec. 13, 1974- (monthly). (Ottawa, Queen's Printer).

54. *Canadiana.* Jan. 15, 1951- (monthly except July and August). (Ottawa: National Library of Canada).

55. *Government of Canada Publications; Quarterly Catalogue.* vol.27- Jan/Mar 1979- (quarterly). (Ottawa: Canadian Government Publishing Centre).

56. *Microlog.* 10- 1988- (monthly) (Toronto: Micromedia). *Microlog Microfiche Collections.* 1983- (monthly) (Toronto: Micromedia). *Microlog on CD.* 1979- (Toronto: Micromedia).

57. Statistics Canada. *Statistics Canada Catalogue.* 1972- (annual). (Ottawa: Statistics Canada).

58. Statistics Canada. *Historical Catalogue of Statistics Canada Publications, 1918-1980.* (Ottawa: Statistics Canada, User Services Division, 1981).

59. *Historical Statistics of Canada.* 2nd ed. (Ottawa: Statistics Canada, 1983).

60. *Canada Handbook.* 46th- 1977- (annual). (Ottawa: Publishing Section, Information Division, Statistics Canada).

61. *Bibliography of Federal Data Sources; Excluding Statistics Canada 1981.* (Ottawa: Statistics Canada, User Services Division, Reference Products Section, 1982).

62. *CANSIM Time Series Main Base.* 1946- Available online from Statistics Canada, Electronic Data Dissemination Division and a number of other vendors; CD-ROM available from Micromedia Ltd.

63. *Canadian Statistics Index.* 1985- (Toronto: Micromedia Ltd.).

64. *Government of Canada Publications; Outline of Classification.* 4th ed. (Ottawa: Canadian Government Publishing Centre, 1984).

65. Peter I. Hajnal. *Guide to United Nations Organization, Documentation & Publishing for Students, Researchers, Librarians.* (Dobbs Ferry, NY: Oceana Publications, 1978).

66. *Everyone's United Nations.* 10th ed. (New York: United Nations, 1986).

67. United Nations. *United Nations Documentation; a Brief Guide* (New York: United Nations, 1981).

68. United Nations. Secretariat. *Instructions for Depository Libraries Receiving United Nations Material.* (New York: U.N. Secretariat, 1981).

69. United Nations. Office of Public Information. *Yearbook of the United Nations.* 1946/47- (annual). (New York: United Nations).

70. *UNDOC Current Index; United Nations Documents Index.* Vol.1- 1979- (monthly except July and August). (New York: United Nations, Dag Hammarskjold Library).

71. *Index to Proceedings of the Economic and Social Council.* 1953- (irregular). (New York: United Nations). *Index to Proceedings of the General Assembly.* 5th session- 1950/51- (irregular). (New York: United Nations). *Index to Proceedings of the Security Council.* 19th- 1964- (annual). (New York: United Nations). *Index to Proceedings of the Trusteeship Council.* 11th- 1952- (annual). (New York: United Nations).

72. *UN Chronicle.* Vol.12, no.4- Apr.1975- (quarterly). (New York: United Nations Office of Public Information).

73. *Treaty Series / United Nations.* Vol.1- 1946- (New York: United Nations).

74. *Demographic Yearbook.* 1st- 1948- (annual) (New York: Department of Economic and Social Affairs, Statistical Office, United Nations).

75. *Yearbook on Human Rights.* 1946- (annual?) (New York: United Nations).

76. *Directory of United Nations Information Systems.* 2nd ed. Vol. II. (Geneva: Inter-Organization Board for Information Systems, 1980).

77. *Electronic Index to United Nations Documents and Publications.* [CD-ROM] 1945- (New Canaan, CT: Readex).

78. *Europe.* 1979- (bimonthly) (Washington, Delegation of the Commission of the European Communities).

79. *Bulletin of the European Communities.* 1968- (monthly) (Brussels, Secretariat General of the Commission).

80. *EUROVOC: Annex to the Index of the Official Journal of the European Communities.* 2nd ed. (Luxembourg: Office for Official Publications of the European Communities, 1987-1990).

81. *European Communities Official Publications* [catalog]. (Lanham, MD: UNIPUB, 1991).

82. Write to the Office for Official Publications of the European Communities, L-2985 Luxembourg for a free copy.

83. *Official Journal of the European Communities.* 1973- (Luxembourg: Office for Official Publications of the European Communities).

84. *COM Documents.* [microfiche] 1983- (Brussels: The Commission of the European Communities).

85. *Session Documents. Series A, Reports.* [microfiche] 1987- (Luxembourg: European Parliament).

86. Ian Thomson. *The Documentation of the European Communities: A Guide.* (London: Mansell, 1989).

87. John A. Jeffries. *Guide to the Official Publications of the European Communities.* 2nd ed. (London: Mansell, 1981).

88. *EC Index.* 1984-1986. (Maastricht, The Netherlands: Europe Data).

89. *SCAD Bulletin.* 1986- (weekly) (Bruxelles: SCAD : Washington, DC: European Community Information Service [distributor]).

90. *SCAD.* Available online through EUROBASES.

91. *European Access.* 1988- (bimonthly) (Cambridge: Chadwyck-Healey Ltd.).

92. *Basic Statistics of the Community.* (annual) (Brussels: Statistical Office of the European Communities).

93. For further information contact the EUROSTAT Helpdesk, Telephone: 43014567 or Facsimile: 43014762.

## FURTHER READING

Cason, Maidel. "African Government Documents in Microform." *Microform Review* 14 (Fall 1985): 223-28.

Fetzer, Mary K. "United Nations Depositories: Status and Prospects." *Drexel Library Quarterly* 16 (October 1980): 87-103.

Ford, Barbara J. "Foreign Country Information from U.S. Government Publications." *Special Libraries* 72 (July 1981): 277-83.

George, Mary W. and Susan B. White. "A Virtual Treasure Hunt: Exploring International Documents on International Education." *Education Libraries* 11 (Spring 1986): 29-43.

Graham, Peter S. "Government Documents and Cataloging in Research Libraries." *Government Publications Review* 10 (January-February 1983): 117-25.

Hajnal, Peter I. "Access to Documents and Publications of International Organizations," in *Public Access to Government Information*, by Peter Hernon and Charles R. McClure, pp.361-84. Norwood, NJ: Ablex Pub. Corp., 1984.

Hallewell, Laurence. "Government Publishing in Brazil." *Government Information Quarterly* 1 (1984): 259-71.

Hinds, Thomas S. "The United Nations as a Publisher." *Government Publications Review* 12 (1985): 297-303.

Johnson, David G. "The British Library Lending Division and British Official Publications." *Government Publications Review* 3 (1976): 277-83.

Lopresti, Robert. "Analogous Reference Tools Produced by the U.S. and Canadian Federal Governments." *Government Publications Review* 18 (May/June 1991): 263-74.

Morton, Bruce and Steven D. Zink. "'We Are Here to Make Sure that Information is Available, Accessible, and Cost-Effective' an interview with Patricia Horner, Director of the Canadian Government Publishing Centre." *Government Publications Review* 17 (September/October 1990): 397-410.

Pfeister, Sue. "Maintenance and Control of an Uncataloged United Nations Documents Collection." *Illinois Libraries* 55 (March 1973): 129-32.

Rozkuszka, W. David. "The Art and Acquisition of Foreign Official Publications," in *Official Publications of Western Europe*, vol.1, edited by Eve Johansson, pp.1-11. London: Mansell, 1984.

Schaaf, Robert W. "Information Policies of International Organizations." *Government Publications Review* 17 (January/February 1990): 49-61.

_____. "International Organizations Documentation: Serving Research Needs of the Legal Community." *Government Publications Review* 13 (January-February 1986): 123-33.

Turner, David. "LC Seeks OK for Iraq Transactions: Publications Not Excluded from President's Embargo." *Library of Congress Information Bulletin* 49 (November 5, 1990): 370-71.

Windheuser, Christine S. "Government Mapping in the Developing Countries." *Government Publications Review* 10 (July-August 1983): 405-9.

Yeh, Thomas Y. "Government Publications of the People's Republic of China." *Government Publications Review* 14 (1987): 405-10.

## EXERCISES

Choose a country or an international organization. Using the sources and/or techniques described in this chapter plus your own ingenuity, compile a bibliography of important publications and documents for that country or IGO. Note how you discovered each title. Include, as appropriate, the following:

Name and address of the government printing office.

Name and address of the authorized distributor.

Title of the primary catalog or publications list.

A "Guide to the Literature" in article, chapter, or book form.

Periodical describing the activities and publications of an IGO.

National bibliography of a country.

Official gazette.

Statistical abstract.

Organization manual.

Yearbook or encyclopedia.

Laws and statutes.

Proceedings and debates.

Court decisions.

Microform availability.

On-line and CD-ROM databases.

List of depository libraries or libraries with large collections.

Other important or interesting items.

# APPENDIX 1
## Publishers, Suppliers, and Vendors of Online Searching

BNA Online
The Bureau of National Affairs, Inc.
1231 25th St., N.W.
Washington, DC 20037
(800) 862-4636, (202) 452-4132

BRS Information Technologies
1200 Route 7
Latham, NY 12110
(800) 345-4BRS, (518) 783-1161
(BRS/After Dark provides cheaper searching on weekends and evenings.)

Commerce Clearing House, Inc.
Electronic Legislative Search System
4025 W. Peterson Ave.
Chicago, IL 60646
(708) 940-4600

Compu-Mark
500 Victory Rd.
North Quincy, MA 02171-1545
(800) 421-7881, (617) 479-1600, FAX (617) 786-8273

CompuServe, Inc.
5000 Arlington Center Blvd.
Columbus, OH 43220
(614) 457-8600

Congressional Information Service, Inc.
4520 East-West Hwy., Suite 800
Bethesda, MD 20814-3389
(800) 638-8380, (301) 654-1550, FAX (301) 654-4033

Congressional Quarterly, Inc.
Washington Alert
1414 22nd St. NW
Washington, DC 20037
(202) 887-6366

Counterpoint Publishing
20 William St., Suite G-70, Box 9135
Wellesley, MA 02181
(617) 235-4667

Data-Star
485 Devon Park Dr., Suite 110
Wayne, PA 19087
(215) 687-6777

Derwent, Inc.
Suite 401, 1313 Dolley Madison Blvd.
McLean, VA 22101
(703) 790-0400, FAX (703) 790-1426

DIALOG Information Services
3460 Hillview Ave.
Palo Alto, CA 94303
(800) 3-DIALOG, in California (800) 982-5838
(Knowledge-Index allows cheaper nighttime searches of thirty-five of DIALOG's databases.)

William S. Hein & Co., Inc.
1285 Main St.
Buffalo, NY 14209-1987
(800) 828-7571, Manhattan (212) 283-3528, Washington (202) 393-3938, FAX (716) 883-8100

Information on Demand, Inc.
8000 Westpark Dr.
McLean, VA 22101
(800) 999-4463, (703) 442-0303

Institute for Scientific Information (ISI)
Genuine Article Service
3501 Market St.
Philadelphia, PA 19104
(800) 523-1850

LEGI-SLATE
777 N. Capitol St.
Washington, DC 20002
(800) 733-1131, (202) 898-2300, FAX (202) 898-3030

Martin Marietta Information Systems Group
Computing Services
4795 Meadow Wood Lane
Chantilly, VA 22021
(703) 802-5700

Mead Data Central
P. O. Box 1830
Dayton, OH 45401
(800) 227-4908

National Standards Association
1200 Quince Orchard Blvd.
Gaithersburg, MD 20878
(301) 590-2300

NERAC, Inc.
One Technology Dr.
Tolland, CT 06084
(203) 872-7000, FAX (203) 875-1749

NewsBank/Readex
58 Pine St.
New Canaan, CT 06840-5408
(800) 762-8182, (813) 263-6004, FAX (813) 263-3004

NISC National Information Services Corp.
Wyman Towers, Suite 6
3100 St. Paul St.
Baltimore, MD 21218
(301) 243-0797

OCLC
6565 Frantz Rd.
Dublin, OH 43017-3395
(800) 848-5878, in Ohio (800) 848-8286

ORBIT Online Products
8000 West Park Dr.
McLean, VA 22102
(800) 456-7248, (800) 421-7229, in Virginia
(703) 442-0900

PAIS
521 West 43rd St.
New York, NY 10036-4396
(800) 288-7247, in New York City (212) 736-6629

Readex Micro-print Corporation
58 Pine St.
New Canaan, CT 06840
(800) 762-8182, (813) 566-9122, FAX (813) 566-9134

Research Publications
Box 2527
Eads Station
Arlington, VA 22202
(800) 336-5010, FAX (703) 685-3987

Questel, Inc.
5201 Leesburg Pike, Suite 603
Falls Church, VA 22201
(800) 424-9600, (703) 845-1133

SDC Search Service
2500 Colorado Ave.
Santa Monica, CA 90406
(800) 421-7229

SilverPlatter
100 River Ridge Dr.
Norwood, MA 02062-5026
(800) 343-0064, in Massachusetts
 (617) 769-2599; FAX (617) 769-8763

STN International
c/o Chemical Abstracts Service
2540 Olentangy River Rd.
P. O. Box 02228
Columbus, OH 43202
(800) 848-6533, Ohio or Canada (800) 848-6538

Thomson & Thomson
500 Victory Rd.
North Quincy, MA 02171-1545
(800) 692-8833, (617) 479-1600, FAX (617) 786-8273

University Microfilms International
Article Clearinghouse
300 N. Zeeb Rd.
Ann Arbor, MI 48106
(800) 521-0600

University Publications of America
4520 East-West Hwy., No. 800
Bethesda, MD 20814-3319
(800) 692-6300, (301) 657-3200

Washington On-Line
Legi-Tech Corp.
1029 J St., Suite 450
Sacramento, CA 95814
(916) 447-1886

West Publishing Co.
Box 64526, 50 W. Kellogg Blvd.
St. Paul, MN 55164-0526
(800) 328-2209, (612) 228-2778

# APPENDIX 2
# For Further Research: Subject Headings
# from *Library Literature**

To search *Library Literature* for additional publications related to the topics covered in this book, the subject headings below will be useful.

*Chapter 1: Introduction to Government Information Resources*
Government Publications (and subheadings)
National Libraries

*Chapter 2: Access to Government Information*
Freedom of Information
Government Publications—History
Information Policy
Surveys—Freedom of Information

*Chapter 3: GPO, The Mother Lode*
Classification—Systems—Superintendent of Documents
Government Publications—Microform Reproductions
United States. Government Printing Office.

*Chapter 4: Depository Libraries: Federal Information Safety Net*
Depository Libraries
Surveys—Depository Libraries

*Chapter 5: Bibliographies and Indexes*
Government Publications—Indexes and Abstracts
Monthly Catalog of United States Government Publications
Periodicals, Government

*Chapter 6: Scientific Information*
Technical Reports
United States. National Agricultural Library.
United States. National Library of Medicine.
United States. National Technical Information Service.

*Chapter 7: Patents, Trademarks, and Copyrights*
Copyright (and subheadings)
Copyright Legislation

Information Systems—Special Subjects—Patents
Ownership of Materials
Patent Literature

*Chapter 8: Legislative Information Sources*
United States. Library of Congress.

*Chapter 9: Regulations*
(none)

*Chapter 10: Executive Branch Information Sources*
United States. National Archives and Records Administration. Libraries.

*Chapter 11: Judicial Information Sources*
United States. Supreme Court.

*Chapter 12: Statistics*
Research Materials—Special Subjects—Census Data

*Chapter 13: Nonprint and Primary Resources*
Archives, Government
Information Storage and Retrieval Systems—Special Subjects—Government Publications
United States. National Archives and Records Administration. National Audiovisual Center.

*Chapter 14: Overcoming Barriers to Access: Using Documents Reference Sources*
Government Publications—Bibliography
Government Publications—(names of states)
Municipal Publications
State Publications
Surveys—Government Publications
Use Studies—Government Publications

*Chapter 15: Foreign and International Documents*
European Economic Community Publications
Government Publications—(names of countries)
Periodicals, Government
United Nations
United Nations Publications

* *Library Literature* has been called "the standard professional index of American librarians . . . often used to the exclusion of all others." Patricia Tegler, "The Indexes and Abstracts of Library and Information Science," *Drexel Library Quarterly* 15 (July 1979), p. 11.

# APPENDIX 3
# SuDocs Numbers

The following is a referral list from many titles mentioned in the text (but not in references or bibliographies) to Superintendent of Documents Classification numbers.

*1900 Federal Population Census* GS 4.2:P 81/2/900
*1910 Federal Population Census* GS 4.2:P 81/2/910
*1980 Census User's Guide* C 3.223:80-nos.

*Abridged Index Medicus* HE 20.3612/2:
*ACCESS EPA* EP 1.8/13:Ac 2
*Administrative Notes* GP 3.16/3-2:
*AGRICOLA User's Guide* A 17.22:Ag 8
*Agricultural Statistics* A 1.47:

*Background Notes on the Countries of the World* S 1.123:
*Biographical Directory of the American Congress, 1774-1989* Y 1.1/3:100-34
*Budget of the U.S.* PrEx 2.8:
*Bureau of the Census Catalog of Publications, 1790-1972* C 56.222/2-2:790-972
*Business Statistics* C 59.11/3:

*Calendars of the House of Representatives* Y 1.2/2:
*Catalog of Copyright Entries* LC 3.6/6:
*Catalog of Government Inventions Available for Licensing* C 51.16/2:
*Census and You* C 3.238:
*Census Bureau Catalog and Guide* C 3.163/3:
*Census User's Guide (1980)* C 3.223:80-nos.
*A Century of Photographs, 1846-1946* LC 1.2:P 56/5/846-946
*CFR Index and Finding Aids* AE 2.106/3-2:
*Classification Definitions* C 21.3/2:
*Climatological Data* C 55.214:
*Code of Federal Regulations* AE 2.106/3:
    *Index and Finding Aids* AE 2.106/3-2:
    *List of CFR Sections Affected, 1964-72* GS 4.108:List/964-72/vol.
    *List of CFR Sections Affected, 1973-1985* AE 2.106/2-2:
*Codification of Presidential Proclamations and Executive Orders* AE 2.113:945-yr.
*Concordance: United States Patent Classification to International Patent Classification* C 21.14/2:C 74/990

*Condition of Education* ED 1.109:
*Congressional Directory* Y 4.P 93/1:1/cong
*Congressional District Atlas* C 3.62/5:
*Congressional Pictorial Directory* Y 4.P 93/1:1P/cong
*Congressional Record Index* X/a.Cong.-sess.:nos./ind.
*Congressional Record* X/a.Cong.-sess.:
*Constitution of the United States, Analysis and Interpretation* Y 1.1/3:99-16; 1990 supplement Y 1.1/3:101-36
*Constitution of the United States of America, as Amended: Analytical Index, Unratified Amendments* X 95-2:doc. 256
*Consumer Information Catalog* GS 11.9:
*Country Demographic Profiles* C 3.205/3:DP-nos.
*Country Study Series* D 101.22:550-no.
*County and City Data Book* C 3.134/2:
*CRS Review* LC 14.19:
*CRS Studies in the Public Domain* LC 14.20:
*Current Index to Journals in Education* ED 1.310/4:

*Daily Depository Shipping List* GP 3.16/3:
*Data User News* C 3.238:
*Decisions of the United States Courts Involving Copyright* LC 3.3/2:
*Decisions of the United States Courts Involving Copyright and Literary Property (1789-1909) with an Analytical Index* LC 3.3/3:
*The Department of Defense Index of Specifications and Standards* D 1.76:
*Dictionary of Occupational Titles* L 37.302:Oc 1
*Digest of Education Statistics* ED 1.113:
*Digest of Public General Bills and Resolutions* LC 14.6:
*Directory of Federal Laboratory and Technology Resources: A Guide to Services, Facilities, and Expertise* C 51.2:T 22/3/
*Directory of Federally Supported Information Analysis Centers* LC 1.31:In 3/979
*Directory of U.S. Depository Libraries* Y 4.P 93/1-10:
*Dispatch* S 1.3/5:
*Document Catalog* GP 3.6:

*Economic Indicators* Y 4.Ec 7:Ec 7/date
*Economic Report of the President* Pr_.9:
*Economic Statistics Data Finders* C 3.163/6:
*Economic Surveys Data Finder* C 3.163/6:Ec 7/2/985
*EIA Publications Directory* E 3.27:

# APPENDIX 4
# A Documents Toolkit

The titles below make up an inexpensive reference collection for information specialists working in non-depository libraries.

1. Because *Library of Congress Publications in Print* (LC 1.12/2:P 96/yr) includes SuDocs numbers and notes GPO availability, it is a quick reference for identifying LC depository items and GPO sales titles. This biennial is free from Library of Congress, Office Systems Services, Printing and Processing Section, Washington, DC 20540.

2. The *List of Classes of United States Government Publications Available for Selection by Depository Libraries* (GP 3.24: ) is a handy guide to depository materials, allowing referral from SuDocs stem to issuing agency and class titles. The list is helpful for quick verification of depository status, SuDocs number stem, or issuing agency (a key step in requesting free copies). Buy a single copy each year or invest slightly more to receive all four quarterly issues (consult Price List 36 for cost).

3. Price List 36, *Government Periodicals and Subscription Services*, (GP 3.9:36/nos.) not only lists government magazines sold by GPO, but also provides brief bibliographic information, including prices, SuDocs numbers, and annotations. Available free, with automatic quarterly updates, this is a handy source for quickly verifying title, SuDocs stem, frequency, or scope of GPO periodicals.

4 and 5. Every reference desk should have a set of **Subject Bibliographies** (GP 3.22/2: ), along with the **Subject Bibliography Index** (SB-599). Here is a quick referral set for identifying government publications on more than 300 topics. Sure, the titles listed are all for sale from GPO, but most are also in depository libraries, where users can consult them free. These short bibliographies offer a quick starting point for documents literature searches and a reminder of the availability of government titles on a topic. Many supply SuDocs numbers and even annotations.

# APPENDIX 5
# Solutions to Exercises

Solutions to exercises provide *suggested* search strategies: Many other approaches may be used to identify answers.

## Solutions to Exercises for Chapter 3

1. SuDocs number for the *Congressional Record*
   ANSWER: Consult Price List 36, alphabetically by title. This free quarterly pamphlet can be received automatically on standing request, and is recommended as part of a basic, free documents reference collection (see Appendix 4, A Documents Toolkit).

2. Sequencing SuDocs Numbers
   ANSWER: The shelf order for the SuDocs numbers exercise is given below. Note that D 101.2.A 8 is an impostor: a SuDocs number lookalike that is actually a Library of Congress class number. Remember that each SuDocs number will have two distinguishing characteristics: a letter or letters at the beginning, and a colon in the middle. With its initial D, this LC number resembles a SuDocs number for the Department of Defense, but it lacks a colon.

   D 101.2:N 56
   I 19.81:40121-B 3-TF-024/991
   J 21.2/10:988
   J 21.22:1
   LC 3.4/2:62 a
   LC 3.4/2:62/991
   Pr 41.8:P 96
   PrEx 2.2:C 86
   Y 3.T 22/2:2 C 73/13/v.2/pt.2/charac
   Y 3.T 22/2:2 T 22/24/v.2/pt.2/China
   D 101.2.A 8 = Library of Congress class number

## Solutions to Exercises for Chapter 4

1. General Information Concerning Patents
   ANSWER: The *List of Classes of United States Government Publications Available for Selection by Depository Libraries* (GP 3.24: ) provides a quick answer to this question. Because there is no title index, some familiarity with government agencies and SuDocs numbers is required: the appendix lists the Patent and Trademark Office as C 21. Skimming the document titles under PTO, you will find *General Information Concerning Patents* listed as Item 0256-A-02, SuDocs stem
   C 21.26/2: .

   The *List of Classes* is also useful for verifying depository document titles, and for determining issuing agency when the SuDocs number stem is known (an initial step in requesting free copies of recent publications).

2. Additional strategies for determining depository status
   ANSWER: OCLC, *Monthly Catalog*, or PRF (for GPO imprints) would all provide information about the depository status of *General Information Concerning Patents*. Depository indicators are "item" numbers (with or without the word item or a black bullet) and depository shipping list notations. Both or either may show up in bibliographic records.

   OCLC offers the advantage of speed (as do the commercial CD-ROM versions of the *Monthly Catalog*). If multiple records are available, chose those from DLC (Library of Congress) or GPO. OCLC 3362926 (1992 edition) notes depository item number in field 074, but omits the word "item." Learning to recognize item number configurations and fields in OCLC makes you independent of omitted clues. GPO's hardcopy *Monthly Catalog* adds the black-bullet crutch, but the commercial *Monthly Catalog* CD-ROMs and the PRF do not. GPO sales catalogs like Subject Bibliography 021 tend to note the SuDocs number, GPO stock number and price, but omit any reference to availability in depository libraries.

## Solutions to Exercises for Chapter 5

1. Depository Use Study
   ANSWER: McClure, Charles R. and Peter Hernon. *Users of Academic and Public GPO Depository Libraries.* GPO, 1989. (GP 3.2:Us 2) Depository status
   TIPS: This information could have been identified using the PRF (as of September 1991), *Monthly Catalog* (89-14241), or an OCLC author search (OCLC 19866610).

2. FBI Library Awareness Program
   ANSWER: House. Committee on the Judiciary. Subcommittee on Civil and Constitutional Rights. *FBI Counterintelligence Visits to Libraries.* GPO, 1989. (Y 4.J 89/1:100/123) Depository status
   TIPS: This information was identified using the *Monthly Catalog* (89-12353). Because no author or title was provided, OCLC could not be used. Because the title is a congressional

hearing, it was also located in PAIS, which identifies its SuDocs number (SD cat. no.) but gives no indication of depository status.

3. USDA "Farmers' Bulletins"
ANSWER: Pre-1976 USDA "Farmers' Bulletins" can be identified using the old-format *Monthly Catalog.*
TIPS: In the old-format *Monthly Catalog*, series numbers follow the entry number and must be appended to the SuDocs stem to complete each title's unique SuDocs number. In the entry below, for example, the complete SuDocs number for *Beef Cattle, Dehorning, Castrating, Branding and Marking* is A 1.9:2141. The series number, 2141, has been added to the SuDocs stem listed at the head of the entry.

```
        Farmers' bulletins.  ● Item 9                          A 1.9:(nos.)
  1214   2141. Beef cattle, dehorning, castrating, branding and marking; [by R. T. Clark,
               A. L. Baker and George E. Whitmore]. [Nov. 1959, slightly revised
               Dec. 1967.] [1967.] 16 p. il. ([Animal Husbandry Research Division,
               Agricultural Research Service.]) [Supersedes Farmers' bulletin 1600.]
               ● Paper, 10c.
  1215   2152. Slaughtering, cutting, and processing lamb and mutton on farm; [prepared
               by Animal Husbandry Research Division, Agricultural Research Service].
               [Aug. 1960, slightly revised Dec. 1967.] [1967.] 16 p. il. [Supersedes
               Farmers' bulletin 1807, Lamb and mutton on farm.] ● Paper, 10c.
  1216  Growth country, living country, remarks by Secretary of Agriculture
               Orville L. Freeman at opening of rural industrialization meeting, History
               and Technology Building, Smithsonian Institution, Washington, D.C.,
               Sept. 27, 1967. [1967.] 11 p. 4° (2859; USDA 3061-67.) †
```

4. Thomas Jefferson's Catalog
ANSWER: Library of Congress. *Thomas Jefferson's Library: A Catalog with the Entries in His Own Order.* GPO, 1989. (LC 1.2:T 36) Depository status
TIPS: This information could have been identified using the PRF (as of September 1991) or the *Monthly Catalog*: subject index under the LCSH "Jefferson, Thomas - 1743-1826 - Library - Catalogs," or keyword index under "Thomas," "Library," or "Catalog" (89-14955). An OCLC author search (Jeff,Tho) would also retrieve it (OCLC 19124971): Note that the number 786 in Field 074 is the item number, indicating depository status.

This title was also listed in the 1991 *Subject Guide to Books in Print* under the subject heading "Jefferson, Thomas, Pres. U. S., 1743-1826" (arrangement under the subject heading is alphabetical by authors' or editors' names; Gilreath, James is the editor). BIP listed USGPO as publisher, but did not note availability for free use in depository libraries. BIP did not list this under Thomas Jefferson as author.

Anyone correctly guessing that the Library of Congress published this title could verify it in the 1991 *Library of Congress Publications in Print* (not knowing the title, you could search under "Jefferson" in the index), which lists Sudocs number, GPO stock number, and price, but gives no indication of depository status.

5. *The KGB and the Library Target*
ANSWER: FBI. *The KGB and the Library Target, 1962-present.* FBI, [1988]. Not depository; no SuDocs number
TIPS: This title was not listed in PRF or *Monthly Catalog*. A title search of OCLC (kgb,an,th,l) located the document (OCLC 22544867), but indicated neither a SuDocs nor item number. The title was also located through an ERIC search, as *The FBI's Library Awareness Program: National Security vs. Government Intrusion into American Libraries [and] The KGB and the Library Target* (EJ 399470). The EJ number indicates this was cited in *Current Index to Journals in Education* and therefore is a journal article.

6. Core Depository Titles

POSSIBLE PITFALL: locating the short GPO Subject Bibliography about a title rather than the title itself. Hints that you've found a SB are: (1) a SuDocs number indicating GPO is the issuing agency (GP 3.22/2: ), (2) collation indicating a title of only a few pages, and (3) a citation that identifies it as a Subject Bibliography and notes SB number.
TIP: Because most of the core depository titles are serials, they can be quickly identified using the *Monthly Catalog* Periodicals Supplement. The Periodicals Supplement gives open entries rather than citing individual issues as the regular *Monthly Catalog* will do.

```
91-2266
                    GP 3.22/2:228/990
United States. Superintendent of Documents.
      Congressional directory. — [Washington, D.C.] : U.S.
G.P.O., Supt. of Docs., [1990]
      [1] leaf ; 28 cm. — (Subject bibliography ; SB-228)  Caption
title.  Shipping list no.: 90-628-P.  "August 21, 1990."  ●Item
552-A
      1. Government publications — United States — Bibliogra-
phy — Catalogs.  2. United States. Congress — Directories —
Bibliography — Catalogs.  I. Title.  II. Series: United States.
Superintendent of Documents. Subject bibliography ; SB-228.
OCLC 22541901
```

## Solutions to Exercises for Chapter 6

1. Bibliographic Verification
SEARCH STRATEGY: Title searches can be performed in the NTIS Bibliographic Database or on the NTIS CD-ROM, but GRA & I does not offer a title index. Unless the separately published, microfiche *NTIS Current Title Index* is available, title searches in GRA & I must be converted to subject searches using the keyword index.

a. Defense Technical Information Center. *How to Get It: A Guide to Defense-Related Information Sources.* NTIS, 1988. AD-A 201 600
ANSWER: The NTIS cite gives no hint that this title is available in depository libraries. OCLC 18436796 notes depository item number, shipping list number, and SuDocs number: clues to the knowledgeable searcher that the title is available for free use in depository libraries. Availability from GPO is not mentioned in the OCLC cite, nor is availability from NTIS.
*Monthly Catalog* notes a non-GPO stock number (S/N AD-A 201 @ Defense Technical Information Center) and a technical report number (STRN: DTIC/TR-89/1), yet does not mention availability from NTIS.

b. FBI. *The KGB and the Library Target, 1962-present.* FBI, [1988]. Available from NTIS - PB88-239645 (FBI is called Performing Organization)
ANSWER: This title could be identified in GRA & I through a subject search (USSR, "Espionage," "Libraries," "Infiltration (Personnel)," and others), or by performing organization.
OCLC (19890918) included no mention of NTIS or a PB number.

c. Gilreath, C. L. *AGRICOLA User's Guide.* NTIS, 1984. PB85-100618.

ANSWER: Note that the first two digits of the PB number give an idea when the title should appear in GRA & I. The GRA & I citation omits SuDocs number (A 17.22:Ag 8).

d. *The Effects of Electronic Recordkeeping on the Historical Record of the U.S. Government: A Report for the National Archives and Records Administration*. NTIS, 1989. PB89-152219

ANSWER: This could be identified by searching GRA & I under performing organization (National Academy of Public Administration), sponsoring organization (NARA), or by subject ("Archives," "Records management," "Document storage," and others). Of course, if the PB number were known it would be a speedy access point.

OCLC (19372104) included no mention of NTIS or a PB number.

e. Hasty, T. J. *Protection of Personal Privacy Interests Under the Freedom of Information Act*. NTIS, 1991. AD-A242 183 (Air Force Academy = performing organization)

Not in OCLC.

f. *Managing Federal Information Resources: Annual Report (1st) Under the Paperwork Reduction Act of 1980*. NTIS, 1982. PB82-194473

ANSWER: This cite was identified through the Corporate Author index, searching Office of Management and Budget. Oddly, none of the following keywords located the cite in the keyword index: "Paperwork Reduction Act," "Information" (or any of its subheadings), "Federal Agencies," or "Government." Although issued more than a decade ago, this title can still be purchased from NTIS. Price can be determined by translating the price code noted in 1982 into today's prices, using a recent GRA & I issue.

While the GRA & I citation omitted SuDocs number (PrEx 2.25: ), it was included in the OCLC record (9752396) along with notation of depository status (853-A-5 microfiche = item number).

g. *Federal Government Information Technology: Electronic Record Systems and Individual Privacy* NTIS, 1986. PB87-100335

ANSWER: This demonstrates the helpfulness of supplying detailed information in technical report citations. The cite could be located in the Report Number index under OTA-CIT-296; in the Corporate Author index under Office of Technology Assessment; and in the Keyword index under "Federal Government," "Electronic Records Systems," or "Privacy." If the PB number were known, it could have been identified in the Order Number index. Note that although the report was issued in 1986, it did not appear in GRA & I until 1987. In online or CD-ROM searches, this would not need to be considered, because these media cumulate all cites for one-stop searching.

OCLC 13845006 includes SuDocs number (Y 3.T 22/2:2 El 2/6), a GPO stock number and price (current availability must be verified in PRF), and notes depository status with an item number (1070-M).

2. STAR: Space Shuttle *Challenger* Accident report Presidential Commission on the Space Shuttle Challenger Acci-

dent. *Report of the Presidential Commission on the Space Shuttle Challenger Accident, Volume 1*. NTIS or GPO, 1986. N86-24726

ANSWER: The STAR citation included the NTIS accession number (N86-24726) and NTIS price code. (GPO price is also given, but would have to be verified in PRF before purchase.)

OCLC 13742794 notes depository item number, shipping list number, GPO stock number, and SuDocs number: clues that the title is available for free use in depository libraries and was for sale from GPO when it was issued (needs verification in PRF for current purchase).

3. NTIS video
ANSWER: No search is necessary to answer this question. PR numbers indicate free brochures describing NTIS products and services. PR-858 tells you that this is free from NTIS.

## Solutions to Exercises for Chapter 7

1. Patent Number Search

Consult the *Official Gazette* weekly issue in which the patent number appears. Patent abstracts are listed in patent number order.

2. Patent Name Search
SEARCH STRATEGY:

**Step One:** Consult the annual *Index of Patents* (C 21.5/2: ), "Part I, List of Patentees," for the year the patent was issued to identify patent number. Or, consult the microfiche *Patentee/Assignee Index* (C 21.27: ) which lists patentees and assignees from the last five or six years, with corresponding patent numbers. For recent patents, CASSIS can be searched by inventor's name to identify patent number.

**Step Two:** The volume of *Official Gazette* in which the patent number appears must be identified before the OG patent abstract can be located. To determine which OG issue the patent number appeared in, consult the table in Part II of the annual *Index of Patents*, "List of Patent, Design, Plant Patent, Reissue and Defensive Publication Numbers Appearing in the Individual Issues of the Official Gazette for [year]."

ANSWERS:

a. # 4,438,032 Unique T-Lymphocyte Line and Products Derived Therefrom *Official Gazette* (March 20, 1984)
b. # 4,704,583 Light Amplifiers Employing Collisions to Produce a Population Inversion *Official Gazette* (November 3, 1987)
c. # 4,736,866 Transgenic Non-Human Mammals *Official Gazette* (April 12, 1988)
d. # 2,415,012 Toy and Process of Use *Official Gazette* (January 28, 1947)
e. # 395,781 Art of Compiling Statistics *Official Gazette* (January 8, 1889)
f. 4,259,444 Microorganisms Having Multiple Compatible Degradative Energy-Generating Plasmids and Preparation Thereof *Official Gazette* (March 31, 1981)

3. The author has mixed his metaphors—one does not "patent a trademark," nor can names or titles be patented. The name BARTLETT was registered as a trademark.

## Solutions to Exercises for Chapter 8

1. Smokey Bear: Historical Search
   ANSWER: S. 2322; P. L. 82-359, accompanied by H. Rpt. [82]-1512 and S. Rpt. [82]-1128; 66 Stat. 92
   SEARCH STRATEGY: 1952 *Monthly Catalog* subject index, under "Smokey Bear," refers to *Monthly Catalog* entry numbers for both the law and the House and Senate reports.
   1952 Senate *Journal:* "Smokey Bear" in index refers to H.R. 5790 in the "House Bills" section, which gives a legislative history and notes that S. 2322 was passed in lieu. In the "Senate Bills" section, the legislative history of S. 2322 notes Public Law number. Similar information could be located using the House *Journal.*
   *Congressional Record Index*, vol. 98, subject search, or "History of Bills and Resolutions" under S. 2322.

2. NTIS Privatization
   ANSWER: House. Committee on Science, Space, and Technology. Subcommittee on Science, Research and Technology. *Hearing on the Privatization of the National Technical Information Service, and H. R. 812, The National Quality Improvement Award Act of 1987* 100-1 March 4, 1987 (No. 5) (Y 4. Sci2:100/5)
   SEARCH STRATEGY: Searching "National Technical Information Service" in *CIS/Index* or its online or CD-ROM equivalents nets several NTIS privatization hearings citations. SuDocs numbers, depository status notation (Item No.), and CIS accession numbers facilitate access to the full text. Hearings are not included in the Serial Set. A *CIS/Index* subject search also unearths P. L. 100-519, the National Institute of Standards and Technology Authorization Act for FY89, which confirmed NTIS's protection from privatization.
   *Monthly Catalog* subject index reveals citations to the hearings, but without abstracts.

3. *Titanic* Investigation: Historical Search
   ANSWER: During the 62nd Congress, the Senate issued Documents 726 and 933, and S. Rpt. 806.
   SEARCH STRATEGY: These can be identified through subject searches of the *Congressional Record Index, CIS Congressional Serial Set Index,* or *Congressional Masterfile 1* (which includes the CIS *Committee Hearings Index),* or the *Document Catalog.*
   Although S. Doc. 726 was a hearing (hearings are not part of the Serial Set), it was ordered printed as a Senate Document, placing it in the Serial Set. Thus, S. Doc. 726 is cited in CIS's *Congressional Committee Hearings Index, Serial Set Index,* and *Congressional Masterfile 1* on CD-ROM.
   The *Congressional Record Index* cites the Senate Report and Documents plus numerous bills, speeches, and remarks in the *Congressional Record* but not incorporated into the Serial Set because they were neither Reports nor Documents.

4. *Congressional Record* Reform
   SEARCH STRATEGY: For activity in the current Congress, subject search any of the following:

*U.S. Code Congressional and Administrative News*
*CIS/Index* or *Congressional Masterfile 2*
House *Calendars*
*Congressional Index*
*Congressional Record Index*
*Digest of Public General Bills and Resolutions*

Retrospective materials: A search of previous Congresses should unearth H. Res. 230 (1985) which mandated that inserted unspoken remarks in the House were distinguished by an alternate typeface during the 99th Congress. This could be identified using *CIS/Index*, 1985 H423-5: *Accuracy in House Proceedings Resolution.* 99-1; H. Rpt. 99-228 (Y 1.1/8:99-228). Note the reflection of the House Report number after the SuDocs stem. The final issue of the House *Calendars* for the 99th Congress gives a legislative history of H. Res. 230.
   Also: *Task Force on the Congressional Record: Prepared for the Committee on House Administration of the U.S. House of Representatives.* 101-2 (Committee Print) GPO, 1990. Y 4.H81/3:C 76/3

5. Hearings—FBI Library Awareness Program
   ANSWER: House. Committee on the Judiciary. Subcommittee on Civil and Constitutional Rights. *FBI Counterintelligence Visits to Libraries.* GPO, 1989. (Y 4.J89/1:100/123)
   SEARCH STRATEGY: This information could have been identified through a subject search of *CIS/Index* or *Congressional Masterfile 2* (1989 H521-64).

6. Disposal of Patent Models: Historical Search
   ANSWER: *Disposition of Old Patent Office Models*, S. Rpt. 1062 and H. Rpt. 1102 (both from the 68th Congress, 2nd session.) These will be in the Serial Set because they are congressional Reports.
   SEARCH STRATEGY: Report and serial numbers can be identified through a subject search of *CIS Congressional Serial Set Index* or *Congressional Masterfile 1* (which also lists historical hearings and committee prints not in the Serial Set but cited in the CIS congressional hearings and committee prints indexes).

7. The Federal Information Resources Management Act of 1989
   ANSWER: It was never enacted into law, and died at the conclusion of the 101st Congress. (If enacted, the final statement in a legislative history will note public law number and approval date.)
   SEARCH STRATEGY: Consult House *Calendars*, final edition for 101-2, "History of Bills and Resolutions" section under bill number: No action was taken on the bill after it was reported from the Senate Governmental Affairs Committee (S. Rpt. 101-487).
   Similar information can be located by searching under bill number in the 1990 editions of:

House or Senate *Journal*
*Congressional Record Index*

8. Free *Congressional Record* from Legislators
   ANSWER: 44 USC 906
   SEARCH STRATEGY: A subject search of the indexes to *U.S. Code*, USCA, or USCS retrieves the "gratuitous copies" sections of Title 44, Chapter 9 - CONGRESSIONAL RECORD.

## Solutions to Exercises for Chapter 9

1.  The FDA's "Top 20"

    ANSWER: The 1991 annual cumulation of the *Federal Register Index* lists the top foods lists as proposed rules under the heading "Food and Drug Administration," citing 56 FR 30468 and 56 FR 43964; the final rules will appear in 21 CFR 101.42, and can also be identified using the *CFR Index*.

2.  FR/CFR Citations

    ANSWER: Do subject searches in either *CIS Federal Register Index, Federal Index, Federal Register Index, Federal Register Abstracts, CFR Index and Finding Aids*, CIS *Index to the CFR*, LEXIS, or WESTLAW.

    a.  Patent models: 37 CFR 1.91 and 37 CFR 1.92

    b.  Circular A-130: A proposed revision appeared in the *Federal Register* in April 1992 to solicit public comments (57 FR 18296). If finalized, the circular will be printed in the FR, but because it is a circular rather than a regulation it will not be incorporated into the CFR.

    c.  Presidential gifts: 12 CFR 264b.3; 3 CFR 100.735-14

    d.  Mayonnaise: 21 CFR 169.140

    e.  Cottage cheese: 21 CFR 133.128

    f.  Carry-on baggage: 14 CFR 91.523

    g.  Child safety seats: 49 CFR 571.213

## Solutions to Exercises for Chapter 10

1.  Patent Cooperation Treaty
    ANSWER: PCT entered into force January 24, 1978; 28 UST 7645, TIAS 8733
    SEARCH STRATEGY: Search *Treaties in Force* subject index ("patents") to identify ratification date, TIAS number, UST citation, plus a list of nations party to PCT. The treaty text can be consulted in either 28 UST 7645 (volume 28, page 7645) or TIAS (by TIAS number).

    For background information, search for legislative history in *CIS/Index* or its electronic equivalents. Remembering that treaties can stagnate for years awaiting congressional action, search backwards from the ratification date (or, more quickly, by treaty title in *Congressional Masterfile 2*). The legislative history for Patent Cooperation Treaty, P.L. 94-131 (1975), lists a House and Senate report and a House hearing (the House and Senate reports will be in the Serial Set.)

2.  Executive Order 9568
    ANSWER: E. O. 9568, "Providing for the Release of Scientific Information," June 8, 1945
    SEARCH STRATEGY: Retrospective search
    E. O. 9568 could quickly be identified using *CIS Index to Presidential Orders and Proclamations, 1789-1983*, by E. O. number, or by searching the subject index ("Demobilization," "Security Classification of Documents," or "Technology transfer"). The section called "Index of Interrelated Orders and Proclamations" lists subsequent, related executive orders.

Both the current Title 3 CFR and *Codification of Presidential Proclamations and Executive Orders, April 13, 1945-January 20, 1989* omit E. O. 9568. Why? Because Truman's executive order was later superseded, losing its legal effect. The "Disposition Tables" list E. O. 9568, citing later executive orders which superseded it. *Code of Federal Regulations, Title 3—The President, 1936-1975 Consolidated Tables* also lists it in the "Disposition Tables," as an inactive E. O.

In libraries with hearty retrospective collections, the text could also be found in the 1945 *U.S. Code Congressional and Administrative News* (search index under "Executive Orders"), *Federal Register*, or in the 1943-1948 Compilation of 3 CFR, in chronological order under issue date.

3.  Geography Awareness Week
    SEARCH STRATEGY:
    To locate a citation, search *Federal Register Index* (use the "Federal Register Pages and Dates" to determine which issue), *Federal Index, U.S. Code Congressional and Administrative News*, or CIS *Federal Register Index* under "Presidential Documents" or subject. Depending on its recency, the text of the proclamation can be found in *Federal Register, Weekly Compilation of Presidential Documents, U.S. Code Congressional and Administrative News* (under Proc. number), Title 3 of the CFR (Proc. number), *Codification of Presidential Proclamations and Executive Orders* (under subject or E.O. number), *Public Papers of the Presidents* (under issue date), *CQ Almanac* (issue date), LEXIS, or WESTLAW. The easiest sources to use for recent proclamations are *Federal Register Index, Federal Index*, USCCAN, or CIS *Federal Register Index*.

    Because many presidential proclamations are triggered by congressional joint resolutions, congressional indexes could also be searched by subject or proclamation title. The joint resolution is usually worded differently than the presidential proclamation, but concludes with the phrase, "*Resolved by the Senate and House of Representatives of the United States of America in Congress assembled*, That [date] is designated as [topic], and the President is authorized and requested to issue a proclamation. . . ." The presidential proclamation is usually issued at about the same time as the joint resolution.

4.  Classification E. O.
    ANSWER: E. O. 12356 (April 2, 1982)
    SEARCH STRATEGY: Because it is still in effect, a subject search ("Security, national") of *Codification of Presidential Proclamations and Executive Orders, April 13, 1945-January 20, 1989* provides the E. O. number and the text of the E. O.

## Solutions to Exercises for Chapter 11

1.  Nixon Papers
    ANSWER: *Nixon* v. *Administrator of General Services*, 433 US 425
    SEARCH STRATEGY: We are seeking a Supreme Court decision rendered in 1977; Richard M. Nixon was the plaintiff, and the United States government was the defendant.

    A logical starting point would be a legal digest, with its indexes to Supreme Court decisions. Searching the "Table of Cases" in the *Digest of United States Supreme Court Reports, Lawyer's Edition* under "Nixon" locates a citation in *United States Reports: Nixon* v. *Administrator of General Services,* 433 US 425. (It helps to realize that the Nixon materials were placed in the custody of the National Archives, a division of the General Services Administration: see Chapter 10.) To read the text of the decision, consult the official or unofficial Supreme Court reporter (the digest notes parallel citations in West and the Lawyers Edition).

2. Census Lawsuit
   ANSWER: 499 US 1068
   SEARCH STRATEGY: We are seeking a decision from an unknown (but probably federal) court; we know only the names of plaintiff and defendant.

   A logical starting point would be *Federal Practice Digest,* since it covers the entire federal court system. Searching the table of cases under the names of the parties locates cites to *United States Reports* and parallel citations in West (SCt) and the Lawyers Edition (LEd2d), where the text of the case can be read. (The text clarifies that Klutznick was the Secretary of Commerce: The Bureau of the Census is a subunit of Commerce.)

3. Verbatim Transcripts
   ANSWER: 771 F.2d 539 (D.C. Cir 1985)
   SEARCH STRATEGY: Consult the "Federal Court Decisions" table in Chapter 11. The abbreviation F.2d refers to decisions from U.S. courts of appeals reprinted in the *Federal Reporter.* The U.S. district courts comprise twelve circuits, one of which is the District of Columbia (D.C. Cir).

4. Supreme Court Citations
   ANSWER:    102 S. Ct. 87
              454 U.S. 812
              77 L.Ed.2nd 317
   STRATEGY: Peruse the citations to identify abbreviations for the official (U.S.) and unofficial (S. Ct. and L.Ed.2nd) Supreme Court reporters.

## Solutions to Exercises for Chapter 12

1. Population of the U.S.
   ANSWER: The answer to this question is ever changing.
   SEARCH STRATEGY: The easiest and quickest answer source is the latest *Statistical Abstract.* A more current answer would be available through CENDATA or a recent Census Bureau population survey.

2. Identify Answers or Probable Answer Sources
   a. Science literacy
      ANSWER SOURCE: *Statistical Abstract of the United States,* "Test Scores-High School Graduates," includes science test results. The *Abstract* notes *Digest of Education Statistics* as the data source. The *Digest* could be also identified using ASI: subject search ("Scientific education," "Educational attainment," or "Educational tests") or Index by Categories (Demographic breakdowns-by age-education).

   b. 1991 Harris privacy poll
      ANSWER: *Harris-Equifax Consumer Privacy Survey 1991*
      ANSWER SOURCE: SRI. First, remember that polls = statistics. Because Harris polls are not government surveys, we are looking for U.S. nonfederal statistics. A subject search ("Right to Privacy" or "Harris, Louis,

   and Associates") retrieves the report (the SRI annotation mentions "level of concern regarding threats to privacy"). It is available from Equifax Inc. or SRI (SRI/MF/complete).

   c. Patents granted to non-Americans
      ANSWER SOURCE: ASI. A subject search ("Patents" or "Patent and Trademark Office") yields the *Commissioner of Patents and Trademarks Annual Report.* The annotation mentions "Patents issued by the U.S. to residents of foreign countries." Remember that because annual reports summarize statistics about agency activities, they are likely to be indexed and abstracted in ASI.

   d. McClure and Hernon's report on depository use of census data
      ANSWER: McClure, Charles R. and Peter Hernon. *Use of Census Bureau Data in GPO Depository Libraries: Future Issues and Trends.* 1990 (C 3.2:D 26/9) is available in depository libraries, and for sale from ASI on microfiche.
      ANSWER SOURCE: ASI, author or subject search. ASI notes depository status (item number), SuDocs number, and ASI microfiche availability (ASI/MF/4). ASI was selected because this study was commissioned by the government. When unsure whether the title sought is federal or nonfederal, use *Statistical Masterfile,* which allows searching across both ASI and SRI.

   e. NTIS titles
      ANSWER: *Directory of Computerized Data Files* was replaced by *Directory of U.S. Government Datafiles for Mainframes and Microcomputers* in 1989.
      ANSWER SOURCE: Although this may not appear to be a "statistics" question, the answer is found in ASI (1991) because computer data files are statistical files. (Moral: never underestimate the scope of ASI.) Search by title (*Directory of U.S. Government Datafiles for Mainframes and Microcomputers*) or subject (NTIS or "Computer Data File Guides") to locate the description under "National Technical Information Service–Annuals and Biennials." The citation not only gives the NTIS PB number, but also notes depository status and SuDocs number. It can be purchased from NTIS or ASI (ASI/MF/5).

## Solutions to Exercises for Chapter 13

1. Challenger Accident Archival Records
   SEARCH STRATEGY: *Guide to the National Archives of the United States* (AE 1.108:N21) appears to be a logical starting point, but is merely a reprint of the 1974 edition, supplemented with an appendix of record groups added between 1970 and 1977—not current enough to answer this question.

   Because many of NARA's finding aids are unpublished and inaccessible outside the Archives, the next step would be to pose your question to NARA directly. Consult "National Archives Primary Reference Contact List," or "Information about the National Archives for Prospective Researchers," (AE 1.113:30) to identify an initial contact. Your NARA expert will advise you that the Challenger records are in Record Group 220: Records of Temporary

Committees, Commissions, and Boards, and are scattered among several NARA units according to their media format. An index to the collection may be consulted at NARA or purchased on paper, microfiche, or computer tape. A handout describing Challenger records, "Information for Researchers: Records of the Presidential Commission on the Space Shuttle Challenger Accident," is free from NARA.

2. Farm Security Administration photos
   SEARCH STRATEGY: *Special Collections in the Library of Congress* (LC 1.6/4:C 68) describes the Farm Security Administration Collection, "probably the most famous pictorial record of American life in the 1930s," held in LC's Prints and Photographs Division. Brochures describing the Division's collections and services are free upon request.
   The *Guide to the Holdings of the Still Picture Branch of the National Archives and Records Administration* (AE 1.108:St 5) indicates that the National Archives also holds a collection of FSA photographs in Record Group 96, Records of the Farmers Home Administration.

3. Government-produced videos
   SEARCH STRATEGY: First, check the *Media Resource Catalog* (AE 1.110/4: ), but remember that it reflects only a partial listing of NAC titles. A comprehensive search requires accessing the NAC Master Data File, conducted by NAC Customer Service staff in response to telephone or written inquiries.

4. NARA most-requested photo
   SEARCH STRATEGY: *Guide to the Holdings of the Still Picture Branch of the National Archives and Records Administration* (AE 1.108:St 5) appears to be a logical starting point, but does not provide an answer. Once again, pose the question directly to NARA by contacting the Still Pictures Branch Research Room. You will discover that a 1970 snapshot of Elvis Presley and President Nixon shaking hands is the National Archives' most-requested photo. (Before this photograph became publicly available in 1980, the favorites were a portrait of Abraham Lincoln and a photo of Pearl Harbor being bombed by the Japanese.) The Nixon/Presley photo is held in the Nixon Presidential Materials Project, which archives Nixon's official presidential papers and the Nixon audiotapes: Nixon Presidential Materials Staff (NLNP), National Archives, Washington, DC 20408; (703)756-5498.

## Solutions to Exercises for Chapter 14

1. Official title of the Watergate report
   ANSWER: *Report, Watergate Special Prosecution Force*, (J 1.2:W 29) and *Final Report, Watergate Special Prosecution Force* (J 1.2:W 29/977). Consult Bernier and Wood's *Popular Names of U.S. Government Reports: A Catalog* (LC 6.2:G 74/984) to translate from the short, popular report name to its official title and issuing agency. This source provides *Monthly Catalog* entry numbers to expedite access to further bibliographic information.
   NOTE: the two titles cited in *Popular Names of U.S. Government Reports* are only two of numerous Watergate materials. A search of *CIS/Index* or *Congressional Masterfile 2*, for example, will yield citations to numerous impeachment hearings and related materials.

2. Ethnic composition of counties
   ANSWER: Consult the statistical compendia that focuses on county-level data: *County and City Data Book* (C 3.134/2:C 83/2/yr.). Another profitable source would be *American Statistics Index*, using the "Index by Categories" to locate tables that include data broken down by (1) county, and (2) race. Remember that although ASI covers federally generated statistics, the federal government gathers statistics on diverse subjects and numerous geographic regions.

3. Foreign country data
   ANSWER: Search the *Statistical Masterfile* or ASI, using the "Index by Categories" to locate tables that include data broken down by foreign countries. Such a search would locate statistical compendia like the CIA's *World Factbook* and *Handbook of Economic Statistics*, plus reports from the Census Bureau's Center for International Research. *Statistical Masterfile* also includes *Index to International Statistics*, indexing statistics issued by international intergovernmental organizations. *PAIS International* indexes international organizations' statistical publications related to public policy issues. The *Statistical Abstract of the United States* includes an appendix, "Guide to Sources of Statistics, State Statistical Abstracts, and Foreign Statistical Abstracts," listing sources of data about foreign countries.

# Index

by Linda Webster

Office for Official Publications (OOPEC), 192
Office of Disease Prevention and Health Promotion (ODPHP), 58-59, 64-65, 151
Office of Educational Research and Improvement (OERI), 148, 151
Office of Federal Supply and Services, 63
Office of Information and Regulatory Affairs (OIRA), 106
Office of Legislative Information, 98, 102
Office of Management and Budget (OMB), 4, 8-9, 43, 50, 106, 123, 135, 164
Office of Scientific and Technical Information (OSTI), 56, 63
Office of Technology Assessment (OTA), 3-4, 11, 33, 100, 102, 106
Office of the Federal Register (OFR), 107, 111, 175
Office of the Publication Board, 50, 51
Office on Smoking and Health, 61
*Official Gazette: Patents*, 68, 72, 74, 75
*Official Gazette: Trademarks*, 79
Official gazettes, 184, 189, 192-93
*Official Journal of the European Communities*, 192-93
OFR. *See* Office of the Federal Register (OFR)
OG. *See* Official Gazette (OG)
O'Hara, Frederic J., 123, 175
OIRA. *See* Office of Information and Regulatory Affairs (OIRA)
OMB. *See* Office of Management and Budget (OMB)
OMB Watch, 14, 111
Ondrasik, 150
Online catalogs, 1, 29, 36
Online Computer Library Center. *See* OCLC
Online databases. *See* Databases; Electronic formats and information
"Online Health Information," 65
Online Library System (EPA), 56
OOPEC. *See* Office for Official Publications (OOPEC)
OPEC, 181
OPRF. *See* Out-of-Print GPO Sales Publications Reference File (OPRF)
ORBIT, 52, 60, 76
Organization of American States (OAS), 181
Organization of Petroleum Exporting Countries (OPEC), 181
*Organization of the Government of Canada*, 189
OSTI. *See* Office of Scientific and Technical Information (OSTI)
OTA. *See* Office of Technology Assessment (OTA)
*OTA Annual Report*, 100, 102
*OTA Publications List*, 100, 102
*Out-of-Print GPO Sales Publications Reference File* (OPRF), 43
*Overseas Business Reports*, 188

Packard, Vance, 11
Paine, Thomas, 8
*PAIS International*, 88, 89, 117, 118, 123, 177-79
*PAIS International in Print*, 45, 183
*PAIS International Online*, 45
*PAIS on CD-ROM*, 45
*PAIS Subject Headings*, 45
Palic, Vladimir, 184
Paperwork Reduction Act (PRA) (1980), 4, 8-9, 43

Paris Convention, 76
Parish, David W., 176, 177, 177, 178
Park Service, 156
Patent and Trademark Office (PTO), 34, 67, 68, 72, 75, 76, 78-80, 82
Patent Cooperation Treaty (PCT), 76
Patent Depository Libraries (PDLs), 72, 75, 78, 80, 82
Patent Licensing Bulletin Board (PLBB), 75, 82
Patent numbers, 68, 75
Patent Office Building, 72
*Patent, Trademark & Copyright Journal*, 82
Patents
    claims, 76
    classification of, 68, 72-73
    components of, 76, 77
    computer searching of, 75-76, 78
    court cases on, 82
    definition of, 67-68
    depository libraries for, 72, 75, 78, 80, 82
    foreign patents, 76, 78
    freebies on, 82, 83
    glossary concerning, 78
    government patents, 75
    issuing agency for, 67
    legal basis of, 67
    length of protection of, 67
    models of, 76
    numbers of, 68, 75
    overlapping protection with copyright and trademarks, 81-82
    searching, 68, 72-78
    translating patent language, 72
Patents and Trademarks Subject Bibliography, 82
*Patents Throughout the World*, 76
PCT. *See* Patent Cooperation Treaty (PCT)
PDLs. *See* Patent Depository Libraries (PDLs)
PDQ, 58
Pemberton, John E., 186
Pentagon, 9, 12
Pergamon Press, 184
Periodicals
    indexes for, 44-46
    list of, 36, 20
    supplement to *Monthly Catalog*, 39, 40
Periodicals Supplement, 39, 40
PGP. *See* Popular Government Publications File (PGP)
PHBB. *See* Project Hermes Bulletin Board (PHBB)
Photographs and prints, 155-57, 165
PHS. *See* Public Health Service (PHS)
*Pictorial Sources in the Washington, D.C. Area*, 157
Pierian Press, 39
Plant Patent Act, 68
Plant patents, 67, 68, 69, 72, 74
PLBB. *See* Patent Licensing Bulletin Board (PLBB)
"Pocket Guide to ERIC, A," 46
*Pocket Guides*, 178
Pocket vetoes, 94
*Politics in America*, 88, 99
Poore, Benjamin, 43-44
Poore's Catalog, 44
POPLINE, 58
*Popular Government Publications File* (PGP), 42

*Popular Names of U.S. Government Reports: A Catalog* (Bernier and Wood), 174
*Population Index*, 183
Posters, Charts, Picture Sets and Decals Subject Bibliography, 168
PRA. *See* Paperwork Reduction Act (PRA) (1980)
Preliminary Prints, 130, 132
Prentiss, Norman D., 177
Preschel, Barbara M., 45
Presidential action, on legislation, 85, 94
*Presidential Executive Orders* (Lord), 117
Presidential libraries, 115, 119-20
Presidential Libraries Act, 115
*Presidential Libraries and Collections* (Veit), 120
Presidential messages, 117-18
Presidential publications
    eras in history of, 114-15
    Executive Office of the President, 123
    Library of Congress Presidential Papers Collection, 114
    National Security Directives, 114
    presidential messages, 117-18
    "privileged" documents, 113-14
    proclamations and executive orders, 115-17
    public statements, 115
    types of, 113-14
Presidential Records Act, 115
*Presidential Vetoes*, 94
Presidential vetoes, 85, 94
Presidents of the United States Subject Bibliography, 124
*President's Papers Index Series*, 114
PRF. *See* Publications Reference File (PRF)
"Price and Availability List of the U.S. Geological Survey Publications," 160, 168
Price List 36, 20, 25, 39, 40
Primary sources, 165-67, 184
Princeton University, 183
Printing Act (1895), 4, 27
Printing and Graphic Arts Subject Bibliography, 25
Prints and photographs, 155-57, 165
Privacy Act, 11-13, 107
*Privacy Act Issuances Compilation*, 12, 13
Private laws, 86
*Proclamation and Executive Orders, Herbert Hoover*, 117
Producer Price Index, 149
Project Blue Book, 8
Project Hermes Bulletin Board (PHBB), 129, 130
*Prologue*, 167
"Protecting Inventions in Europe," 83
PTO. *See* Patent and Trademark Office (PTO)
"Public Access to Government Information: Looking Ahead in 1991," 14
Public Affairs Information Service, Inc. (PAIS), 45
Public Affairs Video Archives, 92
Public Documents Library, 32
*Public Documents of the First Fourteen Congresses, 1789-1817* (Greeley), 44
Public Health Service (PHS), 58, 61
Public Health Service Smoking and Health Bulletin, 61
*Public Land Statistics*, 143
Public Law 95-261, 34
Public libraries, 54, 56, 143